CALL TO APOSTLESHIP

CALL TO APOSTLESHIP

REFLECTIONS ON THE TABLETS OF THE DIVINE PLAN

JANET A. KHAN

Bahá'í
PUBLISHING

Wilmette, Illinois

Bahá'í Publishing

401 Greenleaf Ave, Wilmette, Illinois 60091

Copyright © 2016 by the National Spiritual Assembly
of the Bahá'ís of the United States

All rights reserved. Published 2016

Printed in the United States of America ∞

19   18   17   16   1   2   3   4

Library of Congress Cataloging-in-Publication Data

Names: Khan, Janet A. (Janet Adrienne), 1940– author.
Title: Call to apostleship : reflections on The tablets of the divine
plan /
   Janet Khan.
Description: Wilmette : Bahá'í Publishing, 2016. | Includes bibli-
ographical references and index.
Identifiers: LCCN 2016022103 | ISBN 9781618511102 (hardcover :
alk. paper)
Subjects: LCSH: 'Abdu'l-Bahá, 1844–1921. Alv?a?h-i tabl?i?g?h?i-yi
Amr?ik?a.
   | Bahai Faith.
Classification: LCC BP363.A673 K43 2016 | DDC 297.9/3824—
dc23
LC record available at https://lccn.loc.gov/2016022103

Cover design by Jamie Hanrahan
Cover photo by Lindsey Lugsch-Tehle
Book design by Patrick Falso

Contents

CONTENTS

CONTENTS

CONTENTS

Introduction

One hundred years ago, while the First World War was raging in Europe, 'Abdu'l-Bahá, the son of Bahá'u'lláh, the Prophet-Founder of the Bahá'í Faith, penned fourteen letters to the members of the Bahá'í community in North America during his closing years as head of his Father's religion. In these historic letters, referred to collectively as the Tablets of the Divine Plan, 'Abdu'l-Bahá entrusted the American Bahá'ís with the responsibility of engaging in activities designed to provide a spiritual and moral solution to the problem of war, thereby laying the foundation for a world of unity and peace envisioned in the Revelation of Bahá'u'lláh. Described in the Bahá'í writings as the charter for the promulgation of the worldwide spread of the Bahá'í Faith, these seminal letters set in motion processes designed to bring about, in due course, the spiritual transformation of the planet.[1]

The individual and structural changes envisaged in the Bahá'í writings are profound. The Revelation of Bahá'u'lláh does not aim at "the subversion of the existing foundations of society"; rather, it "seeks to broaden its basis, to remold its institutions in a manner consonant with the needs of an ever-changing world." Describing the potency of the new Revelation and its capacity to effect such change, 'Abdu'l-Bahá writes, "'The Call of God, when raised, breathed a new life into the body of mankind, and infused a new spirit into the whole creation. It is for this reason that the world hath been moved to its depths, and the hearts and consciences of men been quickened. Erelong the evidences of this regeneration will be revealed, and the fast asleep will be awakened.'" The challenge for the Bahá'ís is to embrace the society-building tasks entrusted to them in the Tablets of the Divine Plan and to create the nucleus of the civilization embodied in the teachings of Bahá'u'lláh.[2]

Study of the Tablets of the Divine Plan provides new insights into both the role of religion in social change and in identifying the means for sustaining this change in the long-term. The chapters that follow consist of a series of reflections on themes derived from 'Abdu'l-Bahá's seminal letters.

In light of the enduring relevance of the Tablets of the Divine Plan, the first chapter sets the stage by briefly examining a number of well-known historical documents, such as the Magna Carta, the Constitution of the United States, and the United Nations Declaration of Human Rights. Similar to 'Abdu'l-Bahá's Tablets, each of these documents was written at a particular point in time and addresses a specific historical situation. Because of their visionary character, all have continued to exert influence on social thought and action in our world today. It will be argued that the capacity of the Tablets of the Divine Plan to make a continuing contribution to the transformation of life on this planet derives primarily from their specific strategies and processes designed to translate 'Abdu'l-Bahá's visionary concepts into practical reality. Additionally, the Tablets also contain provisions to ensure that this evolving task is carried out in a systematic and timely manner by assigning responsibility, in the first instance, to the American Bahá'ís for the completion of this unfolding enterprise.

The second chapter considers the relationship between Bahá'u'lláh's proclamation of His mission to the kings and ecclesiastical leaders of the world and 'Abdu'l-Bahá's Tablets of the Divine Plan. As a context for the discussion, some of the features of Bahá'u'lláh's proclamation are described, as well as the failure of the rulers to respond to His invitation to participate in the establishment of peace and unity in the world. It is suggested that, in the Tablets of the Divine Plan, 'Abdu'l-Bahá takes up the unfinished business of promulgating and implementing the salutary message of peace, justice, and unity contained in the Tablets of Bahá'u'lláh proclaiming His Revelation to the world's political and religious leaders. And, because the mission of teaching his Father's Faith was so vital it could not be left to chance, or to the good will of a few dedicated souls, 'Abdu'l-Bahá mobilized the rank and file of the American Bahá'í community and provided for the establishment of the Bahá'í Administrative Order to ensure that the job would be completed successfully. From this perspective, the seminal Tablets of 'Abdu'l-Bahá's Divine Plan might be said to constitute a critical turning point in the progressive elaboration of the instructions contained in the Bahá'í writings concerning the means by which the Bahá'í Faith was to be disseminated and its transformative influence brought to bear on the world at large.

Though written in 1916 and 1917, the majority of the Tablets of the Divine Plan did not arrive in North America until after the end of the war. The third chapter describes the historical context and the events that surrounded the arrival of the Tablets. It draws parallels between the Peace Conference in Paris in 1919 and the Bahá'í Convention held in New York, which was called by 'Abdu'l-Bahá for the purpose of studying the Tablets and mobilizing the Bahá'í community in response to the mandate he was conferring upon its members. Chapter 3 also details the initial steps taken by the Bahá'ís in response to the Tablets of the Divine Plan.

The issue of how new religious movements are spread throughout the world is addressed in the fourth chapter. Using the example of the early spread of Christianity as a context for examining the rise and diffusion of the Bahá'í Faith and the emergence of the Bahá'í Administrative Order, we examine stages in the unfoldment of the Divine Plan and describe how the transformative processes for the spiritual regeneration of the planet were set in motion during the ministries of Bahá'u'lláh, 'Abdu'l-Bahá, Shoghi Effendi,* and more recently under the jurisdiction of the Universal House of Justice.** We then

---

* Grandson of 'Abdu'l-Bahá who became head of the Bahá'í Faith after 'Abdu'l-Bahá's passing.

** Universally elected, nine-member body that is the head of the Bahá'í Faith.

explore how these processes have evolved and become more complex over time as the capacities of the individual, the community, and the Baháʾí Faith's administrative institutions have evolved and matured. In addition, we argue that the guidance contained in the Tablets of the Divine Plan represents a critical stage in the progressive elaboration of the instructions concerning how the Baháʾí Faith should be spread, and we suggest that the significance of these historic Tablets lies in their representing a call by ʿAbduʾl-Bahá to universalize the religion.

Chapter 5 considers a number of parameters that create a context within which to examine the Baháʾí approach to establishing the foundations of social order. The guidance set out in the Tablets of the Divine Plan gives direction to the unfoldment of the processes necessary for the implementation of Baháʾuʾlláh's vision for humankind. ʿAbduʾl-Bahá calls for the propagation of the new Revelation throughout the world as a means of gradually transforming human values and institutional structures as a prerequisite to laying the foundations of a new social order expressing the oneness of humankind and universal peace. At each stage in the evolution of the organic society-building process, the responsibility for implementing the goals of the Tablets is placed upon the individual, the community, and the institutions of the Faith, though the actual functions each one performs may vary with the passage of time, their level of capacity, the conditions in the world, and the maturity of the Baháʾí community. At every stage in the process, these three protagonists are challenged to identify the priorities of the moment and to determine how best to meet their responsibilities.

Knowing the level of responsibility and the long-term nature of the society-building process, ʿAbduʾl-Bahá, to inspire and sustain the motivations of his followers and to encourage them to reflect on the sacred and historic nature of the task in which they are engaged, calls them to the station of apostleship and invites them to become an "Apostle of Baháʾuʾlláh."[3] He links the great enterprise they are striving to achieve in contemporary times to the historic work undertaken by the apostles of Christ.

Chapters 6–8 explore in detail the three conditions specified by ʿAbduʾl-Bahá for attainment to the station of an Apostle of

Bahá'u'lláh—namely, firmness in the Covenant, fellowship and love among the believers, and the act of arising to teach the Cause. 'Abdu'l-Bahá's call to apostleship in the Tablets of the Divine Plan implies the need for commitment and action both to the worldwide promotion of the Faith and to the acquisition of capacities that advance civilization.

Firmness in the Covenant, the first prerequisite to attaining the station of an Apostle of Bahá'u'lláh, is the avenue by which an individual aligns his or her life's purpose to the divine purpose. Its transformative, motivating force sustains the members of the community in their individual and collective endeavors to change the pattern of human society in conformity with the vision set out in the Revelation of Bahá'u'lláh. Chapter 6 discusses a number of issues concerning firmness in the Covenant, including the significance of being a party to the Covenant, the importance of independent investigation of truth and the acquisition of knowledge, the relationship between obedience to the teachings and institutions of the Faith and personal freedom, and the orientation to service. In addition, the society-building ramifications of firmness in the Covenant and its impact on the emerging Bahá'í culture are illustrated with reference to the Universal House of Justice's guidance to the Bahá'í community in Iran concerning the advancement of women and participating in the discourses of society.

When Bahá'u'lláh proclaimed His Message to the world in the nineteenth century, He not only laid out the central purpose of His Revelation, He also made it abundantly clear that the first step essential for the peace and progress of mankind was its unification. In the Tablets of the Divine Plan, 'Abdu'l-Bahá stresses the importance of the practice of the oneness of mankind in daily life. He designates "fellowship and love among the believers" as the "second condition" for attainment to the station of an Apostle of Bahá'u'lláh, and he describes the high standard of conduct associated with this prerequisite. Implementation of the second condition of apostleship, fellowship and love among the believers, involves transformation at the level of spiritual principle and individual and social action. In practical terms, this transformation requires the reexamination of assumptions and existing cultural values and practices in light of the teachings of the Manifestation of God, and concerted action based on the principle of the oneness of mankind. Bahá'ís are, therefore, engaged in a variety of activities aimed at changing both the individual and social institutions. They are striving "to establish a pattern of activity and the corresponding administrative structures that embody the principle of the oneness of humankind and the convictions underpinning it."[4]

Chapter 7 examines the means by which human activity is given focus and organized in the world, through the powers associated with "the Collective Center of the Kingdom"—that is, through the inspirational and educational forces deriving from the teachings of the Manifestation of God.[5] This chapter also calls attention to a number of factors that distinguish the Bahá'í approach to social transformation from an unrealistic utopianism. These factors include the conception of the nature of man, the systematic development of individual and institutional capacity, the structure of the Bahá'í administrative order, an emerging culture of learning, and a process orientation allowing for evolutionary change.

The third condition for the attainment to the station of apostleship involves traveling to teach the Cause of God. Chapter 8 examines the significance of a number of themes and strategies set out in the Tablets of the Divine Plan which have given rise to processes that have influenced and continue to influence the worldwide expansion of the Bahá'í Faith and its involvement in society. The subjects included for consideration in this chapter are the nature of teaching, the qualities of the teacher, the importance of traveling to serve the Faith, the contribution of travel teachers and pioneers to the processes of social transformation through demonstrating the community-building power of the Faith, the strategic emphasis on particular geographical locations, the focus on minority populations, and the unique role of women in the promotion of the Faith.

The opportunity offered to the followers of the Bahá'í Faith to attain to the high station of an Apostle of Bahá'u'lláh through sacrificial and sustained service to the Divine Plan is unique—and potentially within the grasp of each individual. As a means of enhancing individual capacity to respond to the Master's invitation to attain to the station of apostleship, chapter 9 draws on a number of statements in the Bahá'í writings concerning the life of 'Abdu'l-Bahá and reflects on what can be learned from his example, especially as it pertains to the practice of firmness in the Covenant, fellowship and love among the believers, and arising to teach the Cause.

A great deal can be learned from gaining a deeper appreciation of 'Abdu'l-Bahá's unique role in the Covenant, his complete identification with Bahá'u'lláh's Teachings, and his all-embracing love and concern for humankind. His sensitive interactions with people from different backgrounds, races, and classes offer useful insights into the promotion of fellowship, love, and unity, and they have implications for the practice of the principle of the oneness of humankind by the individual, the community, and the institutions of the Faith, as well as the wider society. And, much can be learned from 'Abdu'l-Bahá's approach to service, as it relates to traveling to teach the Faith.

As the transformative processes set in motion by implementation of 'Abdu'l-Bahá's Tablets of the Divine Plan continue to evolve and reshape the spiritual, intellectual, and social lives of individuals, communities, and administrative systems, in line with Bahá'u'lláh's prophetic vision of unity and peace, so too will it continue to evolve and reshape the tasks the Bahá'í community is called upon to undertake in the years ahead. Though future responsibilities will change, what remains is the priceless opportunity afforded the individual to respond to the call of apostleship, and through sacrificial service, to make his or her contribution to the spiritual regeneration of the planet.

1

Seminal Documents

The historical record includes a number of seminal documents that, because of their immediate relevance to the needs of a society at a critical turning point in its evolution, have made important and decisive contributions to human and social development. The influence of these documents may well extend beyond the particular moment in time they were written to address. With the passage of time, an enhanced appreciation of the significance and continuing relevance of these ground-breaking texts tends to emerge as people in different parts of the world become increasingly aware not only of the enduring visionary ideas and prescriptions these documents contain but also of their potential relevance to new situations that develop in different locations and historical eras. Examples of these documents include the Magna Carta, the Constitution of the United States, and the Universal Declaration of Human Rights.

In this chapter we will briefly examine the content and significance of a number of well-known historical documents and introduce the Tablets of the Divine Plan, a set of fourteen visionary letters written by 'Abdu'l-Bahá to the Bahá'ís of North America in 1916 and 1917. Described in the Bahá'í writings as the charter for the promulgation of the worldwide spread of the Bahá'í Faith, these letters, which were penned during the darkest days of World War I, set in motion processes designed to bring about, in due course, the spiritual transformation of the planet. The historical context for the revelation of these unique Tablets will be described, and their major themes will be outlined. We will explore why these letters were, in the first instance, addressed specifically to the Bahá'ís in North America, and we will consider the impact of this assignment on the strategic approach to the ongoing systematic unfoldment of the Bahá'í Faith throughout the world.

Historical Documents

To illustrate the impact of documents that are of a visionary nature and have the potential to dramatically change the course of human history, we begin by briefly considering some of the features of the Magna Carta, of the Constitution of the United States, and of the Universal Declaration of Human Rights. This discussion will provide a context for describing the seminal nature and enduring significance of 'Abdu'l-Bahá's Tablets of the Divine Plan.

THE MAGNA CARTA

The Magna Carta is the Great Charter of English Liberties granted by King John of England in 1215. It was the first document forced onto an English king under threat of civil war by a group of his subjects (the barons). The barons aimed to limit the king's powers by law and thereby protect their own privileges. The provisions of the Magna Carta, which were modified several times during the thirteenth century, related primarily to the social conditions that existed in feudal England in medieval times, and represented a direct challenge to the monarch's absolute authority. For example, the charter required the king to proclaim certain liberties and to accept that his will was not arbitrary—that no freeman could be punished except through the law of the land, a right which is still in existence today.

The circumstances of the granting of the Magna Carta in 1215 following the historic confrontation between the king and the barons on the meadows at Runnymede have given this great charter a unique place in popular imagination. Early on, it became symbolic and a battle cry against oppression, with each successive generation reading into it a projection of their own threatened liberties. The charter was an important part of the extensive and long-term historical process that led to the rule of constitutional law in the English-speaking world.

The contemporary relevance of the Magna Carta is underlined by the launching of plans to mark the 800th anniversary of this document in 2015. A British member of parliament, speaking at a meeting inaugurating the run-up to these celebrations, linked the granting of the Magna Carta to the birth of British—and indeed global—democracy. He made the following observation: "It is probably fair to say that when the barons forced the King to concede limits to his absolute power, they weren't thinking of passing on the benefits of this new 'democracy' to the rest of the people any time soon. But the lesson of Magna Carta is the lesson of history: once you've let the genie out of the bottle, you can't put it back. One thing leads to another and a little democracy tends to gain momentum." He concludes his speech by describing the means by which the "lesson of history" operates. He calls attention to the power of this document to exert an influence beyond the United Kingdom, and suggests how it has the potential to continue to motivate and inspire those who live in areas of the world where the process of building democracy is still in its infancy: ". . . just as Magna Carta spawned our modern democracy, the constitution of the United States and the basic principles of constitutional government across a large part of the world today, so the story of Magna Carta—a gradual opening which becomes an irreversible process—should become a beacon of hope for the billions of our fellow citizens around the world who still live their lives under one sort of tyranny or another."[1]

THE CONSTITUTION OF THE UNITED STATES OF AMERICA

When the English settlers left their homeland for America in the early years of the seventeenth century, they brought with them charters establishing their colonies. These charters defined the rights and responsibilities of the colonists and drew their inspiration from such things as the provisions enshrined in the Magna Carta and in English common law.

In later years, when the American revolutionaries gained independence from Britain and issued their historic Declaration of Independence, one of their critical aims was to preserve the rights and liberties they had enjoyed under the English legal system that they knew and admired. The framers of the basic text of the United States Constitution who gathered at the Constitutional Convention in 1787 wished to ensure that rights they already held, such as those provided by the Magna Carta, were not lost unless explicitly curtailed under the new United States Constitution. [2]

Prior to its final enactment by the national Congress in 1789, the new Constitution had to be formally ratified by the individual states. This process led to demands by a number of states for a Bill of Rights to supplement the provisions of the Constitution. To satisfy this request, Congress proposed ten amendments to the Constitution, which were added in 1791. These ten amendments together comprise the United States Bill of Rights. They ensure such rights as freedom of religion, speech, press, and assembly, the general rights of the accused and due process of law, the right to trial by jury in civil cases, and prohibitions against excessive bail and fines and against cruel and unusual punishments.[3] Additional amendments have subsequently been ratified.

The Constitution of the United States of America is the supreme law of the United States. The Constitution is the framework for the organization of the United States government. It defines in broad terms the principal organs of government—the legislative branch, consisting of the House of Representatives and the Senate; the executive branch, led by the President; and the judicial branch, headed by the Supreme Court—and specifies the powers and duties of each branch. It also sets out the basic rights of citizens and how the document could be amended.

The Constitution of the United States is one of the world's oldest surviving constitutions. It is a living document. While the Supreme Court continually interprets the Constitution so as to reflect a rapidly changing world, its few basic tenets have remained virtually unchanged since its inception. There is, however, scope for future leaders to elaborate the provisions and to fill in necessary details.

While the American Constitution is of continuing importance to the United States and impacts the everyday lives of its citizens, its significance extends beyond the borders of the nation and exerts an influence on forms of governance and human rights on a global level. The U.S. Constitution is regarded as one of the most influential legal documents in existence. The scope of the influence of this seminal document is illustrated by the fact that since its creation some two hundred years ago, over one hundred countries around the world have used it as a model for their own constitutions.[4]

THE UNIVERSAL DECLARATION OF HUMAN RIGHTS

The Universal Declaration of Human Rights was adopted by the United Nations General Assembly on December 10, 1948.[5] Recognition of the need for such a Declaration, which was drafted by the United Nations Commission on Human Rights, arose directly from the experience of the Second World War. The Holocaust, the attempt to annihilate the Jews of Europe, altered forever the way in which people viewed human rights. Prior to World War II, the protection of human rights was considered primarily a domestic concern, the responsibility of individual governments. Following the war, the struggle for human rights became a subject of universal concern.

The adoption of the Declaration by the United Nations in 1948 marked the inauguration of an enduring international commitment to human rights. The community of nations adopted the Universal Declaration of Human Rights without dissent. It represented one of the first collective expressions of an international community. At the time, this momentous action was described as "an historic act, destined to consolidate world peace through the contribution of the United Nations toward the liberation of individuals from the unjustified oppression and constraint to which they are too often subjected."[6]

The Universal Declaration sets out the fundamental and inalienable rights of all members of the human family. It affirms the inherent dignity of the human being, emphasizes the rule of law over the rule of force, and places the well-being of the individual at the center of international law. This influential document reshaped the moral terrain of international relations. Since its inception over sixty years ago, the Declaration has grown in stature and importance: "What began as an articulation of shared values bearing moral weight on U.N. Member states, has become a primary building block of customary international law that demands respect from the entire world community. Direct reference to the Universal Declaration is made in the national constitutions of numerous countries. Human rights advocates worldwide invoke its principles." This historic document has, to date, inspired over sixty international treaties and conventions, which have acquired increasing authority through incorporation into national legal systems.[7]

The three documents described above share a number of features. Each one represents a specific response to the needs of a particular historic moment. Hence, the Magna Carta served as a vehicle for opening the way to democracy in medieval England; the Constitution of the United States embodied the democratic principle in a system of law and a set of institutions of government designed to preserve fundamental rights and liberties in eighteenth-century America; and the Universal Declaration of Human Rights, responding to the conditions existing in the world after the Second World War, sets out, for the first time, fundamental human rights to be universally protected. Furthermore, each document has had an enduring and evolving influence that extends to contemporary times and may well project into the future.

Bahá'í Charter Documents

Embedded in the writings of the Founders of the Bahá'í Faith are a number of documents that set in motion processes that will expand the influence of the religion into the future. Three of these documents have primary significance in relation to the worldwide development of the religion, to the establishment of its system of administration, and the emergence of a just and peaceful social order. The first of these charters is the Tablet of Carmel, revealed by Bahá'u'lláh, which provides the vision and broad guidelines for the establishment of the international headquarters of the Bahá'í Faith. The second is the Will and Testament of 'Abdu'l-Bahá. This document builds on the seminal ideas outlined in Bahá'u'lláh's writings and calls into being the institutions comprising the Bahá'í Administrative Order, which is destined to serve as the vehicle for the diffusion of the Faith's values throughout the world and as the nucleus of world order. The Tablets of the Divine Plan, a set of fourteen letters written by ‘Abdu’l-Bahá to the members of the Bahá’í Faith in North America in 1916–1917, constitute the third of these important charters. These historic letters describe in visionary terms the strategic approach to promoting the influence of the Bahá’í Faith throughout the globe. The implementation of this task is, in the first instance, assigned to the American Bahá’í community.

Addressing the American Bahá’ís, Shoghi Effendi, the Guardian of the Faith, spells out the significance of the Bahá’í charter documents, describes their sphere of operation, and expresses his confident hope that the American Bahá’ís will arise to carry out the function to which they have been called. He writes:

> It is indeed my fervent and constant prayer that the members of this firmly knit, intensely alive, world-embracing Community, spurred on by the triple impulse generated through the revelation of the Tablet of Carmel by Bahá’u’lláh and the Will and Testament as well as the Tablets of the Divine Plan bequeathed by the Centre of His Covenant—the three Charters which have set in motion three distinct processes, the first operating in the Holy Land for the development of the institutions of the Faith at its World Center and the other two, throughout the rest of the Bahá’í world, for its propagation and the establishment of its Administrative Order—may advance from strength to strength and victory to victory. May they hasten, by their present exertions, the advent of that blissful consummation when the shackles hampering the growth of their beloved Faith will have been finally burst asunder . . . when the brightness of its glory will have illuminated the whole earth, and its dominion will have been established over the entire planet.[8]

The primary focus of this book is on processes set in motion by one of these great charters—namely, the Tablets of the Divine Plan, a Plan conceived by ‘Abdu’l-Bahá and entrusted to the Bahá’ís of North America in fourteen letters. To a lesser extent, attention will also be given to key provisions of 'Abdu'l-Bahá's Will and Testament concerning the establishment of the institutions of the Administrative Order with which the systematic propagation of the Faith is organically interconnected.

From a Bahá'í perspective, the significance of this collection of letters cannot simply be confined to the years 1916–1917 in which they were written or to the continent of America. Rather, they represent not only the Plan for the systematic dissemination of the Faith of Bahá'u'lláh throughout the world, a task ultimately to be shared by all Bahá'í communities. In the long term, the guidance contained in these letters is calculated to exert a constructive influence on the spiritual and social unfoldment of the life of humankind.

The Tablets of the Divine Plan

In the evening of his life, 'Abdu'l-Bahá addressed to the Bahá'ís of North America fourteen letters that together form the Tablets of the Divine Plan. As the "supreme charter" for the diffusion of the Bahá'í Faith, these seminal documents fashion in broad outline 'Abdu'l-Bahá's master plan for the spiritual regeneration of the world. He unfolds to the small body of his American followers his conception of their spiritual destiny and invests them with "a mandate to plant the banner of His Father's Faith . . . in all the continents, the countries and islands of the globe." 'Abdu'l-Bahá assures the North American Bahá'ís that their mission is "unspeakably glorious," and he predicts that, should success crown their enterprise, "America will assuredly evolve into a center from which waves of spiritual power will emanate, and the throne of the Kingdom of God, will in the plenitude of its majesty and glory, be firmly established." He makes the following dramatic affirmation: "The moment this Divine Message is carried forward by the American believers from the shores of America, and is propagated through the continents of Europe, of Asia, of Africa and of Australasia, and as far as the islands of the Pacific, this community will find itself securely established upon the throne of everlasting dominion. Then will all the peoples of the world witness that this community is spiritually illumined and divinely guided. Then will the whole earth resound with the praises of its majesty and greatness."[9]

The historic Tablets of the Divine Plan were written during the darkest days of World War I, at a time when all means of communication between 'Abdu'l-Bahá, the head of the Bahá'í Faith residing in Palestine, and the community of its followers around the world, were disrupted and, for a period, severed.

It is interesting to note that 'Abdu'l-Bahá, an astute observer of world events, clearly predicted the outbreak of war. During his travels in the West in 1911–1912, he warned in ominous tones of the catastrophe He saw approaching. His warnings concerning the magnitude of the dangers were very direct. A leading Montreal newspaper contains the following report of 'Abdu'l-Bahá's words: "All Europe is an armed camp. These warlike preparations will necessarily culminate in a great war. The very armaments themselves are productive of war. This great arsenal must go ablaze. There is nothing of the nature of a prophecy about such a view . . . it is based on reasoning solely."[10]

In his public talks in North America 'Abdu'l-Bahá attests that he "cried out in every meeting and summoned the people to the propagation of the ideals of universal peace." He "plainly" said that "the continent of Europe had become like unto an arsenal and its conflagration was dependent upon one spark," and he predicted the flare up would occur "within two years." Against such a background, he emphasized the urgent need for reconciliation and the paramount importance of international peace as a means of alleviating the suffering of humankind and the preservation of civilized values. For example, in an address delivered in California in October 1912, 'Abdu'l-Bahá stated, "The European continent is like an arsenal, a storehouse of explosives ready for ignition, and one spark will set the whole of Europe aflame, particularly at this time when the Balkan question is before the world . . . Therefore, the greatest need in the world today is international peace. The time is ripe. It is time for the abolition of warfare, the unification of nations and governments. It is time for love. It is time for cementing together the East and the West."[11]

WORLD WAR I

Eight months after 'Abdu'l-Bahá's return to Haifa from his sojourn in the West, World War I broke out. The outbreak of the war was precipitated by the assassination of an Austrian archduke in Sarajevo, Bosnia, in 1914. While a factor contributing to the attack was the spread of nationalism in the Balkans, some historians trace the origins of the war to the German victory over France in the Franco-Prussian War of 1870–1871, inasmuch as the newly constituted German Empire sought allies to forestall a French attempt to reverse that outcome. Europe was thus divided into rival camps by a system of alliances.[12]

In his recent book on world order, Henry Kissinger offers the following comment on the causes of the Great War: ". . . the war that overturned Western civilization had no inevitable necessity. It arose from a series of miscalculations made by serious leaders who did not understand the consequences of their planning, and a final maelstrom triggered by a terrorist attack . . . In the end, the military planning ran away with diplomacy. It is a lesson subsequent generations must not forget."[13]

The protagonists in World War I were Austria-Hungary, Germany, and Turkey, who were opposed by Russia, France, and Great Britain. The latter three countries were joined by Japan, Italy, the United States and many smaller nations. All these nations were armed, and conscription was introduced. In the view of historian H. G. Wells, the governments of Europe were "inspired by antiquated policies of hate and suspicion," and given the scientific advances in modern weaponry, "found themselves with unexampled powers both of destruction and resistance in their hands. The war became a consuming fire round and about the world, causing losses both to victors and vanquished out of all proportion to the issues involved."[14]

The main fighting against Germany occurred along the Western front, in Belgium and northern France. It was there, in the view of leaders on both sides, the war would be decided. The fighting was protracted and bloody. For three and a half years, neither side advanced more than a few miles along the line of trenches, despite the use of new weapons such as poison gas and the introduction of tanks. The stalemate was not relieved until the spring of 1918 when the Germans were defeated and thrown back into Belgium.[15]

In addition to the military campaigns on the continent of Europe, battles took place at sea and in the air, and the fighting reached such places as Russia, Turkey, the Caucasus, Palestine, and Mesopotamia. Commenting on the scope of the warfare and its social impact, Wells refers to the vast size of the armies, and the organization of "entire populations . . . for the supply of food and munitions to the front," which gave rise to the "cessation of nearly every sort of productive activity except such as contributed to military operations." According to Wells, "All the able-bodied manhood of Europe was drawn into the armies and navies or into the improvised factories that served them."[16] As a consequence, nations were impoverished; peoples were socially uprooted and transplanted; and trade, shipping, and communications were disrupted.

The entry of the United States into the war on the side of the Allies in 1917 was a major turning point and hastened the end of the conflict. When the war finally came to an end in 1918, the allied powers imposed a vindictive peace treaty on their defeated enemies and demanded ruinous reparations of them. These actions not only served to plant the seeds of another more terrible conflict but also helped "prepare demoralized peoples in Europe to embrace totalitarian promises of relief which they might not otherwise have contemplated."[17]

Assessing the long-term implications of the Great War, Eric Hobsbawm, an eminent historian, offers the sobering view that "the First World War began the descent into barbarism." In his judgment, this war "opened the most murderous era so far recorded in history"; and "the limitless sacrifices which governments imposed on their own men" as they drove them into tragic and wasteful battles "set a sinister precedent." Furthermore, he observes that "the very concept of a war of total national mobilization shattered the central pillar of civilized warfare," by blurring "the distinction between combatants and non-combatants," and he regards the pervasive tendency to demonize the enemy to governments' need to sustain the fighting focus of largely volunteer armies. Beyond its moral and psychological impact, Hobsbawm attests, "the Great War ended in social and political breakdown, social revolution and counter-revolution on an unprecedented scale." In his assessment, the direct impact of this era of breakdown and revolution was felt for the next thirty years.[18]

'ABDU'L-BAHÁ AND THE WAR YEARS

'Abdu'l-Bahá returned to the Holy Land in the latter months of 1913. Palestine, which was then an outpost of the crumbling Ottoman Empire, entered the war on the side of Germany, and soon became caught up in the conflict. The region was surrounded by grave dangers. Shoghi Effendi indicates that, at one time, the threat of the bombardment of Haifa by the Allies was so real that 'Abdu'l-Bahá temporarily evacuated the members of his family and the local Bahá'í community to the inland village of Abú-Sinán.[19]

For the duration of the war, the population of Palestine was subject to severe privations and hardships. The area was isolated, and communication with the rest of the world was cut off. Hunger, exacerbated by the neglect of the ruling authorities and the operation of a strict naval blockade, increased the level of suffering. The plight of the people of Haifa and the surrounding areas was partially alleviated by the distribution of grain, which had been grown and providentially stored by 'Abdu'l-Bahá in anticipation of the outbreak of hostilities. The British government subsequently conferred the title of knighthood on him in recognition of his humanitarian work during the war for the relief of distress and famine. He accepted the honor as the gift of a "just king" but never used the title.[20]

TIMING OF THE TABLETS

'Abdu'l-Bahá was greatly saddened by the failure of the world to respond to the call for universal peace set out in the writings of Bahá'u'lláh and the urgent appeals he himself had uttered in his public addresses in the West. Shoghi Effendi said of 'Abdu'l-Bahá in those days: "Agony filled His soul at the spectacle of human slaughter precipitated through humanity's failure to respond to the summons He had issued, or to heed the warnings He had given. . . ." So critical was the need to alleviate the condition of humanity, 'Abdu'l-Bahá turned to the American Bahá'ís for resolute action and provided them with a long-term strategy for ameliorating the human condition. Shoghi Effendi writes: "And yet during these somber days, . . . 'Abdu'l-Bahá, . . . was moved to confer once again, and for the last time in His life, on the community of His American followers a signal mark of His special favor by investing them, on the eve of the termination of His earthly ministry, through the revelation of the Tablets of the Divine Plan, with a world mission, whose full implications even now, . . . still remain undisclosed, and whose unfoldment thus far, though as yet in its initial stages, has so greatly enriched the spiritual as well as the administrative annals of the first Bahá'í century."[21]

The individual Tablets constituting 'Abdu'l-Bahá's Divine Plan were revealed at two separate points in time. The first eight Tablets were written between March 26 and April 22, 1916. The second group of six Tablets was penned between February 2 and March 8, 1917. The delivery of these historic documents was, however, interrupted and delayed by the war. Nine of the Tablets did not arrive in North America until the cessation of hostilities. It is reported that five of the Tablets revealed in 1916 "had actually reached America and been published in the September 8, 1916, issue of *Star of the West*. After that all communication with the Holy Land was severed, . . . the remainder of the Tablets were kept in a vault in the Shrine of the Báb on Mt. Carmel for the duration of the war. They were dispatched to America at the end of the war where they were unveiled in befitting ceremonies during the 'Convention of the Covenant' held at Hotel McAlpin in New York City on April 26–30, 1919."[22]

The period in which the Tablets of the Divine Plan were written coincides with the time of most intense suffering occasioned by the war. Commenting on the timing of the revelation and the visionary nature of these Tablets, historian Amin Banani writes, "History records this period as one of awesome bloodletting in Europe. It is truly breathtaking to contemplate the devising of the Divine Strategy for the redemption of the planet in the midst of the din and destruction of the old order. The transforming vision of 'Abdu'l-Bahá spreads before us the plans for the spiritual conquest of the globe."[23]

The year 1916 marked the beginning of a renewed offensive on the Western front and the commencement of the tremendous bombardments that were to characterize the ensuing military encounters. At the beginning of this fateful year, a grand total of 139 divisions— thirty-eight British, ninety-five French, and six Belgian divisions were assembled in France to confront 117 German divisions. On February 21, 1916, the battle for Verdun began. By the end of June, when the fighting had died down, the French had lost 315,000 soldiers, and the Germans had lost 281,000. Assessing the outcome of this battle, Taylor writes: "Verdun was the most senseless episode in a war not distinguished for sense anywhere. Both sides at Verdun fought literally for the sake of fighting. There was no prize to be gained or lost, only men to be killed and glory to be won. The conflict at Verdun had a peculiar intensity. At some time during these four months no less than 115 divisions were crammed in by one side or the other on a front that was rarely more than five miles wide. . . . The spirit of the French army was broken, and many units were on the brink of mutiny. On the other hand, the French held Verdun; and this had an inspiring effect on all those who had not fought there. . . . therefore Verdun seemed a French victory."[24]

The first eight Tablets of the Divine Plan, written between March 26 and April 22, 1916, include 'Abdu'l-Bahá's messages to each of five separate regions of the United States and Canada. These regions were Canada and Greenland, and the northeastern, southern, central, and western states of the United States. Three general letters were also addressed collectively to the believers in North America, and they embodied his mandate to diffuse "the fame of the Cause of God . . . throughout the East and the West" and to proclaim "the advent of the Kingdom of the Lord of Hosts . . . in all the five continents of the globe."[25]

The first of the general Tablets named the republics, territories, and islands of the Western Hemisphere and called upon the Bahá'ís to arise to open these regions to the Faith of Bahá'u'lláh. The second was a call to propagate the religion "through the continents of Europe, of Asia, of Africa, and of Australasia, and as far as the islands of the Pacific." And, in the third, 'Abdu'l-Bahá addressed the believers as "Apostles of Bahá'u'lláh" and he specified the conditions on which the attainment of this special station depends. In three of these letters, as in a number of his public addresses in the West, 'Abdu'l-Bahá specifically links the work of promoting the Word of God with creating the conditions for peace and reconciliation. Calling for teachers to travel through all the continents and islands of the globe, he confidently anticipates that ". . . in a short space of time, most wonderful results will be produced. The banner of universal peace will be waving on the apex of the world and the lights of the oneness of the world of humanity may illumine the universe."[26]

During the remaining months of 1916, the engines of war continued to wreak havoc. The disastrous Battle of the Somme (July 1–November 15, 1916), a costly offensive was launched by the British and French along a twenty-mile stretch of the River Somme in northwestern France. On the first day of the military engagement, the British sustained 60,000 casualties, of which 20,000 were killed—the heaviest loss sustained in a single day by any army in the First World War. During these twenty weeks of fighting, the Allies lost 600,000 men, two-thirds of whom were British, while the Germans lost around 450,000. Commenting on the impact of the Battle of the Somme, Taylor writes: "Strategically, the battle of the Somme was an unredeemed defeat. It is supposed to have worn down the spirit of the German army. So no doubt it did, though not to the point of crippling that army as a fighting machine. The German spirit was not the only one to suffer. The British were worn down also. Idealism perished on the Somme. . . . The war ceased to have a purpose. It went on for its own sake, as a contest in endurance. . . . The Somme set the picture by which future generations saw the First World War: brave helpless soldiers; blundering obstinate generals; nothing achieved."[27]

Another tragic highlight of this period was the Battle of Jutland (May 31–June 1, 1916), the principal, though indecisive, naval engagement between the British and German fleets.[28] Despite the brevity of the engagement, the outcome of this battle was highly destructive in the long-term since it gave rise to the strategic use of submarines by the Germans to disrupt all forms of shipping, both military and commercial. As a result, trade and commerce were greatly disrupted and the suffering of civilian populations was dramatically increased.

In January, 1917, the Germans announced the immediate introduction of unrestricted submarine warfare. All shipping, including ships from neutral countries, would be sunk at sight in the war zone of the eastern Atlantic. On 2 February, Woodrow Wilson, President of the United States, who had for some time been trying to mediate peace between the contending parties, broke off relations with Germany. The impact of submarine attacks on shipping brought Britain to its knees and threatened its defeat. Until the introduction of convoys later in the year, it was estimated that one ship out of every four leaving British ports never came home. According to Taylor, "German submarines forced the entry of the United States into the war." It was after the sinking of American ships by German submarines that the United States declared war on Germany on April 6, 1917.[29]

The final six Tablets, penned between February 2 and March 8, 1917, were written against the backdrop of a travailing world and immediately prior to the entry of the United States into the war. In five of these Tablets, 'Abdu'l-Bahá elaborated and reinforced his guidance to the five regions of the United States and Canada. His final general Tablet described the nature of collective centers and the power of unity, and it contained a renewed appeal to the believers to travel throughout the Western Hemisphere. In two of these historic letters, 'Abdu'l-Bahá returns to the theme of universal peace, calling on the American Bahá'ís to unfurl "the flag of the oneness of the world of humanity" so that "the melody of universal peace may reach the ears of the East and the west, all the paths may be cleared and straightened, all the hearts may be attracted to the Kingdom of God, the tabernacle of unity be pitched on the apex of America, the song of the love of God may exhilarate and rejoice all the nations and peoples, the surface of the earth may become the eternal paradise, the dark clouds may be dispelled and the Sun of Truth may shine forth with the utmost intensity."[30]

'Abdu'l-Bahá's concern for the well-being and spiritual transformation of humankind is reflected in the fact that, in all, 120 territories and islands are mentioned by name in these Tablets. He attached particular importance to teaching the Eskimos, and other indigenous Americans, and to establishing the Bahá'í Faith in specific areas such as Alaska, Greenland, Mexico, Panama, and Bahia (Salvador), Brazil. Underlying the spiritual nature of the enterprise, these Tablets also include a number of prayers, specific guidance to teachers, and practical advice concerning the organization of teaching activities.

While the Tablets of the Divine Plan were written at a critical time in the history of humanity and resonate with the particular needs of that era, an examination of the themes included in this collection of letters will demonstrate that their significance extends far beyond the years 1916–1917. The Tablets set out the Plan assigned, in the first instance, to the North American Bahá'ís for the systematic dissemination of the Faith of Bahá'u'lláh throughout the world—an assignment that would ultimately be shared by all Bahá'í communities in the world. Further, the guidance contained in these Tablets that is directed at the individual, the community, and the institutions that administer its affairs—the three protagonists whose transformation and participation are critical to the outcome of the Plan—is, in the long-term, calculated to exert a constructive influence on the spiritual and social unfoldment of the life of humankind.

WHY AMERICA?

While the late entry of the United States of America into World War I undoubtedly insured the protection of its population and also enabled the members of the American Bahá'í community to continue to conduct their affairs in comparative safety and freedom—despite being cut off for a number of years from the head and spiritual center of their Faith—it is suggested that the choice of America may have a deeper spiritual and historical significance. In the writings of the Bahá'í Faith, there are many visionary statements that anticipate that the American Bahá'í community and the North American continent are destined, in the future, to make a preeminent contribution to the transformation of spiritual and social values and to the establishment of world order and peace.

Shoghi Effendi summarizes, in the following passage, some of the most dramatic statements from the writings of the Báb and Bahá'u'lláh, the twin Founders of the Bahá'í Faith, and from 'Abdu'l-Bahá, which illustrate the unique role of America:

The Báb had in His Qayyumu'l-Asmá', almost a hundred years previously, sounded His specific summons to the "peoples of the West" to "issue forth" from their "cities" and aid His Cause. Bahá'u'lláh, in His Kitáb-i-Aqdas, had collectively addressed the Presidents of the Republics of the entire Americas, bidding them arise and "bind with the hands of justice the broken," and "crush the oppressor" with the "rod of the commandments" of their Lord, and had, moreover, anticipated in His writings the appearance "in the West" of the "signs of His Dominion." 'Abdu'l-Bahá had, on His part, declared that the "illumination" shed by His Father's Revelation upon the West would acquire an "extraordinary brilliancy," and that the "light of the Kingdom" would "shed a still greater illumination upon the West" than upon the East. He had extolled the American continent in particular as "the land wherein the splendors of His Light shall be revealed, where the mysteries of His Faith shall be unveiled," and affirmed that "it will lead all nations spiritually." More specifically still, He had singled out the Great Republic of the West, the leading nation of that continent, declaring that its people were "indeed worthy of being the first to build the Tabernacle of the Most Great Peace and proclaim the oneness of mankind," that it was "equipped and empowered to accomplish that which will adorn the pages of history, to become the envy of the world, and be blest in both the East and the West.[31]

'Abdu'l-Bahá recognized the capacity and vitality of the nascent American Bahá'í community, which was the first to respond to the call of the New Day in the Western world. From the outset, he lavished his attention and guidance upon it and fostered its development. At an advanced age, he journeyed to North America and during his extensive travels imparted to the American Bahá'ís a more comprehensive understanding of the spiritual, social, and administrative teachings of the Faith. The Tablets of the Divine Plan addressed to the Bahá'ís of North America constitute 'Abdu'l-Bahá's "mandate to the community which He Himself had raised up, trained and nurtured, a Plan that must in the years to come enable its members to diffuse the light, and erect the administrative fabric, of the Faith throughout the five continents of the globe."[32]

While these historic Tablets singled out the American Bahá'í community for the "unique and imperishable honor" of serving as "the principal custodian and chief executor of 'Abdu'l-Bahá's Divine Plan," the magnitude of the tasks outlined in the Tablets and the long-term nature of the society-building enterprise they envisioned soon necessitated increasing collaboration between the Bahá'í communities in different parts of the world. With the expansion of the worldwide Bahá'í community, its gradual maturing, and the establishment of its evolving administrative structure, more and more communities were progressively called upon to assume their share of responsibility. By May 1953, for example, the Guardian, Shoghi Effendi called upon the United States believers, the "chief executors," the Canadian believers, their "allies," and the Latin American believers, their "associates," to "brace themselves and initiate . . . in other continents of the globe, an intercontinental campaign designed to carry a stage further the glorious work already inaugurated throughout the Western Hemisphere."[33]

While preserving the primacy of the responsibility assigned to the American Bahá'ís, the implementation of 'Abdu'l-Bahá's Plan, his Charter for the systematic expansion of the Bahá'í Faith, and the promulgation of its vision of a peaceful and united world has increasingly involved the active participation of all members of the global Bahá'í community. A later chapter will consider in detail the relationship between the unique role of the American Bahá'í community and the strategic approach to the ongoing systematic unfoldment of the Faith throughout the world.

Themes and Processes

Written at a time when the peoples of the world were suffering the impact of a terrible war, 'Abdu'l-Bahá's Tablets of the Divine Plan tap into the mood of the times and the intense longing for peace that grew out of the conflict. Addressing this urgent yearning, 'Abdu'l-Bahá provides a contrasting and uplifting vision of how the world might be, and he suggests steps to be taken not only to alleviate the existing crisis but also to foster the process of building a lasting and universal peace, a peace based on recognition of the oneness of the human family and the practice of attitudes and values that promote and sustain peace and conduce to the well-being and evolving maturity of humankind. In one of these letters, written on April 11, 1916, 'Abdu'l-Bahá writes: ". . . this world-consuming war has set such a conflagration to the hearts that no word can describe it. In all the countries of the world the longing for universal peace is taking possession of men. There is not a soul who does not yearn for concord and peace. A most wonderful state of receptivity is being realized. This is through the consummate wisdom of God, so that capacity may be created, the standard of the oneness of the world of humanity be upraised, and the fundamental of universal peace and the divine principles be promoted in the East and the West." To initiate this process, 'Abdu'l-Bahá instructed the "believers of God" to exert "an effort and after this war spread ye the synopsis of the divine teachings" throughout Europe.[34]

To understand the vision for the transformation of the world articulated in the Tablets of the Divine Plan, it is important to consider, in brief, some of the major themes embedded in these seminal documents and to examine a number of evolutionary processes that guide the implementation of individual and social transformation. An analysis of these themes will serve both to exemplify the visionary nature of these letters, and to illustrate their continuing and future relevance not only to the world-wide propagation of the Bahá'í Faith but also to the evolution of an orderly, just, and peaceful world.

THE ROLE OF RELIGION IN SOCIETY

From a Bahá'í perspective, the course of history is, in large part, shaped by the intermittent intervention of the Divine Will in the historical process. Religion is, therefore, regarded as playing a critical role in society and the ongoing development of civilization. At the heart of Bahá'í belief is the concept of progressive revelation, which involves the coming of divine Educators, or Manifestations of God, at periodic intervals in various parts of the world over the span of thousands of years. Each of these Manifestations of God, who are the Founders of the world's great religious systems, brings teachings appropriate to the needs of the age in which they appear. These teachings provide the inspiration and values for the advance of civilization and propel humanity forward toward a promised time of world unity, human rights, and peace. The seminal writings and creative impulse, when translated into constructive action, unlock individual potential and stimulate social development. The Báb and Bahá'u'lláh, Whose advent the Báb foretold, are the Founders of the Bahá'í Faith. They are the most recent of these Educators, and as such, fit into this historical process.

Bahá'ís attribute the principal influence in the gradual civilizing of human character to the effect produced on the rational soul by the guidance of the successive Messengers of God. It is They, Who, in each age, have defined the meaning and requirements of modernity. They have been the ultimate Educators of humankind. In a treatise addressed to the people of Iran in 1875, 'Abdu'l-Bahá highlights the impact of the empowerment that derives from the values and ideals promulgated by these spiritual Educators: "Universal benefits derive from the grace of the divine religions, for they lead their true followers to sincerity of intent, to high purpose, to purity and spotless honor, to surpassing kindness and compassion, to the keeping of their covenants when they have covenanted, to concern for the rights of others, to

liberality, to justice in every aspect of life, to humanity and philan-
thropy, to valor and to unflagging efforts in the service of mankind.
It is religion, to sum up, which produces all human virtues, and it is
these virtues which are the bright candles of civilization."[35]

'Abdu'l-Bahá returns to the subject of the historical and transformative role of religion in society in the final Tablet of his Divine Plan.
Written on March 8, 1917, the letter states:

> Consider how the religions of God served the world of human-
> ity! How the religion of Torah became conducive to the glory and
> honor and progress of the Israelitish nation! How the breaths of
> the Holy Spirit of His Holiness Christ created affinity and unity
> between divergent communities and quarreling families! How the
> sacred power of His Holiness Muḥammad became the means of
> uniting and harmonizing the contentious tribes and the different
> clans of Peninsular Arabia—to such an extent that one thousand
> tribes were welded into one tribe; strife and discord were done
> away with; all of them unitedly and with one accord strove in
> advancing the cause of culture and civilization, and thus were
> freed from the lowest degree of degradation, soaring toward the
> height of everlasting glory![36]

'Abdu'l-Bahá characterizes "the sacred religions" as a "divine Collective
Center." He links the capacity of religion to foster unity and transform society and its institutions to "the spirit of the divine teachings,"
introduced by the Prophets and promulgated by the followers of the
religion. The work of spreading the divine teachings, thus, has priority. 'Abdu'l-Bahá exclaims: "This is the most great work! Should you
become confirmed therein, this world will become another world, the
surface of the earth will become the delectable paradise, and eternal
Institutions be founded."[37]

It is, therefore, evident that the importance of this work to which
the Baháʾís are called extends beyond the mere expansion of the
membership of a faith community. Rather, 'Abdu'l-Bahá stresses the
relationship between the actions of the Baháʾís in sharing the teachings

of their Faith to the transformation of the individual and to laying the foundations for enduring social change.

ENGAGEMENT WITH SOCIETY

From the foregoing pages, it is apparent that implicit in the Tablets of the Divine Plan is recognition that the Bahá'í Faith is a religion of change and regards all human beings as having the true purpose of participating in an ever-advancing civilization. The Faith aims to create unity between the diverse elements of humankind. Its teachings include principles that are directed to all aspects of human thought and conduct that promote individual and social development. The concept of change is embedded in the teachings of the Bahá'í Faith. Central to Bahá'í belief is the view that ". . . religious truth is not absolute but relative, that Divine Revelation is a continuous and progressive process, that all the great religions of the world are divine in origin, that their basic principles are in complete harmony, that their aims and purposes are one and the same, that their teachings are but facets of one truth, that their functions are complementary, that they differ only in the non-essential aspects of their doctrines, and that their missions represent successive stages in the spiritual evolution of human society." Hence, the Bahá'í Faith does not aim to belittle the station of the Prophet-Founders of past religions, nor to diminish their teachings. Rather, it seeks "to restate the basic truths which these teachings enshrine in a manner that would conform to the needs, and be in consonance with the capacity, and be applicable to the problems, the ills and perplexities, of the age in which we live."[38]

As a contemporary religion that addresses the issues confronting the modern world, it follows that for the Baha'i Faith to make its contribution to society, its members must not only be aware of what is transpiring in the world but also be actively engaged in sharing ideas and values that serve to ameliorate "the ills and perplexities, of the age" and to take steps to further social evolution. Conscious of the fact that "the civilization that beckons humanity will not be attained through the efforts of the Bahá'í community alone," the religion also actively reaches out and progressively collaborates with like-minded groups and organizations, animated by the spirit of world solidarity, to influence the forces toward peace and order in the world.[39]

Within the above context, it is interesting to observe that the Tablets of the Divine Plan characterize war, which is one of the scourges of the age, as "the destroyer of the foundation of man," and that 'Abdu'l-Bahá compares the distress and anxiety suffered by the peoples of the world to their being submerged in "the abyss of the ocean of hatred and enmity." Likewise, the antidote, peace, is described as "the founder of the prosperity of the human race," and, to initiate the process of individual and social transformation, 'Abdu'l-Bahá assigns the following practical tasks to his followers: "In every city and village they must occupy themselves with the diffusion of the divine exhortations and advices, guide the souls and promote the oneness of the world of humanity. They must play the melody of international conciliation with such power that every deaf one may attain hearing, every extinct person may be set aglow, every dead one may obtain new life and every indifferent soul may find ecstasy. It is certain that such will be the consummation."[40]

ONENESS OF HUMANKIND—
THE ORGANIZING PRINCIPLE FOR ACTION

When Bahá'u'lláh proclaimed His Message to the world in the nineteenth century, He made it abundantly clear that the first step essential for the peace and progress of humankind was its unification. Bahá'u'lláh states that "the fundamental purposing animating" His religion, is "to safeguard the interests and promote the unity of the human race, and to foster the spirit of love and fellowship amongst men." He cautions against making religion "a source of dissension and discord, of hate and enmity," affirming, "This is the straight Path, the fixed and immovable foundation. Whatsoever is raised on this foundation, the changes and chances of the world can never impair its strength, nor will the revolution of countless centuries undermine its structure." And He warns, "The well-being of mankind, its peace and security, are unattainable unless and until its unity is firmly established." The achievement of this unity is Bahá'u'lláh's declared mission and the aim of all Bahá'í activity.[41]

The principle of the oneness of humankind has both philosophical and practical implications.[42] The Universal House of Justice states that "The oneness of mankind . . . is at once the operating principle and ultimate goal" of Bahá'u'lláh's Revelation and, further, that it "implies the achievement of a dynamic coherence between the spiritual and practical requirements of life on earth." Describing this principle as "the pivot round which all the teachings of Bahá'u'lláh revolve," Shoghi Effendi, in the passage cited below, highlights the significance of the principle and underscores some of its far-reaching, long-term ramifications for social transformation. It is, he writes

> . . . no mere outburst of ignorant emotionalism or an expression of vague and pious hope. Its appeal is not to be merely identified with a reawakening of the spirit of brotherhood and good-will among men, nor does it aim solely at the fostering of harmonious cooperation among individual peoples and nations. Its implications are deeper, its claims greater than any which the Prophets of old were allowed to advance. Its message is applicable not only to the individual, but concerns itself primarily with the nature of those essential relationships that must bind all the states and nations as members of one human family. . . . It implies an organic change in the structure of present-day society, a change such as the world has not experienced. . . . It calls for no less than the reconstruction and the demilitarization of the whole civilized world—a world organically unified in all the essential aspects of its life, its political machinery, its spiritual aspiration, its trade and finance, its script and language, and yet infinite in the diversity of the national characteristics of its federated units.[43]

It is recognized that the challenges facing a slowly maturing world are not only inevitable but also potentially difficult to surmount, and that the changes called for are likely to evolve in the centuries to come.[44] Shoghi Effendi underlines some of the tasks that lie ahead in this transformative process. He writes:

> Unification of the whole of mankind is the hall-mark of the stage which human society is now approaching. Unity of family, of tribe, of city-state, and nation have been successively attempted and fully established. World unity is the goal towards which a harassed humanity is striving. Nation-building has come to an end. The anarchy inherent in state sovereignty is moving towards a climax. A world, growing to maturity, must abandon this fetish, recognize the oneness and wholeness of human relationships, and establish once for all the machinery that can best incarnate this fundamental principle of its life.[45]

Alluding to the critical importance of achieving "a dynamic coherence between the spiritual and practical requirements of life on earth," 'Abdu'l-Bahá, in the Tablets of the Divine Plan, refers to various forms of social organization that are conducive to association and unity between peoples as "collective centers." Included among the examples he provides are "patriotism," "nationalism," "identity of interests," "political alliance," and "union of ideals." Stressing the importance of these structures, he states that "the prosperity of the world of humanity is dependent upon the organization and promotion of the collective centers." However, 'Abdu'l-Bahá also observes that such social structures tend to be transitory in nature because of certain inherent limitations. "All the above institutions," he asserts, "are, in reality, the matter and not the substance, accidental and not eternal—temporary and not everlasting. With the appearance of great revolutions and upheavals, all these collective centers are swept away."[46]

'Abdu'l-Bahá allies the infusion of spiritual values into the life of society and its institutions with the achievement of a world-embracing, inclusive, and lasting unity. In this regard, he calls attention to the contribution of "the Collective Center of the Kingdom," which embodies "the institutions and divine teachings." This "eternal Collective Center," he writes,

. . . establishes relationship between the East and the West, organizes the oneness of the world of humanity, and destroys the
foundation of differences. It overcomes and includes all the other
collective centers. Like unto the ray of the sun, it dispels entirely
the darkness encompassing all the regions, bestows ideal life, and
causes the effulgence of divine illumination. Through the breaths
of the Holy Spirit it performs miracles; the Orient and the Occident embrace each other, the North and South become intimates
and associates, conflicting and contending opinions disappear,
antagonistic aims are brushed aside, the law of the struggle for
existence is abrogated, and the canopy of the oneness of the
world of humanity is raised on the apex of the globe, casting its
shade over all the races of men. Consequently, the real Collective
Center is the body of the divine teachings, which include all the
degrees and embrace all the universal relations and necessary laws
of humanity.[47]

EVOLUTIONARY CHANGE

The profound changes called for in the Bahá'í Revelation are
destined to impact the individual, the community, and the structure
of society. Commenting on the nature of this process of change,
Bahá'u'lláh makes the following challenging pronouncement, "is not
the object of every Revelation to effect a transformation in the whole
character of mankind, a transformation that shall manifest itself, both
outwardly and inwardly, that shall affect both its inner life and external
conditions?"[48]

Given the far-reaching transformations envisioned, the Bahá'í writings anticipate that the process of change will be evolutionary in nature.
This civilization-building enterprise is, in the words of the Universal
House of Justice, one "of infinite complexity and scale, one that will
demand centuries of exertion by humanity to bring to fruition." And,
it cautions that "There are no shortcuts, no formulas." Its tasks are
challenging and multifaceted. They include understanding the vision
of the oneness of the human family, transforming human values and
systems of governance, and creating opportunities for peace to emerge.

The way forward will not be smooth. Crises will increase the hunger for security and justice, and will strengthen resolve and intensify the search for creative ways to surmount stubborn obstacles to unity.[49]

While the process of change is evolutionary, it is not haphazard. Rather, the trajectory of evolution and the pace at which it unfolds derive their direction and inspiration from the Bahá'í writings. The Tablets of the Divine Plan illustrate aspects of the conscious strategic approach associated with the promotion of evolutionary change. For example, the Tablets articulate the vision of a peaceful and united world, where "the mirror of the earth may become the mirror of the Kingdom, reflecting the ideal virtues of heaven." To translate this poetic vision into a concrete plan, 'Abdu'l-Bahá specifies that the teachings of the New Day be promulgated throughout all the nations and islands of the world. To assist the American Bahá'ís to approach this massive task in a systematic manner, he not only lists the countries and island groups by name, but he also specifies the order in which this task is to be completed, and he gives priority to certain cities like Bahia, Brazil and geographic areas, such as Alaska and Panama.[50]

To ensure the initiation of the process, 'Abdu'l-Bahá stresses the importance of taking a first step. Recalling the early days of Christianity, he sets out an important principle of growth: "Nearly two thousand years ago, Armenia was enveloped with impenetrable darkness. One blessed soul from among the disciples of Christ hastened to that part, and through his effort, erelong that province became illumined. Thus it has become evident how the power of the Kingdom works!"[51]

Likewise, 'Abdu'l-Bahá instills an awareness of the long-term nature of the enterprise by use of the analogy of farming. He calls upon the believers to become "heavenly farmers and scatter pure seeds in the prepared soil," and promises that "Throughout the coming centuries and cycles many harvests will be gathered." He states, "Consider the work of former generations. During the lifetime of Jesus Christ the believing, firm souls were few and numbered, but the heavenly blessings descended so plentifully that in a number of years countless souls entered beneath the shadow of the Gospel."[52]

Furthermore, 'Abdu'l-Bahá calls for a realistic assessment of the manner in which a particular task is completed, and stresses the importance of having a systematic approach to the work. Assessing the progress of the teaching work in several of the Central States, for example, he observes, "So far the summons of the Kingdom of God and the proclamation of the oneness of the world of humanity has not been made in these states systematically and enthusiastically. Blessed souls and detached teachers have not traveled through these parts repeatedly; therefore these states are still in a state of heedlessness." He goes on to emphasize the spiritual and personal qualities of the teacher that are critical to success. "If it is possible," he states, ". . . send to those parts teachers who are severed from all else save God, sanctified and pure. If these teachers be in the utmost state of attraction, in a short time great results will be forthcoming. The sons and daughters of the kingdom are like unto the real farmers. Through whichever state or country they pass they display self-sacrifice and sow divine seeds. From that seed harvests are produced."[53]

The implementation of the mandate set out in the Tablets of the Divine Plan is itself an evolutionary process, a process that is described by Shoghi Effendi as being "laborious and tremendously long." Indeed, 'Abdu'l-Bahá challenged the North American Bahá'ís to extend the "scope" of their "exertions," promising "The wider its range, the more striking will be the evidence of divine assistance." Further, in another Tablet he foreshadows the long-term nature of the tasks that lie ahead. He writes, "The range of your future achievements still remains undisclosed. I fervently hope that in the near future the whole earth may be stirred and shaken by the results of your achievements. The hope, therefore, which 'Abdu'l-Bahá cherishes for you is that the same success which has attended your efforts in America may crown your endeavors in other parts of the world, that through you the fame of the Cause of God may be diffused throughout the East and the West and the advent of the Kingdom of the Lord of Hosts be proclaimed in all the five continents of the globe." In later chapters, some of the details of the strategies involved in fostering the unfoldment of 'Abdu'l-Bahá's Divine Plan will be explored.[54]

CAPACITY BUILDING

The purpose underlying every Revelation is, in the words of Bahá'u'lláh, "to endue all men with righteousness and understanding, so that peace and tranquillity may be firmly established amongst men." Calling upon His followers to participate in this transformative process, He writes, "Address yourselves to the promotion of the well-being and tranquillity of the children of men. Bend your minds and wills to the education of the peoples and kindreds of the earth, that haply the dissensions that divide it may, through the power of the Most Great Name, be blotted out from its face, and all mankind become the upholders of one Order, the inhabitants of one City." Further, Bahá'u'lláh imposes certain preconditions on those who wish to serve in this way. He cautions, "Whoso ariseth among you to teach the Cause of his Lord, let him, before all else, teach his own self, that his speech may attract the hearts of them that hear him. Unless he teacheth his own self, the words of his mouth will not influence the heart of the seeker. . . ." And, in relation to teaching, He indicates:

Such a deed is acceptable only when he that teacheth the Cause is already a firm believer in God, the Supreme Protector, the Gracious, the Almighty. He hath, moreover, ordained that His Cause be taught through the power of men's utterance, and not through resort to violence. Thus hath His ordinance been sent down from the Kingdom of Him Who is the Most Exalted, the All-Wise. Beware lest ye contend with anyone, nay, strive to make him aware of the truth with kindly manner and most convincing exhortation. If your hearer respond, he will have responded to his own behoof, and if not, turn ye away from him, and set your faces towards God's sacred Court, the seat of resplendent holiness.[55]

Intrinsic to the implementation of this mandate is the development of human resources at the level of the individual, the community, and administrative structures. Education is critical to furthering this transformative process. It serves to promote the spiritual, intellectual, and social aspects of Bahá'í life. On the level of individual capacity building, 'Abdu'l-Bahá's Tablets of the Divine Plan call for the development of spiritual qualities, the acquisition of deep knowledge of the history and teachings of the Faith, and commitment to endeavoring to practice the laws and principles of the Bahá'í Faith in one's personal life. For example, we read: "The teachers of the Cause must be heavenly, lordly, and radiant. They must be embodied spirit, personified intellect, and arise with the utmost firmness, steadfastness and self-sacrifice."[56] To inspire the acquisition of such qualities and to encourage the Bahá'ís to engage in the act of teaching, 'Abdu'l-Bahá provides a number of special prayers for the teachers to recite. In addition, he encourages those who plan to arise to spread the Faith outside of North America to prepare themselves, prior to their departure, by attempting to learn the language and become familiar with the culture and conditions of the country to which they intend to travel.

As a means of fostering capacity-building at the level of the community, 'Abdu'l-Bahá calls for classes to be instituted for training teachers, including the youth, and for the holding of meetings to make known the aims and teachings of the Bahá'í Faith. He calls for the appointment of committees charged with the translation, publication, and distribution of Bahá'í literature, and for the publication of *Star of the West*, a magazine concerned with promoting information and news about the Bahá'í Faith and its worldview.[57]

'Abdu'l-Bahá also foreshadows the emergence of administrative structures that are necessary to sustain and enhance the processes of capacity-building and guide the evolution of a peaceful and united world. In this regard, he refers to the significant contribution to the development of the embryonic administration of the new Faith made by the Bahá'ís of Chicago. This city has the distinction of being the one where the Bahá'í Faith was first mentioned in North America. He calls attention to the establishment of the institution of the Mashriqu'l-Adhkár (Bahá'í House of Worship) in Chicago, the first to be established in the West, and he presages the importance of this city as the future site of the national headquarters of the religion in the United States. Anticipating the consequent efflorescence of institutional capacity, he observes, "Up to the present time, every movement initiated in Chicago, its effect was spread to all parts and to all directions, just as everything that appears in and manifests from the heart influences all the organs and limbs of the body."[58]

THE CALL TO APOSTLESHIP

From the foregoing it is apparent that a complex of personal qualities and skills, and individual, social, and institutional capacities are needed to develop and nurture the processes required for fostering the spiritual regeneration of the planet. 'Abdu'l-Bahá relates the initiation of this great enterprise in contemporary times to the historic work undertaken by the apostles of Christ. Recalling the instructions of Christ, 'Abdu'l-Bahá exhorts the American Bahá'ís to "Travel . . . to the East and to the West of the world and summon the people to the Kingdom of God!"[59]

'Abdu'l-Bahá calls the believers to the station of apostleship, a designation calculated both to inspire action and to underline the sacred, historic nature of their task. At the same time, he informs them that the attainment of "this supreme station," that of "Apostle of Bahá'u'lláh," is "dependent on the realization of certain conditions." Thus, to engage successfully in the challenging work of society-building, the present-day apostles must satisfy three critical and interrelated conditions specified by 'Abdu'l-Bahá—namely, the teachers must be firm in the Covenant of God; demonstrate fellowship and love amongst the believers; and travel to all parts of the globe to spread the teachings of the New Day.[60]

The three prerequisites outlined by 'Abdu'l-Bahá for the attainment to the station of "Apostle of Bahá'u'lláh" are the subject of later chapters. It is, however, useful to mention, in brief, some of their important implications for the transformation of the world of humanity.

The first condition is firmness in the Covenant of God.[61] A Covenant in the religious sense is a binding agreement between God and man, where God requires of man certain behaviors in return for which He guarantees certain blessings. Hence, those who accept the authority of a Messenger of God make a firm commitment to endeavor to put the teachings of the religion into practice in their daily life. This not only contributes to the spiritual development of the individual but also has the potential for illustrating the transformative value of the application of the religion's teachings to community life.

Another form of Covenant is that made by a Messenger of God with His followers concerning their acceptance of His appointed successor and the arrangements for the organization of the religion after the death of its Founder. The terms of the Covenant of Bahá'u'lláh provide for the appointment of 'Abdu'l-Bahá as His designated successor and for the establishment of administrative institutions. These institutions, to which the Bahá'ís owe their loyal and willing support, have the authority to direct the affairs of the Faith. The provisions of this Covenant ensure the continuity of the community and at the same time provide a balance between individual initiative and unified collective action. Its institutions are designed to provide for the progressive clarification and progressive application of the Bahá'í teachings, thereby guaranteeing the flexibility of the religion and preserving its ability to remain a creative agent of change.

The second condition is fellowship and love amongst the believers. At one level, this requirement relates to the quality of the relationships between the members of the community. At a more fundamental level, its practice illustrates the operation of the power of the love of God in creating unity, and the demonstration of its transforming influence serves to attract people to the values of the Bahá'í Faith.

The third condition set out by 'Abdu'l-Bahá calls for teachers to "continually travel . . . to all parts of the world." Implicit in this condition is the expectation that the teacher must manifest and demonstrate certain spiritual qualities. Rather than being motivated by personal ambition and financial rewards, such teachers must be conscious of the exalted task they are called upon to perform. The presence of spiritually developed individuals in diverse countries and cultures acts as a spiritual leaven and inspires others to practice such qualities. It illustrates the universal appeal and relevance of the Teachings of the Faith to the needs of society, and fosters an increased awareness of the intrinsic oneness of humankind and an appreciation of diversity.[62]

Conclusion

The fourteen letters known collectively as Tablets of the Divine Plan share some of the features of the seminal documents described earlier in this chapter. Similar to the Magna Carta, the American Constitution, and the United Nations Declaration of Human Rights, these Tablets were written at a particular point in time and address a specific historical situation, and because of their visionary character, all have continuing relevance. The first three documents have furthered the discourse concerning human dignity and individual rights and freedoms, and they have made a significant contribution to the evolution of the world's legal and political systems. Similarly, 'Abdu'l-Bahá's letters broaden the understanding of the nature of man by emphasizing the essential oneness of the human family and its implications for social organization and governance. Beyond the exposition of visionary ideas, the Tablets call for the adoption of specific strategies aimed at promoting the spiritual, intellectual, and social processes necessary to create the environment in which lasting global peace and unity can emerge.

The Tablets of the Divine Plan articulate an approach to change that is realistic, long-term, evolutionary, and flexible. Their approach is organic, striving to achieve coherence between the spiritual and material aspects of life. Critical to this process is the progressive transformation of values at the level of the individual, the community, and the institutions, and the development of the necessary skills and capacities in these cohorts to tackle and resolve the issues confronting humankind as it continues to evolve toward its stage of maturity.

To initiate the processes associated with the kind of strategic change outlined in his Tablets, 'Abdu'l-Bahá begins by focusing on the most pressing problem facing the world at that time—namely, the establishment of universal peace. He then assigns primary responsibility to the American Bahá'ís for the task of sharing the unifying message of their religion with the peoples of the world in a systematic and phased manner, since this is an effective means by which the values of peace and unity can be diffused throughout the five continents of the globe.

The capacity of the Tablets of the Divine Plan to make a continuing contribution to the transformation of life on this planet derives not only from the fact that these seminal letters outline specific strategies and processes designed to translate 'Abdu'l-Bahá's visionary concepts into practical reality, but that they also contain provisions to ensure the evolving task is carried out in a systematic and timely manner by assigning primary responsibility to the Bahá'í community for the completion of specific phases of this unfolding enterprise.

2

Call to the Nations

The Revelation of Bahá'u'lláh, the Manifestation of God for the modern age, diagnoses the condition of human society and prescribes the necessary remedy to enable humanity to take the next steps in its unfolding destiny. As the inspired Divine Physician, Bahá'u'lláh's assessment of the state of the world and the prescription He offers represent an expression of the Divine Will.

The purpose of the Bahá'í Faith is to present to the world Bahá'u'lláh's message of hope, of love, and of practical reconstruction. The divinely inspired teachings of the religion provide the direction and spiritual impetus to lead humanity to the new age of maturity, unity, and peace, foreshadowed in His writings. Bahá'u'lláh Himself initiated the process of promulgating His message. To this end, He employed a variety of means. Among others, He addressed letters to specific individuals, including the kings and religious leaders of His day, openly proclaiming His station and expounding His teachings. He arranged for the wide dissemination and circulation of His writings both within the nascent Bahá'í community and beyond; and He dispatched Bahá'í teachers to different parts of the Orient and beyond. His approach was strategic and progressive. In the first instance, He disclosed His mission to His close companions, then, more broadly, to the members of the Bahá'í community, and finally to the world at large.

In this chapter, we examine the significance of the mandate set out in the Tablets of the Divine Plan that 'Abdu'l-Bahá addressed to the American Bahá'í community in the light of Bahá'u'lláh's historic public proclamation of His message to the kings and religious leaders of the day. We begin by describing in brief some of the features of Bahá'u'lláh's proclamation, the context in which His Tablets to the kings were revealed, the events that transpired, and the nature of the response to His call. Against this background, we then consider the relationship between Bahá'u'lláh's proclamation and the Divine Plan of 'Abdu'l-Bahá. In particular, we will illustrate how, in the Tablets of the Divine Plan 'Abdu'l-Bahá takes up the unfinished business of promulgating and implementing the salutary message of peace, justice, and unity contained in the Tablets of Bahá'u'lláh addressed to the kings and ecclesiastical leaders of the world. Finally, we explore some of the implications for the role of the Bahá'í community.

Tablets to the Kings

The public proclamation of Bahá'u'lláh's message to the world at large through Tablets He addressed to the kings and rulers of the earth took place over a period of several years. It began in 1863 during Bahá'u'lláh's exile in Constantinople (present-day Instanbul), continued during His stay in Adrianople (present-day Edirne), and reached its climax during His confinement in the prison city of 'Akká. These historic Tablets are published in English translation in a volume titled *The Summons of the Lord of Hosts*.[1]

The messages of Bahá'u'lláh to the kings and religious leaders form an integral part of a new divine Revelation. These Tablets, though addressed to the monarchs, can also be considered as constituting more broadly a general call to all nations and peoples. The major topics outlined in these Tablets include the announcement of Bahá'u'lláh's rank and station, the elucidation of the relationship between His message and the will of God, and the elaboration of the essential principles of the new world order whose advent would mark the coming of age of the human race.

The Tablets to the kings were written in clear and unmistakable language. In brief, they announced the dawning of the long-promised age of world peace and brotherhood and asserted that Bahá'u'lláh Himself was the Bearer of the new message and power from God that would transform the prevailing system of antagonism and enmity between men and create the spirit and form of the destined world order. Bahá'u'lláh foresaw and forewarned of the potential for chaos and conflict inherent in the prevailing social and political order, declaring, "Soon, will the present day order be rolled up and a new one spread out in its stead," and plainly affirmed that the unity of the human race was the essence of His World Order. "The fundamental purpose animating the Faith of God and His Religion," He wrote, "is to safeguard the interests and promote the unity of the human race, and to foster the spirit of love and fellowship amongst men."[2]

Bahá'u'lláh called upon the kings to examine His Cause with fairness and justice. He disclosed to them the uniqueness of the God-given opportunity His call presented to them, to make a significant contribution to the establishment of peace in conformity with the divine vision of the unfolding historical process. He enjoined them to take counsel together, to institute the reign of justice, to compose their differences, and to reduce their armaments in order to end the excessive expenditures that were impoverishing their subjects. To this end, the rulers were instructed to convene a world conference and establish a mechanism for collective security and the maintenance of peace.

In addition, Bahá'u'lláh instructed these rulers to safeguard the rights of the downtrodden and to punish wrongdoers, and He informed them of His afflictions. He warned them that they would be held responsible before God for their actions. Unless the leaders united in their efforts to establish peace and root out social injustice, Bahá'u'lláh cautioned, their countries would be thrown into chaos and power would slip from their hands. At the same time, He assured the kings that His mission was "to seize and possess the hearts of men," disclaiming any intention to lay hands on their kingdoms.[3]

It is significant that Bahá'u'lláh chose to direct the proclamation of His mission to the kings and religious leaders of the world, who, in the words of Shoghi Effendi, "by virtue of the power and authority they wielded, were invested with a peculiar and inescapable responsibility for the destinies of their subjects." Elaborating on this subject, the Guardian states that these rulers "were still, for the most part, wielding unquestioned and absolute civil and ecclesiastical authority over their subjects and followers," and, as a consequence, "the masses . . . dominated and shackled, were robbed of the necessary freedom that would enable them to either appraise the claims and merits of the Message proffered them, or to embrace unreservedly its truth." Shoghi Effendi asserts, "It would be no exaggeration to say that in most of the countries of the European and Asiatic continents absolutism, on the one hand, and complete subservience to ecclesiastical hierarchies, on the other, were still the outstanding features of the political and religious life of the masses."[4]

All the kings and rulers of the earth were collectively addressed by Bahá'u'lláh in His Tablets of proclamation. In addition, specific Tablets were dispatched to individual rulers such as the Sultán of Turkey, the Shah of Persia, Kaiser Wilhelm I, Czar Alexander II, Napoleon III, Queen Victoria, and Pope Pius IX. Furthermore, a wide range of influential civil and religious personages and leaders of thought were, through these same letters and Tablets, informed of the mission and station of Bahá'u'lláh. Expounding on the vast scope of this historic proclamation, Shoghi Effendi writes:

Kings and emperors, severally and collectively; the chief magistrates of the Republics of the American continent; ministers and ambassadors; the Sovereign Pontiff himself; the Vicar of the Prophet of Islam; the royal Trustee of the Kingdom of the Hidden Imam; the monarchs of Christendom, its patriarchs, archbishops, bishops, priests and monks; the recognized leaders of both the Sunní and Shí'ah sacerdotal orders; the high priests of the Zoroastrian religion; the philosophers, the ecclesiastical leaders, the wise men and the inhabitants of Constantinople—that proud seat of both the Sultanate and the Caliphate; the entire company of the professed adherents of the Zoroastrian, the Jewish, the Christian and Muslim Faiths; the people of the Bayán; the wise men of the world, its men of letters, its poets, its mystics, its tradesmen, the elected representatives of its peoples; His own countrymen—all have, at one time or another, in books, Epistles, and Tablets, been brought directly within the purview of the exhortations, the warnings, the appeals, the declarations and the prophecies which constitute the theme of His momentous summons to the leaders of mankind . . .[5]

Such was the breadth of the proclamation of Bahá'u'lláh to humankind. He Himself was moved to testify, "Never since the beginning of the world hath the Message been so openly proclaimed."[6]

An in-depth study and analysis of the contents of the Tablets of proclamation, of the specific guidance provided by Bahá'u'lláh to each of the rulers, the nature of their individual response, and its impact on the life of the kings is beyond the scope of this book. Suffice it to say, while Bahá'u'lláh's Tablets to particular kings and to the pope were delivered, they were either ignored or rejected by their recipients. Indeed, in one instance, the young man who delivered the Tablet to the Persian Shah was cruelly tortured and killed.[7]

The wise counsel and the warnings contained in the Tablets represented both the portentous expression and the judgment of the Divine Will. Had this counsel been implemented by the kings and ecclesiastical leaders, it would have minimized human suffering and given rise to the emergence of a peaceful and united world. However, history shows that it not only went unheeded but precipitated renewed and increased persecution of Bahá'u'lláh and of the Bahá'í community in the East. Only Queen Victoria was reported to have made a sympathetic response. Overall, the reaction of those to whom His message of hope and transformation was addressed was negative and dismissive. Shoghi Effendi provides examples of "the evidences of the treatment meted out by a generation sunk in self-content, careless of its God, and oblivious of the omens, prophecies, warnings and admonitions revealed by His Messengers." He includes the

Unmitigated indifference on the part of men of eminence and rank; unrelenting hatred shown by the ecclesiastical dignitaries of the Faith from which it had sprung; the scornful derision of the people among whom it was born; the utter contempt which most of those kings and rulers who had been addressed by its Author manifested towards it; the condemnations pronounced, the threats hurled, and the banishments decreed by those under whose sway it arose and first spread; the distortion to which its principles and laws were subjected by the envious and the malicious, in lands and among peoples far beyond the country of its origin . . .[8]

Commenting on the implications of the failure of the kings and religious leaders to respond to the prophetic and healing message contained in Bahá'u'lláh's Tablets of proclamation, historian, Geoffrey Nash writes:

. . . the world of 1870–1914 did not accept the principles which Bahá'u'lláh then stated would conduce to its tranquility. That it did not lay down its armaments, convene a world conference and establish a collective security, history attests only too clearly. That in fact it has taken well nigh one hundred years for human agencies to begin to think in universal terms and to tackle the problems of mankind as though there was indeed only one home—the entire earth—is painfully apparent, looking back. The world has only recently caught up with and begun to implement the wonderful principles of this remarkable personage.[9]

The rejection by the kings and ecclesiastics and other important personages of the principles outlined by Bahá'u'lláh in no way negates the relevance of the guidance He proffered for this time in history. Rather, their failure brings into sharp focus the critical continuing needs of a world progressively descending into a condition of conflict and crisis for want of His divinely inspired teachings of unity, justice, and peace. The negligence of the rulers deprived them of the God-given opportunity to be the vehicles for the achievement of Bahá'u'lláh's prophetic vision of world order in accordance with the Divine Will.

The closing years of the nineteenth and early years of the twentieth centuries was a period of tumultuous changes. The Ottoman, Qájár, Austro-Hungarian, and Russian empires were overthrown, the Muslim caliphate was dissolved, and the Vatican was deprived of much of its temporal power. Revolutions swept over a number of countries. Politically, this period was marked by the coming into office of new governments in all the major countries of Europe and many of the smaller ones, allowing for a degree of popular representation and the gradual extension of the right to vote. Historian David Earl observes that, "Policymaking was moving into the hands of the bourgeoisie and the industrialists; social standards also were increasingly dominated by the middle class."[10] Socially, free public, secular education was becoming available to the masses for the first time in history, and the influence of the religious hierarchy began to diminish with the new role and importance accorded to science and technology.[10]

Earl considers that the radical changes in the political, intellectual, and social climate that coincided with and followed Bahá'u'lláh's call to the rulers might well have constituted a turning-point, not only for Europe but for the world as a whole. To this end, he suggests, "It was thus that the closing decades of the nineteenth century played their special role in the general age of crisis, minimizing the power of kings and ecclesiastics, bringing the adolescence of the human race almost to a close, and preparing it for its imminent coming of age."[11]

In the Tablets of the Divine Plan, 'Abdu'l-Bahá takes up the unfinished business of promulgating and implementing the salutary message of peace, justice, and unity contained in the Tablets of Bahá'u'lláh addressed to the kings and ecclesiastical leaders of the world.

Relationship between the Proclamation to the Kings and Religious Leaders and the Tablets of the Divine Plan

While Bahá'u'lláh's proclamation was addressed to the kings and religious leaders of the world, including the "Rulers of America and the Presidents of the Republics therein," 'Abdu'l-Bahá's Tablets of the Divine Plan focused primarily on the members of the North American

Bahá'í community.[12] From an analysis of some of the statements in these historic Tablets of Bahá'u'lláh and 'Abdu'l-Bahá, it is evident that they envision a special mission for the West and indeed for the continent of America.

THE SIGNIFICANCE OF THE WEST

The Bahá'í writings anticipate that the West is destined to play a central and distinctive role in the emergence of a new world order. This critical function dates back to the very outset of the Bahá'í era. It was implicitly initiated by processes set in motion when the Báb, the Herald of the Faith, in His first book, the Qayyúmu'l-Asmá, addressed the peoples of the West and called upon them to "issue forth" from their cities to aid God, and to "become as brethren" in His "one and indivisible religion."[13]

In the Kitáb-i-Aqdas, His Book of Laws, Bahá'u'lláh fanned and gave direction to this creative impulse by addressing "the Chief Magistrates of the entire American continent" and specifically commissioning these Rulers to "bind with the hands of justice the broken," and "crush the oppressor" with the "rod of the commandments" of their Lord. Shoghi Effendi attests that "this remarkable pronouncement" conferred "distinction upon the sovereign rulers of the Western Hemisphere." In this regard, he calls attention to the marked difference in tone between Bahá'u'lláh's address to the rulers of the American continent and His Tablets to the other Kings and Rulers of the world. Underlining this distinction, Shoghi Effendi writes:

Unlike the kings of the earth whom He had so boldly condemned in that same Book, unlike the European Sovereigns whom He had either rebuked, warned or denounced, such as the French Emperor, the most powerful monarch of his time; the Conqueror of that monarch; the Heir of the Holy Roman Empire; and the Caliph of Islám; the Rulers of America were not only spared the ominous and emphatic warnings which He uttered against the crowned heads of the world, but were called upon to bring their

44

corrective and healing influence to bear upon the injustices perpetrated by the tyrannical and the ungodly.[14]

Furthermore, concerning the role of the West and the destiny of America, there are portentous statements of Bahá'u'lláh that foreshadow the sovereignty His Revelation will achieve through the actions of those who will champion His Faith in the West, including the following: "In the East the light of His Revelation hath broken; in the West have appeared the signs of His dominion. Ponder this in your hearts, O people, and be not of those who have turned a deaf ear to the admonitions of Him Who is the Almighty, the All-Praised."[15]

In commenting on the unique importance and the significant role played by the West in the history of religion, 'Abdu'l-Bahá describes, in one of his talks, the operation of a general and dynamic spiritual principle of growth. He testifies that, "From the beginning of time until the present day, the light of Divine Revelation hath risen in the East and shed its radiance upon the West. The illumination thus shed hath, however, acquired in the West an extraordinary brilliancy." To illustrate his point, 'Abdu'l-Bahá refers to the history of the Christian Faith, observing that, "Though it first appeared in the East, yet not until its light had been shed upon the West did the full measure of its potentialities become manifest." He then applies this principle to the development of the Bahá'í Faith, affirming, "The day is approaching when ye shall witness how, through the splendor of the Faith of Bahá'u'lláh, the West will have replaced the East, radiating the light of Divine guidance," and, in the following words, he predicts the spiritual ascendancy of the West: "The East hath, verily, been illumined with the light of the Kingdom. Erelong will this same light shed a still greater illumination upon the West."[16]

Through the revelation of the Tablets of the Divine Plan, 'Abdu'l-Bahá gives further impetus and clarity to the processes set in motion by the Báb and Bahá'u'lláh in relation to the role of the West. His seminal Tablets represent the continuity and extension of the guidance contained in Their Tablets. Underlying the closeness of the relationship between the rationale of Bahá'u'lláh's proclamation and the Tablets of the Divine Plan of 'Abdu'l-Bahá, Shoghi Effendi characterizes the "significant summons to the Chief Magistrates of the New World" as the "forerunner of the Mission with which the North American continent was to be later invested," and he further affirms, "The Divine Plan . . . may be said to have derived its inspiration from, and been dimly foreshadowed in, the injunction so significantly addressed by Bahá'u'lláh to the Chief Magistrates of the American continent."[17]

Elaborating on this theme, Shoghi Effendi also calls attention to the significance of the assignment of responsibility for the execution of the Plan to the American Bahá'í community: "In the Tablets of the Divine Plan, . . . which may be designated as the Charter of the Plan with which He was to entrust them in the evening of His life, He, in a language still more graphic and in terms more definite than those used by either the Báb or Bahá'u'lláh, revealed the high distinction and the glorious work which America, and particularly the United States and Canada, was to achieve in both the Formative and Golden Ages of the Bahá'í Dispensation."[18] Thus, by assigning responsibility to the continent of America, 'Abdu'l-Bahá set in train a strategic plan of action to be executed, in the first instance, by the American Bahá'í community.

Shoghi Effendi also provides insight into the reason 'Abdu'l-Bahá selected the American Bahá'í community to carry out this mission. He indicates that "It [the Divine Plan] was prompted by the contact established by 'Abdu'l-Bahá Himself, in the course of His historic journey, with the entire body of His followers throughout the United States and Canada. It was conceived, soon after that contact was established, in the midst of what was then held to be one of the most devastating crises in human history."[19]

'Abdu'l-Bahá's perception of the potential capacity of the American Bahá'ís to carry out the assigned functions, and his implicit confidence in their future accomplishments, are highlighted in the following prophetic statements from the Tablets of the Divine Plan:

> . . . the continent of America is, in the eyes of the one true God, the land wherein the splendors of His light shall be revealed,

where the mysteries of His Faith shall be unveiled, where the righteous will abide and the free assemble.[20]

Behold the portals which Bahá'u'lláh hath opened before you! Consider how exalted and lofty is the station you are destined to attain, how unique the favors with which you have been endowed.[21]

The full measure of your success is as yet unrevealed, its significance unapprehended.[22]

The moment this Divine Message is carried forward by the American believers from the shores of America, and is propagated through the continents of Europe, of Asia, of Africa and of Australia, and as far as the islands of the Pacific, this community will find itself securely established upon the throne of an everlasting dominion. Then will all the peoples of the world witness that this community is spiritually illumined and divinely guided. Then will the whole earth resound with the praises of its majesty and greatness.[23]

Shoghi Effendi provides additional insight into the investiture of North America with the divine mandate. While the community possessed such "virtues and qualities of high intelligence, of youthfulness, of unbounded initiative, and enterprise," it was at the same time immersed in a culture that was notorious for its "corruption, moral laxity and ingrained prejudice."[24]

Addressing the American Bahá'ís, the Guardian instructs them not to "imagine for a moment that for some mysterious purpose or by any reason of inherent excellence or special merit Bahá'u'lláh has chosen to confer upon their country and people so great and lasting a distinction." The fundamental reason for this special station, he explains, is "precisely" due to the pernicious influence of "an excessive and binding materialism," which gives rise to a number of "patent evils" in American society. In providing the rationale for the seemingly paradoxical operation of the Divine Will, Shoghi Effendi also describes some of the most pressing social issues confronting the nation, and he calls attention to the responsibility of the Bahá'ís to demonstrate the power of the Revelation to transform human behavior, and bring about significant social change. He writes:

> It is by such means as this that Bahá'u'lláh can best demonstrate to a heedless generation His almighty power to raise up from the very midst of a people, immersed in a sea of materialism, a prey to one of the most virulent and long-standing forms of racial prejudice, and notorious for its political corruption, lawlessness and laxity in moral standards, men and women who, as time goes by, will increasingly exemplify those essential virtues of self-renunciation, of moral rectitude, of chastity, of indiscriminating fellowship, of holy discipline, and of spiritual insight that will fit them for the preponderating share they will have in calling into being that World Order and that World Civilization of which their country, no less than the entire human race, stands in desperate need. Theirs will be the duty and privilege, . . . to inculcate, demonstrate, and apply those twin and sorely needed principles of Divine justice and order—principles to which the political corruption and the moral license, increasingly staining the society to which they belong, offer so sad and striking a contrast.[25]

STRATEGIC ASSIGNMENT OF RESPONSIBILITY

The Revelation of Bahá'u'lláh diagnosed the needs of humanity in modern times. As already mentioned, the hallmark of His teachings is the pivotal and world-shaping principle of the oneness of humankind that is destined to give rise to the evolution of a new spiritual and social order. Addressing "the concourse of the kings of the earth," Bahá'u'lláh counsels them to "Give ear unto the Voice of God."[26] He proclaimed His message and unfolded before the eyes of the rulers of the world, and through them to humanity as a whole, the Divine Plan destined to raise mankind to a higher level of development and to create a more spiritually sound civilization.

In His Tablets to the embodiments of authority and power, the kings and religious leaders, Bahá'u'lláh not only articulated His divinely-inspired vision, He also invited them to take a leadership role in executing His plan for the unification of the world. These recipients of Bahá'u'lláh's Tablets of proclamation were offered the unique opportunity to bring about a dramatic and orderly transformation in the fortunes of humanity. The power of the rulers to effect such a beneficial influence on their subjects and on society in general is illustrated by the following guidance addressed to one of the European monarchs:

> Adorn the body of Thy kingdom with the raiment of My name, and arise, then, to teach My Cause. Better is this for thee than that which thou possessest. God will, thereby, exalt thy name among all the kings. Potent is He over all things. Walk thou amongst men in the name of God, and by the power of His might, that thou mayest show forth His signs amidst the peoples of the earth. Burn thou brightly with the flame of this undying Fire which the All-Merciful hath ignited in the midmost heart of creation, that through thee the heat of His love may be kindled within the hearts of His favored ones. Follow in My way and enrapture the hearts of men through remembrance of Me, the Almighty, the Most Exalted.[27]

The refusal of the kings and religious leaders to heed Bahá'u'lláh's call and to take up this God-given opportunity had tragic consequences not only for the rulers themselves, but also for humankind. Their failure to embrace His redemptive plan for the unification and pacification of the world—the convening of a world conference called for by Bahá'u'lláh to consult together about collective security and the creation of mechanisms and administrative structures to ensure peace—set in motion the forces of change foretold by Bahá'u'lláh, forces that contributed to the collapse of their kingdoms and the decline of ecclesiastical structures. In addition, the unwillingness of those in authority to use their power and influence to actively support the execution of the divinely-revealed Plan and to serve as its standard-bearers guiding the masses to the path leading to the coming of age of the human race condemned mankind to a prolonged period of chaos, confusion, and intense suffering.

In weighing the consequences of the rejection of Bahá'u'lláh's call by the rulers of the world, it is important to recognize that although their decision impacted the manner in which Bahá'u'lláh's plan for humankind was to unfold, it was powerless to thwart the intention of the Divine Will. Writing on this theme, Bahá'u'lláh emphasizes the potency of His Revelation and the nature of the relationship between God and mankind: "Regard thou the one true God as One Who is apart from, and immeasurably exalted above, all created things. The whole universe reflecteth His glory, while He is Himself independent of, and transcendeth His creatures. . . . He Who is the Eternal Truth is the one Power Who exerciseth undisputed sovereignty over the world of being, Whose image is reflected in the mirror of the entire creation. All existence is dependent upon Him, and from Him is derived the source of the sustenance of all things." Further, in relation to "the true nature of the Faith of God," Bahá'u'lláh categorically asserts, "To demonstrate the truth of His Revelation He hath not been, nor is He, dependent upon any one." Elaborating on this pronouncement, He stresses the availability of literature about the Faith and the responsibility of the individual to examine it for himself: "Well nigh a hundred volumes of luminous verses and perspicuous words have already been sent down from the heaven of the will of Him Who is the Revealer of signs, and are available unto all. It is for thee to direct thyself towards the Ultimate Goal, and the Supreme End, and the Most Sublime Pinnacle, that thou mayest hear and behold what hath been revealed by God, the Lord of the worlds."[28]

It is therefore apparent that while the rulers had the privilege of "demonstrating the truth of His Revelation" and had both the opportunity and the means to make a significant contribution to its promulgation and to the creation of a new world, this process was not entirely dependent on them. Indeed, the disintegration of the traditional foundations of society, the erosion of its ancient institutions and values, consequent of the failure of the kings and religious leaders, created a unique opportunity for the masses of humanity to assume responsibility for the eventual fulfillment of Bahá'u'lláh's vision and it gave impetus to the establishment of Bahá'í administrative structures that were destined to serve as the nucleus and pattern of a new world order.

THE ROLE OF 'ABDU'L-BAHÁ

'Abdu'l-Bahá dedicated his life to furthering the Faith of his Father. During his almost lifelong incarceration and throughout the course of his extended travels in the West, 'Abdu'l-Bahá made frequent appeals to those in authority and to the public at large to examine the teachings enunciated by Bahá'u'lláh. He also foreshadowed the impending chaos, the approaching upheavals, and the universal conflagration which was beginning to impact human society.

As 'Abdu'l-Bahá's physical life drew to a close, he set in motion a strategic plan for ensuring the implementation of Bahá'u'lláh's vision of a peaceful and creative world order. Assessing the spiritual needs and capacities of the peoples of the world, he assigned the task to the American Bahá'í community. The world mission entrusted to the American Bahá'ís was set out in the Tablets of the Divine Plan. Designated as "the chosen trustees and principal executors of 'Abdu'l-Bahá's Divine Plan," the American Bahá'ís were called upon to assume a preponderating role in taking the message of Bahá'u'lláh to all the countries of the world and for effecting the transformation in values necessary for the emergence of a world order characterized by justice, unity and peace.[29]

It is fascinating to contrast the position of the kings and religious leaders with the dramatically different situation of the members of the American Bahá'í community. The rulers had high status, power, influence, authority over their citizens, and unlimited material, human, and administrative resources at their disposal. While the requisite elements of freedom, initiative, and executive capacity no doubt existed within the American community, it was at the same time small, relatively uninformed, inexperienced, and largely untried. Indeed, it was not until 1893 that the Bahá'í Faith had been first mentioned in North America, and the nascent community was less than twenty-five years old when 'Abdu'l-Bahá invested it with its spiritual mission.

Referring to the conditions that existed in the early years of the American Bahá'í community, Shoghi Effendi states that it was ". . . relatively negligible in its numerical strength; . . . bereft in the main of material resources and lacking in experience and in prominence; ignorant of the beliefs, concepts and habits of those peoples and races from which its spiritual Founders have sprung; wholly unfamiliar with the languages in which its sacred Books were originally revealed; constrained to place its sole reliance upon an inadequate rendering of only a fragmentary portion of the literature embodying its laws, its tenets, and its history." Nevertheless, Shoghi Effendi affirms that the community was able to surmount its inherent limitations in carrying out its assigned responsibility, and he identifies some of the spiritual, personal and administrative qualities that made this possible: "Unsupported by any of the advantages which talent, rank and riches can confer, the community of the American believers, despite its tender age, its numerical strength, its limited experience, has by virtue of the inspired wisdom, the united will, the incorruptible loyalty of its administrators and teachers achieved the distinction of an undisputed leadership among its sister communities of East and West in hastening the advent of the Golden Age anticipated by Bahá'u'lláh."[30]

So it was that 'Abdu'l-Bahá turned to the rank and file members of the Bahá'í community, individuals devoid of material power and influence, to carry out the historic mandate. Inspired by his guidance and encouragement, they became the instruments for implementing the provisions of the Divine Plan.

MOBILIZING COLLECTIVE ACTION

The Tablets of the Divine Plan were the directing and motivating force for spreading, in a strategic, systematic, and evolutionary manner the society-building values and concepts embodied in the teachings of Bahá'u'lláh. While the efforts of dedicated believers at the grassroots of a community provided the human resources for the unfoldment of this historic enterprise, 'Abdu'l-Bahá clearly foresaw the critical importance of some form of organization or administrative structure to provide leadership and sustain long-term systematic and united action. Through his historic travels in the West, 'Abdu'l-Bahá not only strengthened the sense of individual responsibility of the members of the community, he also performed a number of seminal acts that gave impetus to the processes of community and administrative development. Included among these was laying the foundation stone of the Bahá'í House of Worship, fostering the beginnings of the Bahá'í Administrative Order through his participation in the festive gathering, and addressing the newly-founded Bahá'í Temple Unity, the forerunner to the national governing body, the National Spiritual Assembly.

Cognizant of the need to mobilize collective action, in one of the Tablets of the Divine Plan addressed to the Bahá'ís of the United States and Canada, 'Abdu'l-Bahá provides the following visionary elucidation of the importance of unified action. He writes:

> In the contingent world there are many collective centers which are conducive to association and unity between the children of men. For example, patriotism is a collective center; nationalism is a collective center; identity of interests is a collective center; political alliance is a collective center; the union of ideals is a collective center, and the prosperity of the world of humanity is dependent upon the organization and promotion of the collective centers.

Underlying the limitations of all the previous institutions, which, though useful, tend to be temporary and subject to overthrow and to political and social dislocation, 'Abdu'l-Bahá contrasts them with the enduring, transforming, and cohesive power of religion, the "Collective Center of the Kingdom" that embodies "institutions and divine teachings." In relation to the operation of this "eternal Collective Center" and its capacity to mobilize and organize change, he states:

> It establishes relationship between the East and the West, organizes the oneness of the world of humanity, and destroys the foundation of differences. It overcomes and includes all the other collective centers. Like unto the ray of the sun, it dispels entirely the darkness encompassing all the regions, bestows ideal life, and

causes the effulgence of divine illumination. Through the breaths of the Holy Spirit it performs miracles; the Orient and the Occident embrace each other, the North and South become intimates and associates, conflicting and contending opinions disappear, antagonistic aims are brushed aside, the law of the struggle for existence is abrogated, and the canopy of the oneness of the world of humanity is raised on the apex of the globe, casting its shade over all the races of men.[31]

Beyond the general reference to the institutional aspect of the "Collective Center of the Kingdom," in the Tablets of the Divine Plan, 'Abdu'l-Bahá refers specifically to a number of embryonic institutions and functions that foreshadow the emergence of the Bahá'í administrative system. He mentions, for example, the work involved in raising the first Mashríqu'l-Adhkár in the West, the holding of the annual convention and special meetings of consultation to discuss the work of the Faith, the establishment of committees to undertake such functions as the translation of Bahá'í literature, and the publication and circulation of periodicals and books.[32]

Given the emphasis on systematic organized activity implicit in the Tablets of the Divine Plan, it is suggested that these seminal letters might well be considered as anticipating the implementation of the provisions of 'Abdu'l-Bahá's Will and Testament, which were disclosed at the time of his passing in 1921. The Bahá'í Administrative Order, established in the writings of Bahá'u'lláh, was brought into being by the Master's Will. It gave rise to the formation of institutions and delineated the features of the Faith's administrative machinery. At a later time, under the guidance of Shoghi Effendi, the Guardian of the Faith, these institutions were to become "the agencies" for the "proper and systematic execution" of the provisions of the Divine Plan.[33]

It is useful to note, in passing, that there are a number of unique and innovative provisions governing the organization of the Bahá'í community. Of particular significance is the fact that the Bahá'í Faith is a lay religion, devoid of a clerical class. Within the Bahá'í community there are no figures comparable to the rabbis, priests, ministers, or mullas who exercise individual authority over the mass of the faithful and enjoy rights and privileges not accorded to their fellow-believers. Although the Bahá'í Faith has no priesthood and no ordained clerical class, it does assign responsibility for administrative actions to certain institutions and individuals. The international governing body, the Universal House of Justice, is the head of the Bahá'í Faith. The affairs of the community are administered by a system of democratically elected Spiritual Assemblies, operating at the local and national levels of society, and they are assisted by individuals who are appointed to provide a counseling and educational function. The Bahá'ís who serve in these capacities, however, do not have episcopal authority over the other members of the community, nor do they constitute an inherently superior and privileged class.

At the local level, for example, the leadership of the Bahá'í community is primarily vested in the elected Local Spiritual Assembly. It serves as the point of authority and unity and is the vehicle for directing the activities of the community. Working in close collaboration with the members of its Bahá'í community, the Local Spiritual Assembly serves as the primary agency for the efficient and systematic prosecution of the plans and activities designed to meet the needs of the evolving community. The National Spiritual Assembly, on the other hand, directs, unifies, coordinates, and stimulates the activities of individuals as well as local Assemblies within its jurisdiction.

Prior to the disclosure of the provisions of 'Abdu'l-Bahá's Will and Testament in 1921, the Bahá'í administrative system existed, at best, in embryonic form. It was the role of Shoghi Effendi, the appointed Guardian of the Bahá'í Faith, to begin to translate into visible form the guidance set out in the writings of Bahá'u'lláh and 'Abdu'l-Bahá concerning the Bahá'í administrative structure.

As part of the development of the Bahá'í Administrative Order, Shoghi Effendi called for the systematic introduction of elected Assemblies operating at local and national levels of society. To ensure the efficient functioning of these institutions, the Guardian initiated a period of training to increase the capacity of these embryonic Assemblies. Indeed, the implementation of the mandate contained in the Tablets of the Divine Plan is inextricably linked to the evolution of the Bahá'í Administrative Order. Stressing the indispensability of the Administrative Order, Shoghi Effendi describes it as "a divinely appointed agency for the operation of that Plan." He further attests that while the response of individual believers to the call of 'Abdu'l-Bahá was sacrificial and immediate, the official and large-scale initiation of the Plan ". . . had, for well-nigh twenty years, been held in abeyance, while the processes of a slowly emerging administrative Order were, under the unerring guidance of Providence, creating and perfecting the agencies for its efficient and systematic prosecution."[34]

The full implementation of the Divine Plan of 'Abdu'l-Bahá was formally launched in 1937 when Shoghi Effendi conferred on the North American Bahá'í community the mission of the First Seven Year Plan (1937–44), the first of a series of plans designed to carry out its provisions in increasingly fuller degrees. These "epoch-making Tablets" are the motivating force which rally the community "to implant the banner, and lay an unassailable basis for the administrative structure of the Faith of Bahá'u'lláh."[35]

Concluding Remarks

While the failure of the kings and religious leaders created the need for a change in the way in which the purpose of Bahá'u'lláh was to unfold, their rejection of Bahá'u'lláh's summon also created the opportunity for the masses of humanity to participate in the mighty enterprise calculated to give rise to the emergence of peace and tranquility in the world. The Tablets of the Divine Plan represented not only a strategic assignment of responsibility but also mandated a structured and orderly approach to the task. The mission was so vital it could not be left to chance, to the goodwill of a few dedicated souls. It required the establishment of the Bahá'í Administrative Order, the mobilization of the rank and file of the members of the Faith, and their engagement in systematic action to ensure the job was done. From this perspective, the seminal Tablets of 'Abdu'l-Bahá's Divine Plan might be said to constitute a critical turning point in the progressive elaboration of the instructions contained in the Bahá'í writings concerning the means by which the Faith was to be disseminated and its transformative influence brought to bear on the world at large.

3

An Epoch-Making Gathering

This chapter examines the historical context of and the events that surrounded the arrival of the Tablets of the Divine Plan in North America at the end of the First World War, the great conference called by 'Abdu'l-Bahá for the study of these Tablets, and the mobilization of the Bahá'í community in response to the mandate he conferred upon its members.

Historical Context

The signing of the armistice with Germany on November 11, 1918 brought the Great War to an end. The protagonists, exhausted by years of suffering and economic hardship, were keen not only to create a lasting peace but also to set in place mechanisms that eventually took the form of a League of Nations, designed to prevent war. People everywhere longed for the speedy arrival of a general peace between all the nations of the world and for the establishment of a closer bond of union among the races. The embryonic Bahá'í community shared in the universal spirit of optimistic euphoria and rejoiced in the dawning of peace.

The Bahá'ís in the West were, in addition, greatly excited to receive a telegram in October 1918, published in a Bahá'í journal, *Star of the West*, announcing the safety of 'Abdu'l-Bahá.[1] The arrival of the victorious

British army in Haifa brought stability to the Holy Land and hastened the ultimate demise of the Ottoman Empire. It also ensured the protection of the Master and his family and opened the way for the reestablishment of direct communication between 'Abdu'l-Bahá and the Bahá'ís throughout the world, which for a number of years had been cut off during the war. Once the postal services were restored, the flow of letters from 'Abdu'l-Bahá—many of which has been written long before—began to reach his devoted followers in the West. A letter written by 'Abdu'l-Bahá's secretary to an American Bahá'í illustrates the excitement associated with the resumption of contact between East and West:

My dear sister in the holy Cause:

This letter was written to you nearly two years ago, but returned to me from Constantinople because war was declared between the United States and Germany. Because it contains the words of 'Abdu'l-Bahá as well as the translation of His Tablet to you, I only change the envelope, add these few words of greeting and mail it again, hoping that this time it may reach you safely. During this long period of silence we have been waiting for this day, so that we might correspond with each other with the utmost freedom. Praise be to God, 'Abdu'l-Bahá and all the friends are well and are longing to look on the faces of the believers. . . .[2]

The opening of the doors of communication between 'Abdu'l-Bahá and the outside world paved the way for him to send to North America an emissary who would bring with him copies of the remaining nine Tablets of the Divine Plan that had been written in the years 1916–17 but could not, until now, be delivered. The person nominated to travel to America was Mírzá Ahmad Sohrab, a secretary of 'Abdu'l-Bahá who had resided in Haifa during the war years. The news of his impending arrival was announced in *Star of the West*.[3]

'Abdu'l-Bahá instructed Sohrab to arrive in time for the annual Bahá'í Convention and Congress, which was scheduled to take place at the Hotel McAlpine in New York City on April 26–30, 1919. The

Master further instructed that his Tablets of the Divine Plan were to be made available and distributed to the participants of this Convention. Despite the challenges of travel, Sohrab managed to reach the United States in good time and went first to Washington D.C., where he set about translating into English the remaining Tablets he carried with him from Haifa.[4]

The letter of invitation to this gathering, written by the secretary of the Convention Committee, conveys both a sense of anticipation and a burgeoning awareness of the potential historic significance of the event, and contains the following appeal:

> All past Conventions have been a preparation for this gathering which is now being made ready in New York, and it is the desire of 'Abdu'l-Bahá that the largest possible number shall attend.
>
> This attendance should not be limited to delegates, but should include everyone who is attracted to the universality of the divine teachings. The doors are flung open to the lovers of Truth everywhere. The greatest possible publicity should be given in each city so that the largest number of souls who are attracted may attend. . . .
>
> To a degree never before known these gatherings are being planned and carried forward under the direct guidance of 'Abdu'l-Bahá. In a more wonderful sense than ever before realized it is the Convention of 'Abdu'l-Bahá. The program for the Convention and Congress will revolve around these great messages which will be brought forward in nine presentations.
>
> It is sufficient to suggest that everyone who attends these meetings will be astonished at the import and significance of these messages. No words can describe them, for they are the Creative Word, itself. They are the illumination of the world of humanity, the essence of hope to every despondent one, the full explanation, the radiant, powerful traces of the brilliant Sun of Truth. Wonderful constructive days are now beginning of which these messages are the pivot. . . .
>
> This is an epoch-making gathering, not alone to the Bahá'ís, but to the entire world. All are in His Assembly. . . .

In these gatherings the heavenly feast will be spread and all who long for this sustenance are invited, from the highways and byways of the world of existence.

In the name of 'Abdu'l-Bahá, we bid ye welcome . . . The doors are open, the call is raised, the sacrificing hearts are yearning for servitude. Will ye come?[5]

The Bahá'í Convention of 1919 was taking place at a critical point in time. It coincided with a near-universal longing for lasting peace in the world at large and with a growing consciousness on the part of the Bahá'ís of the extent of the opportunity and the challenge confronting them to devise a systematic means for applying the remedy set out in the teachings of the Faith for the establishment of universal brotherhood, peace, and justice throughout the world. The details of what transpired at this gathering will be outlined below.

Those gathered at the Bahá'í Conference were acutely conscious of the juxtaposition in time of their meeting in New York and the Peace Conference in Paris, which was tasked with deciding on the terms of the peace settlement and whose deliberations led to the formation of the League of Nations. A subsequent report of the Bahá'í Conference suggests that the participants' awareness of these parallel events was a source of reflection and inspiration; it strengthened their resolve to take action and underlined the nature of the unique contribution the Bahá'ís were to make to the necessary transformation of human values required for the attainment of peace: "The fact that while we were gathered discussing plans for spiritual union and harmony throughout the world, the delegates at Paris, in the Peace Conference, were meeting to establish the new world conditions politically, economically and socially, lent a peculiar power and significance to the gathering of the friends in the metropolis of the new world."[6]

PARIS PEACE CONFERENCE

During the first six months of 1919, the allied victors converged in Paris to set the peace terms for the defeated powers. The Paris Peace Conference opened on January 18, 1919. Though diplomats from some thirty-two countries were involved, the proceedings were dominated by the leaders of the four great powers: Great Britain, France, the United States, and, to a lesser extent, Italy. Although at the outset, the desire for peace was paramount, with the passage of time old rivalries—both political and economic—emerged and dominated the proceedings.

The Paris Peace Conference was not a conference between the victors and the vanquished of the First World War. The victors decided among themselves the terms to be imposed on the defeated enemy, and Germany and its former allies were not invited to attend until the details of the peace treaties had been elaborated and agreed upon. In this environment, the peacemakers carved up and reshaped the map of Europe, and new nation-states emerged from the ruins of former empires.

The conference gave rise to a number of historic treaties, including the Treaty of Versailles. The terms of the treaties were often harsh and vindictive. A central feature of the Treaty of Versailles, for example, was the imposition of exorbitant reparation payments on the vanquished, and a clause requiring the defeated nations to accept full responsibility for causing a war for which all parties had been, to one degree or another, responsible. It is also interesting to note that this same treaty incorporated the visionary decision to establish the League of Nations, an institution that, it was hoped, would adjudicate future disputes between nations and harmonize international affairs.

Commenting on the limitations of the Treaty of Versailles, Henry Kissinger averred, "Rarely has a diplomatic document so missed its objective as the Treaty of Versailles," and he underlined the potential weaknesses of the League of Nations, observing,

> The major powers attempted to institutionalize their revulsion to war into a new form of peaceful international order. A vague formula for international disarmament was put forward, though the implementation was deferred for later negotiations. The League of Nations and a series of arbitration treaties set out to replace power contests with legal mechanisms for the resolution of disputes. Yet while membership in these new structures was

nearly universal and every form of violation of the peace formally banned, no country proved willing to enforce the terms. Powers with grievances or expansionist goals . . . soon learned that there were no serious consequences for violating the terms of membership or simply for withdrawing.[7]

The idealism that initially underpinned the peace process was undermined by the realities of the postwar economic situation. The war had disrupted the fabric of international trade and investment, and as a result, economic crisis precipitated political crisis. The resulting unemployment inflamed nationalism and gave rise to militant, ruthless, authoritarian movements, and the emergence of dictatorships. Reporting on the challenge of the times, commentators later observed that "Europe needed more drastic and deliberate reconstruction than was possible in the desperate conditions of the immediate post-war years."[8]

Furthermore, the League of Nations, whose purpose was to harmonize international relations and preserve order, was gravely weakened at its birth by the exclusion of Germany and Soviet Russia from its membership and by the failure of its chief sponsor, the United States, to join the League or to ratify the Treaty of Versailles. A document prepared at the request of the Universal House of Justice underscores the potential significance of an opportunity which the political leadership failed to grasp: ". . . at precisely the moment in human history when an unprecedented outbreak of violence had undermined the inherited bulwarks of civilized behavior, the political leadership of the Western world had emasculated the one alternative system of international order to which experience of this catastrophe had given birth and which alone could have alleviated the far greater suffering that lay ahead."[9]

The Convention of the Covenant

The Tablets of the Divine Plan, the Charter of the New Age, were unveiled in befitting ceremonies during a Bahá'í Convention held at the Hotel McAlpin in New York City on April 26–30, 1919.

'Abdu'l-Bahá's guiding hand was felt throughout the Convention. During the course of the sessions, he dispatched a number of cables containing guidance to the gathering. In one, he instructed, "Let this be the Convention of the Covenant!"[10] Above all, however, it was the Tablets of the Divine Plan themselves whose world-embracing vision and far-reaching guidance inspired the hearts and minds of those in attendance. The participants were also energized by the presence at the convention of Mírzá Ahmad Sohrab, the bearer and translator of these Tablets, who played a central role in its proceedings.

The convention began with a reception and celebration of the Bahá'í Festival of Riḍván, marking the Declaration by Bahá'u'lláh of His prophetic mission to be the Manifestation of God for the Day in which we live. It is estimated that over six hundred persons were present. A striking feature of the Feast of Riḍván was the participation of several clergymen and leaders of thought, who contributed to the discussions. A number of these distinguished individuals had had the pleasure of meeting 'Abdu'l-Bahá during his travels in the United States and Canada in 1912.

In describing the purposes and hopes of the Convention, Mr. Harlan Ober, a member of the organizing committee, elevated the vision of his audience, imbued in them a sense of history, spelled out the responsibility of the North American Bahá'ís, and linked the mandate set out in 'Abdu'l-Bahá's Tablets of the Divine Plan with the resolution of the problems facing society. He states:

> From the vantage point of that high mountain, Carmel, 'Abdu'l-Bahá, the Center of the Covenant of God, has turned his eyes and is looking towards this group of people to see to what extent they will respond to this tremendous call which has come through, from out of the heart of the war, yes, further than that, from the heart of peace and love and spirituality. The Word of God is the divine solvent. There is no other. The Word of God is the solution for the vexing problems which are facing the globe today. . . .
>
> Everything in this Congress revolves around these divine instructions. Can you imagine what it would have meant if in the

days of Jesus Christ tremendous Tablets, revelations from Christ, has been presented to the body of the Christian people? . . . [T]hrough the progress of the world and through the bounty of God and through the requirements of this illumined day and through the greatness of the problems themselves just exactly that thing has happened. . . .

Let us, therefore, as we approach these great unveilings, turn our hearts to God and know that we are living through the mercy of God, at a time in the history of the world, which is absolutely epoch-making. In no past age or cycle of which we have record did such great events transpire. Realizing this, let us in our minds and hearts prepare that at the end we shall not go away from these sessions without a definite plan of action which shall spread the bounties of God to every last individual on the face of the globe.[11]

The working sessions of the convention were nine in number. The first five sessions were devoted to the study of Tablets addressed to a particular region of North America—the northeastern, southern, central, and western states, respectively—to Canada and Greenland, and to the United States and Canada. The remaining sessions focused on themes drawn from the Tablets addressed collectively to the Bahá'ís of the United States and Canada.[12]

Each day speeches were delivered highlighting major themes of a particular Tablet or Tablets. Ahmad Sohrab, the secretary of 'Abdu'l-Bahá who had been present when the Tablets were revealed, read each Tablet aloud and then commented on the unique background of that particular Tablet. Following a musical interlude, two children came forward and, with a dramatic flourish, drew aside the curtains covering the beautifully illuminated and framed original Tablet in Persian, thereby presenting it to public view for the first time. Finally, the prayer at the end of the Tablet was read in English, then chanted in Persian. The dawning impact of this unfolding process on the participants has been captured in the following report: ". . . as the Tablets were read which represent the Charter of the new Age, and which outline in no uncertain terms the part America is to play in the spiritualization of the world—there was joy abundant and hope unbounded, to offset all the doubt and uncertainly which the epoch of reconstruction brings to those lacking the spiritual insight and the hope of the age."[13]

Immediate Impact of the Convention

In her address to the convention, May Maxwell, a distinguished early Bahá'í, highlighted the supreme challenge confronting those in attendance. While reflecting on the history of religion and the distinguished services of the disciples of Christ, which were well familiar to all, she cautioned the participants about the danger of failing to appreciate the true significance of the present moment. She called attention to the fact that it is only when we look back upon past events and periods in the world that we realize their greatness. However, she observed, "It may be that the most difficult thing for the soul is to become conscious of the greatness of events with which we are contemporaneous."[14]

From a perusal of the reports of the convention sessions, it is possible to identify a number of themes that reflect the participants' growing understanding of the significance of the gathering and the nature of the response that it demanded.

HISTORICAL CONSCIOUSNESS

Presentations at the convention demonstrated an awareness of the historical moment, that it was a time of change in the world and within the Bahá'í community itself, and that such circumstances called for creative and innovative responses.

The current state of the world and the fundamental changes resulting from the recently concluded war were uppermost in people's minds and provided both a context and a starting-point for many of the subjects discussed in the sessions. It was observed, for example, that "Most every one feels that we are today standing on the threshold of an age of material, and intellectual and spiritual regeneration. All the hidden forces of humanity are being stirred; political, social and economic principles of the last two generations are more or less set at naught and the wise men of every nation are thinking to reconstruct the body politic from top to bottom."[15]

Another speaker posed the following question: "You know, we are living in such an astounding day of tumult and endeavor, a day when all the old world is so absolutely falling to pieces that sometimes we are in despair, sometimes we say how can any great edifice ever lift its head out of this ruin and catch the light of the sun once more?"[16]

This awareness of the historical moment extended to the conviction that the advent of Bahá'u'lláh and the teachings of the Bahá'í Faith provided the remedy for the issues facing contemporary society and that the guidance contained in 'Abdu'l-Bahá's Tablets of the Divine Plan were critical to effecting the necessary regeneration of human society. Speaking on this theme, one participant stated:

> The brief span of our lives upon earth is contemporaneous with the most marvelous event that has ever happened in all the ages. This event has been the dream and promise of wise men, prophets and seers, in past centuries and ages. How glorious to be living in the day of its fulfillment, when the whole earth is illumined by the face of its Lord! By obedience to the divine commands we become conscious of the divine power. It is the privilege of all who hear this Message to become instruments in the hands of God of quickening flesh with the spiritual power and of receiving the peace, harmony and security of the world of existence. . . .
>
> Truly, if a man lived upon this earth one hundred thousand years, no higher hope, no brighter destiny could be his, than to be an instrument in the hands of God of bringing universal happiness to man. . . .[17]

AWARENESS OF RESPONSIBILITY

Associated with an understanding of the needs of contemporary society was a growing realization of the nature and scope of the spiritual enterprise to which the American Bahá'ís were being called and the heavy responsibility they were being asked to accept.

The scope of the mandate was world-embracing. The Tablets of the Divine Plan called for the Bahá'ís to spread the teachings of their

Faith not only throughout the length and breadth of North America but to all the countries and islands of the globe, many of which were specifically named in the Tablets themselves. For example, in a Tablet addressed to the Bahá'ís of the United States and Canada, 'Abdu'l-Bahá called for

> A party speaking their languages, severed, holy, sanctified and filled with the love of God, must turn their faces to and travel through the three great island groups of the Pacific Ocean—Polynesia, Micronesia and Melanesia, and the islands attached to these groups, such as New Guinea, Borneo, Java, Sumatra, Philippine Islands, Solomon Islands, Fiji Islands, New Hebrides, Loyalty Islands, New Caledonia, Bismarck Archipelago, Ceram, Celebes, Friendly Islands, Samoa Islands, Society Islands, Caroline Islands, Low Archipelago, Marquesas, Hawaiian Islands, Gilbert Islands, Moluccas, Marshall Islands, Timor and the other islands.[18]

One can only imagine the impact the reading of the names of these faraway places, names that were likely unfamiliar and exotic sounding, must have had on those present!

In relation to the nature of the task, while the Bahá'ís were familiar with the general outline of the teachings of Bahá'u'lláh, this Convention helped them to better appreciate that the promulgation of these teachings was calculated to set in motion processes to minister to the needs of humanity, to transform individual and social values, and to lay the foundation of a new civilization that gave expression to the oneness of humanity. Reflecting on the civilizing power inherent in the Word of God, its vital role in the transformation of human values and social reconstruction, one of the speakers provided the following analysis:

> Bahá'u'lláh taught the actual oneness of the religions of the world, the oneness of all humanity, the universal brotherhood of man, universal peace: the perfect harmony of religion and science. He enjoined men to search diligently for truth and to

abolish all prejudices, religious, national, racial, social. He proclaimed the equality of the sexes, commanded equal educational advantages for both, besides vast equitable social readjustments, the equalization of the means of livelihood and the complete establishment of justice among men. He proclaimed the urgency of a universal language to bring men into closer relationship and mutual understanding. He emphasized the incumbency of a Parliament of Man—a universal tribunal of justice and arbitration for the adjustment of international affairs. And unequivocally, he taught the power of the Holy Spirit in the life of humanity.

In brief: The Holy Spirit revealed by the Manifestation of God, Bahá'u'lláh, is the mysterious force of civilization in the new age.[19]

In the words of one of those who addressed the gathering, the challenge confronting the Bahá'ís was to convey the vision of the new age to the peoples of the world,

to fill the hearts with the new ideals of God, love, beauty, constancy and happiness as portrayed in the writings of Bahá'u'lláh and 'Abdu'l-Bahá.

This means that we are called upon to solve some of the most crucial problems of this age. In order to render this service, we must not lag behind, but be in the vanguard of the forces of this new ideal civilization. We must universalize our aims, spiritualize our thoughts, renew our beings, exalt our ambitions and dedicate ourselves to the service of humanity.[20]

As the scope of the enterprise gradually dawned on the participants, it became evident that the task would not be completed within a short period of time. Speaker after speaker called attention to the long-term nature of the work, and the extent of the responsibility involved. Thus the participants were reminded: "It is not the work of one or two or ten or twenty years but for a long stretch of years. It is indeed a divine responsibility. . . ."[21]

THE KINGDOM OF GOD ON EARTH

By the last session of the Convention, the participants were both thrilled and galvanized by the realization that the task on which they were about to embark involved the establishment of the Kingdom of God on earth. Underlining this theme the speaker noted that "For nineteen centuries the Kingdom of Heaven has been largely considered by man merely a parable," and he went on to say that through these "wonderful Tablets of 'Abdu'l-Bahá" which had been unveiled at this gathering, "the fruit of this Kingdom" had been offered to all "in a heavenly banquet."[22]

Building on the image of a Kingdom, the speaker observed that a "Kingdom naturally implies organization." However, he distinguished between "the world of affairs" where "organization in itself is power" and is likely to give rise to disharmony, and "the world of the Kingdom, where love is the law of organization" and "unity radiates from its power."[23] Finally he lay before his audience an inspiring vision of the connection between the Tablets of the Divine Plan, the unfoldment of the Kingdom, and the unique role of the American Bahá'ís in its establishment:

My dearest, dearest friends: We have had revealed to us in these sublime Tablets, a whole new order of life. We have had presented to us with its great opportunity the chance to rise and to serve God in His world. I believe in this day that disciples choose themselves, that all may be disciples, that we are all called to the station of discipleship in this new and glorious kingdom; that God Himself has incarnated in, the world and founded the great Spiritual Magna Charta and its laws, its joys and its happiness, and has placed them in the hands of the friends of America. He has given to America the station of the illumination of the world, and now, we must build deep that it may be high, we must build outside of time that it may withstand time. Peter and Paul built beyond the empire of Rome, they built beyond the time of the life of all emperors because they built deep and they built high. It is our privilege, it is our greatest joy, it is the supreme happiness now of our lives to dedicate them to this service to the Kingdom.[24]

Mobilization for Action

To provide a backdrop against which to examine the initial impact of this epoch-making gathering and the immediate actions taken by the Bahá'ís in their desire to implement the heavy responsibilities laid on their shoulders, it is useful to reflect briefly on the recent origins of the Bahá'í community in North America and the embryonic state of its development in 1919.

THE ORIGINS OF THE NORTH AMERICAN BAHÁ'Í COMMUNITY

It might be said that, from the outset, Bahá'u'lláh viewed His religion as a universal creed that, with the passage of time, was destined to spread throughout the whole world. During the ministries of Bahá'u'lláh and 'Abdu'l-Bahá, emphasis was therefore placed on spreading information about the existence of the new Revelation and on endeavoring to increase the religion's membership and its geographical spread. Summarizing the sequence in which the earliest Bahá'í communities emerged, Peter Smith notes that initially, this "expansion was concentrated in Iran, but also came to include the Caucasus (1860s), Egypt (1860s), India and Burma (1870s), Russian Turkistan (1880s), and North America and Europe (1890s)." And, he further observes, "The idea of worldwide expansion was given special emphasis in 'Abdu'l-Bahá's *Tablets of the Divine Plan*. The establishment of Bahá'í communities in the West bore a particular significance as a major 'cultural breakthrough,' indicating the potential universality of the Bahá'í Cause."[25]

America first received word of the new religion at the World Parliament of Religions in 1893, one year following the passing of Bahá'u'lláh. The Parliament was part of the Colombian Exposition held in Chicago to commemorate the 400th anniversary of America's discovery by Christopher Columbus. Shoghi Effendi describes this historic event:

It was on September 23, 1893, a little over a year after Bahá'u'-lláh's ascension, that, in a paper written by Rev. Henry H. Jessup, D.D., Director of Presbyterian Missionary Operations in North Syria, and read by Rev. George A. Ford of Syria, at the World Parliament of Religions, . . . it was announced that "a famous Persian Sage," "the Bábí Saint," had died recently in 'Akká, and that two years previous to His ascension "a Cambridge scholar" [Professor E. G. Browne] had visited Him, to whom He had expressed "sentiments so noble, so Christ-like" that the author of the paper, in his "closing words," wished to share them with his audience.[26]

These "closing words" are as follows: "That all nations should become one in faith and all men as brothers; that the bond of affection and unity between the sons of men should be strengthened; that diversity of religions should cease and differences of race be annulled. What harm is there in this? Yet so it shall be. These fruitless strifes, these ruinous wars shall pass away, and 'the Most Great Peace' shall come. Do not you in Europe need this also? Let not a man glory in this, that he loves his country; let him rather glory in this, that he loves his kind."[27]

Little did the Reverend George Ford and the Reverend Henry Jessup know that on that day—September 23rd 1893—they had opened a new page in the history of the West. Indeed, the portent of that day was barely noticed when it came to pass. Pondering the unusual manner in which this first public reference to the Founder of the Bahá'í Faith took place, Shoghi Effendi writes, "Of pomp and circumstance, of any manifestations of public rejoicing or of popular applause, there were none to greet this first intimation to America's citizens of the existence and purpose of the Revelation proclaimed by Bahá'u'lláh. Nor did he who was its chosen instrument profess himself a believer in the indwelling potency of the tidings he conveyed, or suspect the magnitude of the forces which so cursory a mention was destined to release."[28]

While the moment passed without apparent fanfare, the news of the Bahá'í teachings spread. By the turn of the twentieth century, Bahá'í communities were flourishing in several metropolitan areas, including Chicago, Montreal, New York, and Washington D.C., and news of the Faith had been spread to the West Coast and the Hawaiian Islands.[29]

In 1898, the first group of American pilgrims traveled to the Holy Land to visit 'Abdu'l-Bahá and to learn firsthand more about the Bahá'í teachings. The expansion of the Faith in North America received special impetus from the activities of these pilgrims who, after meeting 'Abdu'l-Bahá, were inspired to share the Message of the new day with their fellow citizens upon returning to their homes. Shoghi Effendi captures the impact of their meeting with 'Abdu'l-Bahá and the importance of their services: "I can never pay sufficient tribute to that spirit of unyielding determination which the impact of a magnetic personality and the spell of a mighty utterance kindled in the entire company of these returning pilgrims, these consecrated heralds of the Covenant of God, at so decisive an epoch of their history."[30]

To facilitate the process of spreading the teachings of the religion, 'Abdu'l-Bahá dispatched teachers from the East to North America, and he addressed a constant stream of letters to his followers in that continent, "embodying in passionate and unequivocal language His instructions and counsels, His appeals and comments, His hopes and wishes, His fears and warnings."[31] His letters were translated, collected, published, and circulated within the community, and were, for a time, the only available Bahá'í literature. They served to formulate and clarify the basic tenets of the Faith. In due course, the literature of the Faith was enriched with works by Bahá'í authors, and the Bahá'í Publishing Society and a number of periodicals were established as a means of providing information about the teachings of the religion to the general public.

The process of expansion was furthered by American Bahá'ís arising to teach their religion to their fellow citizens in other parts of the nation, and by some undertaking teaching efforts by pioneering to a number of European countries, including France, Great Britain, and Germany, and also to the Pacific islands, China, and Japan.

'Abdu'l-Bahá's travels in North America lent further impetus to the expansion of the Bahá'í Faith in that continent. In the United States and Canada, he spoke about the teachings of the Faith before a large number of religious, humanitarian, and educational groups. His presentations served to clarify the vision of the Faith and its socially developmental mission.[32] 'Abdu'l-Bahá's presence in North America also helped the American Bahá'ís gain a greater awareness of the need both to put the spiritual and social teachings of the religion into practice in their daily lives as well as to develop Bahá'í community life and its embryonic administrative institutions. These activities gave rise to the introduction of study classes and summer schools, which were aimed at increasing the general level of understanding of the religion and equipping individual members of the community to share the teachings of the Faith with others. Classes were also instituted for the Bahá'í education of children. A regular community meeting, known as the Nineteen Day Feast, designed to enhance the spiritual, social, and administrative aspects of Bahá'í community life, gradually became an integral part of the life of the community.

As the Bahá'í community grew in size and the number of activities proliferated, the need increased for a system of organization, consonant with Bahá'í principles, to give direction to the work of the Cause. In some instances, committees or some other designated groups were appointed or elected to take care of a wide range of functions, and the Bahá'í Temple Unity, which was to evolve into the National Spiritual Assembly of the Bahá'ís of the United States and Canada, was established in 1909 for the all-important task of planning for the construction of the first Bahá'í House of Worship in the Western world. Nevertheless, there was no single designated administrative body with the necessary authority to direct all facets of the work of the small but rapidly diversifying North American Bahá'í community. During 'Abdu'l-Bahá's lifetime, a small number of embryonic consultative groups existed in the East and to a lesser extent in the West. However, there were no uniform procedures governing such features as how they were to be elected, the number of members, or even the title by which they were to be known.[33]

Such was the state of affairs that existed within the small embryonic American Bahá'í community in 1919 when its members convened in New York for the Convention of the Covenant. This community "despite its tender age, its numerical strength, its limited experience" was challenged to fulfill the global mission set out in the Tablets of the Divine Plan. This community, acting progressively in collaboration with its co-religionists in the West, was called upon to be "the standard-bearers of the emancipation and triumph of the Bahá'í Faith."[34]

As a footnote, it should be noted in passing that the year 1921 marked a critical transition point in the evolution of the Bahá'í Faith and the unfoldment of its administrative structure. The Formative Age of the Faith was ushered in by the death of 'Abdu'l-Bahá and the disclosure of the contents of his Will and Testament, a document which, together with Bahá'u'lláh's Book of Laws, constitutes the Charter of the New World Order and defines the major institutions that are to serve as the nucleus and pattern of this new Order. It was the role of Shoghi Effendi, the appointed Guardian of the Bahá'í Faith, to begin to translate into visible form the guidance set out in the writings of Bahá'u'lláh and 'Abdu'l-Bahá concerning the Bahá'í administrative structure. And it was the immediate and positive response of the American Bahá'í community to this new stage in the development of the Faith and its institutions that earned it the designation from Shoghi Effendi as "the cradle and stronghold of the Administrative Order of the Faith of Bahá'u'lláh." This community was, in the words of the Guardian, "the first among all other Bahá'í communities in East and West to arise and champion the cause of that Order, to fix its pattern, to erect its fabric, to initiate its endowments, to establish and consolidate its subsidiary institutions, and to vindicate its aims and purposes."[35]

RESPONSE ON THE HOME FRONT

The tasks assigned to the American Bahá'ís in the Tablets of the Divine Plan called for actions to be taken to spread the Bahá'í message progressively and systematically on the home front—within the five specified regions of the United States and Canada, as well as internationally.

From the outset, it was evident that the scope of the assignment required a system of organization capable of developing human resources and coordinating the progress of the plans. This gave rise to the establishment of a two-pronged approach. On a national level, a National Teaching Committee and Regional Committees were established to give direction to the work, while the international work was usually pursued by individuals who, of their own initiative, arose and made their way to various countries of the globe.

In relation to the work within North America, during the sessions of the Convention itself, individuals were encouraged to arise to undertake teaching activities in the particular area of the country in which they lived. However, within a year, at the next National Convention held in Chicago in 1920, the delegates voted to institute a number of measures to ensure a more systematic approach to the work. A National Teaching Committee was established. One of its first actions was to divide the country into the five sections or divisions designated by 'Abdu'l-Bahá in his Tablets of the Divine Plan, and to appoint separate Committees to oversee the work in the five regions—the Northeast, Southern, Central, and Western States, and Canada. It further decided to publish a monthly bulletin to provide information concerning the various activities of the teachers in the field all over America and Canada, as well as a financial report.[36]

Springing into action, the Committee for the Central States, one of the new regional teaching committees, decided within the course of the year to launch "at least one concentrated teaching campaign, consisting of an adequate advertisement scheme, a series of lectures and to arrange for the maintenance of one or more competent teachers who are able to do follow-up work for a short period after the campaign is concluded." Participating teachers were also asked to report the details of their activities to the Teaching Committee and to cooperate with their local Bahá'í administrative bodies, the Houses of Spirituality, wherever they existed.[37]

Likewise, a Committee for the Southern States was established and immediately set about planning its activities and putting in place processes to facilitate the general work and contribute to the work of the individuals who arose to serve. In addition to holding meetings to introduce the teachings of the Faith to the general public in all the larger towns throughout the South, the plan also called for placing books in libraries, publishing interesting articles on the Faith in newspapers, and devoting careful attention to the work of following up with individuals interested in the new Faith. The Southern States were to be the field of the heroic travels and teaching activities of Mr. Louis Gregory and Mrs. Dorothy Baker, and of the initiation of the inter-racial amity conventions, the first of which took place in Washington D.C. in 1921 under the patronage of Mrs. Agnes S. Parsons. A report describing these historic gatherings referred to the Washington meeting as "the first convention for amity between white and colored races in America and so far as we know, the world." The uniqueness of these meetings involving both "the white and colored races" and the overall approach adopted in their conduct was described in the following terms: "Founded upon the principle of spiritual oneness revealed by Bahá'u'lláh as the underlying social law of this cycle, the meetings for Inter-Racial Amity have endeavored to meet the problem without compromise, asserting and demonstrating the possibility of justice and fellowship between these long opposed branches of the human family."[38]

The success of the plans and goals set by the Teaching Committees depended on the support of the rank and file members of the community and their participation in the implementation of the goals. One of the challenges confronting these fledgling bodies was to gain the support of the individual who was more used to operating as a free agent. Initially, devoted Bahá'ís who were inspired by the mandate set out in the Tablets of the Divine Plan and the overall sense of purpose generated by the great Convention of the Covenant arose to teach the Faith. Some increased their activities within their local areas, while others were able to travel to other parts of the country. With time, the Committees were able to focus the attention of the individuals on the priority goals mentioned in the Tablets of the Divine Plan and thereby make the most productive use of scarce human resources.

As will be described below, it was not until the basic administrative structure of the Faith was established under the guidance of Shoghi Effendi with the formation of National and Local Spiritual Assemblies that human and material resources could be effectively harnessed, thereby opening the way for a new stage in the systematic implementation of 'Abdu'l-Bahá's Divine Plan.

INAUGURATION OF INTERNATIONAL RESPONSE

At first "a handful of men and women . . . arose to carry out the mandate which 'Abdu'l-Bahá had issued." "Forsaking home, kindred, friends and position" these "enterprising ambassadors of the Message of Bahá'u'lláh" were instrumental in spreading the Bahá'í Faith to the far corners of the earth.[39]

The first to arise in response to the call contained in the Tablets of the Divine Plan was Miss Martha Root, the intrepid star-servant of the Cause of Bahá'u'lláh. In 1919, she embarked on the first of four historic world-encircling journeys around the globe, in the initial phase of which she visited many of the important cities in South America. Two years later, Leonora Holsapple Armstrong settled in the Brazilian town of Bahia (Salvador).[40]

In 1920, a new continent was opened to the Faith when John and Clara Hyde-Dunn, then in their late middle-age, left the United States and settled as Bahá'í pioneers in Australia. Despite limited means, they succeeded not only in carrying "the Message to no less than seven hundred towns throughout that Commonwealth" but also in making a significant contribution to the establishment of the Bahá'í community in New Zealand. In that same year, Miss Fanny Knobloch arrived in Cape Town and became the first Bahá'í teacher to visit South Africa. She spent the next two years traveling to many parts of the country to teach the Faith and to nurture the embryonic Bahá'í communities.[41]

John and Louise Bosch, a Swiss couple living in California, were attracted by 'Abdu'l-Bahá's call to take the Faith to the islands of Polynesia in the Pacific Ocean. Eager to assist in this enterprise, and being fluent in the French language, they chose Tahiti, in the Society Islands, as their post. In 1920, they taught for five months in the capital, Papeete, and also visited the island of Moorea. Though confronted by many challenges, including lack of adequate accommodation, illness, the rigors of the tropical climate, and communication difficulties, they were able to introduce the Faith to several people.

The brief examples mentioned above serve to illustrate the exploits of the small band of individuals whose response to the Tablets of the Divine Plan was immediate. Shoghi Effendi attests to the importance of the heroic and exemplary services of these early believers who, "fired with a zeal and confidence which no human agency can kindle, arose to carry out the mandate which 'Abdu'l-Bahá had issued." The accomplishments of "these intrepid heralds of the Faith of Bahá'u'lláh," he states, are "unique and eternal." And he provides the following tribute to those souls:

In the face of almost insurmountable obstacles they have succeeded in most of the countries through which they have passed or in which they have resided, in proclaiming the teachings of their Faith, in circulating its literature, in defending its cause, in laying the basis of its institutions and in reinforcing the number of its declared supporters. It would be impossible for me to unfold in this short compass the tale of such heroic actions. Nor can any tribute of mine do justice to the spirit which has enabled these standard-bearers of the Religion of God to win such laurels and to confer such distinction on the generation to which they belong.[42]

INITIATION OF COLLECTIVE ACTION

As referred to above, the Divine Plan of 'Abdu'l-Bahá "underwent a period of incubation, after His ascension, while the machinery of a divinely appointed Administrative Order was being laboriously devised and its processes set in motion." Once the administrative institutions were functioning with some degree of efficiency and unity, Shoghi Effendi directed the North American Bahá'ís assembled at the 1936 National Bahá'í Convention to devise and inaugurate a systematic campaign to begin to implement systematically the provisions of

'Abdu'l-Bahá's Divine Plan. Calling attention to the deepening gloom of the world situation and the healing potential of the message of Bahá'u'lláh to alleviate the ills of a declining age, the Bahá'ís were encouraged to open to the Faith every state within North America and every republic in the American continent and to establish the basis of its administrative structure before the end of the first Bahá'í century in 1944. Commenting on the significance and scope of such an enterprise, and its potential impact, Shoghi Effendi writes:

> The promulgation of the Divine Plan . . . is the Key which Providence has placed in the hands of the American believers whereby to unlock the doors leading them to fulfil their unimaginably glorious Destiny. As the proclamation of the Message reverberates throughout the land, as its resistless march gathers momentum, as the field of its operation widens and the numbers of its upholders and champions multiply, its potentialities will correspondingly unfold, exerting a beneficial influence, not only on every community throughout the Bahá'í world, but on the immediate fortunes of a travailing society.[43]

The full implementation of the Divine Plan of 'Abdu'l-Bahá was formally launched in 1937 when Shoghi Effendi conferred on the North American Bahá'í community the mission of the First Seven Year Plan (1937–1944), the first of a series of plans designed to carry out its provisions to increasingly fuller degrees. The charter and motivating force of the First Seven Year Plan and of all subsequent future plans are 'Abdu'l-Bahá's Tablets of the Divine Plan, since these "epoch-making Tablets" call for the American Bahá'ís to carry the banner of the Faith "to the utmost ends of the earth" and to "lay an unassailable basis for the administrative structure of the Faith of Bahá'u'lláh."[44]

4

Diffusing the Light

Historical accounts of the birth of a new religion and the means by which it is spread are replete with stories of heroism and sacrifice, of spiritual transformation. These accounts are often inspired by contact with the Founder of the faith and by waves of persecution directed towards the new movement by those in authority who attempt to stem the flow of new ideas, to preserve the status quo, and to overcome what is typically seen as a threat to the power and influence of the prevailing social and ecclesiastical systems.

In this chapter, we begin by reflecting briefly on factors involved in the diffusion of new religious movements, with special emphasis on the early spread of Christianity as a context for examining the rise of the Bahá'í Faith. We then consider the uniqueness of 'Abdu'l-Bahá's mandate, addressed to the followers of the Bahá'í community and contained in Tablets of the Divine Plan, "to diffuse the light, and erect the administrative fabric, of the Faith throughout the five continents of the globe."[1] Central to this examination are such themes as what happens after the passing of the Founder of the Faith in terms of succession and who has the authority to make decisions regarding issues of doctrine and strategies for how a religion should be disseminated. Finally we argue that the guidance contained in the Tablets of the Divine Plan represents a critical stage in the progressive elaboration of the instructions concerning how the Bahá'í Faith should be spread;

and we suggest that the significance of these historic Tablets lies in their representing a call by 'Abdu'l-Bahá to universalize the religion.

The Context—The Birth of New Religious Movements

By way of introduction, we call attention to several general themes, drawn from the sacred literature of the Bahá'í Faith, that pertain to the appearance of new religious movements. For example, the Báb, the One Who announced the coming of Bahá'u'lláh, attests that the birth of each of the great religions of the world is a testimony to the unfailing love of the Creator for humankind: "The Lord of the universe hath never raised up a prophet nor hath He sent down a Book unless He hath established His covenant with all men, calling for their acceptance of the next Revelation and of the next Book; inasmuch as the outpourings of His bounty are ceaseless and without limit."[2]

Each new religious movement occurs at a critical point in time and sets in motion processes and reactions that influence the course of history, infuse a dynamic creative power and energy into individual and social life, and become the basis for new civilizations and social order. As mentioned in an earlier chapter, at the heart of Bahá'í belief is the concept of progressive revelation, which involves the coming of divine Educators, or Manifestations of God, at periodic intervals in different parts of the world over the span of many thousands of years. These Manifestations of God are the Founders of the world's great religious systems and bring teachings appropriate to the age in which they appear. Bahá'ís hold, as a fundamental principle of their Faith, that "religious truth is not absolute but relative, that Divine Revelation is a continuous and progressive process, that all the great religions of the world are divine in origin, that their basic principles are in complete harmony, that their aims and purposes are one and the same, that their teachings are but facets of one truth, that their functions are complementary, that they differ only in the non-essential aspects of their doctrines, and that their missions represent successive stages in the spiritual evolution of human society."[3] Foundational concepts such as these impact understanding about the role of the divine Educators in the world of existence, Their relationship with humankind and with each other, and Their creative contribution to the processes of social evolution

Each of the divine Educators can well be regarded as an "All-Knowing Physician" who has placed "His finger on the pulse of mankind." Expanding on this medical analogy, Bahá'u'lláh describes how the skilled physician "perceiveth the disease, and prescribeth, in His unerring wisdom, the remedy." And commenting on the inevitability of change and the uniqueness of each new era, He observes that as "Every age hath its own problem, and every soul its particular aspiration. The remedy the world needeth in its present-day afflictions can never be the same as that which a subsequent age may require." Underlining this important notion, Bahá'u'lláh advises humanity to be "concerned with the needs of the age ye live in, and center your deliberations on its exigencies and requirements."[4]

The particular historical period in which the divine Messenger lives not only has distinctive problems and needs, it also has unique spiritual and creative potential. The "remedy" prescribed by the divine Physician is characterized as the "Water of Life" to humankind. To illustrate some of the dynamic qualities involved, we draw upon a number of statements from the writings of the Faith. For example, Bahá'u'lláh indicates that "every age in which a Manifestation of God hath lived is divinely ordained, and may, in a sense, be characterized as God's appointed Day." The advent of the Manifestation of God, therefore, sets in motion spiritual processes that enable humankind to recognize the new Messenger of God. Depicting the operation of the Divine Will at the dawn of a new Revelation, the Báb explains that God

> . . . hath . . . deposited within the realities of all created things the emblem of His recognition, that everyone may know of a certainty that He is the Beginning and the End, the Manifest and the Hidden, the Maker and the Sustainer, the Omnipotent and the All-Knowing, the One Who heareth and perceiveth all

things, He Who is invincible in His power and standeth supreme in His Own identity, He Who quickeneth and causeth to die, the All-Powerful, the Inaccessible, the Most Exalted, the Most High. Every revelation of His divine Essence betokens the sublimity of His glory, the loftiness of His sanctity, the inaccessible height of His oneness and the exaltation of His majesty and power. His beginning hath had no beginning other than His Own firstness and His end knoweth no end save His Own lastness.[5]

Bahá'u'lláh likewise testifies that, as an expression of His justice and mercy, God has "endowed every soul with the capacity to recognize the signs of God." He, thus, categorically affirms, "How could He, otherwise, have fulfilled His testimony unto men, if ye be of them that ponder His Cause in their hearts. He will never deal unjustly with any one, neither will He task a soul beyond its power. He, verily, is the Compassionate, the All-Merciful."[6]

While all are assured the capacity to recognize and respond to the new message, it is also evident that the degree of individual receptivity may vary from person to person. In light of this reality, Bahá'u'lláh offers the following constructive encouragement to action: "The whole duty of man in this Day is to attain that share of the flood of grace which God poureth forth for him. Let none, therefore, consider the largeness or smallness of the receptacle. The portion of some might lie in the palm of a man's hand, the portion of others might fill a cup, and of others even a gallon-measure."[7]

Those who respond to the call of the new day are urged to express gratitude to God for this great spiritual gift and for the inestimable privilege of serving the Faith. "Render thanks unto thy Lord," Bahá'u'lláh advises, "for having aided thee to embrace His Cause, enabled thee to recognize the Manifestation of His Own Self and raised thee up to magnify Him Who is the Most Great Remembrance in this glorious Announcement."[8]

There are potentially many different reasons why an individual might choose to recognize the truth of the mission of the Manifestation of God, such as an appreciation of the exalted quality of the life of the

Founder of the new religion, the nature of His writings, the relevance and timeliness of His teachings for the current state of the world, and the impact of these teachings on the life of the faith community.

There are likewise many ways and approaches of presenting the new message to an individual, and the greatest care should be taken to avoid forcing one's beliefs on another. Those who embrace the new message in the days of the Manifestation of God are eager to share it with family, friends, and members of the wider community. Bahá'u'lláh provides the following guidance concerning some of the personal attitudes and qualities that are critical to the interaction between the one who is endeavoring to share the teachings with another soul: "Show forbearance and benevolence and love to one another. Should any one among you be incapable of grasping a certain truth, or be striving to comprehend it, show forth, when conversing with him, a spirit of extreme kindliness and good-will. Help him to see and recognize the truth, without esteeming yourself to be, in the least, superior to him, or to be possessed of greater endowments."[9]

Guidance such as this is not only conducive to fostering an understanding of spiritual truth, but critically, it leaves the response entirely to the person with whom the message is being shared. Stressing the importance of such an approach, Bahá'u'lláh advises, "The wise are they that speak not unless they obtain a hearing."[10] Care needs to be exercised at all times to avoid forcing the teachings on unwilling listeners. Likewise, as a mark of respect for the rights of the individual, it is important for a teacher to refrain from exerting undue pressure upon someone to change his or her Faith, from issuing threats, or from offering material benefits as an inducement to conversion.

The advent of the new Manifestation of God gives rise to a spiritually charged and creative environment within which individuals are attracted to the Person of the new Messenger, begin to respond to His teachings, and arise to teach the religion and to build a new faith community. While the Manifestation of God is alive, the unfoldment and diffusion of the new religious community takes place under His guidance and direction. The death of the Founder deprives the religion of His inspiring presence that had attracted new followers and kept the believers united. The Founder's passing thus raises practical issues concerning how to sustain the continued expansion of the religion and how to maintain its spiritual and social cohesion.

The Rise of Early Christianity

A brief survey of the diffusion of Christianity in its earliest days will serve to illustrate some of the general themes examined in the foregoing section.

During the lifetime of Christ, a number of outstanding followers were attracted to the new religious movement and became its active supporters. In the words of 'Abdu'l-Bahá,

> When Christ appeared, certain blessed souls followed His example. They were with their Master, ever watching and observing His conduct, movements and thoughts. They witnessed the persecutions which were heaped upon Him and were informed of all the events appertaining to that marvelous life—recipients of His kindness and favors. After the ascension of Christ they hastened to various regions of the world, scattering broadcast the teachings and instructions which He had given them. Through their devotion and efforts other places and remote nations became informed of the principles revealed by Him.[11]

A description of the initiation of this seminal process is captured in the Gospel of Matthew 4:18–22. The Gospel describes how Jesus was walking beside the Sea of Galilee. Seeing two fishermen, the brothers Peter and Andrew, casting their net into the water, Jesus called upon them to leave their nets behind and to follow Him, promising to make them fishers of men. Their response was instant. They abandoned their nets and embraced His Cause. Going on from there, Jesus saw two other brothers, James and John, who were in a boat with their father Zebedee, preparing their nets. Jesus called them, and immediately they left the boat and their father and followed Him.

These four fishermen, called by Christ to devote their lives to serving His Cause and spreading the gospel, were among His chosen body of twelve apostles. They were to play a significant role in the beginnings of the Christian ministry and would help rally many others to the discipleship of Jesus Christ.

The exploits of the apostles were legendary. The earliest expansion of Christianity was due to their heroic efforts. They arose in response to the call to take their Faith to all nations.[12] Their tasks included preaching the gospel and administering the newly founded churches. Convening in Jerusalem after the resurrection, they took counsel together and, with renewed confidence, began publicly preaching the message. Large numbers of people embraced the teachings of Christ.

The influx of Jewish converts was viewed as a potential threat by the religious and governmental authorities in the Holy Land. It resulted in fierce opposition to the nascent Christian community. Many of the early Christians fled from Jerusalem and Palestine and took refuge in Damascus and other places. Commenting on the challenges confronting the early Christians, 'Abdu'l-Bahá invites us to "consider how at the beginning of the Christian era the Apostles were afflicted, and what torments they endured in the pathway of Christ. Every day of their lives they were targets for the Pharisees' darts of mockery, vilification and abuse. They bore great hardship; they saw prison; and most of them carried to their lips the sweet cup of martyrdom."[13]

The dissemination of Christianity beyond Palestine, had, in the first instance, occurred without detailed planning or the direction of its leaders, but rather as a result of persecution—scattered by this persecution, the Christians had carried the gospel with them and started preaching—initially among the Jews and then also among the Gentiles, thereby increasing the diversity of the Christian community. The apostle Paul is credited with transforming Christianity from "a Jewish sect to a gentile movement."[14]

The apostle Paul is also recognized as having made a significant contribution to the systematic expansion of the gospel. The master plan he proposed for establishing Christian communities in the main centers of the Greco-Roman world lent a degree of organization and a particular focus to the diffusion of Christianity.[15]

Great missionary journeys were undertaken by the disciples for the purpose of spreading the gospel and organizing new churches. A report of Paul's journeys conveys something of the range and extent of his activities: "On his first journey, he sailed to the island of Cyprus, traveled through it from end to end, embarked for Asia Minor, and established self-propagating Christian groups at Perga, Antioch in Pisidia, Iconium, Lystra, and Derbe. On his second journey, he revisited the churches he had already established, and then proceeded to . . . ancient Troy, whence he sailed to Macedonia on the continent of Europe. After establishing congregations in the principal cities along the coast, he went south to Athens, and then to Corinth, where he founded an important church. On his return, he sailed to Ephesus, in Ionia, before going home. His third journey took him around the same circuit."[16]

The introduction of Christianity to Armenia in the first century is likewise traced to the missionary work of Bartholomew, one of the disciples of Christ. In the Tablets of the Divine Plan, 'Abdu'l-Bahá refers briefly to this episode and underlines the spiritual impact of such activity: "Nearly two thousand years ago, Armenia was enveloped with impenetrable darkness. One blessed soul from among the disciples of Christ hastened to that part, and through his effort, erelong that province became illumined. Thus it has become evident how the power of the Kingdom works!"[17]

The early missionary work experienced rapid success. It is reported that within a century after the death of Christ, "churches came into existence in many parts of Asia Minor, in Greece, in Italy, in Egypt, almost certainly in France and Spain, and perhaps even as far away as India. To this day, the Thomas Christians in Kerala claim that their church was founded by the apostle Thomas in person."[18]

EMERGENCE OF ORGANIZATIONAL STRUCTURE

While the missionary journeys served to extend the influence of Christianity across the world, the establishment of churches in the newly opened communities required the emergence of an organizational structure.

In the absence of clear written guidance in the Gospels concerning how the church should be organized after the death of Christ, the apostles—including Peter, the first among the apostles, whose faith was extolled by Jesus—and the apostle Paul assumed responsibility for the affairs of the new faith. However, as the number of communities and churches proliferated and the geographic spread of the religion increased, the work of preaching and administering the affairs of the faith was gradually delegated to an emergent clerical class.

Shoghi Effendi includes among the causes, in later years, of the decline in "the unity of the Church of Christ" and the gradual undermining of its influence the facts that "the Edifice which the Fathers of the Church reared after the passing of His First Apostle was an Edifice that rested in nowise upon the explicit directions of Christ Himself," and that the "authority and features of their administration were wholly inferred, and indirectly derived, with more or less justification, from certain vague and fragmentary references which they found scattered amongst His utterances as recorded in the Gospel."[19]

It is beyond the scope of this chapter to deal in detail with the events that transpired in the course of the emergence of the functions of a clergy and the rise of the Christian ecclesiastical hierarchy following the crucifixion. Nevertheless, suffice it to say that during the lifetime of the apostles, their personal authority and the expectation of Christ's imminent return forestalled questions of church governance. However, as the apostles died and the church's membership expanded and diversified, the need became more acute for a system of organization with well-defined authority and a means of resolving disputes about doctrines and the specialization of functions. By the mid-second century of the Christian Era, the three-tiered ministry of bishops, presbyters or priests, and deacons was well established and widely accepted.

Typically, the bishop was the overseer, having full responsibility for the ministry of preaching the word and administering the sacraments of the church. The presbyter or priest, as a fellow minister, helped the bishop in performing the rites and sacraments of the church, while the deacons assisted the bishop with the administrative work and the maintenance of the welfare of the community.

With the passage of the centuries, as the church became institutionalized, the bishop emerged as a leading figure with responsibility for a geographical area extending beyond that of one local church. In time, the bishop of Rome, who is regarded by tradition as standing in direct line from Peter the apostle, came to be considered as the first among equals. The primacy of the pope was widely acknowledged by the fifth century and was maintained in the West until the Reformation in the sixteenth century challenged the legitimacy of the authority of the pope and the Roman Curia. The Protestants "turned away from papal authority to the authority of the Bible," challenged "ecclesiastical legalism," and attempted "to restore a more biblical pattern of church and ministry."[20]

OFFICIAL RECOGNITION

The official recognition accorded Christianity within the Roman Empire by Emperor Constantine in 313 AD gave further impetus to the process of institutionalization of the religion. In addition to granting to Christianity equality of status with the other religious cults practiced within the Roman Empire, Constantine's proclamation also granted civic privileges to the Christian clergy.[21]

Commenting on the contribution of the Emperor to Christianity, 'Abdu'l-Bahá notes that "This great king was the first Roman ruler to champion the Cause of Christ. He spared no efforts, dedicating his life to the promotion of the principles of the Gospel."[22]

As to the significance of Constantine's actions for the future growth of the Christian religion, Montgomery, in his study of the diffusion of Christianity makes the following interesting observations:

At the time of Constantine's legitimization of Christianity in 313, Christians probably constituted between one-tenth and one-fifth of the population . . . the majority of whom lived in the Eastern Mediterranean. Official approval meant that the growth curve shot up in the fourth century to reach perhaps one-half of the population by the end of the century. . . .

By the end of the fifth century, Christianity was not only protected, but also was made the official religion and actively sponsored by the government . . . It took some seven hundred years for Christianity to spread throughout Europe, the Scandinavians and the people on the Baltic Sea being the last to accept Christianity.[23]

PATTERNS OF GROWTH

In reflecting on the pattern of growth that emerges from this all-too-brief summary of some of the processes involved in the spread of Christianity in its earliest years, a number of themes emerge, including the spiritually charged moment when the Manifestation of God appears; His diagnosis of the pressing needs of society; the cogency of His prescription; the attraction of the apostles and disciples to their Beloved; their desire to share His message; their willingness to withstand persecution, to leave their homes, and to travel to distant lands; and their determination to ensure that the Christian teachings are securely embedded in the life of the newly emerging communities, which would ultimately result in the emergence of an organizational structure. These and similar themes are also reflected in the rise and spread of the earliest days of the Bahá'í Faith.

Stages in the Unfoldment of the Bahá'í Faith

To more fully appreciate the divinely propelled processes of growth that direct and energize the unfoldment of the Bahá'í Faith, it is useful to reflect briefly on the unique vision of the Revelation and the scope of its all-encompassing mission. While space does not permit a detailed historical treatment of the growth of the Bahá'í Faith and a comprehensive analysis of the specific Plans for its advancement issued by successive Heads of the Faith, we devote the remainder of this chapter to a consideration of the nature and requirements of some of the important initiatives undertaken by the Bahá'ís to promote the interests of the Faith at different stages in its history.

UNIQUENESS OF REVELATION AND ITS SUPREME MISSION

A unique feature of the Bahá'í Faith is that it is blessed with twin Manifestations, the Báb and Bahá'u'lláh, each of Whom brought divine teachings to guide humanity. Shoghi Effendi portrays the Báb as "standing at the confluence of two universal prophetic cycles, the Adamic Cycle stretching back as far as the first dawnings of the world's recorded religious history and the Bahá'í Cycle destined to propel itself across the unborn reaches of time for a period of no less than five thousand centuries."[24] Within this Cycle, the Bahá'í Dispensation itself is anticipated to last for at least one thousand years.

The "supreme mission" of the Revelation of Bahá'u'lláh is far-reaching. "It calls for profound change not only at the level of the individual but also in the structure of society." The Guardian attests that it aims to achieve the "organic and spiritual unity of the whole body of nations"; it signalizes "through its advent the coming of age of the entire human race"; it marks "the last and highest stage in the stupendous evolution of man's collective life on this planet"; it will give rise to the "emergence of a world community, the consciousness of world citizenship, the founding of a world civilization and culture."[25]

The task assigned to the members of the Bahá'í community in the realization of this historic mission is to create a pattern for future society, thereby laying the foundations for the new civilization that is destined to emerge with the passage of time. A number of interconnected processes are involved, including diffusing the teachings of the Faith throughout the world and demonstrating the capacity of the community and its institutions to serve as the nucleus and pattern of the new world order.

The 2010 Riḍván Message of the Universal House of Justice underlines the extent of the fundamental transformations required to achieve the Faith's historic mission. The House of Justice emphasizes the evolutionary nature of such an enterprise and calls attention to the tasks to be accomplished by the Bahá'í community over the centuries:

Bahá'u'lláh's Revelation is vast. It calls for profound change not only at the level of the individual but also in the structure of society. . . . The work advancing in every corner of the globe today represents the latest stage in the ongoing Bahá'í endeavor to create the nucleus of the glorious civilization enshrined in His teachings, the building of which is an enterprise of infinite complexity and scale, one that will demand centuries of exertion by humanity to bring to fruition. There are no shortcuts, no formulas. Only as effort is made to draw on insights from His Revelation, to tap into the accumulating knowledge of the human race, to apply His teachings intelligently to the life of humanity, and to consult on the questions that arise will the necessary learning occur and capacity be developed.[26]

Clearly the mission is immense. It would be naïve to think otherwise. Its completion will require the best thinking of humankind over long periods of time.

DIVINELY PROPELLED PROCESS OF GROWTH

The progress of the Bahá'í Faith since its earliest days has been directed by a divinely propelled process of growth. The expansion of the Bahá'í community over time has evolved and will continue to evolve through successive stages.

A distinctive feature of this divinely propelled process of growth is the fact that, at each successive stage in the evolution of the community, the Head of the Faith has established the overall priorities and strategies to be adopted for the preservation of the unity and advancement of the Cause. During Their lifetimes, first the Báb and then Bahá'u'lláh directed the course of the Faith's activities. Bahá'u'lláh's authentic writings not only contained clear provisions concerning immediate successorship, they also described the role of the supreme institution, the Universal House of Justice, in ensuring the continuing flow of guidance to humanity through which the achievement of the purpose of Bahá'u'lláh's Revelation is assured.

Unique to the Bahá'í Faith are its provisions to avoid the enduring schisms that have grievously diminished the strength and cohesion of many religions as a consequence of disagreements over authority and organization after the passing of the Founders. These provisions are contained in the Covenant of Bahá'u'lláh, which sets out explicitly and in writing the arrangements for authority and the organization of the Faith after His passing.

In contrast to the religions that originated in the distant past, succession of authority and the form of organization in the Bahá'í Faith are explicitly specified by Bahá'u'lláh in His Book of the Covenant and in related passages of His writings. Such specific provisions assure unity in these vital aspects of Bahá'í community life, since deviation from such an explicit prescription can only be accomplished by the self-contradictory rejection by a Bahá'í of a portion of the authentic writings of the Founder of the religion.

The Covenant of Bahá'u'lláh designates the appointed successor and provides for the establishment of Bahá'í administrative institutions to guide the affairs of the religion. Hence, Bahá'u'lláh appointed His eldest son, 'Abdu'l-Bahá, as His successor and head of the religion. In His Will and Testament, 'Abdu'l-Bahá appointed his eldest grandson, Shoghi Effendi, as Guardian of the Bahá'í Faith. Shoghi Effendi performed the prescribed functions—which included that of authentic interpretations—until his death in 1957.

The Bahá'í Administrative Order, founded and anticipated in the Kitáb-i-Aqdas and elaborated by 'Abdu'l-Bahá in His Will and Testament, has as its principal institutions the Guardianship and the Universal House of Justice. These institutions can thus be seen to be the "Twin Successors" of Bahá'u'lláh and 'Abdu'l-Bahá.[27] To bring into being the Bahá'í administrative structure specified in the Covenant of Bahá'u'lláh, Shoghi Effendi gave special attention to establishing and consolidating the administrative institutions throughout the world and to elucidating both the principles and methods of operation of this evolving administrative system. By discharging his functions, which included acting as the authorized interpreter of the Faith, Shoghi Effendi successfully completed his mission to expand and protect the fledgling Faith by the time of his own passing in 1957. The Universal House of Justice, which was first elected in 1963 and which renews its membership by election every five years, is now the Head of the Bahá'í

Faith. Included within its clearly prescribed functions are the authority to enact laws and ordinances that are not expressly set out in the Bahá'í writings and the authority to elucidate questions that are obscure in the teachings of Bahá'u'lláh.

Briefly, the Bahá'í Administrative Order, functioning under the direction of the Universal House of Justice, consists, on the one hand, of elected National and Local Spiritual Assemblies, which guide and coordinate the activities of the Bahá'í community. The Administrative Order also includes, on the other hand, eminent and devoted believers who are appointed to provide a vital counseling and advisory function to the Spiritual Assemblies and to the believers generally. These individuals are known as Counselors and Auxiliary Board members, and along with their assistants are organized into five boards of Counselors, one for each continental area of the world. Their work is coordinated and supervised by the International Teaching Center, whose members are designated as International Counselors. The Institution of the International Teaching Center functions under the guidance of the Universal House of Justice; its seat is located at the Bahá'í World Center.

The provisions of the Bahá'í Covenant briefly outlined above have significance beyond the establishment of the administrative institutions of the Faith. They have, for example, a critical ongoing impact on such things as the preservation of the integrity of the Faith's teachings, the emergence of a creative, organically evolving community, and the establishment of the Most Great Peace in the distant future. A later section will explore a number of the ongoing implications of the Covenant for the diffusion of the Faith.

TIME AND THE BAHÁ'Í DISPENSATION

In projecting the course of the unfoldment of the one-thousand-year long Bahá'í Dispensation, Shoghi Effendi divides it into three ages: the Heroic Age, the Formative Age, and the Golden Age. The Heroic Age began in 1844, was inaugurated by the declaration of the Báb, and closed with 'Abdu'l-Bahá's passing in 1921. It is the age associated with the turbulent years of the birth of the religion, with the exploits of its saints and martyrs in the land of its birth, and with the initial spread of its teachings throughout the world.

The second of the three ages in the Dispensation of Bahá'u'lláh is the Formative Age, with its distinguishing feature being the establishment throughout the world by Bahá'ís of an Administrative Order for their Faith. This system of organization and administration of the Bahá'í community is based on principles laid down by Bahá'u'lláh and further elaborated by 'Abdu'l-Bahá, in his Will and Testament within his capacity as authorized interpreter of his father's writings. The Formative Age is also destined to witness the establishment by the nations of the world of the Lesser Peace, characterized as a binding treaty for the political unification of the world. It will lead to the emancipation of the Bahá'í Faith from the fetters of religious orthodoxy and to the universal recognition of its independent status as a world religion.[28]

The third and final age of the Bahá'í Dispensation is its Golden Age, which lies hundreds of years in the future, when the transformation of human society through the influence of the Bahá'í teachings and as a practical consequence of the spiritualization of the world will give rise to the Most Great Peace and to the birth and efflorescence of a world civilization having a dazzling splendor far beyond our capacity to visualize.[29]

Given the projected length of the Bahá'í Dispensation, it is evident that the needs and capacity of the Bahá'í community will change with the passage of time and that tasks assigned to the members of the community will also change. While the particular activities that are undertaken may depend on such things as the specific historical circumstances, the degree of development of the Bahá'í community, and its capacity to take on increasingly complex functions, the underlying mission of the Faith remains the same—namely, setting in place transformative processes that are progressively bringing the Faith into more direct contact with the life of society that will give rise to the establishment of a divine civilization.

THE BIRTH OF THE BAHÁ'Í ERA

The beginning of the Heroic Age of the Faith coincides with the birth of the Bahá'í Era. It was ushered in on May 23, 1844 by the declaration of the Báb that He was the bearer of a divine message, "the mouthpiece of God Himself, promised by the Prophets of bygone ages . . . the Herald of One immeasurably greater than Himself." In addition, He summoned the kings of the earth to investigate His claim, warned the corrupt government officials concerning their behavior, and challenged the rulers of the world to acknowledge the value of His Cause and to deliver His message "to lands in both the East and the West."[30] This momentous declaration took place in the city of Shíráz during a meeting with the young Mullá Ḥusayn, who was the first person to believe in the Báb.

A comprehensive treatment of the history of the inception of the Faith of the Báb and Bahá'u'lláh has been recounted in the inspirational chronicle by Nabíl entitled *The Dawn-Breakers: Nabíl's Narrative of the Early Days of the Bahá'í Revelation* (Wilmette: Bahá'í Publishing Trust, 1999), which details in graphic language the saga of the birth of the Bahá'í religion, and in *God Passes By* (Wilmette: Bahá'í Publishing Trust, 1974), Shoghi Effendi's sweeping history of the first one hundred years of the Bahá'í Era, which describes the circumstances surrounding the subsequent expansion of the nascent religion, the development of its Administrative Order and the emergence of the Bahá'í Faith as a world-embracing religious movement.

Drawing on the material in *Nabil's Narrative,* historian Hasan Balyuzi provides a graphic account of the epic meeting between the Báb and Mullá Ḥusayn.[31]

Mullá Ḥusayn was a man of profound scholarship and determination. He was a disciple of Siyyid Káẓim-i-Rashtí, a spiritually learned man whose studies and acute sensitivity led him to anticipate the imminent appearance in the world of the promised Lord of the Age whose advent had for centuries been the hope of countless millions. Following the dying counsel of Siyyid Káẓim to his disciples to scatter far and wide and to seek the Promised One, Mullá Ḥusayn, together with his brother and nephew, arrived at the gates of Shíráz in the afternoon of May 22, 1844. It was as though a magnet had drawn them to this city.

On reaching the gates of Shíráz, Mullá Ḥusayn sent his companions into the city to obtain lodgings, while he himself stayed behind for a while in the fields, his mind preoccupied with the purpose of his quest. Taking up the narrative, Balyuzi describes the first moment of contact between Mullá Ḥusayn and the Báb:

> As he walked and pondered he came face to face with a Youth of striking appearance. That young Man, who was gentle and gracious and whose turban proclaimed His descent from the Prophet Muhammad, greeted him with great kindness. Mullá Ḥusayn was amazed and overwhelmed by the warmth of this unexpected welcome. It was the courtesy coupled with the dignified mien of this young Siyyid which particularly impressed him. Then the young Man invited him to be His guest and to partake of the evening meal at His house. Mullá Ḥusayn mentioned that his companions had gone ahead and would be awaiting him, to which the young Siyyid replied: "Commit them to the care of God; He will surely protect and watch over them."[32]

While Mullá Ḥusayn did not imagine that the Youth might be the Promised One, he nevertheless suspected that the unexpected encounter might in some way bring him closer to the end of his quest. In the course of the evening, the Báb and His guest prayed together and engaged in conversation, during which the Báb suddenly inquired if Siyyid Káẓim had given his disciples any detailed information concerning the distinguishing features of the Promised One. When Mullá Ḥusayn finished reciting the list of requirements, there was a pregnant silence, which was broken by the stunning declaration of the Báb: "Behold, all these signs are manifest in Me."[33]

Taken aback by the Báb's announcement, Mullá Ḥusayn marshaled his arguments, even presenting the Báb with a copy of a treatise he had written on some of the abstruse doctrines of his mentors. He requested the Báb to peruse the document and elucidate the mysteries it contained. After looking quickly at the dissertation, the Báb not only shed light on its contents but greatly expanded His comments to other subjects. Then, suddenly, the Báb started to reveal a commentary on a most difficult allegorical chapter in the Qur'án—namely, the Surih of Joseph. Mullá Ḥusayn had previously requested his teacher, Siyyid Káẓim, to write such a commentary. However, the latter had refused, informing Mullá Ḥusayn that he did not have the capacity to complete this task and foreshadowing that the Promised One, would, unasked, reveal it for Mullá Ḥusayn.

By the time the Báb had completed the revelation of the first chapter of His commentary on the Surih of Joseph, Mullá Ḥusayn was convinced of the station of the Báb and aware of the significance of the events he had witnessed. He recorded for posterity the exact moment in time the birth of the new Dispensation took place, noting, "At that moment, the clock registered two hours and eleven minutes after sunset."[34]

The Báb, addressing Mullá Ḥusayn with the following words, acknowledged his faith and set out the initial processes by which His Revelation was to be diffused: "O thou who art the first to believe in Me! Verily I say, I am the Báb, the Gate of God, and thou art the Bábu'l-Báb, the gate of that Gate. Eighteen souls must, in the beginning, spontaneously and of their own accord, accept Me and recognise the truth of My Revelation. Unwarned and uninvited, each of these must seek independently to find Me. And when their number is complete, one of them must needs be chosen to accompany Me on My pilgrimage to Mecca and Medina. There I shall deliver the Message of God to the Sharif of Mecca."[35]

During the following forty days, seventeen other individuals accepted the Báb's claim, and together with Mullá Ḥusayn, they constitute the group known as the "Letters of the Living," the Báb's chosen disciples. Shoghi Effendi provides the following insight into this fascinating and mystical process and underlines the particular significance of two of these early disciples, both of whom were destined to play an important role in the early history of the religion: "Gradually, spontaneously, some in sleep, others while awake, some through fasting and prayer, others through dreams and visions, they discovered the Object of their quest, and were enlisted under the banner of the new-born Faith. The last, but in rank the first, . . . was the erudite, the twenty-two year old Quddús . . . Immediately preceding him, a woman [Ṭáhirih], the only one of her sex, who, unlike her fellow-disciples, never attained the presence of the Báb, was invested with the rank of apostleship in the new Dispensation."[36]

The Báb summoned to His presence these disciples, assigned to each a specific task and prior to their departure, He prepared them for their mission with the following words of counsel and encouragement: "O My beloved friends! You are the bearers of the name of God in this Day. You have been chosen as the repositories of His mystery. It behooves each one of you to manifest the attributes of God, and to exemplify by your deeds and words the signs of His righteousness, His power and glory." He called to mind the words Jesus addressed to His disciples as they set out to teach His Cause:

Ye are even as the fire which in the darkness of the night has been kindled upon the mountain-top. Let your light shine before the eyes of men. Such must be the purity of your character and the degree of your renunciation, that the people of the earth may through you recognize and be drawn closer to the heavenly Father who is the Source of purity and grace. For none has seen the Father who is in heaven. You who are His spiritual children must by your deeds exemplify His virtues, and witness to His glory. You are the salt of the earth, but if the salt have lost its savor, wherewith shall it be salted?[37]

In this same address, the Báb stressed the magnitude of their responsibility and emphasized the greatness of the New Day. He counseled His followers in these terms:

O My Letters! Verily I say, immensely exalted is this Day above the days of the Apostles of old. Nay, immeasurable is the difference! You are the witnesses of the Dawn of the promised Day of God. You are the partakers of the mystic chalice of His Revelation. . . . The days when idle worship was deemed sufficient are ended. The time is come when naught but the purest motive, supported by deeds of stainless purity, can ascend to the throne of the Most High and be acceptable unto Him. . . . You have been called to this station; you will attain to it, only if you arise to trample beneath your feet every earthly desire, and endeavor to become those "honored servants of His who speak not till He hath spoken, and who do His bidding."[38]

Finally the Báb informs His disciples that He is preparing them for the advent of an even mightier Day to come. He calls upon them to put their trust in God and to "Scatter throughout the length and breadth of this land, and, with steadfast feet and sanctified hearts, prepare the way for His coming."[39]

Thus, the divinely propelled process of growth was set in motion as thousands responded to the summons of a New Day.

The Báb's disciples were galvanized into action by the mandate conferred upon them. They scattered throughout the provinces of Iran, attracting receptive individuals, especially from the clerical and merchant classes, to the religion of the Báb. Indeed, as the fame of the Báb spread, the "wave of passionate inquiry" that swept the whole country resulted not only in widespread interest in the new Revelation but also provoked a countervailing negative reaction.[40]

The men and women in Iran who recognized the station of the Báb as the bearer of a new divine message, and who witnessed the dawning influence of His Revelation and participated in the turbulent events that marked its advent in the land of its birth, are referred to in the Bahá'í writings as the "dawn-breakers," those who were present at the beginning of the new day. The dramatic impact of the Báb's prophetic mission on His early followers and the tenor of this stirring period are captured in the following description: "We behold, as we survey the episodes of this first act of a sublime drama, the figure of its Master Hero, the Báb, arise meteor-like above the horizon of Shíráz, traverse the somber sky of Persia from south to north, decline with tragic swiftness, and perish in a blaze of glory. We see His satellites, a galaxy of God-intoxicated heroes, mount above that same horizon, irradiate that same incandescent light, burn themselves out with that self-same swiftness, and impart in their turn an added impetus to the steadily gathering momentum of God's nascent Faith."[41]

The heroic and sacrificial actions of the dawn-breakers made a direct contribution to the diffusion of the Báb's message. Through their actions they made known the very existence of the new Faith. Their fearless and wise presentation of the teachings of the Faith attracted spiritually minded individuals to the Cause. The early believers demonstrated by their personal conduct the power and efficacy of the spiritually and socially transforming teachings of God, and they established the identity of the Faith as an independent religion. Their willingness to withstand vicious persecution in order to plant the seeds of the new Manifestation of God in Persia not only ensured the continuity of the new Message in Persia but attracted the attention and sympathy of historians, intellectuals, scholars, and other prominent thinkers in Europe, thereby spreading the knowledge and influence of the new Revelation beyond the land of its birth. The power of the Faith to grow and to overcome challenges, in the face of active opposition, and despite a lack of human and material resources, illustrated its cohesive strength and potential as a society-building force.

SPREAD OF THE FAITH BEYOND PERSIA

The second phase of the Heroic Age coincides with the ministry of Bahá'u'lláh. His voluminous writings set forth the pathway to a divine civilization that would ensure peace and prosperity for all by offering the means for individual, spiritual transformation and the final unification of human society. As mentioned in an earlier chapter, Bahá'u'lláh urged the kings and rulers of His time to recognize and assist in bringing the promised peace into existence. His visionary teachings aroused opposition and precipitated His exiles and final confinement in the Most Great Prison.

From the early days of the Faith, a number of outstanding believers had been traveling throughout Persia to teach the Faith. By the time Bahá'u'lláh entered the city of 'Akká in 1868, the Faith had reached a few of the neighboring countries and attracted the hearts of some of their inhabitants. Toward the end of Bahá'u'lláh's ministry, the Faith had been introduced into fifteen countries, mainly the Islamic lands stretching from Turkmenistan in the East to Egypt and Sudan in the West. Among others, eminent Bahá'ís such as Nabíl-i-Akbar and Mírzá Abu'l-Faḍl traveled through these territories.[42]

The divinely propelled process of growth "received impetus through the exertions made by early believers to carry the message of Bahá'u'lláh to neighboring countries in the East and scattered pockets in the West."[43] This gave rise to the next significant stage in the expansion of the Faith.

The spread of the Faith beyond the Islamic world was critical to demonstrating the efficacy of the core Bahá'í principle of the oneness of humanity. To promote the diffusion of the Faith beyond the Islamic heartlands, Bahá'u'lláh dispatched, among others, the renowned travel teacher Jamál Effendi (Sulaymán Khán-i-Tunukábání) to the vast subcontinent of India, the majority of whose inhabitants were mainly non-Muslim. He arrived in Bombay in 1878 and began his teaching activities. He traveled extensively in India, then went to Ceylon—where he encountered great opposition from Buddhist leaders—and also to Burma. Over the course of the next twenty years, his travels for the Faith took him to Punjab (Pakistan), Malaya, Thailand, Indonesia, Kashmir, Afghanistan and Tibet. In the course of his travels, he met many leaders of thought and men of culture from every background and religion. People from all walks of life turned to Jamál Effendi for enlightenment. He succeeded in converting peoples of various religions to the Faith. Among them were Muslims of the Sunni and Shí'ih sects, Ismá'ílís, and Hindus and Buddhists. In the islands of Java, many people were attracted to the Cause, and some rulers and dignitaries were influenced by his teaching work.[44]

In Madras, Jamál Effendi taught the Faith to a young man named Siyyíd Muṣṭafáy-i-Rúmí, who was of 'Iraqi background. Muṣṭafáy-i-Rúmí served the Cause with distinction, mainly in Burma, and was posthumously named by Shoghi Effendi as one of the Hands of the Cause. After his death, Shoghi Effendi, in a cable to the Bahá'í world, referred to him as a "DISTINGUISHED PIONEER" of the Faith of Bahá'u'lláh, a "STAUNCH AND HIGH-MINDED SOUL," the record of whose "SUPERB SERVICES IN BOTH TEACHING AND ADMINISTRATIVE FIELDS SHED LUSTRE ON BOTH THE HEROIC AND FORMATIVE AGES OF BAHAI DISPEN-SATION," and whose resting-place "SHOULD BE REGARDED FOREMOST SHRINE IN THE COMMUNITY OF BURMESE BELIEVERS."[45]

The expansion of Bahá'í activity in India and Burma was remark-able. The steadily growing community included among its members representatives of all the main religious Faiths, and during the lifetime of 'Abdu'l-Bahá, the village of Daidanaw in Burma had eight hundred Bahá'í residents and possessed "a school, a court, and a hospital of their own, as well as land for community cultivation, the proceeds of which they devoted to the furtherance of the interests of their Faith."[46]

While the Bahá'í Faith had its origins in the East and was embedded in an Islamic context, the travels of the Faith's early itinerant teachers helped to demonstrate the appeal of Bahá'u'lláh's teachings to people from different religious, ethnic, and cultural backgrounds. Their labors took place against the backdrop of the slide of the world into the horrors of World War I. The establishment of the foundations of embryonic Bahá'í communities represents the initiation by the believers of an attempt to introduce and apply society-building processes based on the teachings of the Manifestation.

The stage was set for the next phase in the evolution of the Faith, a stage characterized by a strategic approach to the expansion of the Faith and the establishment of its administrative structures. Under the leadership of 'Abdu'l-Bahá, through the Tablets of the Divine Plan that he penned in 1916–17, and through the provisions of his Will and Testament, the divinely ordained process of growth acquired greater structure and coherence.[47]

THE MINISTRY OF 'ABDU'L-BAHÁ

The third stage of the Heroic Age (1892–1921) coincides with the ministry of 'Abdu'l-Bahá. As mentioned in chapter 3, in 1893, a year after the passing of Bahá'u'lláh, mention of His advent and the major focus of His Revelation was made in the West, in a paper written by a Presbyterian minister that was read during a presentation at the World Parliament of Religions held in Chicago. The spread of the Faith in North America, together with 'Abdu'l-Bahá's extended visits to the West in 1911–12, gave rise to the establishment of embryonic Bahá'í communities in the United States and Canada, the laying of the foundation stone for the Mother Temple of the West, and the establishment of nascent communities in France, England, and Germany. The Tablets the Master addressed to these communities deepened the believers' knowledge of the Faith, and his constant encouragement reinforced their attempts to teach the Faith and to begin to attempt to organize and consolidate the foundations of these newly established communities.

Vital to this stage of development are 'Abdu'l-Bahá's Tablets of the Divine Plan which unfold to the eyes of the believers his Plan for the mission he wished them to undertake—a Plan that, in the words of Shoghi Effendi, "must in the years to come enable its members to diffuse the light, and erect the administrative fabric, of the Faith throughout the five continents of the globe."[48] The thrust of the Divine Plan is twofold and involves both the systematic spread of the Faith to all parts of the world and the erection of institutions to administer its affairs. While the Tablets of the Divine Plan underline, in a general way, the need for administrative structures and committees to organize and give direction to the work of spreading knowledge of the Faith and of increasing its influence, it is 'Abdu'l-Bahá's Will and Testament, whose contents were made known after his passing in 1921, that gave rise to the establishment of the Faith's administrative institutions.

The response of the believers to this call during the lifetime of 'Abdu'l-Bahá lent "an unprecedented impetus to the work which the enterprising ambassadors of the Message of Bahá'u'lláh had initiated in distant lands." Shoghi Effendi describes what happened:

> Forsaking home, kindred, friends and position a handful of men and women, fired with a zeal and confidence which no human agency can kindle, arose to carry out the mandate which 'Abdu'l-

Bahá had issued. Sailing northward as far as Alaska, pushing on to the West Indies, penetrating the South American continent to the banks of the Amazon and across the Andes to the southernmost ends of the Argentine Republic, pressing on westward into the island of Tahiti and beyond it to the Australian continent and still beyond it as far as New Zealand and Tasmania… these men and women have been instrumental in extending, to a degree as yet unsurpassed in Bahá'í history, the sway of Bahá'u'lláh's universal dominion. In the face of almost insurmountable obstacles they have succeeded in most of the countries through which they have passed or in which they have resided, in proclaiming the teachings of their Faith, in circulating its literature, in defending its cause, in laying the basis of its institutions and in reinforcing the number of its declared supporters. . . .

The Cause of Bahá'u'lláh had by that time encircled the globe. Its light, born in darkest Persia, had been carried successively to the European, the African and the American continents, and was now penetrating the heart of Australia, encompassing thereby the whole earth with a girdle of shining glory. . . . How deep a satisfaction 'Abdu'l-Bahá must have felt, while conscious of the approaching hour of His departure, as He witnessed the first fruits of the international services of these heroes of His Father's Faith![49]

Though knowledge of the existence of the Cause of Bahá'u'lláh had indeed "encircled the globe," the execution of the mandate contained in the Tablets of the Divine Plan was far from complete. 'Abdu'l-Bahá's Tablets added a specifically global dimension to the mission of the Faith by naming individual countries and island groups that were to receive the message of Bahá'u'lláh. Furthermore, the Tablets of the Divine Plan, together with the Master's Will and Testament, set out systematic strategies to enable the Faith to become truly universal, and they put in place processes that lay the foundations of the administrative structure necessary to give direction to the evolving worldwide community. The guidance contained in these seminal documents provided the means for stimulating its worldwide expansion and for laying the foundations of community life. It thus represented a strategic shift in the approach used to diffuse the Faith.

The call to universalize the growth and spread of the Faith and to create a cohesive global community may well reflect 'Abdu'l-Bahá's confidence in the efficacy of the provisions of the Bahá'í Covenant and the operation of the administrative institutions to maintain the Faith's identity, unity, and the integrity of its teachings, while reaching out to peoples of all different ethnic, social, and religious backgrounds and cultures.

The processes and procedures put in place by such provisions of the Covenant serve to protect the Faith from fragmenting into schisms— such as an American Bahá'í Faith, a Persian Bahá'í Faith, or an African Bahá'í Faith—as a result of either the dominant or diverse cultures it encounters. Among other things, these provisions serve to retain focus and guard against such hazards as surrendering to cultural influences, the pressures of a particular majority or ethnic group, or the temptation to violate one's principles in order to gain converts or influence.

Writing in the "Declaration and Trust," the preamble to its Constitution, the Universal House of Justice summarizes the provisions put in place by Bahá'u'lláh to ensure the continuity of the divinely appointed authority after His passing, and it describes its relationship to the Bahá'í Covenant:

Bahá'u'lláh, the Revealer of God's Word in this Day, the Source of Authority, the Fountainhead of Justice, the Creator of a new World Order, the Establisher of the Most Great Peace, the Inspirer and Founder of a world civilization, the Judge, the Lawgiver, the Unifier and Redeemer of all mankind, has proclaimed the advent of God's Kingdom on earth, has formulated its laws and ordinances, enunciated its principles, and ordained its institutions. To direct and canalize the forces released by His Revelation He instituted His Covenant, whose power has preserved the integrity of His Faith, maintained its unity and stimulated its world-wide expansion throughout the successive ministries of 'Abdu'l-Bahá and Shoghi Effendi. It continues to fulfil its life-giving purpose through the agency of the Universal House of Justice whose fundamental object, as one of the twin successors of Bahá'u'lláh and 'Abdu'l-Bahá, is to ensure the continuity of that divinely-appointed authority which flows from the Source of the Faith, to safeguard the unity of its followers, and to maintain the integrity and flexibility of its teachings.[50]

COVENANTAL PROVISIONS AND WORLD-WIDE EXPANSION

Based primarily on the execution of principles laid down by Bahá'u'lláh and the provisions of 'Abdu'l-Bahá's Will and Testament, the Bahá'í administrative structure derives its authority from the Covenant of Bahá'u'lláh. However, the Administrative Order is much more than a mere system of organization for the Bahá'í community. Shoghi Effendi indicates that it is destined to be "at once the harbinger, the nucleus and pattern" of the future World Order of Bahá'u'lláh.[51] Further, the Bahá'í Covenant plays a critical role in setting in place principles and processes governing interpersonal and social relationships, for example, between individuals, between the individuals and the institutions, and between individuals and the community. It is therefore useful to examine the connections between the operation of the Bahá'í administrative structure and the function of the Covenant in preserving the unity and integrity of the Bahá'í community and in fostering social transformation.

'Abdu'l-Bahá links the implementation of the oneness of humankind to the Covenant. He states: ". . . the pivot of the oneness of mankind is nothing else but the power of the Covenant." Elaborating on the significance and practical importance of the Covenant, the Universal House of Justice asserts that the Bahá'í Covenant "drives the accelerating transition from the old order to the new World Order envisaged by Bahá'u'lláh." The House of Justice sets out some of the elements involved, explaining that "Its spiritual dynamic and cohesive power, its unifying principles and practical institutional provisions are a pattern for the healing of the ills afflicting our fractured societies and defective social systems."[52]

How, then, do these elements translate into the requisite practical mechanisms and institutional provisions that are necessary to foster and ensure the Faith's commitment to embrace peoples from all backgrounds and cultures within one unified universal community? What will protect the Faith from departing from its core mission of establishing the oneness of humankind? How will these provisions help to counteract the compelling pull toward fragmentation and particularism?

As previously noted, the teachings of the Manifestation of God define the new social reality and provide the spiritual motivation for individual and institutional transformation. Included among Bahá'u'lláh's teachings are His Book of Laws and the fundamentals for a New World Order, which include seminal teachings concerning the oneness of the humanity and the attainment of its maturity.

In contrast to the religions that originated in the past, the authentic writings of Bahá'u'lláh, many of which are written in His own hand, were recorded and collected during His lifetime. His writings are preserved for the future. Many of His works have been published and translated into the diverse languages of the world. Hence, when issues arise about exactly what the teachings of the Bahá'í Faith say on a particular subject, reference can be made to the original texts. The written word is and will continue to be the guide and the standard against which actions are and will be measured. This obviously has implications for the practice of the principle of the oneness of humankind over time.

While the essential spiritual teaching is unchanging, Bahá'u'lláh, in His writings, sets out the principle of progressive revelation, both in relation to the advent of successive Manifestations of God and to the gradual unfoldment and implementation of the Revelation within the ministry of each individual Prophet. Bahá'u'lláh explains:

Know of a certainty that in every Dispensation the light of Divine Revelation hath been vouchsafed unto men in direct proportion to their spiritual capacity. Consider the sun. How feeble its rays the moment it appeareth above the horizon. How gradually its warmth and potency increase as it approacheth its zenith, enabling meanwhile all created things to adapt themselves to the growing intensity of its light. How steadily it declineth until it reacheth its setting point. Were it, all of a sudden, to manifest the energies latent within it, it would, no doubt, cause injury to all created things. . . . In like manner, if the Sun of Truth were suddenly to reveal, at the earliest stages of its manifestation, the full measure of the potencies which the providence of the almighty hath bestowed upon it, the earth of human understanding would waste away and be consumed; for men's hearts would neither sustain the intensity of its revelation, nor be able to mirror forth the radiance of its light. Dismayed and overpowered, they would cease to exist.[53]

Not only did Bahá'u'lláh elaborate His laws and teachings during His lifetime, the designation and appointment of authorized Interpreters of His Revelation created further opportunity for the progressive elucidation of His teachings.

In addition to the principle of progressive revelation, Bahá'u'lláh provided the following guidance concerning the implementation of His laws. In one of His Tablets, He set out the principle of progressive implementation of the laws, stating: "Indeed the laws of God are like unto the ocean and the children of men as fish, did they but know it. However, in observing them one must exercise tact and wisdom . . . One must guide mankind to the ocean of true understanding in a spirit of love and toleration."[54] The establishment of the principles of progressive clarification and progressive implementation of the laws of the Faith has implications for the nature of the process of the spiritual transformation of humanity. Such gradual implementation would seem to mandate planned change, instituted under the guidance of the Head of the Faith.

In addition to laying down His teachings, Bahá'u'lláh, in the book of His Covenant, confirmed the appointment of His eldest son, 'Abdu'l-Bahá, as the Head of the Faith, the Interpreter of His Word, and the Center of His Covenant. What is the practical significance of such appointments and designations? How do they relate to social transformation, to the achievement of the mandate to universalize the Bahá'í community? The Universal House of Justice explains that as the interpreter, 'Abdu'l-Bahá became "the living mouth of the Book, the expounder of the Word."[55] In other words, his designated function was to answer questions about the meaning and intention of the text, to expound on the seminal teachings of Bahá'u'lláh. This he did, often in response to questions, but also in the course of describing and presenting the teachings of the Faith on a particular subject. The significance of this designated function for social transformation is that it provided a means for clarifying the meaning of a text and for resolving differences of opinion. Furthermore, 'Abdu'l-Bahá's interpretations have continuing relevance and application.

What is the significance of 'Abdu'l-Bahá's appointment as the Center of the Covenant for the preservation of unity and social transformation? The Universal House of Justice explains that "He became the incorruptible medium for applying the Word to practical measures for the raising up of a new civilization."[56] Hence, 'Abdu'l-Bahá not only expounded the meaning and intention of Bahá'u'lláh's teachings, but he also fostered the application of these teachings in the everyday lives of the adherents of the Faith. He progressively guided the practice of the teachings even when their practice challenged the prevailing traditional cultural patterns. Beyond the Bahá'í community, he promoted understanding of the relevance of Bahá'u'lláh's teachings for the modern age, thus contributing to the forces for social change.

In addition to conferring on 'Abdu'l-Bahá the necessary authority to fulfill the requirements of his office, Bahá'u'lláh "vested in Him the virtues of perfection in personal and social behavior, that humanity may have an enduring model to emulate."[57] This important provision also contributes significantly to preserving the essential unity and identity of the expanding Bahá'í community in that 'Abdu'l-Bahá's life serves as an example and model of how to apply the principles of the Faith to daily life. His example illustrates how to translate abstract spiritual principles into a visible reality. He is a recent historical figure whose life is well-documented, and he lived and traveled in the East and the

West and related to people from diverse backgrounds and cultures. Both his attitudes and behaviors, and his reactions to situations and people have relevance to contemporary life, and he exemplified a way of life that was not bound by culture. Reference to the example of his life can both inspire and motivate and also help to resolve perplexity concerning how to behave.

The twin institutions of the Guardianship and the Universal House of Justice are the chosen successors designated in the writings of Bahá'u'lláh and 'Abdu'l-Bahá. Shoghi Effendi explains that these institutions are ". . . destined to apply the principles, promulgate the laws, protect the institutions, adapt loyally and intelligently the Faith to the requirements of progressive society, and consummate the incorruptible inheritance which the Founders of the Faith have bequeathed to the world." Briefly, the Guardian of the Faith has been made the interpreter of the Word of God, and the Universal House of Justice has been invested with the function of legislating on matters not expressly revealed in the teachings. The House of Justice explains this significance, indicating that, as the appointed interpreter, the "Guardian reveals what the Scripture means; his interpretation is a statement of truth which cannot be varied." It is "he and he alone who can authoritatively state what the Book means." Hence, "Unity of doctrine is maintained by the existence of the authentic texts of Scripture and the voluminous interpretations of 'Abdu'l-Bahá and Shoghi Effendi. The appointment of the designated interpreter "preserves the identity of His Faith, and guards the integrity of His law." The interpreter is the point of authority for explaining the meaning and intention of the text and thus removes the potential for distortion of the meaning with the passage of time.[58]

Upon the Universal House of Justice, "has been conferred the exclusive right of legislating on matters not expressly revealed in the Bahá'í writings." The House of Justice itself further clarifies, "Its [The Universal House of Justice's] pronouncements, which are susceptible of amendment or abrogation by the House of Justice itself, serve to supplement the law of God. Although not invested with the function of interpretation, the House of Justice is in a position to do everything

necessary to establish the World Order of Bahá'u'lláh on this earth."
In practical terms, the significance of the Universal House of Justice
having the right to legislate on matters that are obscure and causing
confusion, assures "unity of administration,"—i.e., of action. While
the sacred text is the highest authority and delimits the sphere of action
of the House of Justice, Shoghi Effendi explains that the process of
elucidation by the House of Justice enables the revealed Word "even as
a living organism, to expand and adapt itself to the needs and requirements of an ever-changing society."[59]

In one of his Tablets, 'Abdu'l-Bahá underlines the importance of
the legislative function of the Universal House of Justice. He states,
"Those matters of major importance which constitute the foundation
of the Law of God are explicitly recorded in the Text, but subsidiary
laws are left to the House of Justice. The wisdom of this is that the
times never remain the same, for change is a necessary quality and an
essential attribute of this world and of time and space. Therefore the
House of Justice will take action accordingly."[60]

The right of the Universal House of Justice to clarify matters that
are obscure and causing conflict not only assures flexibility and unity
of action over time but also serves to illustrate the means by which
the community is protected from the machinations of charismatic
individuals with strong views who seek to impose their views on the
life of the community. Indeed, this provision of the Covenant is an
important mechanism for the release of creativity. People can feel free
to express their opinions as their own personal understandings without
having to worry about causing disunity. They can be confident that the
Universal House of Justice will, as necessary, take any steps that might
be required to ensure the essential unity of the Faith.

As outlined above, the specific provisions of the Bahá'í Covenant
that preserve the essential identity and unity of the Faith while fostering
and safeguarding social change include the fact that the original writings of Bahá'u'lláh are extant and remain the standard against which
the application of His teachings is to be weighed. In addition, the
appointment of authorized interpreters and institutions with authority
to resolve obscure issues allows for the progressive elucidation of the

meaning of Bahá'u'lláh's teachings and the progressive application of these teachings in the life of the community. 'Abdu'l-Bahá and Shoghi Effendi have revealed the meaning and implications of Bahá'u'lláh's seminal teachings. Their interpretations are fundamental statements of truth that have enduring application and authority. The Universal House of Justice clarifies issues that are obscure, directs the application of the teachings, and ensures that there is no continued departure from the practice of the teachings.

Finally, two other aspects of the Covenant should be mentioned, both of which contribute to the implementation of 'Abdu'l-Bahá's mandate to implement the pivotal principle of unity in diversity. The first relates to the individual believer, the second to Bahá'í elected Spiritual Assemblies. In relation to the former, when an individual becomes a member of the Bahá'í Faith, he or she becomes a party to the Covenant and accepts responsibility for endeavoring to put into practice the teachings of the Faith he or she embraced. Writing on this theme, the Universal House of Justice states, "The Covenant is the 'axis of the oneness of the world of humanity' because it preserves the unity and integrity of the Faith itself and protects it from being disrupted by individuals who are convinced that only their understanding of the Teachings is the right one—a fate that has overcome all past Revelations. The Covenant is, moreover, embedded in the writings of Bahá'u'lláh Himself. Thus, as you clearly see, to accept Bahá'u'lláh is to accept His Covenant; to reject His Covenant is to reject Him."[61] Furthermore, in relation to the second point, Bahá'í elected Spiritual Assemblies, Bahá'í institutions and communities are expected to take initiatives to foster the practice of Bahá'í teachings and values. In this regard, the Universal House of Justice offers the following guidance:

Unity of mankind is the pivotal principle of His Revelation; Bahá'í communities must therefore become renowned for their demonstration of this unity. In a world becoming daily more divided by factionalism and group interests, the Bahá'í community must be distinguished by the concord and harmony of its relationships. The coming of age of the human race must be foreshadowed by the mature, responsible understanding of human problems and the wise administration of their affairs by these same Bahá'í communities. The practice and development of such Bahá'í characteristics are the responsibility alike of individual Bahá'ís and administrative institutions . . .[62]

It is therefore evident that the explicit provisions of the Bahá'í Covenant provide both the spiritual motivation and institutional structures to guarantee individual and social transformation. These provisions are the means by which "the foundations of a global society that can reflect the oneness of human nature" can be laid, progressively established, and preserved.[63]

INCEPTION OF THE FORMATIVE AGE— ACCELERATION OF GROWTH

The Formative Age of the Bahá'í Dispensation was ushered in by the passing of 'Abdu'l-Bahá in November, 1921. It stands between the Heroic Age (1844–1921), which is associated with the ministries of the Báb (the Prophet-Herald of the Bahá'í Faith), Bahá'u'lláh, and 'Abdu'l-Baha; and the Golden Age, which will witness the dawning of the Most Great Peace, the emergence of a commonwealth of all the nations of the world, and the advent of the Kingdom of God on earth.

Since the inception of the Formative Age, the activities of the Bahá'í community have been underpinned by a number of interacting processes set in place by the Tablets of the Divine Plan and the covenantal provisions specified in 'Abdu'l-Bahá's Will and Testament and elsewhere in the writings of the Faith. These include a global orientation—the call to diffuse the teachings of the Faith to all five continents, the progressive emergence of an evolving institutional structure, and the fostering of community-building processes.

The implementation of these underlying processes proceeds in an organic manner, depending on the size of the community, its administrative capacity, its ability to empower individuals, and its capacity for service. In this regard, we have seen how, by naming specific geographical areas, the Tablets of the Divine Plan gave direction and impetus to the systematic spread of the Faith. However, the acceleration of the divinely-propelled processes of growth required the creation of administrative structures to channel the work of the Bahá'ís. It was not until the friends spread out systematically across the globe under the direction of the Guardian to establish small centers of Bahá'í activity and erect the first pillars of the Administrative Order did the process of growth gain significant momentum.

A major thrust of the Formative Age is the shaping, development, and consolidation of the local, national, and international institutions of the Faith. The Formative Age consists of a number of epochs of unequal length, with the timing of each epoch being determined by the Head of the Faith, and reflects a stage in the progressive evolution of the organic Bahá'í community and the maturation of its institutions.[64]

The full-scale implementation of the Tablets of the Divine Plan had to be held in abeyance for almost twenty years until the machinery of the Administrative Order had been devised and forged under the guidance of Shoghi Effendi, and until the elected Local and National Spiritual Assemblies more clearly understood their purpose and functions and had acquired the necessary experience to discharge their responsibilities in an efficient manner. The launching of the Plan was preceded by an intensive period of preparation, ensuring that both the machinery and administrative capacity necessary for the conduct of future systematic teaching activities were in place. Shoghi Effendi's secretary, writing on his behalf, underlines the vital role of the Spiritual Assemblies in furthering the development of the religion at this transitional stage: "Now that they have erected the administrative machinery of the Cause they must put it to its real use—serving only as an instrument to facilitate the flow of the spirit of the Faith out in the world. Just as the muscles enable the body to carry out the will of the individual, all Assemblies and Committees must enable the believers to carry forth the Message of God to the waiting public, the love of Bahá'u'lláh, and the healing laws and principles of the Faith to all men."[65]

The formal initiation of the systematic implementation of the Tablets of the Divine Plan began in 1937 when Shoghi Effendi called upon the North American Bahá'í community to launch the First Seven Year Plan

(1937–1944). This Plan, drawing its inspiration from the Tablets of the Divine Plan, represented the first systematic teaching campaign of the Bahá'í community and inaugurated the initial stage of the execution of 'Abdu'l-Bahá's Divine Plan in the Western Hemisphere.

TEACHING PLANS OF SHOGHI EFFENDI

A distinguishing feature of the execution of the Divine Plan under the direction of Shoghi Effendi was the simultaneous and often spontaneous prosecution of Bahá'í national Plans by National Spiritual Assemblies in both the East and the West, including the United States, British, Indian, Persian, Australian and New Zealand, and 'Iráqí National Assemblies.[66] The Plans derived their direction from 'Abdu'l-Bahá's Divine Plan. The goals were assigned by Shoghi Effendi from the World Center of the Faith, and the prosecution of the Plans involved the mobilization of the Bahá'í community by the National Spiritual Assemblies. The overall aims of the national Plans were to introduce the teachings of the Faith to specific geographic areas in a systematic and planned way, and to strengthen the Bahá'í community.

The internal consolidation and the administrative experience gained by the National Assemblies in the implementation of these national Plans was utilized and mobilized by the Guardian with the launching of the Ten Year World Crusade (1953–1963), a global teaching initiative involving the simultaneous prosecution of twelve national Plans. The culminating event of this global plan was the election of the Universal House of Justice in 1963.

The Plans undertaken during the ministry of Shoghi Effendi not only increased the membership of the community but also served to strengthen and expand the foundations of its administrative structure in the newly opened geographic areas, and to begin to shape Bahá'í community life. They demonstrated the more effective and coordinated use of the administrative machinery to prosecute the goals of the first global spiritual crusade. The Ten-Year Spiritual Crusade will long be remembered for the critical role of hundreds of Bahá'ís who arose as pioneers to settle in goal areas abroad and to open to the Faith specific areas on the homefront.[67]

The outstanding accomplishments of the Bahá'ís during the ministry of Shoghi Effendi were achieved against the backdrop of a decline in the political, economic, and social conditions of the world. They illustrate the resilience and creativity of the Bahá'í community. The Ten Year Spiritual Crusade, for example, coincided with the confluence of such world-shaping events as the lowering of the Iron Curtain onto Europe, the rise of the Cold War, the outbreak of hostilities on the Korean Peninsula, and the rise of opposition to colonial powers in Africa and parts of Asia. In addition, there was a renewed outbreak of persecutions against the Bahá'í community in Iran in 1955, which, for a time hindered the progress of the Plan in that land.

The Guardian's Plans challenged the Bahá'ís to arise to play their part in the current stage of the evolution of the Bahá'í community and to understand their role in this ongoing historical process. They empowered the Bahá'ís and instilled a sense of personal responsibility in them for the fate of the Faith and humanity as a whole, including the recognition that one person can indeed make a difference in the fate of humanity. This stood in sharp contrast to the increasing paralysis of will and disengagement that was afflicting society at large. Commenting on the practical implications of an emergent Bahá'í identity and the willingness of the friends to accept personal responsibility, Shoghi Effendi wrote:

> Conscious of their high calling, confident in the society-building power which their Faith possesses, they press forward, undeterred and undismayed, in their efforts to fashion and perfect the necessary instruments wherein the embryonic World Order of Bahá'u'lláh can mature and develop. It is this building process, slow and unobtrusive, to which the life of the world-wide Bahá'í Community is wholly consecrated, that constitutes the one hope of a stricken society. For this process is actuated by the generating influence of God's changeless Purpose, and is evolving within the framework of the Administrative Order of His Faith.[68]

At the level of the community, the Plans initiated a more systematic approach to capacity-building within the worldwide Bahá'í community and demonstrated faith in the ability of all peoples and cultures to make a contribution to social development. They interwove a number of interacting society-building processes—expansion and consolidation, individual spiritual transformation, and administrative development. They resulted in an enormous growth in the size and diversity of the Bahá'í community and provided a more concrete demonstration of the viability and reality of the oneness of the human family. The nature of the transformative and socially cohesive power inherent in the Faith is illustrated by the Guardian:

> The Faith of Bahá'u'lláh has assimilated, by virtue of its creative, its regulative and ennobling energies, the varied races, nationalities, creeds and classes that have sought its shadow, and have pledged unswerving fealty to its cause. It has changed the hearts of its adherents, burned away their prejudices, stilled their passions, exalted their conceptions, ennobled their motives, coordinated their efforts, and transformed their outlook. . . .
>
> Of such men and women it may be truly said that to them "every foreign land is a fatherland, and every fatherland a foreign land." For their citizenship, it must be remembered, is in the Kingdom of Bahá'u'lláh.[69]

Such initiatives lay the foundations of a new culture based on the practice of spiritual values and the teachings of the Faith and helped to cement the unity and social cohesion of the community.

On an institutional level, the Plans formulated by Shoghi Effendi fostered international cooperation and the collaboration between National Spiritual Assemblies in the fulfillment of the goals of the Plans. Furthermore, the efforts exerted by the Spiritual Assemblies in defense of the persecuted believers in Iran helped raise significantly the profile of the Faith in the world at large. The crowning point of the Crusade was the completion of the basic structure of the Faith's administrative system through the election of the Universal House of Justice, that divinely ordained and supreme institution of the Bahá'í Administrative Order whose institutions are destined to be "at once the harbinger, the nucleus and pattern" of the future World Order of Bahá'u'lláh.[70] The significance of the growing administrative maturity is underlined in the following prophetic statement of Shoghi Effendi:

> In a world the structure of whose political and social institutions is impaired, whose vision is befogged, whose conscience is bewildered, whose religious systems have become anaemic and lost their virtue, this healing Agency, this leavening Power, this cementing Force, intensely alive and all-pervasive, has been taking shape, is crystallizing into institutions, is mobilizing its forces, and is preparing for the spiritual conquest and the complete redemption of mankind. Though the society which incarnates its ideals be small, and its direct and tangible benefits as yet inconsiderable, yet the potentialities with which it has been endowed, and through which it is destined to regenerate the individual and rebuild a broken world, are incalculable.[71]

Further, it is interesting to note that Shoghi Effendi clearly foreshadowed the significance of the Ten Year Crusade in anticipating the emergence of the Faith from obscurity and in hastening the successive stages in the evolving relationship between the Faith and the world at large:

> This present Crusade, . . . will, moreover, by virtue of the dynamic forces it will release and its wide repercussions over the entire surface of the globe, contribute effectually to the acceleration of yet another process of tremendous significance which will carry the steadily evolving Faith of Bahá'u'lláh through its present stages of obscurity, of repression, of emancipation and of recognition—stages one or another of which Bahá'í national communities in various parts of the world now find themselves in—to the stage of establishment, the stage at which the Faith of Bahá'u'lláh will be recognized by the civil authorities as the state religion, similar to that which Christianity entered in the years following the death of the Emperor Constantine, a stage which

must later be followed by the emergence of the Bahá'í state itself, functioning, in all religious and civil matters, in strict accordance with the laws and ordinances of the Kitáb-i-Aqdas, the Most Holy, the Mother-Book of the Bahá'í Revelation, a stage which, in the fullness of time, will culminate in the establishment of the World Bahá'í Commonwealth, functioning in the plenitude of its powers, and which will signalize the long-awaited advent of the Christ-promised Kingdom of God on earth—the Kingdom of Bahá'u'lláh—mirroring however faintly upon this humble handful of dust the glories of the 'Abhá Kingdom.[72]

BECOMING THE NUCLEUS AND PATTERN
OF THE NEW WORLD ORDER

The completion of the Ten Year Spiritual Crusade in 1963 coincided with the election of the Universal House of Justice, the supreme international governing body of the Bahá'í Faith. As the Head of the Faith, the House of Justice has directed the continuing unfoldment and evolution of the worldwide Bahá'í community through an increasingly complex series of global Plans, which initially succeeded in increasing the size and diversity of the Faith's membership, establishing a clearer Bahá'í identity, and strengthening the administrative capacity of the Bahá'í institutions to foster a pattern of life that reflected the values of the Faith and enabling communities progressively to pursue projects aimed at enhancing the social and economic life of the people.

The renewal of the persecution of the Bahá'ís in Iran in 1979 marked the beginning of the Bahá'í Faith's emergence from obscurity, and resulted in the greater exposure of the Faith to the world at large, increased public awareness concerning the relevance of the teachings of the Faith to current social problems, and raised expectations that the Bahá'í community take a more active part in public affairs. To meet this need, the Bahá'í agencies at the United Nations were reinforced and the Universal House of Justice progressively introduced processes to increase the capacity of National Spiritual Assemblies in the field of external affairs. External affairs became "a vital factor in enabling the Faith to manage the consequences of its emergence from obscurity."

Its diplomatic activities mobilized in the defence of and for the emancipation of the persecuted Bahá'í communities, brought the institutions of the Faith into working relationships with the United Nations and its agencies, and with governments and a wide variety of NGOs, thereby enhancing their status and demonstrating the integrity of their functioning. Meanwhile the systematic program of public information promoted Bahá'í perspectives on such issues as human rights, the advancement of women, global prosperity and moral development, and facilitated collaboration with like-minded individuals and agencies, thereby contributing to the mobilization of the forces leading to order in the world.[73]

Confronted with the need to support and further develop the emergence of the Faith from obscurity, to find effective means for the Bahá'í community to deal adequately with the challenges of large-scale growth, and to enhance the community's capacity to make a more direct contribution to the resolution of issues facing society, the community, under the guidance of the Universal House of Justice, developed a framework for action and formulated experience-based strategies for sustaining the process of large-scale expansion and consolidation, and for increasing the ability of the community and its members to demonstrate more notably the "society building power" inherent in the Faith.[74]

Highlighting some of the challenges associated with the large-scale expansion of the Bahá'í Faith during this period, the following summary called attention to the practical difficulties that had arisen when large numbers of people entered the Faith in groups, rather than one at a time, a process described as "entry by troops":

> . . . the process of entry by troops that began during the ministry of Shoghi Effendi continued to gather momentum in other countries. Many had tens of thousands of new believers; a few surpassed one hundred thousand, while the Indian community grew by hundreds of thousands to some two million. Such rapid growth, however, often carried out by a relatively small core of dedicated believers, could not be matched by a pattern of consolidation that would adequately deepen such vast numbers, edu-

cate their children, raise institutions, and lay the foundations of community life. Although large-scale expansion was initiated in country after country, it could not be sustained. The challenge was not simply to place emphasis on activities for consolidation, which, alone, would lead to an inward-looking orientation and the potential stagnation of the Bahá'í community. Rather, what was needed was a capacity to maintain the balance between expansion and consolidation in a pattern of systematic action over time.[75]

Addressing the imperative needs of this stage in the evolution of the processes driving the unfoldment of the Bahá'í community, and capitalizing on the invaluable experience gained by the Bahá'í community in its efforts to cope with the challenges of absorbing large numbers of new believers, the Universal House of Justice issued a series of global Plans, beginning with the Four Year Plan (1996–2000), and subsequently followed by a series of global Five Year Plans, scheduled to finish in 2021. The current framework for action set out in these Plans is focused explicitly on advancing the process of entry by troops and creating a system for the development of human resources at the level of the cluster.[76]

Announcing the goals of the Four Year Plan, the Universal House of Justice expanded on the importance and timeliness of the major goal of the Plan, namely, "a significant advance in the process of entry by troops," and the means by which the aim was to be achieved, in light of current circumstances. This phrase, the House of Justice states:

accommodates the concept that current circumstances demand and existing opportunities allow for a sustained growth of the Bahá'í world community on a large scale; that this upsurge is necessary in the face of world conditions; that the three constituent participants in the upbuilding of the Order of Bahá'u'lláh—the individual, the institutions, and the community—can foster such growth first by spiritually and mentally accepting the possibility of it, and then by working towards embracing masses of new believers, setting in motion the means for effecting their spiritual and administrative training and development, thereby multiplying the number of knowledgeable, active teachers and administrators whose involvement in the work of the Cause will ensure a constant influx of new adherents, an uninterrupted evolution of Bahá'í Assemblies, and a steady consolidation of the community.[77]

And, the House of Justice reiterated that "such an advance is to be achieved through marked progress in the activity and development of the individual believer, of the institutions, and of the local community."[78]

To enhance the capacity of individuals, the Bahá'í community, and its administrative institutions to undertake the functions such as those outlined in the passage above, the Universal House of Justice called for the establishment of training institutes charged with systematizing the learning process by providing educational and training opportunities for acquiring the competencies and skills necessary to serve the Faith, as well as the skills required to enable the believers to plan, in the light of experience, the next stages of its development at a local or regional level.

In the course of the global Plans, subsequent to the Four Year Plan, a framework for action has been outlined, consisting of a number of core activities, including participation in the sequence of training institute courses, the holding of devotional gatherings, and the provision of educational programs for children and junior youth. The Universal House of Justice attests that it is through according priority to the processes associated with the core activities outlined in the global Plans that "the worldwide Bahá'í community has acquired the capacity to enable thousands, nay millions, to study the writings in small groups with the explicit purpose of translating the Bahá'í teachings into reality, carrying the work of the Faith forward into the next stage: sustained large-scale expansion and consolidation."[79]

In relation to advancing the process of entry by troops, the focus on the cluster as the geographic area represents a significant stage in the unfoldment of the Faith. During the ministries of Bahá'u'lláh and 'Abdu'l-Bahá, the priority was to introduce the Faith to individual continents, then specific regions of the world; in the time of Shoghi Effendi, the task was to progressively open specific countries to the Cause. Now that the Bahá'í Faith has spread to all countries and significant island groups, the designation of smaller discrete areas as clusters serves as a practical means for both the development of administrative capacity and for systematically and progressively ensuring the fulfillment of 'Abdu'l-Bahá's mandate to diffuse the light of Bahá'u'lláh's Revelation to all corners of the globe. Commenting on the significance of the cluster for the expansion of the Faith and its potential for enhancing administrative capacity, the Universal House of Justice states:

The introduction of the concept of the cluster made it possible for the friends to think about the accelerated growth of the community on a manageable scale and to conceive of it in terms of two complementary, reinforcing movements: the steady flow of individuals through the sequence of institute courses and the movement of clusters from one stage of development to the next. This image helped the believers to analyze the lessons being learned in the field and to employ a common vocabulary to articulate their findings. Never before have the means for establishing a pattern of activity that places equal emphasis on the twin processes of expansion and consolidation been better understood.[80]

It is suggested that the mode of operation described in the above passage from the message of the Universal House of Justice has the potential to foster a realistic approach to planning, one that appreciates the complexity of the situation, gives attention and coherence to the multiplicity of tasks associated with growth, and promotes an awareness of the organic nature of change.

Recent letters of the House of Justice stress the continuing importance of the cluster as the focus of Bahá'í activity and its potential role in community-building—observing, for example, that as the Bahá'í community increases in size, and as the human and administrative resources within the cluster are expanded, the cluster will be drawn more and more into the life of society, and new fields of activity, such as social action and participation in the prevalent discourses of society will become a systematic and coherent part of its functions.

The Five Year Plans 2011–2016 and 2016–2021, will complete the 25 year period, which began in 1996, a period designated by the Universal House of Justice for giving particular attention to the importance of accelerating the processes of growth by mobilizing large numbers of people in the field of service. These Plans also call for the Bahá'ís to identify and reach out to receptive populations (see chapter 8), to adopt regular cycles of activity as a means of retaining focus and systematizing the planning and implementation of their collective activities (chapter 6), and to launch intensive teaching activities designed to hasten both the growth of the Bahá'í community and the day when the Faith has sufficient resources to minister to the well-being of their fellow citizens by engaging in social action and sharing a Bahá'í perspective on the solution of the problems and issues confronting the wider society. "New frontiers of learning," the House of Justice affirms, "are now open to the friends, who are asked to dedicate their energies to the creation of vibrant communities, growing in size and reflecting in greater and greater degrees Bahá'u'lláh's vision for humanity."[81]

AN EMERGING BAHÁ'Í CULTURE

The divinely-propelled processes of growth that, under the direction of the Head of the Faith, has been progressively shaping the evolution of the organic Bahá'í community from the earliest days of its existence, has, with the introduction of the systematic framework for action of the Universal House of Justice, given rise to the emergence of an embryonic Bahá'í culture. The framework of the global Plans issued by the House of Justice

> . . . has succeeded in establishing a pattern of Bahá'í life that promotes the spiritual development of the individual and channels the collective energies of its members towards the spiritual revival of society. It has acquired the capacity to reach large

numbers of receptive souls with the message, to confirm them, and to deepen their understanding of the essentials of the Faith they have embraced. It has learned to translate the principle of consultation enunciated by its Founder into an effective tool for collective decision-making and to educate its members in its use. It has devised programs for the spiritual and moral education of its younger members and has extended them not only to its own children and junior youth but also to those of the wider community. With the pool of talent at its disposition, it has created a rich body of literature which includes volumes in scores of languages that address both its own needs and the interest of the general public. It has become increasingly involved in the affairs of society at large, undertaking a host of projects of social and economic development. Particularly since the opening of the fifth epoch in 2001, it has made significant strides in multiplying its human resources through a program of training that reaches the grassroots of the community and has discovered methods and instruments for establishing a sustainable pattern of growth.[82]

The emerging Bahá'í culture is fostered by a systematic educational process that encourages and supports the participation of "the three protagonists in the Divine Plan," i.e. individuals, communities and institutions, in a wide range of activities.[83] These activities increase understanding of the transforming vision of the Faith, build capacity for service, increase motivation, instill confidence, and increase willingness to accept responsibility for engaging in the society-building activities of the community.

The Universal House of Justice calls attention to the importance of the adoption by the "three protagonists in the Divine Plan" of "learning as a mode of operation," a mode of operation that has far reaching transformative potential, observing

The individual, the institutions, and the community—the three protagonists in the Divine Plan—are being shaped under the direct influence of His Revelation, and a new conception of each, appropriate for a humanity that has come of age, is emerging. The relationships that bind them, too, are undergoing a profound transformation, bringing into the realm of existence civilization-building powers which can only be released through conformity with His decree. At a fundamental level these relationships are characterized by cooperation and reciprocity, manifestations of the interconnectedness that governs the universe.[84]

As the capacities of the individual, the community, and the Bahá'í institutions increase to articulate and apply the teachings of Bahá'u'lláh both within the Bahá'í community and to their interactions with the surrounding society and its institutions, so too will the potential of the three protagonists to contribute to the emergence of social order also increase. As the maturity of their functioning progressively evolves, it will demonstrate the Faith's cohesive strength and the potency of its society-building power. The Bahá'í institutions will provide an alternative approach to the dysfunctional systems of governance existing in the world at large, and the Bahá'í community will serve as a model of unity and peace in an otherwise crumbling and divided world.

Learning as a mode of operation not only builds individual capacity, it is the key to sustaining growth and to building the collective and administrative capacity necessary to take on enlarged and more complex functions that will hasten the evolution of world order. Stressing the uniqueness and significance of the culture developing within the Bahá'í community, the Universal House of Justice writes, "That the Bahá'í world has succeeded in developing a culture which promotes a way of thinking, studying, and acting, in which all consider themselves as treading a common path of service—supporting one another and advancing together, respectful of the knowledge that each one possesses at any given movement and avoiding the tendency to divide the believers into categories such as deepened and uninformed—is an accomplishment of enormous proportions. And therein lies the dynamics of an irrepressible movement."[85]

Chapter 6 will provide further consideration of the Bahá'í perspective on the role of knowledge and will explore certain aspects of the dynamic relationships between the educational process, service, and the emergence of a Bahá'í culture of learning.

Conclusion

The processes involved in diffusing the Message of Bahá'u'lláh, set in motion by the Tablets of the Divine Plan, are dynamic, diverse, and strategic. The tasks to which they give rise are destined to continue to change and unfold as the Bahá'í community grows in size and acquires the capacity to assume a greater and more direct role in collaborating with constructive movements in the wider society to lay the foundations of the emerging social order, an order enlightened by the vision of unity, peace, and prosperity embodied in the writings of the Bahá'í Faith.

5

Fostering the Spiritual Regeneration
of the Planet

The divine purpose for the world of humanity is, in the words of 'Abdu'l-Bahá, for it to become "a Garden of Eden, an earthly paradise." 'Abdu'l-Bahá's vision of the world of the future centers attention on the nature of the profound transformation destined to accompany the achievement of the spiritual regeneration of the planet. Writing in one of his Tablets, 'Abdu'l-Bahá states, "The Lord of all mankind hath fashioned this human realm to be a Garden of Eden, an earthly paradise. If, as it must, it findeth the way to harmony and peace, to love and mutual trust, it will become a true abode of bliss, a place of manifold blessings and unending delights. Therein shall be revealed the excellence of humankind, therein shall the rays of the Sun of Truth shine forth on every hand."[1]

The guidance set out in the Tablets of the Divine Plan gives direction to the unfoldment of the processes necessary for the implementation of the Bahá'í vision for humankind. 'Abdu'l-Bahá calls for the propagation of the life-giving teachings of Bahá'u'lláh throughout the world as a means of gradually bringing about the transformation of human values and institutional structures, thereby laying the foundations of a new social order and civilization expressing the oneness of humankind and universal peace. "This is the most great work!"

'Abdu'l-Bahá assures those who arise to play their part, "Should you become confirmed therein, this world will become another world, the surface of the earth will become the delectable paradise, and eternal Institutions be founded."[2]

The indispensability of individual action is underlined in 'Abdu'l-Bahá's Will and Testament. For example, he stresses the urgency of striving "to diffuse the sweet savors of God, and to guide all the peoples of the world," observing that it is "the light of Divine Guidance that causeth all the universe to be illumined." Concerning the pressing nature of this activity, he likewise asserts, "To disregard, though it be for a moment, this absolute command which is binding upon everyone, is in no wise permitted, that the existent world may become even as the Abhá Paradise, that the surface of the earth may become heavenly, that contention and conflict amidst peoples, kindreds, nations and governments may disappear, that all the dwellers on earth may become one people and one race, that the world may become even as one home."[3]

The realization of the mandate set out in the writings of the Bahá'í Faith provides, on the one hand, a unique spiritual opportunity offered to the followers of the Faith and, on the other, the challenging responsibility of realizing the nature and scope of the visionary transformation set forth in the writings of the Faith. Shoghi Effendi's secretary, writing on his behalf, highlights both the extent of individual responsibility and the assurance of ultimate victory:

In the *Bayan* the Báb says that every religion of the past was fit to become universal. The only reason why they failed to attain that mark was the incompetence of their followers. He then proceeds to give a definite promise that this would not be the fate of the revelation of "Him Whom God would make manifest," that it will become universal and include all the people of the world. This shows that we will ultimately succeed. But could we not, through our shortcomings, failures to sacrifice and reluctance to concentrate our efforts in spreading the Cause, retard the realization of that ideal? And what would that mean? It shall mean that we will be held responsible before God, that the race will remain longer in its state of waywardness, that wars would not be so soon averted, that human suffering will last longer.[4]

The transformation of the planet to an "earthly paradise" is a far-reaching undertaking requiring a complex of spiritual qualities and skills, the development of individual and administrative capacities, and an active posture of learning. In the previous chapter, we saw how the transformative processes for the spiritual regeneration of the planet that were set in motion during the ministries of Bahá'u'lláh, 'Abdu'l-Bahá, Shoghi Effendi, and more recently under the jurisdiction of the Universal House of Justice have evolved and become more complex over time as the capacities of the individual, the community, and its administrative institutions have evolved and matured.

At each stage in the evolution of the organic society-building process, the weight of responsibility is placed upon the individual, the community, and the institutions, though the actual functions each perform may vary with the passage of time, their level of capacity, the conditions in the world, and the maturity of the Bahá'í community. At every stage in the process, the three protagonists are challenged to identify the priorities of the moment and to determine how best to meet their responsibilities. In a letter addressed to the American Bahá'ís, Shoghi Effendi illustrates the critical ongoing nature of individual responsibility and links the actions of the individual to the evolution of the Bahá'í community and the establishment of its administrative agencies. He writes:

This challenge, so severe and insistent, and yet so glorious, faces no doubt primarily the individual believer on whom, in the last resort, depends the fate of the entire community. He it is who constitutes the warp and woof on which the quality and pattern of the whole fabric must depend. He it is who acts as one of the countless links in the mighty chain that now girdles the globe. He it is who serves as one of the multitude of bricks which support the structure and ensure the stability of the administrative edifice now being raised in every part of the world. Without his support, at once whole-hearted, continuous and generous, every measure adopted, and every plan formulated, by the Body which acts as the national representative of the community to which he belongs is foredoomed to failure. The World Centre of the Faith itself is paralyzed if such a support on the part of the rank and file of the community is denied it. The Author of the Divine Plan Himself is impeded in His purpose if the proper instruments for the execution of His design are lacking. The sustaining strength of Bahá'u'lláh Himself, the Founder of the Faith, will be withheld from every and each individual who fails in the long run to arise and play his part.[5]

CALL TO APOSTLESHIP

To inspire and sustain the motivations of the Bahá'ís and to cause them to reflect on the sacred and historic nature of the task in which they are engaged, 'Abdu'l-Bahá calls his followers to the station of apostleship, to become an "Apostle of Bahá'u'lláh." He links the great enterprise they are striving to achieve in contemporary times to the historic work undertaken by the apostles of Christ. Recalling the instructions of Christ, 'Abdu'l-Bahá exhorts the Bahá'ís to "Travel . . . to the East and to the West of the world and summon the people to the Kingdom of God!"[6]

The call to apostleship is no mere poetic expression of praise, nor is it an empty elevated form of address. Rather, it is a "station" earned by individuals who strive to attain a spiritual condition and who are actively engaged in contributing to the spiritual regeneration of the planet. Such people are, according to 'Abdu'l-Bahá

> . . . delivered from human qualities and the defects of the world of nature, are characterized with the characteristics of God, and are attracted with the fragrances of the Merciful. Like unto the apostles of Christ, who were filled with Him, these souls also have become filled with His Holiness Bahá'u'lláh; that is, the love of Bahá'u'lláh has so mastered every organ, part and limb of their bodies, as to leave no effect from the promptings of the human world. . . .
>
> Any soul from among the believers of Bahá'u'lláh who attains to this station will become known as the Apostle of Bahá'u'lláh.

Therefore strive ye with heart and soul so that ye may reach this lofty and exalted position, be established on the throne of everlasting glory, and crown your heads with the shining diadem of the Kingdom, whose brilliant jewels may irradiate upon centuries and cycles.[7]

Attainment to the "station" of Apostle of Bahá'u'lláh not only requires sustained effort on the part of each individual, it is also "dependent on the realization of certain conditions" specified by 'Abdu'l-Bahá. These conditions inform both the nature of the work undertaken and the approach to the tasks to be performed. Therefore, to engage successfully in the challenging society-building work of transforming the spiritual life of the planet, the present-day apostles must satisfy three critical and interrelated conditions identified by 'Abdu'l-Bahá—namely, that the teachers must be firm in the Covenant of God; that they demonstrate fellowship and love amongst the believers; and that they travel to all parts of the globe to spread the teachings of the New Day.[8]

The three prerequisites outlined by 'Abdu'l-Bahá for the attainment to the station of "Apostle of Bahá'u'lláh" are the subject of this and later chapters.

Context for the Emergence of Social Order

Before beginning the analysis of the conditions outlined by 'Abdu'l-Bahá for attaining the station of "Apostle of Bahá'u'lláh," it is useful to consider briefly a number of parameters that create a context within which to examine the Bahá'í approach to laying the foundations of social order. These include the means for realizing spiritual development—in other words, the pathways to spiritual development; the dynamic relationships between the three prerequisites for apostleship set out in the Tablets of the Divine Plan; and the motivating and energizing force for achieving action and change.

PATHWAYS TO SPIRITUAL DEVELOPMENT

The teachings of the Manifestations of God define the paths to spiritual development. Reflecting on the purpose of "true religion,"

'Abdu'l-Bahá notes that it "promotes the civilization and honor, the prosperity and prestige, the learning and advancement of a people," and he foreshadows the far-reaching impact of the Revelation of Bahá'u'lláh on the future of humankind, observing that Bahá'u'lláh "has provided the remedy for the ailments which now afflict the human world, solved the difficult problems of individual, social, national and universal welfare and laid the foundation of divine reality upon which material and spiritual civilization are to be founded throughout the centuries before us."[9]

In previous ages, the quest for spiritual development was all too often marked by an ascetic life devoted exclusively to prayer and study, undertaken alone, away from the distractions of everyday life and the company of others. It was believed that the surest means of attaining the highest form of spiritual development required withdrawal from the material world and its preoccupying concerns, separating oneself from human society, and living in a monastery or some remote and inaccessible physical location.[10]

The teachings of the Bahá'í Faith redefine the pathway to spiritual development in contemporary times. The course it delineates stands in sharp contrast to the traditions of the past. While acknowledging the "pious deeds" of monks and priests, Bahá'u'lláh calls upon such individuals to "give up the life of seclusion and direct their steps towards the open world and busy themselves with that which will profit themselves and others."[11] 'Abdu'l-Bahá's description of "a religious individual" reflects this change of perspective about the means for attaining the highest form of spiritual development. Thus, such an individual

must disregard his personal desires and seek in whatever way he can wholeheartedly to serve the public interest; and it is impossible for a human being to turn aside from his own selfish advantages and sacrifice his own good for the good of the community except through true religious faith. For self-love is kneaded into the very clay of man, and it is not possible that, without any hope of a substantial reward, he should neglect his own present material good. That individual, however, who puts his faith in God and believes in the words of God . . . will for the sake of God abandon his own peace and profit and will freely consecrate his heart and soul to the common good.[12]

It is clear that there is a spiritually constructive and intimate interconnection between individual personal transformation and service to humanity. "Peace," 'Abdu'l-Bahá states, "must first be established among individuals, until it leadeth in the end to peace among nations." He informs us that the "task" is to strive with all our might "to create, through the power of the Word of God, genuine love, spiritual communion and durable bonds among individuals."[13]

In a letter written in 1935 to a group of youth, Shoghi Effendi elaborated on the critical linkage between spiritual practice and the social milieu, and he called attention to the fact that "the core of religious faith is that mystic feeling that unites man with God" and further indicated that "This state of spiritual communion can be brought about and maintained by means of meditation and prayer." He then spelled out the implications of this principle for the actions of the individual and indeed for the ultimate unfoldment of the Bahá'í Faith:

For the core of religious faith is that mystic feeling that unites man with God. This state of spiritual communion can be brought about and maintained by means of meditation and prayer. And this is the reason why Bahá'u'lláh has so much stressed the importance of worship. It is not sufficient for a believer to merely accept and observe the teachings. He should, in addition, cultivate the sense of spirituality, which he can acquire chiefly by the means of prayer. The Bahá'í Faith, like all other Divine religions, is thus fundamentally mystic in character. Its chief goal is the development of the individual and society, through the acquisition of spiritual virtues and powers. It is the soul of man that has first to be fed. And this spiritual nourishment prayer can best provide. Laws and institutions, as viewed by Bahá'u'lláh, can become

really effective only when our inner spiritual life has been perfected and transformed. Otherwise religion will degenerate into a
mere organization, and become a dead thing.[14]

The Universal House of Justice provides further insight into the
dynamic underlying the interdependence of the spiritual and the
social. It takes as an illustration the importance of upholding Bahá'í
law and writes:

> Just as there are laws governing our physical lives, requiring
> that we must supply our bodies with certain foods, maintain
> them within a certain range of temperatures, and so forth, if we
> wish to avoid physical disabilities, so also there are laws governing
> our spiritual lives. These laws are revealed to mankind in each
> age by the Manifestation of God, and obedience to them is of
> vital importance if each human being, and mankind in general,
> is to develop properly and harmoniously. Moreover, these various
> aspects are interdependent. If an individual violates the spiritual
> laws for his own development he will cause injury not only to
> himself but to the society in which he lives. Similarly, the con-
> dition of society has a direct effect on the individuals who must
> live within it.[15]

Commenting on the operation of the "communal aspects of the
godly life," in a recent letter, the Universal House of Justice observes,
"The spiritual growth generated by individual devotions is reinforced
by loving association among the friends in every locality, by worship
as a community and by service to the Faith and to one's fellow human
beings." And, they note that "the holding of regular meetings for
worship open to all and the involvement of Bahá'í communities in
projects of humanitarian service are expressions of this element of
Bahá'í life . . ."[16]

Given the link between worship, service, the attainment of individual spiritual development, and social transformation, it follows that
the path to spiritual development also requires the emergence of Bahá'í

administrative structures and engagement with the world at large. Indeed, there is a close and growing interaction between the establishment of the embryonic Bahá'í Administration—even though it is as yet at an early stage in its evolution—and the spiritual regeneration of the planet. Writing on this theme, Shoghi Effendi cautioned the friends never to "mistake the Bahá'í administration for an end in itself." "It is," he affirmed, "merely the instrument of the spirit of the Faith," and he underlined its all-inclusive society-building potential:

> It is designed to benefit the entire human race, and the only way it can do this is to re-form the community life of mankind, as well as seeking to regenerate the individual. The Bahá'í Administration is only the first shaping of what in future will come to be the social life and laws of community living. As yet the believers are only just beginning to grasp and practice it properly. So we must have patience if at times it seems a little self-conscious and rigid in its workings. It is because we are learning something very difficult but very wonderful—how to live together as a community of Bahá'ís, according to the glorious teachings.[17]

The following extract from a letter dated May 19, 1994 from the Universal House of Justice provides a glimpse into the operation of the dynamic interactions of the processes set in motion by the individual, the community, and the administrative institutions of the Faith:

> . . . the importance of the Bahá'í administration is its value in serving as a facilitator of the emergence and maintenance of community life in a wholly new mode, and in catering to the requirements of the spiritual relationships which flow from love and unity among the friends. This touches upon a distinguishing characteristic of Bahá'í life which such spiritual relationships foster, namely, the spirit of servitude to God, expressed in service to the Cause, to the friends and to humanity as a whole. The attitude of the individual as a servant, an attitude pre-eminently exemplified in the life and person of 'Abdu'l-Bahá, is a dynamic

that permeates the activities of the Faith; it acquires collective, transformative force in the normal functioning of a community. In this regard, the institutions of the Faith stand as channels for the promotion of this salient characteristic."[18]

Not only is there a complex interaction between the processes engaged in by the individual, the community, and the evolving institutions of the Faith, but each of these three protagonists are also at the same time actively involved in a systematic process of learning, action, and reflection, which contributes in its own way, and in the long-term, to the emergence of a new social order.

When asked by an individual for advice about how to attain spiritual development, Shoghi Effendi's secretary, writing on his behalf, stressed the imperatives of study and action and linked his guidance to the organic unfoldment of the Faith:

His brotherly advice to you, and to all loyal and ardent young believers like you, is that you should deepen your knowledge of the history and of the tenets of the Faith, not merely by means of careful and thorough study, but also through active, wholehearted and continued participation in all the activities, whether administrative or otherwise, of your community. The Bahá'í community life provides you with an indispensable laboratory, where you can translate into living and constructive action the principles which you imbibe from the Teachings. By becoming a real part of that living organism you can catch the real spirit which runs throughout the Bahá'í Teachings. To study the principles, and to try to live according to them, are, therefore, the two essential mediums through which you can ensure the development and progress of your inner spiritual life and of your outer existence as well.[19]

Likewise, the administrative institutions of the Faith have the responsibility to foster the spiritual education of the Bahá'í community and to assist its members to acquire the necessary capacities to undertake the functions appropriate to the community's level of evolution. Hence, in delineating "the supreme objectives" for "the edification, the progress and consolidation" of its community, Shoghi Effendi established the following priorities to be addressed by a National Spiritual Assembly: "The deepening and enrichment of the spiritual life of the individual believer, his increasing comprehension of the essential verities underlying this Faith, his training in its administrative processes, his understanding of the fundamentals of the Covenants established by its Author and the authorized Interpreter of its teachings . . ."[20]

A recent letter of the Universal House of Justice highlights the continuing importance of the coherence of study and practice to the present stage in the evolution of the Bahá'í community, a stage where the Faith is becoming progressively more engaged in the prevalent discourses of society, and where there are evidences of an emerging Bahá'í culture, a culture where learning is the mode of operation. The House of Justice writes:

> To read the writings of the Faith and to strive to obtain a more adequate understanding of the significance of Bahá'u'lláh's stupendous Revelation are obligations laid on every one of His followers. All are enjoined to delve into the ocean of His Revelation and to partake, in keeping with their capacities and inclinations, of the pearls of wisdom that lie therein. . . . But understanding the implications of the Revelation, both in terms of individual growth and social progress, increases manifold when study and service are joined and carried out concurrently. There, in the field of service, knowledge is tested, questions arise out of practice, and new levels of understanding are achieved. . . .
>
> That the Bahá'í world has succeeded in developing a culture which promotes a way of thinking, studying, and acting, in which all consider themselves as treading a common path of service—supporting one another and advancing together, respectful of the knowledge that each one possesses at any given moment

and avoiding the tendency to divide the believers into categories such as deepened and uninformed—is an accomplishment of enormous proportions. And therein lie the dynamics of an irrepressible movement.[21]

From the foregoing, it is clear that the pathway to spiritual development for an Apostle of Bahá'u'lláh is far from being a solitary enterprise, undertaken in isolation from the surrounding society. While there is a high degree of individual responsibility, the call to apostleship brings the individual squarely into intimate contact with the community and its administrative structures. Further, the relationship between the individual, the community, and the administrative institutions is dynamic, shaped by systematic learning, and is service oriented. It evolves with time, as the Faith demonstrates its inherent society-building capacity.

INTERRELATIONSHIPS BETWEEN THE THREE CONDITIONS FOR APOSTLESHIP

Attainment to the "supreme station" of apostleship is "dependent on the realization of certain conditions" which are stipulated by 'Abdu'l-Bahá in the Tablets of the Divine Plan. Thus, the present-day Apostles of Bahá'u'lláh must be firm in the Covenant of God; must be the cause of fellowship and love amongst the believers; and must travel to all parts of the globe to spread the teachings of the New Day.[22]

While each of the prerequisites makes its own unique contribution to the advancement of the interests of the Faith and to the process of social transformation, it is important to recognize that all three conditions specified by 'Abdu'l-Bahá are interrelated and critical to the course of action. Hence, steps toward the successful realization of one condition simultaneously impacts and reinforces the realization of the other two. Likewise, failure to address one of the pre-requisites reduces the outcomes of efforts exerted in relation to the other two.

The operation of the dynamic processes underpinning the interactions between the three conditions for apostleship referred to by 'Abdu'l-Bahá is briefly illustrated by the following extracts from his writings. The selected passages highlight the result of firmness in the

Covenant on the person who strives to fulfill this condition, and they provide a glimpse of the impact of the individual's effort on the realization of the other two conditions—namely, fellowship and love among the believers, and the promotion of the Faith.

In sketching out this example, it is noteworthy that 'Abdu'l-Bahá relates an individual's efforts to attain firmness in the Covenant to the attraction of divine assistance. He stresses the primary importance of this condition and its influence on the individual. In the Tablets of the Divine Plan, he writes, "in the beginning the believers must make their steps firm in the Covenant so that the confirmations of Bahá'u'lláh may encircle them from all sides, the cohorts of the Supreme Concourse may become their supporters and helpers . . ."[23]

As to the relationship between firmness in the Covenant and the second condition, fellowship and love among the believers, "it is indubitably clear," 'Abdu'l-Bahá attests, "that the pivot of the oneness of mankind is nothing else but the power of the Covenant." He links firm adherence to the Covenant of God to social cohesion and the preservation of unity. Thus, "Today no power can conserve the oneness of the Bahá'í world save the Covenant of God; otherwise differences like unto a most great tempest will encompass the Bahá'í world. It is evident that the axis of the oneness of the world of humanity is the power of the Covenant and nothing else."[24]

Finally, the mutual interaction of the processes involved in the realization of firmness in the Covenant and arising to teach the Faith, the third condition, is illustrated by the following passages. In the first, 'Abdu'l-Bahá identifies the act of teaching as an aspect of firmness in the Covenant: "O ye loved ones of God! Out of gratitude for firmness in the eternal Covenant arise to serve the threshold of the omnipotent Lord, observe obligatory prayer and fasting, and spend your time in diffusing the sweet savors of God and in spreading the Divine verses. Tear asunder the veils, remove the obstacles, proffer the life-giving waters, and point out the path of salvation. This is what 'Abdu'l-Bahá admonisheth you every morn and eve." In the second passage, he refers to the connection between teaching the Cause and attracting the power of divine assistance, which derives from firmness in the Covenant:

"Walk, therefore, with a sure step and engage with the utmost assurance and confidence in the promulgation of the divine fragrances, the glorification of the Word of God and firmness in the Covenant. Rest ye assured that if a soul ariseth in the utmost perseverance and raiseth the Call of the Kingdom and resolutely promulgateth the Covenant, be he an insignificant ant he shall be enabled to drive away the formidable elephant from the arena, and if he be a feeble moth he shall cut to pieces the plumage of the rapacious vulture."[26]

MOTIVATING FORCE

The three conditions defining the path to present-day apostleship and the dynamic interrelationship between the processes and strategic actions to which they give rise challenge the individual to reflect on the means by which he or she can attain the necessary spiritual state to carry out the socially transformative tasks laid out in the Bahá'í writings.

The underlying question becomes, how can one meet one's responsibilities? How can one become an Apostle of Bahá'u'lláh? Central to the matter is the issue of motivation—how to take a first step and how to sustain motivation in the long-term—and support. In this regard, 'Abdu'l-Bahá calls attention to the supreme importance of the spiritually and socially transformative influence of the Holy Spirit in the world. He refers to the Holy Spirit as "the energizing factor in the life of man." He promises that "Whosoever receives this power is able to influence all with whom he comes into contact," and his writings set out the means for attracting this power. The following passage from one of the prayers included in the Tablets of the Divine Plan clearly illustrates the dynamic relationship between the influence of the Holy Spirit and the attainment of individual spiritual transformation, personal motivation to act, and success of one's efforts to serve: "O my God! O my God! Thou seest me in my lowliness and weakness, occupied with the greatest undertaking, determined to raise Thy word among the masses and to spread Thy teachings among Thy peoples. How can I succeed unless Thou assist me with the breath of the Holy Spirit, help me to triumph by the hosts of Thy glorious kingdom, and shower upon me Thy confirmations, which alone can change a gnat into an eagle, a drop of water into rivers and seas, and an atom into lights and suns? O my Lord! Assist me with Thy triumphant and effective might, so that my tongue may utter Thy praises and attributes among all people and my soul overflow with the wine of Thy love and knowledge."[27]

Given the importance of the power of the Holy Spirit as an energizing and motivating force in both the life of the individual and society, it is useful to consider briefly the Bahá'í perspective on this subject. What, then, is the power of the Holy Spirit? How does it work? What are the outcomes?

'Abdu'l-Bahá describes the Holy Spirit as "the outpouring grace of God and the effulgent rays that emanate from His Manifestations." The advent of a Manifestation of God is intimately linked to a great effusion of spiritual powers from the Holy Spirit: "Whensoever it [the Holy Spirit] appears, the world is revived, a new cycle is ushered in, and the body of humanity is clothed in a fresh attire." 'Abdu'l-Bahá depicts the operation of some of the processes involved in the following:

> It is the same with the manifestation of the Holy Spirit: Whensoever it appears, it invests the world of humanity with a new life and endows human realities with a new spirit. It clothes all existence with a glorious attire, disperses the darkness of ignorance, and causes the light of human perfections to shine resplendent. It is with such a power that Christ renewed this cycle—whereupon the divine springtide pitched its tent, with utmost vitality and grace, in the realm of humanity and perfumed the senses of the enlightened souls with its life-giving breezes.
>
> In the same way, the manifestation of Bahá'u'lláh was a new springtide which appeared with the sweet savors of holiness, with the hosts of everlasting life, and with a power born of the celestial kingdom. He established the throne of God's sovereignty in the midmost heart of the world and, through the power of the Holy Spirit, revived the souls and ushered in a new cycle.[28]

Concerning the means by which the power of the Holy Spirit has the potential to transform the individual, 'Abdu'l-Bahá takes as an example the events that transpired immediately after the crucifixion of Christ. He states:

> After the death of Christ, the Apostles were troubled and diverged in their thoughts and opinions; later they became steadfast and united. At Pentecost they gathered together, detached themselves from the world, forsook their own desires, renounced all earthly comfort and happiness, sacrificed body and soul to their Beloved, left their homes, took leave of all their cares and belongings, and even forgot their own existence. Then was divine assistance vouchsafed and the power of the Holy Spirit manifested. The spirituality of Christ triumphed, and the love of God took hold. On that day, they received divine confirmations, and each departed in a different direction to teach the Cause of God and unloosed his tongue to set forth the proofs and testimonies.
>
> Thus the descent of the Holy Spirit means that the Apostles were attracted by the messianic Spirit, attained constancy and steadfastness, found a new life through the spirit of God's love, and saw Christ to be their everliving helper and protector. They were mere drops and became the ocean; they were feeble gnats and became soaring eagles; they were all weakness and became endowed with strength. They were like mirrors that are turned towards the sun: It is certain that the rays and the effulgence of the sun will be reflected therein.[29]

Not only do the Bahá'í writings call attention to the life-giving and society-building potential of the power of the Holy Spirit, they also set out a range of actions that constitute the means for attracting its transformative influence. In the 1988 Riḍván message of the Universal House of Justice, the House of Justice summoned "Every individual believer—man, woman, youth and child" to the "field of action," explaining that, "it is on the initiative, the resolute will of the individual to teach and to serve, that the success of the entire community depends. Well-grounded in the mighty Covenant of Bahá'u'lláh, sustained by daily prayer and reading of the Holy Word, strengthened by a continual striving to obtain a deeper understanding of the divine Teachings, illumined by a constant endeavor to relate these Teachings to current issues, nourished by observance of the laws and principles of His wondrous World Order, every individual can attain increasing measures of success in teaching." In all cases, some form of active service is the magnet that attracts the Holy Spirit. For example, writing on his behalf, the Guardian's secretary stated, "There is nothing that brings success in the Faith like service. Service is the magnet which draws the Divine Confirmations. Thus, when a person is active, they are blessed by the Holy Spirit. When they are inactive, the Holy Spirit cannot find a repository in their being, and thus they are deprived of its healing and quickening rays."[30]

Critical to the success of the teaching enterprise, Shoghi Effendi's secretary noted, is that the active servant is called upon to strive to demonstrate certain spiritual qualities in his or her efforts: "What is needed to achieve success in the teaching field is a complete dedication on the part of the individual, consecration to the glorious task of spreading the Faith, and the living of the Bahá'í life, because that creates the magnet for the Holy Spirit, and it is the Holy Spirit which quickens the new soul. Thus the individual should be as a reed, through which the Holy Spirit may flow, to give new life to the seeking soul."[31]

Furthermore, one of the challenges for the present-day apostle engaged in the spiritual regeneration of the planet—an enterprise likely to take centuries to achieve—is how to sustain motivation in the long-term and how to overcome barriers to progress. The Iranian Bahá'í community provides many inspiring examples of persistence in active service in the face of obstacles and persecution over a long period of time.

To take but one contemporary example, reference is made to a letter from the Universal House of Justice dated March, 1997 addressed to the Bahá'ís of Iran, a community that has for decades suffered persecution in their devoted efforts to serve the Faith. The House of Justice described both the response of the youth in that community to their exclusion from university studies by the authorities and the reaction of the whole Iranian Bahá'í community to the severe restrictions imposed on them. The letter also called attention to the quality of the spiritual and social transformations achieved by the efforts of the Iranian Bahá'ís, and it linked these outcomes to the success of their dedicated actions in attracting the outpourings of the Holy Spirit:

> The youth . . . did not sit idle. They busied themselves with the acquisition of human perfections. They endured every discomfort and persevered until they excelled their peers even in the achievement of academic excellence. The attainment of this high station and bounty became possible when the friends in Iran, old and young, women and men, even very young children, realized that the remedy of all their ills was the remembrance of God. They started to study the Writings regularly and systematically. It was through their study that the outpourings of the Holy Spirit, enshrined in every Word of the Sacred Writings, came to their assistance and made of that community a new creation for which the world and whatever it contains is worth nothing when compared with servitude to the Divine Threshold, attainment of Bahá'u'lláh's good pleasure, and eternal life in all the worlds of God. Therefore they patterned their lives on the life-giving Teachings contained in the Sacred Writings. Consequently, they became admired in this world and in the next, succeeding in spreading the fame of the cause of God in the far corners of the world and among the highest institutions of humankind.[32]

Result of Becoming an Apostle of Bahá'u'lláh

The significant contribution to be made by the Apostles of Bahá'u'lláh to the spiritual regeneration of the planet is foreshadowed in the writings of 'Abdu'l-Bahá. Like the pattern of a golden thread in a tapestry, the dynamic interrelationship between the processes set in motion by the Tablets of the Divine Plan and the actions of those who arise to further its aims is progressively becoming more visible.

Concerning the means by which the spiritual regeneration of the individual is attained, 'Abdu'l-Bahá employs a biblical image to describe the life-giving quality of the Covenant and the operation of the Holy Spirit: "Today the pulsating power in the arteries of the body of the world is the spirit of the Covenant—the spirit which is the cause of life. Whosoever is vivified with this spirit, the freshness and beauty of life become manifest in him, he is baptized with the Holy Spirit, he is born again. . . . Praise thou God that thou art firm in the Covenant and the Testament and art turning thy face to the Luminary of the world, His Highness Bahá'u'lláh." 'Abdu'l-Bahá also outlines the path to the development of skills and capacities necessary for the fulfillment of the functions of an apostle. He affirms that the individual's efforts to develop capacities for service and to overcome limitations and obstacles not only assure an increase in capacity but are also an important way to attract the power of the Holy Spirit. Writing to an individual, 'Abdu'l-Bahá provides the following encouragement: "Day and night I entreat and supplicate to the Kingdom of God and beg for you infinite assistance and confirmation. Do not take into consideration your own aptitudes and capacities, but fix your gaze on the consummate bounty, the divine bestowal and the power of the Holy Spirit—the power that converteth the drop into a sea and the star into a sun."[33]

Concerning the pattern for the future spiritual regeneration of the planet, 'Abdu'l-Bahá stresses the relevance of the application of the teachings of Bahá'u'lláh to the needs of the contemporary world, and he foreshadows the eventual victory of those who arise to serve:

For every era hath a spirit; the spirit of this illumined era lieth in the teachings of Bahá'u'lláh. For these lay the foundation of the oneness of the world of humanity and promulgate universal brotherhood. They are founded upon the unity of science and religion and upon investigation of truth. They uphold the principle that religion must be the cause of amity, union and harmony among men. They establish the equality of both sexes and propound economic principles which are for the happiness of individuals. They diffuse universal education, that every soul may as much as possible have a share of knowledge. They abrogate and nullify religious, racial, political, patriotic and economic prejudices and the like. Those teachings that are scattered throughout the Epistles and Tablets are the cause of the illumination and the life of the world of humanity. Whoever promulgateth them will verily be assisted by the Kingdom of God.[34]

Returning to 'Abdu'l-Bahá's vision for the future of the world, that "this human realm . . . be a Garden of Eden, an earthly paradise," it is clear from the Tablet of the Divine Plan that the Apostles of Bahá'u'lláh have a vital role in bringing this vision into reality. Thus, 'Abdu'l-Bahá writes that "the teachers of the Cause must be heavenly, lordly and radiant. They must be embodied spirit, personified intellect, and arise in service with the utmost firmness, steadfastness and self-sacrifice. In their journeys they must not be attached to food and clothing. They must concentrate their thoughts on the outpourings of the Kingdom of God and beg for the confirmations of the Holy Spirit. With a divine power, with an attraction of consciousness, with heavenly glad tidings and celestial holiness they must perfume the nostrils with the fragrances of the Paradise of Abhá."[35]

6

The First Condition of Apostleship

Addressing the Bahá'ís of the United States and Canada, 'Abdu'l-Bahá extols the "supreme station" of the Apostles of Bahá'u'lláh, and he places the attainment to such an exalted position firmly within the hands of each individual. Indeed, 'Abdu'l-Bahá issues an open invitation to "Any soul from among the believers of Bahá'u'lláh," encouraging him or her to strive "with heart and soul so that ye may reach this lofty and exalted position, be established on the throne of everlasting glory, and crown your heads with the shining diadem of the Kingdom, whose brilliant jewels may irradiate upon centuries and cycles." To assist the individual to attain to this noble station, he called attention to the importance of "the realization of certain conditions," namely, "firmness in the Covenant of God," "fellowship and love among the believers," and arising to teach the Faith throughout the world.[1]

Describing the Covenant as the "fortified fortress," the "firm pillar of the religion of God," whose power is "the axis of the oneness of the world of humanity," 'Abdu'l-Bahá accords primary importance to the realization of "firmness in the Covenant of God." He designates it the "first condition," to which attention needs to be given. Thus, 'Abdu'l-Bahá instructs, "in the beginning the believers must make their steps firm in the Covenant so that the confirmations of Bahá'u'lláh may encircle them from all sides, the cohorts of the Supreme Concourse may become their supporters and helpers, and the exhortations and advices of 'Abdu'l-Bahá, like unto the pictures engraved on stone, may remain permanent and ineffaceable in the tablets of all hearts."[2]

The relevance of the call to firmness in the Covenant is not confined to the early years of the twentieth century, the time of the revelation of the Tablets of the Divine Plan. It has continuing significance in the present day. It is a prerequisite for those striving to attain the station of apostleship in contemporary times and critical to the successful implementation of the Divine Plan. In 1996, the Universal House of Justice urged the American Bahá'ís "to manifest unwavering adherence to the provisions of the Covenant, while ever striving for a deeper understanding of its challenging features and of its implications, which far transcend the familiar arrangements of present society."[3]

In earlier chapters—in particular chapter 4, we referred to various aspects of the Bahá'í Covenant, and we illustrated how the term *Covenant* is used with a number of meanings in the literature of the Faith. For example, the Covenant is related to the implicit agreement set in motion by the process of progressive revelation—the advent of Manifestations of God, at different times in history, in fulfillment of the eternal promise of the divine never to leave humankind without a source of guidance, and the concomitant responsibility of humanity to give attention to the teachings of the spiritual Educator.

The term *Covenant* is also applied to the unique provisions made by Bahá'u'lláh, the Founder of the religion, to preserve the unity of His Faith and the integrity of its teachings following His death through the naming of His successor. Bahá'u'lláh's Will and Testament, written in His own handwriting, specifically named His son, 'Abdu'l-Bahá, as His successor and gave him the authority to explain the meaning of His teachings. Addressing an audience in New York City in 1912, concerning "certain new teachings" of Bahá'u'lláh, "which are not found in any of the sacred Books of former times," 'Abdu'l-Bahá highlights the significance of this unique aspect of the Covenant. He states:

> As to the most great characteristic of the revelation of Bahá'u'lláh,
> a specific teaching not given by any of the Prophets of the past:

It is the ordination and appointment of the Center of the Covenant. By this appointment and provision He has safeguarded and protected the religion of God against differences and schisms, making it impossible for anyone to create a new sect or faction of belief. To ensure unity and agreement He has entered into a Covenant with all the people of the world, including the interpreter and explainer of His teachings, so that no one may interpret or explain the religion of God according to his own view or opinion and thus create a sect founded upon his individual understanding of the divine Words. The Book of the Covenant or Testament of Bahá'u'lláh is the means of preventing such a possibility, for whosoever shall speak from the authority of himself alone shall be degraded. Be ye informed and cognizant of this.[4]

Concerning the progressive unfoldment of the Covenant, we have already examined the critical relationship between the Will and Testament of 'Abdu'l-Bahá and his Tablets of the Divine Plan, and considered the significance of a number of covenantal provisions for the worldwide expansion of the Faith. Briefly, 'Abdu'l-Bahá in his Will and Testament, safeguarded the continued unity and integrity of the Faith into the future. He specified twin successors. He named his grandson, Shoghi Effendi, as his successor and the person with authority to interpret and explain the meaning of the sacred text, and he designated the Universal House of Justice as the institution with the authority to legislate on matters not specifically mentioned in the Bahá'í writings and to elucidate issues that were the cause of confusion. This divinely ordained institution thereby serves as a source of authoritative guidance for the development of the Cause into the future. Shoghi Effendi in his lifetime brought into being the Bahá'í Administrative Order, which derives its authority from the provisions of the Covenant of Bahá'u'lláh. Drawing inspiration and direction from the Tablets of the Divine Plan, he fostered the systematic worldwide expansion of the Bahá'í community and thereby set the scene for the election of the Universal House of Justice in 1963. The Universal House of Justice is now the Head of the Bahá'í Faith. It directs and will continue to direct the affairs of the religion and its interactions with the world at large.

The Covenant not only provides the necessary institutional structures, it also serves as the source of spiritual motivation and continuing guidance to those who arise to support it. It offers thereby the means to ongoing individual and social transformation. In this chapter, our focus will be on "firmness in the Covenant of God," which is the "first condition" of apostleship. In particular, we will explore a number of issues associated with the "realization" of this condition that pertain specifically to relationships between the individual and society and that exert a constructive influence on the evolution of the spiritual and social unfoldment of the life of humankind.[5]

In a letter addressed to the Bahá'ís of the world in 1989, the Universal House of Justice underscored the important contribution of loyalty to the Covenant to individual and social transformation. The letter states, "It is not enough to proclaim the Bahá'í message, essential as that is. It is not enough to expand the rolls of Bahá'í membership, vital as that is. Souls must be transformed, communities thereby consolidated, new models of life thus attained. Transformation is the essential purpose of the Cause of Bahá'u'lláh, but it lies in the will and effort of the individual to achieve it in obedience to the Covenant. Necessary to the progress of this life-fulfilling transformation is knowledge of the will and purpose of God through regular reading and study of the Holy Word." This passage sets out the responsibilities of individuals who embrace the Message of Bahá'u'lláh and, as parties to His Covenant, arise and commit themselves to its support. Hence, the realization of the life-fulfilling transformation envisaged in the Revelation of Bahá'u'lláh depends on "the will and effort of the individual to achieve it in obedience to the Covenant," and critical to the "progress" of the transformative process is attaining "knowledge of the will and purpose of God."[6]

Being a Party to the Covenant

Man, in the estimation of Bahá'u'lláh, "the noblest and most perfect of all created things," has a definite purpose in life, namely to know and to worship God and "to carry forward an ever advancing civilization." To fulfill this high purpose, man must recognize the Messenger of God within whose dispensation he lives and "observe every ordinance of Him Who is the Desire of the world. These twin duties are inseparable. Neither is acceptable without the other." Elaborating on the "foundation" of Bahá'í belief, the Universal House of Justice stresses the importance of personal choice and the role of the Covenant in the practical fulfillment of one's purpose in life. The House writes:

> The foundation of our belief rests on our recognition of the sovereignty of God, the Unknowable Essence, the Supreme Creator, and on our submission to His will as revealed for this age by Bahá'u'lláh. To accept the Messenger of God in His Day and to abide by His bidding are the two essential, inseparable duties which each soul was created to fulfil. One exercises these twin duties by one's own choice, and by so doing performs an act which may be regarded as the highest expression of free will with which every human being is endowed by an all-loving Creator. The vehicle in this resplendent age for the practical fulfilment of these duties is the Covenant of Bahá'u'lláh. It is the instrument by which belief in Him is translated into constructive deeds.[7]

The process of investigating the reality of the claim of the new Messenger to be the Bringer of truth and the Source of all good calls for freedom from prejudice, the unfettered search after truth, and man's use of the power of reason. 'Abdu'l-Bahá states, "God has not intended man to imitate blindly his fathers and ancestors. He has endowed him with mind, or the faculty of reasoning, by the exercise of which he is to investigate and discover the truth, and that which he finds real and true he must accept. He must not be an imitator or blind follower of any soul. He must not rely implicitly upon the opinion of any man without investigation; nay, each soul must seek intelligently and independently, arriving at a real conclusion and bound only by that reality." The Universal House of Justice, in a letter written on its behalf dated April 19, 2013, explains the significance of taking this step of Faith and describes the dynamic relationship between divine law and the progress of both the individual and society: "In recognizing the Manifestation of God for today, a believer also acknowledges that His laws and exhortations express truths about the nature of the human being and the purpose of existence; they raise human consciousness, increase understanding, lift the standard of personal conduct, and provide the means for society to progress. His teachings serve, then, to empower humanity; they are the harbinger of human happiness, whose call, far from compelling obedience to an arbitrary and dictatorial regimen of behavior, leads to true freedom."[8]

As a party to the Covenant, the individual is not only duty-bound to search after truth prayerfully and without prejudice until he or she comes to recognize the Manifestation of God for the age and embraces His Cause, but beyond that, as a token of love for God, the individual is called upon to undertake to obey and implement the laws and teachings of the new Messenger.[9]

'Abdu'l-Bahá describes the dynamic transformative processes arising from obedience to the commands of God and the benefits that accrue to the individual and society:

> It is certain that man's highest distinction is to be lowly before and obedient to his God; that his greatest glory, his most exalted rank and honor, depend on his close observance of the Divine commands and prohibitions. Religion is the light of the world, and the progress, achievement, and happiness of man result from obedience to the laws set down in the holy Books. Briefly, it is demonstrable that in this life, both outwardly and inwardly the mightiest of structures, the most solidly established, the most enduring, standing guard over the world, assuring both the spiritual and the material perfections of mankind, and protecting the happiness and the civilization of society—is religion.[10]

Obedience to the laws and teachings of the Manifestation of God is the second of the twin duties that underpin the condition of firmness to the Bahá'í Covenant. In this regard, it is important to recognize that

Bahá'ís are encouraged to use their intellectual capacities to endeavor to understand the guidance, to avoid unthinking responses and unexamined habits of thought and blind fanaticism, and to continue to seek additional knowledge to deepen their understanding of the teachings of the new day. In relation to the standard set by Bahá'u'lláh, Shoghi Effendi's secretary, observed, "He does not ask us to follow Him blindly; as He says in one of His Tablets, God has endowed man with a mind to operate as a torchlight and guide him to the truth. Read His words, consider His Teachings and measure their value in the light of contemporary problems and the truth will surely be revealed to you. Read books such as the Íqán, *Some Answered Questions, Nabil's Narrative*, and you will appreciate the truth of His Mission, as well as the true spirit He creates in whosoever follows His ways."[11]

In contemporary society, the concept of obedience is all too often associated with religious fanaticism, dictatorship, tyranny, prejudice and intolerance. In modern times, historians have documented the appalling results of blind obedience to various political regimes and religious movements, and any review of these results might generate suspicion and anxiety among thoughtful people about any group that demands obedience to its commands.

While such reactions are understandable, and indeed often reflect the course of greatest wisdom, Adib Taherzadeh calls attention to the motive underlying an alternative response to the requirement of obedience. He observes that "in his daily life a human being wholeheartedly obeys the directives of many individuals or institutions that speak with the voice of truth. He is willing to accept authority that appears credible and trustworthy. For instance . . . a patient will willingly allow a surgeon to operate on a cancerous growth because he has faith in the doctor's diagnosis." Applying this insight to the behavior of one who accepts the station of Bahá'u'lláh, Taherzadeh writes, "A similar response results from an individual's recognition of the truth of the Cause of God. Once he sees the teachings as credible, he will not find it difficult to obey them. And since man's part in the Covenant of God is obedience to God's teachings, it is clear that he cannot fulfil his obligation unless he recognizes the truth of His Revelation." And in the passage cited below, Taherzadeh conceptualizes the interacting processes of recognition of the Messenger and motivation to uphold His laws that are likely to unfold in the life of an individual and thereby set the stage for social transformation:

> Every person who becomes a Bahá'í must investigate the truth until he becomes assured in his heart that Bahá'u'lláh is the Manifestation of God for this age. When the individual reaches this stage, he will then want to follow His commandments. And as he deepens his knowledge of the Faith and turns to Bahá'u'lláh to draw from His power, his heart will become the recipient of the knowledge which God can bestow upon a believer. It is then that he can realize the wisdom behind all the laws and teachings which are binding on him. It is then that obedience to the commandments of Bahá'u'lláh becomes coupled with a deep understanding of their purpose, their wisdom, their excellence and their need. It is then that carrying out the teachings of Bahá'u'lláh becomes a source of joy for the individual, and he will find that his thoughts, his aspirations, his words and his deeds are in harmony with the provisions of the Covenant of God with man.[12]

THE QUESTION OF FREEDOM

Individual freedom is an element essential to human existence. Indeed freedom in its various manifestations—freedom of thought, freedom of expression, freedom of action, and the like—has been the focus of social theorists and commentators through the ages. Given the relationship of obedience to the condition of firmness in the Covenant, one might well inquire how the question of freedom is to be viewed in Bahá'í thought and action.

By way of introduction, it is important to note that, while calling for a reexamination of current assumptions concerning the nature of divine law and the means of attaining freedom itself, the teachings of Bahá'u'lláh recognize the invaluable contribution of freedom, in its broadest sense, to constructive social processes. Writing on this theme, the Universal House of Justice invites us to "Consider, for instance,

Bahá'u'lláh's proclamation to the kings and rulers. Can it not be deduced from this alone that attainment of freedom is a significant purpose of His Revelation? His denunciations of tyranny and His urgent appeals on behalf of the oppressed provide unmistakable proof. But does not the freedom foreshadowed by His Revelation imply nobler, ampler manifestations of human achievement? Does it not indicate an organic relationship between the internal and external realities of man such as has not yet been attained?"[13]

The key to understanding the Bahá'í perspective on freedom lies in confronting an apparent paradox inherent in the conception and practice of Bahá'í law. In The Kitáb-i-Aqdas, His Book of Laws, Bahá'u'lláh underlines the dynamic, transformative and socially constructive quality of His laws. He instructs His followers thus: "Think not that We have revealed unto you a mere code of laws. Nay, rather, We have unsealed the choice Wine with the fingers of might and power."[14]

In this same book, Bahá'u'lláh comments on the nature of "true liberty," and He links human happiness and the attainment of "perfect liberty" to obedience to His laws:

> Say: True liberty consisteth in man's submission unto My commandments, little as ye know it. Were men to observe that which We have sent down unto them from the Heaven of Revelation, they would, of a certainty, attain unto perfect liberty. Happy is the man that hath apprehended the Purpose of God in whatever He hath revealed from the Heaven of His Will that pervadeth all created things. Say: The liberty that profiteth you is to be found nowhere except in complete servitude unto God, the Eternal Truth. Whoso hath tasted of its sweetness will refuse to barter it for all the dominion of earth and heaven.[15]

Understood in this way, obedience to the law of God, rather than being a straightjacket and imposing rigid constraints on creativity and progress, is a means to attaining true freedom, human happiness and prosperity.

The Universal House of Justice links the advent of the Revelation of Bahá'u'lláh with the spread of the "spirit of liberty" in recent times.

In elucidating this subject, the House of Justice begins by citing the words of Bahá'u'lláh's commentary on the purpose of His sufferings, then poses a question and offers a compelling perspective concerning His contribution to the freedom of humankind:

> The spirit of liberty which in recent decades has swept over the planet with such tempestuous force is a manifestation of the vibrancy of the Revelation brought by Bahá'u'lláh. His own words confirm it. "The Ancient Beauty," He wrote in a soul-stirring commentary on His sufferings, "hath consented to be bound with chains that mankind may be released from its bondage, and hath accepted to be made a prisoner within this most mighty Stronghold that the whole world may attain unto true liberty."
>
> Might it not be reasonably concluded, then, that "true liberty" is His gift of love to the human race? Consider what Bahá'u'lláh has done: He revealed laws and principles to guide the free; He established an Order to channel the actions of the free; He proclaimed a Covenant to guarantee the unity of the free.
>
> Thus, we hold to this ultimate perspective: Bahá'u'lláh came to set humanity free. His Revelation is, indeed, an invitation to freedom—freedom from want, freedom from war, freedom to unite, freedom to progress, freedom in peace and joy.[16]

The constructive view of freedom embedded in the Bahá'í writings not only sets out a framework for achieving true individual and societal freedom, it also imposes some degree of limitation. However, it is important to acknowledge that in civil society itself, the need to restrict certain freedoms has long been recognized. For example, societies have enacted laws against sedition and hate-mongering in order to protect itself and its citizens against behavior when it becomes socially destructive.

Concerning the limitations to individual freedom, 'Abdu'l-Bahá, for example, describes "the moderate freedom which guarantees the welfare of the world of mankind and maintains and preserves the universal relationships." Such freedom, he asserts, "is found in its fullest power and extension in the teachings of Bahá'u'lláh." Further, the Universal House of Justice, addressing the question of "the latitudes of freedom in the Bahá'í community," offers the following general perspective: "Because human beings have been created to 'carry forward an ever-advancing civilization,' the exercise of freedom, it may be deduced, is intended to enable all to fulfil this purpose in their individual lives and in their collective functioning as a society. Hence whatever in principle is required to realize this purpose gauges the latitudes or limits of freedom."[17]

Applying these principles to Bahá'í community life, the House of Justice continues, "Within this framework of freedom a pattern is set for institutional and individual behavior which depends for its efficacy not so much on the force of law, which admittedly must be respected, as on the recognition of a mutuality of benefits, and on the spirit of cooperation maintained by the willingness, the courage, the sense of responsibility, and the initiative of individuals—these being expressions of their devotion and submission to the will of God. Thus there is a balance of freedom between the institution, whether national or local, and the individuals who sustain its existence." The Universal House of Justice comments further on the society-building importance of the relationship between individual and institutional behavior. It observes:

> This relationship, so fundamental to the maintenance of civilized life, calls for the utmost degree of understanding and cooperation between society and the individual; and because of the need to foster a climate in which the untold potentialities of the individual members of society can develop, this relationship must allow "free scope" for "individuality to assert itself" through modes of spontaneity, initiative and diversity that ensure the viability of society. Among the responsibilities assigned to Bahá'í institutions which have a direct bearing on these aspects of individual freedom and development is one which is thus described in

the Constitution of the Universal House of Justice: "to safeguard the personal rights, freedom and initiative of individuals." A corollary is "to give attention to the preservation of human honor."[18]

Understanding the Will and Purpose of God

Given the dynamic relationship between personal and social transformation, it follows that the individual's recognition of the divine authority and the station of the Manifestation of God and his or her nascent willingness to obey the teachings of the Faith needs to be followed by ongoing efforts to gain a deeper, more systematic knowledge of the will and purpose of God and a clearer understanding of the "life-fulfilling" transformative vision contained in the writings of the Faith.[19] Having embraced the truth of the new Message, the individual continues to engage in a lifelong process of striving to obtain a deeper understanding of the significance and application of this Message, a process that represents the fruits of his or her intellectual capacities and that emerges from action and reflection on experience.

Throughout the course of history, the will and purpose of God have been made known to man through the revelation of the Manifestations of God. God's purpose has guided the direction of the development of both the individual and society at large. "Is not the object of every Revelation," Bahá'u'lláh asks "to effect a transformation in the whole character of mankind, a transformation that shall manifest itself, both outwardly and inwardly, that shall affect both its inner life and external conditions?" And stressing the significance of the transformative power of the Revelation to bring about change, He affirms, ". . . if the character of mankind be not changed, the futility of God's universal Manifestations would be apparent."[20]

The Revelation of Bahá'u'lláh calls for a profound change not only at the level of the individual but also in the very structure of society, and is destined to create "the nucleus of the glorious civilization enshrined in His teachings." Commenting on the emergence of this visionary civilization, the Universal House of Justice notes that it represents "an enterprise of infinite complexity and scale, one that will demand centuries of exertion by humanity to bring to fruition," and the House of Justice calls attention to a number of processes, skills, and capacities that need to be developed in order to ensure the fulfillment of the Divine Will in the long-term. It notes, "Only as effort is made to draw on insights from His Revelation, to tap into the accumulating knowledge of the human race, to apply His teachings intelligently to the life of humanity, and to consult on the questions that arise will the necessary learning occur and capacity be developed."[21]

While recognition of the Manifestation of God satisfies the first of the twin duties outlined by Bahá'u'lláh as prerequisites to the fulfillment of man's purpose in life, the second calls for adherence to the ordinances outlined in His Revelation. The fulfillment of this second prerequisite involves gaining knowledge of the teachings of the Manifestation and being committed to the practice of the guidance they contain in daily life.

The investigation of reality does not come to an end with the recognition of the Manifestation of God. The act of recognizing the truth of the new Messenger is only the beginning of a lifelong process of learning, transformation, and growth. A letter dated October 6, 1954, written on behalf of Shoghi Effendi to an individual believer, captures the seminal moment when a person takes an initial step of faith: "When a person becomes a Bahá'í, actually what takes place is that the seed of the spirit starts to grow in the human soul. This seed must be watered by the outpourings of the Holy Spirit. These gifts of the spirit are received through prayer, meditation, study of the Holy Utterances and service to the Cause of God."[22]

This first step on the path to spiritual development is a transformative moment for the individual soul; with it come new responsibilities and opportunities for service. "Those who declare themselves as Bahá'ís," writes the Universal House of Justice, "should become enchanted with the beauty of the teachings, and touched by the love of Bahá'u'lláh. The declarants need not know all the proofs, history, laws, and principles of the Faith, but in the process of declaring themselves they must in addition to catching the spark of faith, become basically informed about the Central Figures of the Faith, as well as the existence of laws they must follow and an administration they must obey."[23]

Rather than constituting an isolated event, becoming an informed Bahá'í may well involve a gradual process. In addition to being committed to acquiring a more detailed knowledge of the Cause, the newly declared believers must also be willing to follow and obey the spiritual and administrative guidance set forth in the teachings of the Faith, to support the agencies of its institutional structure, to acquire the capacities and skills required to serve the community, and to engage with the world at large to promote the well-being of humankind.

The twin duties prescribed by Bahá'u'lláh for individuals who embrace His Faith not only set out the path to individual spiritual transformation but also give insight into God's purpose for humankind and the means for its fulfillment. The linking of the pursuit of knowledge and its application might well represent a mode of learning that gives direction to a pattern of growth that has the potential to foster and sustain social transformation. The scope of this task is vast. The House of Justice cautions "never to lose sight of the aim of the Faith to effect a transformation of society, remolding its institutions and processes, on a scale never before witnessed." To engage in this activity, the friends must acquire an adequate understanding of the Revelation of Bahá'u'lláh, which sets out His vision and outlines some of the basic features of the New World Order, and the capacity to apply this understanding to the amelioration of the social condition. Enshrined in His Revelation is a pattern for future society, which in the words of the Universal House of Justice is "radically different from any established in the past." It follows that "the promotion of His laws and exhortations constitute an inseparable part of the effort to lay the foundations of such a society."[24]

CENTRAL ROLE OF KNOWLEDGE

The acquisition of knowledge is an important aspect of firmness in the Covenant. Emphasized by 'Abdu'l-Bahá in the Tablets of the Divine Plan in relation to the preparation and training of teachers, the process of acquiring and generating knowledge, as mentioned in chapter 4, now represents an important element in the emerging culture of learning evolving within the Bahá'í community.

The acquisition of knowledge is critical to the ongoing Bahá'í approach to community-building. The approach draws its primary inspiration from the knowledge and application of the laws and teachings of the Faith. It is a fundamentally spiritual enterprise based on acceptance of the guidance contained in the Revelation and on a systematic application of this guidance to individual and collective lives. The following extract from a letter dated June 12, 1984, written on behalf of the Universal House of Justice, identifies the "the establishment of the oneness of the world of humanity" as the "central purpose" of the Bahá'í Dispensation and describes the operation of the society-building processes involved: " . . . it is a Bahá'í teaching that the spiritual development of the soul requires not merely prayer and meditation, but also active service to one's fellowmen in accordance with the laws and principles of the Revelation of God. The reconstruction of human society and the spiritual advancement of individual souls go hand in hand."[25]

Education plays a vital role in sustaining change and growth. The educational initiatives currently undertaken within the Bahá'í community not only emphasize individual study of the sacred writings, they also stress the importance of education at all levels of the community—devotional gatherings, classes for children, junior youth groups, and study circle programs for adults. These activities seek "to raise the capacity within a population to take charge of its own spiritual, social and intellectual development."[26]

The Bahá'í approach to study of the writings is linked to action. It is driven by recognition that "in the field of service, knowledge is tested, questions arise out of practice, and new understandings are achieved." The activities associated with the training institute provide opportunities for individuals not only to engage in systematic study of the Bahá'í writings but also to engage in acts of service. Describing the processes involved in this approach to learning the Universal House of Justice observed:

Thousands upon thousands, embracing the diversity of the entire human family, are engaged in systematic study of the Creative Word in an environment that is at once serious and uplifting. As they strive to apply through a process of action, reflection and consultation the insights thus gained, they see their capacity to serve the Cause rise to new levels. Responding to the inmost longing of every heart to commune with its Maker, they carry out acts of collective worship in diverse settings, uniting with others in prayer, awakening spiritual susceptibilities, and shaping a pattern of life distinguished for its devotional character. As they call on one another in their homes and pay visits to families, friends and acquaintances, they enter into purposeful discussion on themes of spiritual import, deepen their knowledge of the Faith, share Bahá'u'lláh's message, and welcome increasing numbers to join them in a mighty spiritual enterprise. Aware of the aspirations of the children of the world and their need for spiritual education, they extend their efforts widely to involve ever-growing contingents of participants in classes that become centres of attraction for the young and strengthen the roots of the Faith in society. They assist junior youth to navigate through a crucial stage of their lives and to become empowered to direct their energies toward the advancement of civilization. And with the advantage of a greater abundance of human resources, an increasing number of them are able to express their faith through a rising tide of endeavors that address the needs of humanity in both their spiritual and material dimensions.[27]

This dynamic approach to learning not only increases understanding, it also aims to build individual and collective capacity and advances the growth process. Commenting on the empowering and transformative impact of this approach, the Universal House of Justice writes, "the worldwide Bahá'í community has acquired the capacity to enable thousands, nay millions, to study the writings in small groups with the explicit purpose of translating the Bahá'í teachings into reality, carrying the work of the Faith forward into its next stage: sustained large-scale expansion and consolidation."[28]

To sustain this unfolding evolutionary process into the future and to lay the foundations of a new civilization, the long-term challenge is to create within the community an environment conducive to the spiritual empowerment of individuals "who will come to see themselves as active agents of their own learning, as protagonists of a constant effort to apply knowledge to effect individual and collective transformation."[29]

The approach to learning through action is critical to the development of administrative capacity. It is central to certain aspects of decision making related to expansion and consolidation and enables planning and implementation to become more responsive to circumstances on the ground. To provide a space for the development of such skills, people engaged in similar fields of service or in activities at the cluster (or other) level are, from time to time, invited to assemble at a reflection meeting "in order to reach consensus on the current status of their situation, in light of experience and guidance from the institutions, and to determine their immediate steps forward."[30]

To heighten administrative capacity and to retain focus on the task of advancing the process of entry by troops, the Universal House of Justice has called upon the Bahá'í community to institute quarterly cycles for the systematic organization of its work. Typically, each cycle begins with a reflection meeting during which a short expansion phase is planned, to be followed by a longer period of consolidation. The precise objectives of each expansion phase vary depending on conditions in the cluster and the circumstances of the Bahá'í community. The introduction of quarterly cycles of activity capitalizes on the emerging capacity to learn through action and allows it to be steadily reinforced. In this regard, the House of Justice notes that "as learning accelerates, the friends grow more capable of overcoming setbacks, whether small or large—diagnosing their root causes, exploring the underlying principles, bringing to bear relevant experience, identifying remedial steps, and assessing progress, until the process of growth has been fully reinvigorated."[31]

SECULAR KNOWLEDGE

The achievement of the far-reaching social and structural changes necessary to produce a society embodying the recognition and practice of the oneness of humanity will engage the Bahá'í community in earnest consultation with scholars, experts, and other like-minded individuals from all walks of life concerned with the betterment of the life of humankind. The Universal House of Justice notes that the "world civilization now on humanity's horizon must achieve a dynamic coherence between the material and spiritual requirements of life."[32] As the Bahá'í community increases in size and capacity and is drawn further and further into the life of society, it will be challenged to widen the range of human endeavors, to engage in activities aimed at the betterment of their people. And, as Spiritual Assemblies mature and continue to develop, the process of society-building will be accelerated.

Knowledge, both spiritual and secular, is critical to the Bahá'í community's active involvement in the wider society, including social action and participation in the prevalent discourses of society. Those engaged in the processes of social change are encouraged to "learn to apply with increasing effectiveness elements of Bahá'u'lláh's Revelation, together with the contents and methods of science, to their social reality. This reality they must strive to read in a manner consistent with His teachings—seeing in their fellow human beings gems of inestimable value and recognizing the effects of the dual process of integration and disintegration on both hearts and minds, as well as on social structures."[33]

The Bahá'í approach to community-building addresses issues at the fundamental level of values and attitudes and calls for a reassessment of assumptions underlying prevailing social and organizational practices. It proceeds at an evolutionary pace consistent with the level of development, capacity, and size of the unfolding Bahá'í community. It is characterized by commitment to the search for and application of knowledge, together with efforts to correlate insights derived from a careful study of the laws and teachings of the Bahá'í Revelation with current secular thought, and the longing to contribute to social development to which this knowledge gives rise. This approach builds capacity for effective social action within the Bahá'í community and among the diverse populations of the planet, and opens the way for effective collaboration with like-minded individuals and groups eager to contribute to the forces for order in the world.

Commenting on the outward looking orientation of the Bahá'í community's long-term process of capacity-building, the Universal House of Justice writes, "All are welcome to enter the community's warm embrace and receive sustenance from Bahá'u'lláh's life-giving message. No greater joy is there, to be sure, than for a soul, yearning for the Truth, to find shelter in the stronghold of the Cause and draw strength from the unifying power of the Covenant." While membership of the Bahá'í community is not a requirement for participating in the community-building activities initiated by the Bahá'ís, the House of Justice also observes that "every human being and every group of individuals, irrespective of whether they are counted among His [Bahá'u'lláh's] followers, can take inspiration from His teachings, benefiting from whatever gems of wisdom and knowledge will aid them in addressing the challenges they face." Beyond the recognition of the inspirational value of the Bahá'í perspective to such individuals and groups, the House of Justice underlines the indispensability of their contribution to the process of civilization-building and highlights the critical interaction between the parts played by the Bahá'í and wider community, affirming:

> Indeed, the civilization that beckons humanity will not be attained through the efforts of the Bahá'í community alone. Numerous groups and organizations, animated by the spirit of world solidarity that is an indirect manifestation of Bahá'u'lláh's conception of the principle of the oneness of humankind, will contribute to the civilization destined to emerge out of the welter and chaos of present-day society. It should be clear to everyone that the capacity created in the Bahá'í community over successive global Plans renders it increasingly able to lend assistance in the manifold and diverse dimensions of civilization building, opening to it new frontiers of learning.[34]

CULTURE OF LEARNING

The Bahá'í approach to mobilizing social support for change is unique. It is much more than a series of specific techniques. Rather, it addresses this challenging issue at the level of culture.

The 2010 Riḍván letter of the Universal House of Justice sets out in visionary terms the process of civilization-building in which the Baháʾís around the world are engaged, and it describes the relationship between the unfoldment of this evolutionary process and the emerging Baháʾí culture arising from the practice of core activities and the institute process. The House of Justice provides an assessment of the progress made, to date, by the Baháʾí community, and, focusing on the requirements of the future, it reminds the friends of the scope and long-term nature of the challenging mission set out for them in the writings of Baháʾuʾlláh: "The work advancing in every corner of the globe today represents the latest stage of the ongoing Baháʾí endeavor to create the nucleus of the glorious civilization enshrined in His teachings, the building of which is an enterprise of infinite complexity and scale, one that will demand centuries of exertion by humanity to bring to fruition."[35]

To ensure continuing individual and social transformation critical to the implementation of this centuries-long enterprise, the Baháʾí world must have the ability to build and harness human capacity and energy. In its message, the Universal House of Justice describes "the dynamics of an irrepressible movement," an approach to capacity-building that enables the Baháʾí community to sustain its activities without its members succumbing to the challenges of debilitating fatigue and burnout, and without resorting to the use of domination and approaches to leadership that are dictatorial, manipulative, or appeal to such things as fear, greed, or guilt. Indeed, the House of Justice asserts that the Baháʾís have succeeded in laying the foundation of this "irrepressible" process of change by "developing a culture which promotes a way of thinking, studying, and acting, in which all consider themselves as treading a common path of service—supporting one another and advancing together, respectful of the knowledge that each one possesses at any given moment and avoiding the tendency to divide the believers into categories such as deepened and uninformed."[36]

The advance in culture is not confined to the relations among individuals; it also impacts the conduct of the administrative affairs of the Faith, where "learning has come to distinguish the community's mode of operation." The Universal House of Justice views the "evolving relationships" between the institutions and agencies of the Bahá'í administrative structure and their ability "to manage . . . growing complexity with greater and greater dexterity" as "both a sign and a necessity of their steady maturation." And anticipating the continuation of this unfolding process into the future, the House of Justice points to "an important characteristic" of Bahá'í administration, writing, "Even as a living organism, it has coded within it the capacity to accommodate higher and higher degrees of complexity, in terms of structures and processes, relationships and activities, as it evolves under the guidance of the Universal House of Justice."[37]

THE PROCESS OF ACCOMPANIMENT

A key element of the emergent Bahá'í culture, to which the Universal House of Justice now directs our attention, is the process of accompanying an individual on his or her efforts to serve. In everyday usage, the idea of accompanying tends to signify, among other things, the action of being a companion to, of acting with, and of going along with another person. It can also refer to escorting (for safety), attending (as a servant), and playing (in music) an additional part in support of a singer. A number of these definitions implicitly suggest an inherent inequality in the relationship and a certain degree of passivity on the part of one of the participants, and they appear to confine the act of accompanying to the interaction between two people.

The Universal House of Justice calls attention to the fact that within the Bahá'í community, the concept of accompaniment is "being endowed with new meaning as it is integrated into the vocabulary of the Bahá'í community." Highlighting the uniqueness of the enlarged meaning of the word *accompany*, the House of Justice states that, as used by Bahá'ís, "It signals the significant strengthening of a culture in which learning is the mode of operation, a mode that fosters the informed participation of more and more people in a united effort to apply Bahá'u'lláh's teachings to the construction of a divine civilization. . . ."[38]

Reflecting on this broader definition a number of points emerge. From a Bahá'í perspective, accompanying is a relationship that goes far beyond two individuals. It makes a critical contribution to "the significant strengthening of a culture," to the transformation of society. Since "learning" is the "mode of operation" driving the relationship, there is the potential for greater equality among the participants and for the discovery of new insights and solutions, along with the realization that there is no single predetermined answer. Answers arise from reflection on experience, and new knowledge is created. Since the "mode of operation" fosters "informed participation" of increasing number of people, rather than passive acquiescence or submission to the pressures of charismatic or manipulative leaders, those involved are free to exercise their creativity and are more likely to reach knowledge-based conclusions. Since the participants are engaged in "a united effort to apply Bahá'u'lláh's teachings to the construction of a divine civilization," their perspective is service-oriented and forward-looking, motivated by a desire to contribute to the evolution of a new social order that gives requisite consideration to the blending of the spiritual and material dimensions of life.

In immediate practical terms, the implications of accompaniment are far-reaching. Accompaniment is a critical factor in strengthening the emerging culture of learning. It finds expression in the quality of the interactions among the Bahá'ís, and it affects the conduct of the administrative affairs of the Faith where learning has come to distinguish the community's mode of operation.

The dynamic relationship between an approach to society-building where learning is the primary mode of operation and the act of accompaniment is described by the Universal House of Justice. The House of Justice begins by calling attention to the importance of certain underlying spiritual values: "Learning as a mode of operation requires that all assume a posture of humility, a condition in which one becomes forgetful of self, placing complete trust in God, reliant on His all-sustaining power and confident in His unfailing assistance, knowing that He, and He alone, can change the gnat into an eagle, the drop into a boundless sea." And it explains the outcome of such behavior on human motivation, observing that when these primary spiritual, attitudinal conditions are satisfied, the friends are motivated and eager to "labor together ceaselessly, delighting not so much in their own accomplishments but in the progress and services of others. So that their thoughts are centered at all times on helping one another scale the heights of service to His Cause and soar in the heaven of His knowledge."[39]

The dynamic processes outlined above highlight the uniqueness of the Bahá'í concept of accompaniment as a means of mobilizing support for social change. In the words of the Universal House of Justice, "Such an approach offers a striking contrast to the spiritually bankrupt and moribund ways of an old social order that so often seeks to harness human energy through domination, through greed, through guilt or through manipulation."[40]

As a key element of the emerging Bahá'í culture, the act of accompaniment is critical to enhancing capacity-building and to sustaining participation in the processes of society-building.

SUSTAINING GROWTH

One of the challenges confronting any growing social movement is to find a way to sustain growth, to preserve the movement's creativity, and to avoid the corruption of its leadership. Typically, a new movement grows quickly at first. Then, people get tired, become complacent, or feel disappointed or alienated from the wider society. Then, it often happens that a strong leader comes along and that he or she encourages, cajoles, threatens, or bribes the members of the group to take action.

In the Bahá'í community, the provisions of the Bahá'í Covenant and the processes set in motion by 'Abdu'l-Bahá's Tablets of the Divine Plan address the challenge of sustaining growth and facilitate the continuing participation of its members at the level of cultural and administrative values. The Bahá'í approach begins by confronting patterns of behavior that act as barriers to change. For example, the Universal House of Justice calls attention to the impact of the following aspects of present-day society: "Passivity is bred by the forces of society. A desire to be entertained is nurtured from childhood, with increasing efficiency, cultivating generations willing to be led by whoever proves skilful at appealing to superficial emotions. Even in many educational systems students are treated as though they were receptacles designed to receive information."[41]

As described above, the emerging Bahá'í culture is fostered by an educational process that encourages and supports individual partic-ipation in a wide range of core activities—study circles, classes for children, junior youth groups, devotional gatherings, and the like. These activities increase understanding of the transforming vision of the Faith, build capacity for service, increase motivation, instill confi-dence, and increase the willingness of individuals to accept responsi-bility for engaging in the society-building activities of the community.

As parties to the Covenant, all members of the Bahá'í community assume responsibility for pursuing the aims of the Cause. The stan-dard to which the Faith aspires is universal participation. Within the Bahá'í community, there is no separate class of clergy whose members claim superior knowledge and rank and assume major responsibility for the direction of the affairs of the community. This removes the hierarchical distinction between clergy and laypeople found in other religious systems.

Leadership within the Bahá'í community is provided by the insti-tutions of the evolving Bahá'í Administrative Order. These divinely ordained institutions are critical to furthering the growth of the Bahá'í community. Citing the guidance of Shoghi Effendi, the Universal House of Justice states:

The Bahá'í administrative machinery, he [Shoghi Effendi] reiter-ated again and again, "is to be regarded as a means, and not an end in itself." It is intended, he made clear, "to serve a twofold purpose." On the one hand, "it should ensure the internal consol-idation of the work already achieved." And he went on to explain: "It should both provide the impulse whereby the dynamic forces latent in the Faith can unfold, crystallize, and shape the lives and conduct of men, and serve as a medium for the interchange of thought and the coordination of activities among the divers ele-ments that constitute the Bahá'í community.[42]

Participation in the Bahá'í Administrative Order is therefore an important aspect of community-building. To be elected or appointed to serve on the institutions and agencies of the Faith is viewed not only as a great privilege but also as a unique opportunity for service to humanity. The members of these administrative bodies are called to a high standard of ethical conduct—"to exemplify rectitude of conduct," and "to observe its requirements in their uncompromising adherence to the laws and principles of the Faith." By these means, the members will demonstrate the distinctiveness of the Bahá'í institutions and highlight the condition of the rudderless and rapidly declining institutions in the world at large where "the very conception of states-manship has been drained of meaning, as policies have come to serve the economic interests of the few in the name of progress, as hypocrisy has been allowed to undermine the operation of social and economic structures."[43]

It is evident that service on Bahá'í institutions not only enhances the processes of growth within the Bahá'í community. In addition, the quality of functioning of the Bahá'í institutions serves as an alternative model to the increasingly dysfunctional systems of governance preva-lent in the world at large, and thereby contributes to society-building in the wider society.

The capacity of the Bahá'í community to sustain growth and remain dynamic and relevant to the evolving needs of an ever-changing world depends on nurturing the elements of the emerging Bahá'í culture and enhancing the capacity of the Faith's administrative institutions to engage in consultation and collaborate with like-mined groups working for the good of humanity at large.

Laying the Foundations of a New Civilization

The processes set in motion by the Tablets of the Divine Plan for the worldwide expansion and consolidation of the Faith have given rise to patterns of growth that have evolved, through a series of global plans initiated by Shoghi Effendi and the Universal House of Justice, at a pace commensurate with the size and level of capacity of the Bahá'í community and in conformity with the specific requirements of the day. While the tasks undertaken by the Bahá'ís have expanded and changed from time to time, the overall objective has remained the same—to lay the foundations of a new civilization envisioned in the Revelation of Bahá'u'lláh. Commenting on this objective, the Universal House of Justice clarified that

> Bahá'ís do not believe the transformation thus envisioned will come about exclusively through their own efforts. Nor are they trying to create a movement that would seek to impose on society their vision of the future. Every nation and every group—indeed, every individual—will, to a greater or lesser degree, contribute to the emergence of the world civilization towards which humanity is irresistibly moving. Unity will progressively be achieved, as foreshadowed by 'Abdu'l-Bahá, in different realms of social existence. . . . As these come to be realized, the structures of a politically united world, which respects the full diversity of culture and provides channels for the expression of dignity and honor, will gradually take shape.[44]

Addressing the Bahá'ís of Iran in March, 2013, the Universal House of Justice describes the actions needed to sustain the unfoldment of the transformative processes, and it establishes priorities for the current work of the worldwide Bahá'í community:

> The question that occupies the worldwide Bahá'í community, then, is how it can best contribute to the civilization-building process as its resources increase. It sees two dimensions to its contribution. The first is related to its own growth and development, and the second to its involvement in society at large.
>
> Regarding the first, Bahá'ís across the globe, . . . are striving to establish a pattern of activity and the corresponding administrative structures that embody the principle of the oneness of humankind and the convictions underpinning it. . . . Translating ideals such as these into reality, effecting a transformation at the

level of the individual and laying the foundations of suitable social structures, is no small task, to be sure. Yet the Bahá'í community is dedicated to the long-term process of learning that this task entails, an enterprise in which increasing numbers from all walks of life, from every human group, are invited to take part.[45]

ENGAGING IN DISCOURSE WITH THE WIDER SOCIETY

As the Bahá'í community grows in size and capacity, it is in a stronger position to become involved in various forms of social action aimed specifically at the promotion of public welfare and to engage in the prevalent discourses of society. The Universal House of Justice describes the dynamic relationship between the Revelation of Bahá'u'lláh and the progress of the Bahá'í community, foreshadowing that ". . . the new throb of energy now vibrating throughout the Cause will empower it to meet the oncoming challenges of assisting, as maturity and resources allow, the development of the social and economic life of peoples, of collaborating with the forces leading towards the establishment of order in the world, of influencing the exploitation and constructive uses of modern technology, and in all these ways enhancing the prestige and progress of the Faith and uplifting the conditions of the generality of mankind."[46]

In the Tablets of the Divine Plan, 'Abdu'l-Bahá lends support to the systematic unfoldment of the dynamic processes alluded to above. Referring to his journeys in North America where he "opened the door of teaching," 'Abdu'l-Bahá defined the immediate task of the believers as nurturing and building upon the work he had begun: "Now the believers of God and the maidservants of the Merciful must irrigate these fields and with the utmost power engage themselves in the cultivation of these heavenly plantations so that the seeds may grow and develop, prosperity and blessing be realized and many rich and great harvests be gathered in."[47]

With the expansion and increase in capacity of the Bahá'í community over the years and the intensification of growth within clusters, the Universal House of Justice has called for an increasingly strategic approach to the involvement of the Bahá'í community in the life of society. Central to such involvement is an understanding of the current state of the world and the nature of the required response.

Highlighting the condition of the world, the House of Justice called the believers' attention to the contemporary relevance of *The Secret of Divine Civilization*, a letter addressed by 'Abdu'l-Bahá to the people of His native land Persia in 1875 and which was described by Shoghi Effendi as 'Abdu'l-Bahá's "outstanding contribution to the future reorganization of the world." While this historic letter "prophetically laid out . . . the challenge of modernity," the House of Justice affirms, today this challenge "has become the inescapable preoccupation of populations throughout the planet, not least the peoples of the Islamic world." The "meaning of modernity and the features of that rising flood of cultural revolution [that] were explicitly identified in the Master's message" were "constitutional and democratic government, the rule of law, universal education, the protection of human rights, economic development, religious tolerance, the promotion of useful sciences and technologies and programs of public welfare." In sum, the Universal House of Justice attests, the message of 'Abdu'l-Bahá's treatise was ". . . a summons—to the country's leaders and the population alike—to free themselves from blind submission to dogma and to accept the need for fundamental changes in behavior and attitude, most particularly a willingness to subordinate personal and group interests to the crying needs of society as a whole."[48]

THE CASE OF IRAN—FOSTERING THE ADVANCEMENT OF WOMEN

To illustrate the processes involved in the Bahá'í community engaging in discourse with the wider society, it is useful to focus on a particular opportunity for having discussions with like-minded people concerning an issue of concern to society at large that is current in Iran. We can then examine the guidance provided by the Universal House of Justice to the Iranian Bahá'í community to assist it to take full advantage of this opportunity. While the letter is addressed to a particular Bahá'í community, it is suggested that the guidance of the House of Justice sets out broad principles and strategies that potentially have relevance to Bahá'í communities in other parts of the world.

As background to this consideration, it is important to note that since the birth of the Bahá'í Faith in Persia in the middle of the nineteenth century, and continuing to the present day, the Bahá'ís in that land have been subjected to wave after wave of persecution.[49] Despite attacks on their integrity, the destruction of sacred sites associated with the history of its Founders, the ban of Bahá'í administrative institutions, exclusion from educational and employment opportunities, the gross violation of their human rights, the Iranian Bahá'ís, while seeking all legal means to secure their civil rights, have continued to engage in a wide range of activities designed to foster the spiritual, intellectual, and social advancement of the individual members of the community. They have attempted to reach out to the wider society and to be of service to their fellow citizens.

In June, 2008, the Universal House of Justice wrote to the members of the Iranian Bahá'í community encouraging them to consider ways they could "promote the common weal and . . . engage in discourse with the people of Iran on matters of concern to them."[50] The letter set out a number of strategies the community might pursue in responding to the opportunity for service identified by the House of Justice— strategies that both enhanced the potential for success and increased capacity for future initiatives.

As a first step in the process, the House of Justice suggested the Bahá'ís assess the needs of the society in which they resided. It called upon the members of the community to reflect on the "pressing issues" preoccupying their "fellow citizens as they strive to promote the prosperity and well-being" of their nation, and it identified as the "foremost among these . . . the critical need to remove the barriers hindering the progress of women in society."[51]

To assist the Iranian Bahá'í community to formulate its strategic response, the letter of the Universal House of Justice sets out a number of fundamental concepts the Bahá'ís might articulate as a contribution to the discourse about women in society. These concepts address the matter at the level of principle and go to the heart of the underlying problems of contemporary Iranian society. In addition, the guidance contained in the House of Justice's letter prepares the Bahá'ís to confront the criticism often raised in discussions about the equality of women and men, namely that such an issue is not relevant in the East, but purely a matter of interest in the Western world, that the equality of women is contrary to Eastern culture and is something imposed by the West. Countering this potential argument the House of Justice embeds the principle of equality within an Iranian context—it was promulgated by Bahá'u'lláh in Iran—and emphasizes its universal application. The letter states:

> For you [the Iranian Bahá'ís], the equality of men and women is not a Western construct but a universal spiritual truth about an aspect of the nature of human beings, promulgated nearly one hundred and fifty years ago in His homeland, Iran. It is, above all, a requirement of justice. The principle is consonant with the highest rectitude of conduct, its application strengthens family life, and it is essential to the regeneration and progress of any nation, the peace of the world, and the advancement of civilization. As 'Abdu'l-Bahá explained: "The world of humanity has two wings—one is women and the other men. Not until both wings are equally developed can the bird fly. Should one wing remain weak, flight is impossible. Not until the world of women becomes equal to the world of men in the acquisition of virtues and perfections, can success and prosperity be attained as they ought to be."[52]

These words of 'Abdu'l-Bahá cited by the Universal House of Justice underline the practical importance of the equality of women and men to personal, social, and economic development—the promotion of the prosperity and well-being of the nation.

For a Bahá'í community to engage successfully in the prevalent discourses of the wider society, it must be of sufficient size and possess the requisite skills and capacities to undertake such a function. In this regard, the letter of the Universal House of Justice assures the members of the Iranian Bahá'í community that they are "particularly qualified to be of assistance." To reinforce its general reassurance and encouragement, the House of Justice also provided specific examples drawn from the evolution of the Bahá'í Faith in Iran—from its birth until the present day—that illustrate the community's commitment to apply the principle of equality of the sexes together with its evolving capacity and accumulating experience to deal with issues concerning the advancement of women at the level of community-building. Thus the Universal House of Justice refers to

> Ṭáhirih, that peerless heroine of Iranian history, courageously advocated the emancipation of women in 1848, at a time when activity related to this principle was only beginning to gather momentum in parts of the world. From that time on, you have raised generation after generation of your children—both boys and girls—to value and express in every facet of their lives this fundamental tenet of the Faith. In 1911, nearly a century ago, you founded the Tarbíyat School for Girls in Ṭihrán, thereby making an indelible mark on society by providing to girls of all backgrounds the opportunity for education and enlightenment. For almost half a century now, Bahá'í women have participated fully in all the administrative affairs of your community at the local, regional, and national level. And decades ago, you effectively eliminated illiteracy among Bahá'í women under the age of forty.[53]

The examples cited in the passage above could well be used as a broad outline for studying in depth the efforts of the Iranian Bahá'ís to build the capacity of its members to serve their fellow citizens. Regrettably, only a brief sketch of some of the highlights must suffice.

Ṭáhirih, the immortal Bábí heroine, was inspired by the teachings of the New Day. Her courage, dramatic exploits, keen intelligence, and poetic prowess inspired her coreligionists and often shocked the Iranian ruling elites. Ṭáhirih was a Persian native, a truly indigenous role model whose ideas about women and their role in religion and society were far ahead of her time. During her lifetime, her fame and news of her violent martyrdom spread far beyond Iran, electrifying many of the thinking women in Europe and other places.[54]

In relation to the systematic processes of individual and social transformation, Bahá'u'lláh's Revelation provided the spiritual impetus for the removal of barriers hindering the progress of women in society. Among other things, His writings articulated the principle of equality, established it as an integral aspect of the oneness of humankind, made its application a spiritual responsibility, called for equality of rights and opportunity for women and men, set out the role for women in religion and society, promoted education for girls and women, and prohibited violence against women. As parties to the Bahá'í Covenant, the early followers of Bahá'u'lláh in Iran—both women and men—accepted the challenge of beginning to put the teachings into practice in their daily lives, irrespective of the prevailing cultural constraints. The practice of the equality of the sexes required changes in the values and behavior of both men and women. The initiation of their conscious efforts to abide by this principle gave rise, over time, to the dawning of an increased understanding of the implications of the practice of equality for individual and social transformation.

Reinforcing the processes set in motion during the lifetime of Bahá'u'lláh, 'Abdu'l-Bahá gave special attention to the education and advancement of women. Adopting a strategic approach, he focused attention on Iran, which at the time was the largest Bahá'í community in the world and which lacked adequate educational opportunities for the systematic education of girls.

As a result of 'Abdu'l-Bahá's encouragement, modern schools for girls, including the Tarbíyat School for Girls in Ṭihrán, were established in Iran as a means to prepare girls not only for family life but also to enable them to contribute to the advancement of the Bahá'í community and to serve society at large. These schools were renowned for their emphasis on moral and spiritual training, the attitude of respect and dedication shared by students and teachers, high academic standards, progressive curriculum, and the use of modern educational methods, including laboratory-based science classes and gymnastics. To facilitate the introduction of the progressive curriculum and the social acceptance of schools for girls in a cultural environment where systematic attention to the education of girls and women was not customary, 'Abdu'l-Bahá recruited highly-qualified teachers from North America. The Bahá'í schools for girls were open to the general public, and their high reputation attracted the daughters of prominent people. These schools made a unique contribution to the education of girls and the advancement of Iranian women.[55]

Beyond the focus on schools, 'Abdu'l-Bahá also encouraged the formation of women's assemblages in order to raise the capacity of adult women and to prepare them for involvement in society. These gatherings were designed to raise the level of general knowledge and personal competence. They served as a training ground for the development of intellectual and administrative skills necessary for women's confident and effective participation in a wide range of activities within the family and society. Included among the activities were discussions of the application of the Bahá'í teachings to everyday life and its problems. Women's assemblages helped raise the status of women within the Bahá'í community and foster the practice of equality among all its members.[56]

During the ministry of Shoghi Effendi, particular attention was given to the establishment and consolidation of the Bahá'í administrative system throughout the world. The Guardian encouraged the Spiritual Assemblies in Iran to explore ways to promote the social and economic development of the Bahá'í community and to increase the role of women within it. Assemblies were called upon to give leadership to the emancipation and advancement of women. A number of processes were set in motion to achieve this aim. For example, in 1944, the National Spiritual Assembly of Iran established a National Committee for the Advancement of Women, and in 1946, it adopted a four-year plan involving nationwide training programs to prepare women to serve successfully as members of Spiritual Assemblies. In April, 1954, full rights were accorded the Bahá'í women in Iran to participate in the membership of the National and Local Spiritual

Assemblies, removing thereby, in the words of Shoghi Effendi, "the last remaining obstacle to the enjoyment of complete equality of rights in the conduct of the administrative affairs of the Persian Bahá'í community."[57] In this regard, it is interesting to note that in civil society, it was not until 1963 that women in Iran were granted the right to vote and to stand for election.

Since its inception in 1963, the Universal House of Justice has actively fostered the advancement of women and their systematic involvement in all fields of service within the Iranian Bahá'í community. The community has gained a great deal of experience in learning how to apply the principle of equality within the life of the community. Today, women are engaged in promoting the development of the spiritual, social, and economic aspects of Bahá'í community life. They are involved in the world of work and in humanitarian activities, and they are supported in their initiatives by the men in the Bahá'í community.

ELEMENTS OF A STRATEGIC APPROACH

The operation of the systematic processes briefly described above have progressively contributed to the Iranian Bahá'ís acquiring the necessary skills and capacities to understand, explain, and apply the teachings of the Faith to individual and social transformation. On the strength of such learning, the Universal House of Justice thus determined that the Bahá'í community had sufficient capacity to engage with its fellow citizens "to learn together how to promote, step by step, the conditions that will enable the women of Iran to overcome all obstacles and participate fully, as equals of men, in all arenas of human endeavor."[58]

To facilitate and sustain the learning process, the Universal House of Justice sketched out a broad strategic framework to assist the Iranian Bahá'ís. As the heart of its suggested approach is recognition of the need for humility, for ongoing individual and community effort, for a deeper understanding of the principle of the equality of men and women and the challenges associated with achieving fundamental attitudinal and behavioral change, for reflecting and learning from experience, for appreciating the value of collaborative efforts, and for nurturing a culture of learning.

The guidance in the 2008 letter of the House of Justice rejoices in the past accomplishments of the Iranian Bahá'í community and cautions against complacency. If the community is to contribute to the social good, the House of Justice warns, it must continue its efforts "to transcend those cultural practices that impede the progress of women." It reminds the Bahá'ís that the difficulty of changing such long-standing attitudes and behaviors is great, that "The goal of true equality is not easily attained; the transformation required is difficult for men and women alike."[59]

To achieve the fundamental change in the attitudes of women and men and to bring about the cultural change so necessary for the participation of women in all areas of Iranian society, the House of Justice suggests a threefold strategy. The first is directed to changes within the Bahá'í community itself and relates to the high standard of behavior to which its members and community are called to attain; the second relates to sharing with the wider community practical knowledge derived from the experience of attempting to apply the Bahá'í principle of the equality of men and women to everyday life; and the third relates to forging a collaborative relationship with like-minded people to work together to learn how to promote the conditions necessary for social change. The letter states:

> we warmly encourage you to continue to enhance your understanding of this principle and strive to uphold it more fully in your families and in your community. You can, in addition, draw upon your experience to discuss with your friends, neighbors, and co-workers challenges and effective solutions and participate in projects that have this same worthy aim, whether sponsored by the government or originating in civil society.
>
> Many among the people of your country aspire to this universal ideal and will no doubt welcome your joining them to learn together how to promote, step by step, the conditions that will

enable the women of Iran to overcome all obstacles and participate fully, as equals of men, in the arenas of human endeavor.[60]

While the implementation of the strategies outlined by the Universal
House of Justice for the promotion of the advancement of women in
Iran is an ongoing process, there is much that can be learned from the
experience of the Bahá'ís in Iran. Of particular interest is the fact that,
though calling for broad strategic action and a culture of learning,
the approach suggested by the House of Justice is flexible and not
prescriptive. While individuals and communities are required to be
aware of the state of the society in which they live and to be willing to
take responsibility to promote the common good, the approach of the
House of Justice allows for individual initiative and decision-making
at the grassroots that takes into consideration local conditions and
insights derived from experience.

The overall strategy recognizes the underlying role of religion and
spiritual values in social transformation and acknowledges that in the
age of maturity of humankind being ushered in by the Revelation
of Bahá'u'lláh, all cultures require change. The relationship between
spiritual or moral attitudes and the willingness to work for change are
clearly explained by the Universal House of Justice in its letter on peace
addressed to the peoples of the world in 1985. Taking the example of
peace, the House of Justice observes that "the primary challenge in
dealing with issues of peace is to raise the context to the level of principle, as distinct from pure pragmatism. For, in essence, peace stems
from an inner state supported by a spiritual or moral attitude, and
it is chiefly in evoking this attitude that the possibility of enduring
solutions can be found." Generalizing the application of this principle
to other social problems, the House of Justice goes on to describe the
dynamic link between "spiritual principle" and "the discovery and
implementation of practical measures." It writes:

> There are spiritual principles, or what some call human val-
> ues, by which solutions can be found for every social problem.
> Any well-intentioned group can in a general sense devise practi-

cal solutions to its problems, but good intentions and practical knowledge are usually not enough. The essential merit of spiritual principle is that it not only presents a perspective which harmonizes with that which is immanent in human nature, it also induces an attitude, a dynamic, a will, an aspiration, which facilitate the discovery and implementation of practical measures. Leaders of governments and all in authority would be well served in their efforts to solve problems if they would first seek to identify the principles involved and then be guided by them."[61]

The orientation of the Bahá'í community to individual and social transformation is realistic and optimistic, long-term and evolutionary in nature, and driven by commitment to learning. While not discounting the challenges involved in laying the foundations of a new civilization, the writings of the Faith call attention to "the power latent in human endeavor," to the critical role of "ceaseless endeavor" and "indomitable determination" to the achievement of challenging goals.[62]

The engagement of the Bahá'í community with like-minded people in the wider society for the purposes of exchanging ideas and sharing practical experiences of community-building activities provides a learning environment within which ongoing, step by step collaboration can take place and mature as new capacities and skills are acquired for taking on progressively and systematically more complex issues impacting the well-being of fellow citizens. Such an environment will be conducive to the spiritual empowerment of its participants—individuals who, as characterized by the Universal House of Justice, "will come to see themselves as active agents of their own learning, as protagonists of a constant effort to apply knowledge to effect individual and collective transformation."[63]

The long-term contribution of the Bahá'í community to the civilization-building process as its resources continue to increase is assured by the Universal House of Justice. Despite the formidable challenge of translating Bahá'í ideals into reality, and acknowledging that "effecting a transformation at the level of the individual and laying the foundations of suitable social structures, is no small task," the House of Justice nevertheless makes the following commitment: "Yet the Bahá'í community is dedicated to the long-term process of learning that this task entails, an enterprise in which increasing numbers from all walks of life, from every human group, are invited to take part."[64]

Conclusion

The Revelation of Bahá'u'lláh sheds new light on the purpose of God for humankind. Writing on this subject, the Universal House of Justice states, "it refreshes our thoughts; it clarifies and expands our conceptions. His Teachings imbue us with the abundance of God's love for His creatures; they impress upon us the indispensability of justice in human relations and emphasize the importance of adhering to principle in all matters; they inform us that human beings have been created 'to carry forward an ever-advancing civilization' and that the virtues that befit the dignity of every person are: 'forbearance, mercy, compassion and loving-kindness towards all the peoples and kindreds of the earth.'" Commenting further on the purpose of Bahá'u'lláh's Revelation and on the uniqueness of the Bahá'í approach to civilization-building, the Universal House of Justice observes that:

Throughout history, the masses of humanity have been, at best, spectators at the advance of civilization. Their role has been to serve the designs of whatever elite had temporarily assumed control of the process. Even the successive Revelations of the Divine, whose objective was the liberation of the human spirit, were, in time, taken captive by "the insistent self," were frozen into man-made dogma, ritual, clerical privilege and sectarian quarrels, and reached their end with their ultimate purpose frustrated.

Bahá'u'lláh has come to free humanity from this long bondage, and the closing decades of the twentieth century were devoted by the community of His followers to creative experimentation with the means by which His objective can be realized. The prosecution of the Divine Plan entails no less than the involvement of the entire body of humankind in the work of its own spiritual, social and intellectual development.[65]

'Abdu'l-Bahá's call to apostleship in the Tablets of the Divine Plan is, therefore, not only a call to the attainment of a new level of understanding of the divine purpose. It goes further and implies the need for commitment and action both for the worldwide promotion of the Faith and the acquisition of capacities that advance civilization. Firmness in the Covenant, the first prerequisite to attaining the station of Apostle of Bahá'u'lláh, is the avenue by which an individual aligns his or her life's purpose to the divine purpose. The Covenant's transformative motivating force sustains the members of the community in their individual and collective endeavors to change the pattern of human society in conformity with the vision set out in the Revelation of Bahá'u'lláh. The capacity created in the Bahá'í community over time, as illustrated by the example of Iran, renders it "increasingly able to lend assistance in the manifold and diverse dimensions of civilization building."[66]

Highlighting the importance of the contribution of the worldwide Bahá'í community to the long-term processes of social change, the Universal House of Justice states, "The work advancing in every corner of the globe today represents the latest stage of the ongoing Bahá'í endeavor to create the nucleus of the glorious civilization enshrined in His teachings, the building of which is an enterprise of infinite complexity and scale, one that will demand centuries of exertion by humanity to bring to fruition."[67]

It is the Covenant—in the form of the guidance contained in the Bahá'í writings and the counsels of the Institutions of the Faith—that preserves the clarity of vision and mobilizes the united action necessary to accomplish such an inspiring objective.

7

The Second Condition of Apostleship

When Bahá'u'lláh proclaimed His Message to the world in the nineteenth century, He not only laid out the central purpose of His Revelation but also made it abundantly clear that the first step essential for the peace and progress of mankind was its unification: "My object is none other than the betterment of the world and the tranquillity of its peoples. The well-being of mankind, its peace and security, are unattainable unless and until its unity is firmly established. This unity can never be achieved so long as the counsels which the Pen of the Most High hath revealed are suffered to pass unheeded."[1]

In his summary of the principles enshrined in the Tablets revealed by Bahá'u'lláh during the latter years of His life, Shoghi Effendi refers to "the principle of the oneness and wholeness of the human race" as the "most vital," and he characterizes it as "the hall-mark of Bahá'u'lláh's Revelation and the pivot of His teachings." Elaborating on the "cardinal importance" of the principle of unity, the Guardian cites the words of Bahá'u'lláh to highlight its significance:

it is expressly referred to in the Book of His [Bahá'u'lláh's] Covenant, and He unreservedly proclaims it as the central purpose of His Faith. "We, verily," He declares, "have come to unite and weld together all that dwell on earth." "So potent is the light of unity," He further states, "that it can illuminate the whole earth." . . . Unity, He states, is the goal that "excelleth every goal" and an aspiration which is "the monarch of all aspirations." "The world," He proclaims, "is but one country, and mankind its citizens." He further affirms that the unification of mankind, the last stage in the evolution of humanity towards maturity is inevitable, that "soon will the present day order be rolled up, and a new one spread out in its stead," that "the whole earth is now in a state of pregnancy," that "the day is approaching when it will have yielded its noblest fruits, when from it will have sprung forth the loftiest trees, the most enchanting blossoms, the most heavenly blessings." He deplores the defectiveness of the prevailing order, exposes the inadequacy of patriotism as a directing and controlling force in human society, and regards the "love of mankind" and service to its interests as the worthiest and most laudable objects of human endeavor.[2]

Explicating the importance of the principle of the oneness of humankind and emphasizing its scope and the potential impact of its application, Shoghi Effendi writes:

Let there be no mistake. The principle of the Oneness of Mankind—the pivot round which all the teachings of Bahá'u'lláh revolve—is no mere outburst of ignorant emotionalism or an expression of vague and pious hope. Its appeal is not to be merely identified with a reawakening of the spirit of brotherhood and good-will among men, nor does it aim solely at the fostering of harmonious cooperation among individual peoples and nations. Its implications are deeper, its claims greater than any which the Prophets of old were allowed to advance. Its message is applicable not only to the individual, but concerns itself primarily with the nature of those essential relationships that must bind all the states and nations as members of one human family. . . . It implies an organic change in the structure of present-day society, a change such as the world has not experienced. . . . It calls for no less than the reconstruction and the demilitarization of the whole civilized world—a world organically unified in all the essential aspects of its life, its political machinery, its spiritual aspiration, its trade and finance, its script and language, and yet infinite in the diversity of the national characteristics of its federated units.[3]

The centrality of the principle of the oneness of humankind to individual and social transformation is further articulated by the Universal House of Justice in its letter on peace addressed to the peoples of the world: "Acceptance of the oneness of mankind is the first fundamental prerequisite for reorganization and administration of the world as one country, the home of humankind. Universal acceptance of this spiritual principle is essential to any successful attempt to establish world peace. It should therefore be universally proclaimed, taught in schools, and constantly asserted in every nation as preparation for the organic change in the structure of society which it implies."[4]

In chapter 5 mention was made of the dynamic interrelationships between the three conditions for apostleship outlined by 'Abdu'l-Bahá in his Tablets of the Divine Plan—how the first condition—firmness in the Covenant—is intimately connected to the achievement of the other two—fellowship and love among the believers and teaching the Cause. Concerning the relationship between firmness in the Covenant and fellowship and love among the believers, 'Abdu'l-Bahá attests, "It is indubitably clear, that the pivot of the oneness of mankind is nothing else but the power of the Covenant." He, thereby, links firm adherence to the Covenant of God to social cohesion and the preservation of unity: "Today no power can conserve the oneness of the Bahá'í world save the Covenant of God; otherwise differences like unto a most great tempest will encompass the Bahá'í world. It is evident that the axis of the oneness of the world of humanity is the power of the Covenant and nothing else."[5]

The Universal House of Justice has likewise stressed the society-building power of the Covenant and its dynamic connection to unity, asserting that "The pivot of the oneness of humankind is the power of the Covenant, and this power quickens every distinguishing element of Bahá'í life."[6]

The Practice of Oneness

In the Tablets of the Divine Plan, 'Abdu'l-Bahá stresses the importance of the practice of the oneness of mankind in daily life. He designates "fellowship and love among the believers" as the "second condition" for attainment to the station of Apostle of Bahá'u'lláh and the successful achievement of the Divine Plan. And he describes the high standard of conduct associated with this prerequisite: "The divine friends must be attracted to and enamored of each other and ever be ready and willing to sacrifice their own lives for each other. Should one soul from amongst the believers meet another, it must be as though a thirsty one with parched lips has reached to the fountain of the water of life, or a lover has met his true beloved." He also directly links the implementation of the second condition of apostleship to the Covenant by calling attention to the creative and transformative impetus provided by the appearance of the Manifestations of God. "For one of the greatest divine wisdoms regarding the appearance of the holy Manifestations is this," writes 'Abdu'l-Bahá, that

The souls may come to know each other and become intimate with each other; the power of the love of God may make all of them the waves of one sea, the flowers of one rose garden, and the stars of one heaven. This is the wisdom for the appearance of the holy Manifestations! When the most great bestowal reveals itself in the hearts of the believers, the world of nature will be transformed, the darkness of the contingent being will vanish, and heavenly illumination will be obtained. Then the whole world will become the Paradise of Abhá, every one of the believers of God will become a blessed tree, producing wonderful fruits.

O ye friends! Fellowship, fellowship! Love, love! Unity, unity!— so that the power of the Bahá'í Cause may appear and become manifest in the world of existence.[7]

The impassioned call raised by 'Abdu'l-Bahá in the final years of the First World War—for the creation of a united and peaceful world, one characterized by implementation of the principle of oneness, resonates with the needs of contemporary society. In the Tablets of the Divine Plan, he issued the following plea to the American Bahá'ís:

> O ye friends of God! Exert ye with heart and soul, so that association, love, unity and agreement be obtained between the hearts, all the aims may be merged into one aim, all the songs become one song and the power of the Holy Spirit may become so overwhelmingly victorious as to overcome all the forces of the world of nature. Exert yourselves; your mission is unspeakably glorious. Should success crown your enterprise, America will assuredly evolve into a center from which waves of spiritual power will emanate, and the throne of the Kingdom of God will, in the plentitude of its majesty and glory, be firmly established. . . .
>
> Continually my ear and eye are turned toward the Central States; perchance a melody from some blessed souls may reach my ears—souls who are the dawning-places of the love of God, the stars of the horizon of sanctification and holiness—souls who will illumine this dark universe and quicken to life this dead world. The joy of 'Abdu'l-Bahá depends upon this! I hope that you may become confirmed therein.[8]

One hundred years after it was raised, 'Abdu'l-Bahá's plea to the American Bahá'ís has continuing relevance to the whole world. The need for "association, love, unity and agreement" and for concerted unified action is, today, universal. The call to action contained in the Tablets of the Divine Plan, initially addressed to America and now directed to the members of the worldwide Bahá'í community, set in motion civilization-building processes that have evolved over time and are beginning to impact the shape of individual thought and social institutions.[9]

The Promotion of Unity

In the Tablets of the Divine Plan, 'Abdu'l-Bahá did more than simply issue a call for unity. He also provided insight into the means by which human activity is given focus and organized in the world by describing the operation of "collective centers which are conducive to association and unity between the children of men." He takes as examples of this concept "patriotism," "nationalism,' "identity of interests," "political alliance," and "the union of ideals." And he explains that "the prosperity of the world of humanity is dependent upon the organization and promotion of the collective centers."[10]

In broad terms, a collective center functions as a focus for individual and group identity and serves as a rallying point for activity. Individuals derive a sense of identity, purpose, and values from associating themselves with a collective center. These values in turn define the goals and activities of the members of the group. In relation to patriotism, for instance, patriotism is an expression of positive feelings toward one's homeland, the source of the individual's identity as a citizen, and a mobilizing force for collective action. "Membership" bestows certain privileges and responsibilities, such as the rights of citizenship and the responsibility of loyalty and obedience to the law.

While it is an individual's identification with something larger than self that brings people together and allows for civilization to occur, institutions such as nationalism and political alliances tend to be potentially divisive and inherently limited when compared to the Bahá'í standard of the oneness of mankind. Nationalism, for example, embraces the citizens of only one country and excludes the bulk of humankind; it creates boundaries between "self" and "others," and its exclusivity may well give rise to conflict and disunity with other nations. Political alliances, too, often reflect vested interests and are often created to protect narrow partisan interests or to exaggerate the fear of an enemy. Also, as national priorities change, alliances have the potential for instability. Association between the parties is maintained only so long as members continue to derive benefit from the alliance. Commenting on such institutions that, though useful, are capable of achieving lesser degrees of unity, 'Abdu'l-Bahá indicates that they "are, in reality, the matter and not the substance, accidental and not eternal—temporary and not everlasting. With the appearance of great revolutions and upheavals, all these collective centers are swept away."[11]

Contrasting the various limited forms of collective centers with "the real Collective Center," which derives from the Manifestation of God, 'Abdu'l-Bahá is also calling attention to the need for some mechanism to organize and promote "the prosperity of the world of humanity." Identification with the Faith of Bahá'u'lláh and acceptance of its hallmark principle, the oneness of humankind, enlarges one's sense of identity and modifies perceptions of others. The "real Collective Center," 'Abdu'l-Bahá states, will bring about an inclusive and enduring unity, since it encompasses "the body of the divine teachings, which include all the degrees and embrace all the universal relations and necessary laws of humanity." He offers the following explanation concerning how the teachings of the Faith of Bahá'u'lláh, the "Collective Center of the Kingdom," brings about unity:

It establishes relationship between the East and the West, orga- nizes the oneness of the world of humanity, and destroys the foundation of differences. It overcomes and includes all the other collective centers. Like unto the ray of the sun, it dispels entirely the darkness encompassing all the regions, bestows ideal life, and causes the effulgence of divine illumination. Through the breaths of the Holy Spirit it performs miracles; the Orient and the Occi- dent embrace each other, the North and South become intimates and associates, conflicting and contending opinions disappear, antagonistic aims are brushed aside, the law of the struggle for existence is abrogated, and the canopy of the oneness of the world of humanity is raised on the apex of the globe, casting its shade over all the races of men.[12]

The Dynamic Powers of the Collective Center

Before examining themes associated with the dynamic powers of "the Collective Center of the Kingdom" to achieve the oneness of human- kind, it is interesting to note that 'Abdu'l-Bahá not only designates the "power of the Covenant" as "the pivot of the oneness of mankind," he also calls attention to the fundamental means by which change occurs through the operation of the inspirational and educational forces deriving from the teachings of the Manifestation of God. "The power of the Covenant," he writes, "is as the heat of the sun which quickeneth and promoteth the development of all created things on earth. The light of the Covenant, in like manner, is the educator of the minds, the spirits, the hearts and souls of men."[13]

While the pivot of the oneness of humankind is the power of the Covenant, it is this same power which "quickens every distinguishing element of Bahá'í life." In the passage concerning the "Collective Center of the Kingdom," cited above, 'Abdu'l-Bahá outlines a number of interacting processes pertaining to the attainment of unity which are associated with the Collective Center and which derive from the practice of the teachings of Bahá'u'lláh. These processes define an approach to individual and social change and give direction to actions to be taken by the believers as they strive to implement 'Abdu'l-Bahá's second condition of apostleship, namely unity and fellowship.[14]

IDENTIFYING AND DESTROYING
THE FOUNDATION OF DIFFERENCES

The degree of unity and the scope of individual and social change described in the Revelation of Bahá'u'lláh is vast. The fundamental change envisioned by Bahá'u'lláh is at the level of values and action, requiring "a transformation in the whole character of mankind, a transformation that shall manifest itself both outwardly and inwardly, that shall affect both its inner life and external conditions."[15]

In relation to the attainment of the degree of unity implied by the principle of the oneness of humankind, the approach to change suggested in the Bahá'í writings involves identifying the fundamental causes of disunity and focusing on removing the barriers that keep people apart by applying the relevant spiritual principles and teachings. In this regard, 'Abdu'l-Bahá includes among the transformative powers associated with the Collective Center its ability to destroy "the foundation of differences." While differences between peoples may well be due to many diverse causes, the Universal House of Justice asserts that, at a fundamental level, the underlying factor common to all is some form of prejudice: "World order can be founded only on an unshakable consciousness of the oneness of mankind, a spiritual truth which all the human sciences confirm. Anthropology, physiology, psychology, recognize only one human species, albeit infinitely varied in the secondary aspects of life. Recognition of this truth requires abandonment of prejudice—prejudice of every kind—race, class, color, creed, nation, sex, degree of material civilization, everything which enables people to consider themselves superior to others." Having identified "prejudice of every kind" as the fundamental cause and "the oneness of mankind" as the relevant spiritual principle needed to destroy "the foundation of differences," the House of Justice prescribes "abandonment of prejudice" as the necessary remedial action, noting, "Acceptance of the oneness of mankind is the first fundamental prerequisite for reorganization and administration of the world as one country, the home of humankind."[16]

While change is addressed at the level of principle, it does not stop there. It demands more than the mere articulation of an ideal. It requires acquiring new habits and behaviors and committed concerted action over a long period of time. Identifying the oneness of humankind as "the principle that is to infuse all facets of organized life on the planet," the Universal House of Justice writes "That humanity constitutes a single people is a truth that, once viewed with scepticism, claims widespread acceptance today. The rejection of deeply ingrained prejudices and a growing sense of world citizenship are among the signs of this heightened awareness. Yet, however promising the rise in collective consciousness may be, it should be seen as only the first step of a process that will take decades—nay centuries—to unfold." Commenting on the nature and extent of the transformation required the House of Justice observes: "the principle of the oneness of humankind, as proclaimed by Bahá'u'lláh, asks not merely for cooperation among people and nations. It calls for a complete reconceptualization of the relationships that sustain society." The House of Justice offers the following examples of contemporary social relationships and institutional structures in need of reexamination and change:

The deepening environmental crisis, driven by a system that condones the pillage of natural resources to satisfy an insatiable thirst for more, suggests how entirely inadequate is the present conception of humanity's relationship with nature; the deterioration of the home environment, with the accompanying rise in the systematic exploitation of women and children worldwide, makes clear how pervasive are the misbegotten notions that define relations within the family unit; the persistence of despotism, on the one hand, and the increasing disregard for authority, on the other, reveal how unsatisfactory to a maturing humanity is the current relationship between the individual and the institutions of society; the concentration of material wealth in the hands of a minority of the world's population gives an indication of how fundamentally ill-conceived are relations among the many sectors of what is now an emerging global community. The principle of the oneness of humankind implies, then, an organic change in the very structure of society.[17]

The mobilization of support necessary to bring about change on a global level, and the unfoldment of the transformations envisioned in the writings of the Faith are illustrated in the following statement from a letter of the Universal House of Justice:

Every nation and every group—indeed, every individual—will, to a greater or lesser degree, contribute to the emergence of the world civilization towards which humanity is irresistibly moving. Unity will progressively be achieved, as foreshadowed by 'Abdu'l-Bahá, in different realms of social existence for instance, "unity in the political realm," "unity of thought in world undertakings," "unity of races" and the "unity of nations." As these come to be realized, the structures of a politically united world, which respects the full diversity of culture and provides channels for the expression of dignity and honor, will gradually take shape.[18]

'Abdu'l-Bahá's call to fellowship, unity, and love among the believers in the Tablets of the Divine Plan might well be seen as representing an admonition to unity of action. In one of his talks, he describes the spiritual foundation of the bond that must unite the believers and the practical courses of action to which this bond gives rise:

> The great and fundamental teachings of Bahá'u'lláh are the oneness of God and unity of mankind. This is the bond of union among Bahá'ís all over the world. They become united among themselves, then unite others. It is impossible to unite unless united. . . .
>
> Now must we . . . bind ourselves together in the utmost unity, be kind and loving to each other, sacrificing all our possessions, our honor, yea, even our lives for each other. Then will it be proved that we have acted according to the teachings of God, that we have been real believers in the oneness of God and unity of mankind.[19]

To be effective, change in consciousness must be accompanied both by a firm commitment to action and by action itself. 'Abdu'l-Bahá stresses the importance of spreading "the spirit of the divine teachings" which derives from "the Collective Center of the sacred religions," so that "the world of humanity may become enlightened." Emphasizing the importance of such action, he states, "Should you become confirmed therein, this world will become another world, the surface of the earth will become the delectable paradise, and eternal Institutions be founded."[20]

Implementation of the second condition of apostleship, fellowship and love among the believers, involves transformation at the level of spiritual principle and individual and social action. In practical terms, it requires the reexamination of assumptions and existing cultural values and practices in light of the teachings of the Manifestation of God, and concerted action based on the principle of the oneness of mankind. Bahá'ís are, therefore, engaged in a variety of activities aimed at changing both individuals and social institutions. They are striving "to establish a pattern of activity and the corresponding administrative structures that embody the principle of the oneness of humankind and the convictions underpinning it."[21]

To understand the complexity of the task and the potential challenges involved in effecting fundamental change in social behavior and institutions, it is necessary to examine some of the "convictions" that underlie the principle of the oneness of humankind, and to reflect on their society-building implications. A recent letter of the Universal House of Justice highlights the significance of these underlying convictions, lists a number of barriers that stand in the way of unity, describes the social implications of these particular barriers, and suggests actions that might be taken to bring about change. In the extract, cited below, the House of Justice includes among these foundational convictions:

that the rational soul has no gender, race, ethnicity or class, a fact that renders intolerable all forms of prejudice, not the least of which are those that prevent women from fulfilling their potential and engaging in various fields of endeavor shoulder to shoulder with men; that the root cause of prejudice is ignorance, which can be erased through educational processes that make knowledge accessible to the entire human race, ensuring it does not become the property of a privileged few; that science and religion are two complementary systems of knowledge and practice by which human beings come to understand the world around them and through which civilization advances; that religion without science soon degenerates into superstition and fanaticism, while science without religion becomes the tool of crude materialism; that true prosperity, the fruit of a dynamic coherence between the material and spiritual requirements of life, will recede further and further out of reach as long as consumerism continues to act as opium to the human soul; that justice, as a faculty of the soul, enables the individual to distinguish truth from falsehood and guides the investigation of reality, so essential if superstitious beliefs and outworn traditions that impede unity are to be eliminated; that, when appropriately brought to bear on social issues, justice is the single most important instrument for the establishment of unity; that work performed in the spirit of service to one's fellow human beings is a form of prayer, a means of worshipping God.[22]

The Bahá'í community does not underestimate the challenges involved. Recognizing that it is "no small task," to translate "ideals such as these into reality, [thereby] effecting a transformation at the level of the individual and laying the foundations of suitable social structures," the Bahá'ís are dedicated to a long-term learning process aimed at forging a new set of relationships binding the individual, the community, and the institutions of society.[23] Rather than being competitive and adversarial in nature, the new relationships that are emerging are governed by the principle of cooperation.

PROMOTING UNITY IN DIVERSITY

The "Collective Center of the Kingdom," not only has the means to remove the foundations of disunity it also has the capacity to bring about an enduring and more inclusive unity, a unity that transcends the inherent limitations of other collective centers—"national," "patriotic," "political," and the "cultural and intellectual collective center." The "potency of the Word of God" serves as a force for unity of thought and promotes social and institutional change. Through it 'Abdu'l-Bahá states, "this world will become another world, the surface of the earth will become the delectable paradise, and eternal Institutions be founded."[24]

While the Bahá'í principle of the oneness of mankind calls for recognition of the oneness of the members of the human family, it does not seek to impose a narrow uniformity. To describe the seminal power of religion to transform cultures, 'Abdu'l-Bahá uses the analogy of a garden to illustrate the application of the concept of unity in diversity and the means by which it is attained. He invites us to

> Consider the flowers of a garden. Though differing in kind, color, form, and shape, yet, inasmuch as they are refreshed by the waters of one spring, revived by the breath of one wind, invigorated by the rays of one sun, this diversity increaseth their charm, and addeth unto their beauty. How unpleasing to the eye if all the flowers and plants, the leaves and blossoms, the fruits, the branches and the trees of that garden were all of the same

shape and color! Diversity of hues, form and shape, enricheth and adorneth the garden, and heighteneth the effect thereof. In like manner, when divers shades of thought, temperament and character, are brought together under the power and influence of one central agency, the beauty and glory of human perfection will be revealed and made manifest. Naught but the celestial potency of the Word of God, which ruleth and transcendeth the realities of all things, is capable of harmonizing the divergent thoughts, sentiments, ideas, and convictions of the children of men.[25]

The Bahá'í principle of the oneness of humankind is broad and inclusive and welcomes diversity. Nevertheless, its application mandates a change in consciousness and action to transcend limited views and to accommodate an enlargement of perspective. Shoghi Effendi makes it clear that the "call of Bahá'u'lláh is primarily directed against" "all forms of provincialism, all insularities and prejudices." He clarifies that, in no way, does the Faith aim at subverting the "existing foundations of society," rather, "it seeks to broaden its basis, to remold its institutions in a manner consonant with the needs of an ever-changing world. . . . It does not ignore, nor does it attempt to suppress, the diversity of ethnical origins, of climate, of history, of language and tradition, of thought and habit, that differentiate the peoples and nations of the world. It calls for a wider loyalty, for a larger aspiration than any that has animated the human race. It insists upon the subordination of national impulses and interests to the imperative claims of a unified world. . . . Its watchword is unity in diversity . . ."[26]

Responding to questions about cultural diversity and the application of the principle of oneness, the Universal House of Justice, in a letter written on its behalf, outlined the standard to be upheld within the Bahá'í community: "It is abundantly evident, from innumerable passages in Bahá'u'lláh's Revelation, that His Message is intended for the whole of mankind and that every nation and race in human society should regard Him as a Manifestation of God Whose teachings are directed to their upliftment and happiness. . . . The Bahá'í community should regard itself as having been commissioned by Bahá'u'lláh to deliver His Message to the whole of humankind, in obedience to His injunction to 'Proclaim the Cause of thy Lord unto all who are in the heavens and on the earth." And, addressing the "issue of cultural diversity within the Bahá'í community," the House of Justice stated, "The Faith seeks to maintain cultural diversity while promoting the unity of all peoples. Indeed, such diversity will enrich the tapestry of human life in a peaceful world society. The House of Justice supports the view that in every country the cultural traditions of the people should be observed within the Bahá'í community as long as they are not contrary to the Teachings."[27]

In a subsequent letter, the Universal House of Justice stressed the universal application of the standard referred to above and described its long-term implications for change:

People everywhere have customs which must be abandoned so as to clear the path along which their societies must evolve towards that glorious, new civilization which is to be the fruit of Bahá'u'lláh's stupendous Revelation. Indeed, in no society on earth can there be found practices which adequately mirror the standards of His Cause. His own truth-bearing Words clarify the matter: "The summons and the message which We gave were never intended to reach or to benefit one land or one people only. Mankind in its entirety must firmly adhere to whatsoever hath been revealed and vouchsafed unto it. Then and only then will it attain unto true liberty. The whole earth is illuminated with the resplendent glory of God's Revelation."[28]

The application of the principle of the oneness of humankind at an individual and collective level calls for an enlargement of context with new thinking and new patterns of activity. In striving for change, individual rights and cultural diversity must be upheld. The Universal House of Justice offers the following elucidation:

. . . the oneness of mankind will not be based on forced assimilation, but upon protection of cultural diversity. At the same time, however, we should beware of inadvertently settling upon a limited model, such as the one sometimes associated in contemporary discourse on multiculturalism. A distinctively Bahá'í culture will welcome an infinite diversity in regard to secondary characteristics, but also firmly uphold unity in regard to fundamental principles, thereby achieving a vigorous complementarity. For example, in *Selections from the Writings of 'Abdu'l-Bahá* (Haifa: Bahá'í World Centre, 1982), page 260–1, we find the following intriguing statement:

> "What a blessing that will be—when all shall come together, even as once separate torrents, rivers and streams, running brooks and single drops, when collected together in one place will form a mighty sea. And to such a degree will the inherent unity of all prevail, that the traditions, rules, customs and distinctions in the fanciful life of these populations will be effaced and vanish away like isolated drops, once the great sea of oneness doth leap and surge and roll."

The point is neither to minimize differences, nor to make of unity and diversity a false dichotomy, but ever to keep in mind that the Bahá'í standard is very high and grounded in divine love.[29]

ORGANIZING THE ONENESS OF THE WORLD OF HUMANITY

Implementation of the principle of the oneness of humankind defines the context and gives direction to the pursuit of the second condition of apostleship, which is fellowship and love among the believers. In addition to impacting individual consciousness, the civilization-building processes fostered by the Tablets of the Divine Plan are progressively remolding the relationships that bind the individual, the community, and the institutions of society. In the words of 'Abdu'l-Bahá, "The greatest of instrumentalities for achieving the advancement and the glory of man, the supreme agency for the enlightenment and the redemption of the world, is love and fellowship and unity among all the members of the human race. Nothing can be effected in the world, not even conceivably, without unity and agreement, and the perfect means for engendering fellowship and union is true religion."[30]

As noted above, in the Tablets of the Divine Plan, 'Abdu'l-Bahá refers to the society-building implications of oneness and suggests the need for a vehicle to organize and promote unity and agreement. He identifies the unique organizational potential of religion, the "Collective Center of the Kingdom," as a force both for achieving unity of thought and for bringing together people from different cultural backgrounds. Confirming the capacity of the "Collective Center of the Kingdom" to overcome barriers and to promote change, 'Abdu'l-Bahá states that it "organizes the oneness of the world of humanity" and it "overcomes and includes all the other collective centers."[31]

The Bahá'í approach to the systematic promotion and organization of the oneness of the world of humanity draws inspiration and overall direction from the teachings of the Faith and the guidance of its institutions. The success of this undertaking requires attending to a number of interacting processes that further the development of the "three protagonists in the Divine Plan"—the individual, the institutions, and the community. Stressing the importance of such a multifaceted strategy in light of the often fractious relationships between the individual, the institutions, and the community in contemporary society, the Universal House of Justice observes:

Throughout human history, interactions among these three have been fraught with difficulties at every turn, with the individual clamoring for freedom, the institution demanding submission, and the community claiming precedence. Every society has defined, in one way or another, the relationships that bind the three, giving rise to periods of stability, interwoven with turmoil. Today, in this age of transition, as humanity struggles to attain its collective maturity, such relationships—nay, the very conception of the individual, of social institutions, and of the community— continue to be assailed by crises too numerous to count. The worldwide crisis of authority provides proof enough. So grievous

209

have been its abuses, and so deep the suspicion and resentment it now arouses, that the world is becoming increasingly ungovernable—a situation made all the more perilous by the weakening of community ties.[32]

The Universal House of Justice offers the following view of the way in which the teachings of the Faith are beginning to reshape relationships and social institutions:

Every follower of Bahá'u'lláh knows well that the purpose of His Revelation is to bring into being a new creation. No sooner had "the First Call gone forth from His lips than the whole creation was revolutionized, and all that are in the heavens and all that are on earth were stirred to the depths." The individual, the institutions, and the community—the three protagonists in the Divine Plan—are being shaped under the direct influence of His Revelation, and a new conception of each, appropriate for a humanity that has come of age, is emerging. The relationships that bind them, too, are undergoing a profound transformation, bringing into the realm of existence civilization-building powers which can only be released through conformity with His decree. At a fundamental level these relationships are characterized by cooperation and reciprocity, manifestations of the interconnectedness that governs the universe.[33]

The emphasis on cooperation, love, and unity among the believers and beyond is, if anything, of even greater importance in the present chaotic state of the world than it was in the days of 'Abdu'l-Bahá. Everywhere, "people are longing for an example—proof that harmony and love can actually exist in a community—and it is one of the primary duties of the Bahá'ís to demonstrate these great principles in their relations with each other."[34]

Taking up this duty, the Bahá'í community has, over time, engaged in a series of global plans whose inspiration derives from the Tablets of the Divine Plan and whose most recent action priorities and provisions are established by the Universal House of Justice and implemented under the direction of the institutions of the Faith. The major focus of these plans is on expanding the size of the Bahá'í community, developing capacity-building, and enabling collective action. As noted in chapter 6, in addressing this task, the community has progressively adopted a learning mode of operation characterized by action, reflection, consultation, and study, a kind of study that involves not only constant reference to the writings of the Faith but also the scientific analysis of the unfolding patterns of growth.

At the center of the learning process are the core activities associated with the training institute (the establishment of study circles, devotional meetings, classes for children, and junior youth groups) and enhancing the degree of coherence of action achieved among them. The Universal House of Justice stresses the importance of such coherence since it "provides the initial impulse for growth in a cluster, an impulse that gathers strength as these core activities multiply in number." "It is evident," the House of Justice states, "that a systematic approach to training has created a way for Bahá'ís to reach out to the surrounding society, share Bahá'u'lláh's message with friends, family, neighbours and co-workers, and expose them to the richness of His teachings. This outward-looking orientation is one of the finest fruits of the grassroots learning taking place. The pattern of activity that is being established in clusters around the globe constitutes a proven means of accelerating expansion and consolidation. Yet this is only a beginning."[35]

The Universal House of Justice describes the nature of the individual and collective transformation that accompanies the evolution of the pattern of action emerging within the cluster:

> Central to the pattern of action evolving in a cluster is the individual and collective transformation effected through the agency of the Word of God. From the beginning of the sequence of courses, a participant encounters Bahá'u'lláh's Revelation in

considering such weighty themes as worship, service to humanity, the life of the soul, and the education of children and youth. As a person cultivates the habit of study and deep reflection upon the Creative Word, this process of transformation reveals itself in an ability to express one's understanding of profound concepts and to explore spiritual reality in conversations of significance. These capacities are visible not only in the elevated discussions that increasingly characterize interactions within the community, but in the ongoing conversations that reach well beyond . . . Through exchanges of this kind, consciousness of spiritual forces is raised, apparent dichotomies yield to unexpected insights, a sense of unity and common calling is fortified, confidence that a better world can be created is strengthened, and a commitment to action becomes manifest. Such distinctive conversations gradually attract ever-larger numbers to take part in a range of community activities. Themes of faith and certitude surface naturally, prompted by the receptivity and experiences of those involved. What is clear, then, is that as the institute process in a cluster gains momentum, the act of teaching comes to assume greater prominence in the lives of the friends.[36]

Beyond extending the influence of the Bahá'í Faith, one's participation in the activities of the Bahá'í community provides a matrix within which one can effect true and lasting change and has the potential to impact the wider society. For example, in response to questions about steps the Bahá'í community could take to address the challenge of racial prejudice, the Universal House of Justice underlined the assets existing within the framework of action currently being pursued by the Bahá'í community and suggested a multifaceted approach. The House of Justice stressed the value of the core activities and the mode of learning employed by the community; it called attention to the importance of developing personal responsibility, of drawing on the guidance in the writings, and of maintaining a loving environment; and it cautioned about the need for flexibility and spelled out the role of the administrative institutions. It wrote:

The pattern of spiritual and social life taking shape in clusters that involves study circles, children's classes, junior youth groups, devotional meetings, home visits, teaching efforts, and reflection meetings, as well as Holy Day observances, Nineteen Day Feasts, and other gatherings, provides abundant opportunities for engagement, experience, consultation, and learning that will lead to change in personal and collective understanding and action. Issues of prejudice of race, class, and color will inevitably arise as the friends reach out to diverse populations, especially in the closely knit context of neighborhoods. There, every activity can take a form most suited to the culture and interests of the population, so that new believers can be quickened and confirmed in a nurturing and familiar environment, until they are able to offer their share to the resolution of the challenges faced by a growing Bahá'í community. For this is not a process that some carry out on behalf of others who are passive recipients—the mere extension of a congregation and invitation to paternalism—but one in which an ever-increasing number of souls recognize and take responsibility for the transformation of humanity set in motion by Bahá'u'lláh. In an environment of love and trust born of common belief, practice, and mission, individuals of different races will have the intimate connection of heart and mind upon which mutual understanding and change depend. As a result of their training and deepening, a growing number of believers will draw insights from the Writings to sensitively and effectively address issues of racial prejudice that arise within their personal lives and families, among community members, and in social settings and the workplace. As programs of growth advance and the scope and intensity of activities grow, the friends will be drawn into participation in conversations and, in time, initiatives for social action at the grassroots where issues pertaining to freedom from prejudice naturally emerge, whether directly or indirectly. And, at the national level, the National Assembly will guide, through its Office of External Affairs, the engagement of the Faith with other agencies and individuals in the discourse pertaining to race unity.[37]

At its core, the Bahá'í effort to discover the nature of a new set of relationships among the individual, the institutions, and the community is animated by a vision of a future society that derives inspiration from the analogy used by Bahá'u'lláh, in which He compares the world to the human body. Illustrating the application of this analogy, the Universal House of Justice identifies "cooperation" as "the principle" that governs the functioning of both the human and social systems:

> Just as the appearance of the rational soul in this realm of existence is made possible through the complex association of countless cells, whose organization in tissues and organs allows for the realization of distinctive capacities, so can civilization be seen as the outcome of a set of interactions among closely integrated, diverse components which have transcended the narrow purpose of tending to their own existence. And just as the viability of every cell and every organ is contingent upon the health of the body as a whole, so should the prosperity of every individual, every family, every people be sought in the well-being of the entire human race. In keeping with such a vision, institutions, appreciating the need for coordinated action channeled toward fruitful ends, aim not to control but to nurture and guide the individual, who, in turn, willingly receives guidance, not in blind obedience, but with faith founded on conscious knowledge. The community, meanwhile, takes on the challenge of sustaining an environment where the powers of individuals, who wish to exercise self-expression responsibly in accordance with the common weal and the plans of institutions, multiply in unified action.[38]

While the learning process embarked upon by the Bahá'í community is ongoing and much more needs to be accomplished before the desired set of interactions emerge, nevertheless, the systematic civilization-building efforts taking place within the community are, step by step, remolding relationships in accord with the visionary teachings of Bahá'u'lláh. These efforts are gradually giving rise to a pattern of life that is distinguished by adherence to the principle of the oneness of humankind.

It is evident that attainment to the second condition of apostleship—the practice of fellowship, unity, and love among the believers, and ultimately in relation to humanity as a whole—involves a great deal more than a spiritual and emotional response on the part of concerned, well-meaning individuals. The three protagonists—the individual, the institutions, and the community—are all challenged to uphold the "high ideals" of the Faith and to "become their embodiment."[39] Whether as individuals or as a community, Bahá'ís endeavor to put into practice the commands of Bahá'u'lláh. Furthermore, each protagonist also has a unique role to play in creating a united world. To achieve a coherent pattern of life renowned for adherence to the principle of oneness, the institutions of the Faith give specific focus and direction to promoting and organizing the capacity-building processes engaged in by the three protagonists—individuals, institutions, and community.

ROLE OF THE BAHÁ'Í ADMINISTRATIVE ORDER

In earlier chapters, we have described elements of the Bahá'í Administrative Order, its major institutions and functions, its evolution over time, and its capacity to deal with increasing levels of complexity as it expands and consolidates itself and engages more and more with society at large. Anticipating the unfolding contribution of the Administrative Order to the processes leading to the emergence of social order, Shoghi Effendi affirms, "It will, as its component parts, its organic institutions, begin to function with efficiency and vigor, assert its claim and demonstrate its capacity to be regarded not only as the nucleus but the very pattern of the New World Order destined to embrace in the fullness of time the whole of mankind."[40]

The Administrative Order contributes to the promotion of unity and the organization of the oneness of humankind. As an integral aspect of Bahá'u'lláh's Revelation and deriving their authority from the writings of the Faith, the institutions of the Administrative Order might be regarded as constituting part of the Collective Center of the Kingdom.

The administrative institutions act as a channel for the spirit released by Bahá'u'lláh. They serve as a point of authority in the community, a rallying point for community members, and a focus for collective activity. The institutions provide leadership for the community, foster adherence to spiritual laws and practices, seek out diversity, and devise programs for the orderly and systematic advancement of the community and for the spiritual, social, and intellectual education of all its members. They also actively foster the participation of community members in the spiritual maturation of society by providing service opportunities for the development of the capacities and skills necessary to effect individual and social transformation.

The institutions of the Administrative Order not only perform a dynamic organizational and decision-making function, but the manner in which these institutions operate is also directly related to the quality of the relationships they develop with individuals and the community at large. Conscious of the impact of their communications on the emergence of constructive relationships reflecting the principle of the oneness of humankind, Bahá'í institutions also focus on the development of their own functioning. For example, the letter of the Universal House of Justice cited below describes the operation of a Local Spiritual Assembly and highlights the complexity of the interacting community-building processes binding the individual, the Spiritual Assembly, and the Bahá'í community:

> The divinely ordained institution of the Local Spiritual Assembly operates at the first levels of human society and is the basic administrative unit of Bahá'u'lláh's World Order. It is concerned with individuals and families whom it must constantly encourage to unite in a distinctive Bahá'í society, vitalized and guarded by the laws, ordinances and principles of Bahá'u'lláh's Revelation. It protects the Cause of God; it acts as the loving shepherd of the Bahá'í flock.

Strengthening and development of Local Spiritual Assemblies is a vital objective . . . Success in this one goal will greatly enrich the quality of Bahá'í life, will heighten the capacity of the Faith to deal with entry by troops which is even now taking place and, above all, will demonstrate the solidarity and ever-growing distinctiveness of the Bahá'í community, thereby attracting more and more thoughtful souls to the Faith and offering a refuge to the leaderless and hapless millions of the spiritually bankrupt, moribund present order. . . .

The friends are called upon to give their whole-hearted support and cooperation to the Local Spiritual Assembly, first by voting for the membership and then by energetically pursuing its plans and programs, by turning to it in time of trouble or difficulty, by praying for its success and taking delight in its rise to influence and honor. This great prize, this gift of God within each community must be cherished, nurtured, loved, assisted, obeyed and prayed for.

Such a firmly founded, busy and happy community life as is envisioned when Local Spiritual Assemblies are truly effective, will provide a firm home foundation from which the friends may derive courage and strength and loving support in bearing the Divine Message to their fellow-men and conforming their lives to its benevolent rule.[41]

The institutions of the Bahá'í Administrative Order have a critical role in facilitating "the emergence and maintenance of community life in a wholly new mode, and in catering to the requirements of the spiritual relationships which flow from love and unity among the friends." Described by the House of Justice, as "a distinguishing characteristic of Baha'i life," such spiritual relationships "foster . . . the spirit of servitude to God, expressed in service to the Cause, to the friends and to humanity as a whole. The attitude of the individual as a servant, an attitude pre-eminently exemplified in the life and person of 'Abdu'l-Bahá, is a dynamic that permeates the activities of the Faith; it acquires collective, transformative force in the normal functioning of a community. In this regard, the institutions of the Faith stand as channels for the promotion of this salient characteristic."[42]

CONTRIBUTION OF THE BAHÁ'Í COMMUNITY

A major goal of a Spiritual Assembly is the appearance of a united, firmly-based, and self-sustaining community, a community committed to the practice of the principle of the oneness of humankind. Not only does the Spiritual Assembly share responsibility for the promotion of such a community with the individual believer, but beyond that, the achievement of unity requires the collective action of the members of the community to demonstrate in their constructive relationships with each other and with the institutions the distinctive Bahá'í way of life.

'Abdu'l-Bahá identifies the "supreme need of humanity," as "cooperation and reciprocity." "The stronger the ties of fellowship and solidarity amongst men," he asserts, "the greater will be the power of constructiveness and accomplishment in all the planes of human activity. Without cooperation and reciprocal attitude the individual member of human society remains self-centered, uninspired by altruistic purposes, limited and solitary in development . . ."[43]

Stressing the importance of this collective transformation, the Universal House of Justice writes:

> Wherever a Bahá'í community exists, whether large or small, let it be distinguished for its abiding sense of security and faith, its high standard of rectitude, its complete freedom from all forms of prejudice, the spirit of love among its members and for the closely knit fabric of its social life. The acute distinction between this and present-day society will inevitably arouse the interest of the more enlightened, and as the world's gloom deepens the light of Bahá'í life will shine brighter and brighter until its brilliance must eventually attract the disillusioned masses and cause them to enter the haven of the Covenant of Bahá'u'lláh, Who alone can bring them peace and justice and an ordered life.[44]

The maintenance of a climate of love and unity is dependent on cooperative interactions between both the individual members of the community and the Spiritual Assembly. The quality of the relationship between both the institution and their fellow believers encourages "a spirit of enterprise invigorated by an awareness of the revolutionizing purpose of Bahá'u'lláh's Revelation, by a consciousness of the high privilege of their being associated with efforts to realize that purpose, and by a consequent, ever-present sense of joy." "In such a climate," the Universal House of Justice states, "the community is transformed from being the mere sum of its parts to assuming a wholly new personality as an entity in which its members blend without losing their individual uniqueness."[45]

The contribution of the Bahá'í community to society-building is clear. It is called upon to accomplish a spiritual transformation of its members and institutions and offer to the world a model of a united and peaceful society destined to come into being through the power of the Revelation of Bahá'u'lláh. With a membership reflecting a diversity of backgrounds, talents, and interests, and the emergence of a pattern of constructive interactions between the Assembly and the body of the believers, characterized by a common commitment to service and a sense of partnership, the Bahá'í community may well be seen as a tangible example of an enlarging unity, as a step toward the evolution of a civilization renowned for adherence to the principle of the oneness of humankind.

While the development of the Bahá'í community is very much a work in progress, in its statement on peace addressed to the peoples of the world, the Universal House of Justice offered the experience of the Bahá'í community to the world as "a model for study":

It is a community of some three to four million people drawn from many nations, cultures, classes and creeds, engaged in a wide range of activities serving the spiritual, social and economic needs of the peoples of many lands. It is a single social organism, representative of the diversity of the human family, conducting

219

its affairs through a system of commonly accepted consultative principles, and cherishing equally all the great outpourings of divine guidance in human history. Its existence is yet another convincing proof of the practicality of its Founder's vision of a united world, another evidence that humanity can live as one global society, equal to whatever challenges its coming of age may entail. If the Bahá'í experience can contribute in whatever measure to reinforcing hope in the unity of the human race, we are happy to offer it as a model for study.[46]

PROMOTING THE WELL-BEING OF HUMANITY

In the Tablets of the Divine Plan, reflecting on the condition of the world, 'Abdu'l-Bahá characterizes war as "the destroyer of the foundation of man," and peace as "the founder of the prosperity of the human race." He directly links "the prosperity of the world of humanity" to "the organization and promotion of collective centers." It follows, then, that the interacting processes giving rise to the pattern of collaborative relationships between the individual, the institutions, and the community do more than contribute to a mere climate of love and unity, they also have significant practical social implications. They promote and contribute to the material well-being of society and the attainment of peace. As the Bahá'í community increases in size and its members and institutions develop the necessary capacities, they progressively engage with the wider community in efforts to deal with the problems confronting society. They "enter into collaboration, as their resources permit, with an increasing number of movements, organizations, groups and individuals, establishing partnerships that strive to transform society and further the cause of unity, promote human welfare, and contribute to world solidarity."[47]

The mission of the Faith of Bahá'u'lláh is to establish world unity. The achievement of this transformative mission involves not only a profound change in human values—the emergence of a deep and abiding appreciation of the oneness and wholeness of humankind, but also the creation of global institutions necessary for the establishment of just and unified relationships between the peoples and nations of the world. War must be eliminated and universal peace firmly established. This far-reaching vision of the future of humanity, set out in the Bahá'í writings, is referred to as the World Order of Bahá'u'lláh. The Bahá'í Administrative Order constitutes the first shaping of the future World Order. It represents the "nucleus" and "pattern" of a new social order destined to bring about the unification of humankind. It laws and institutions are "destined to be a pattern for future society, a supreme instrument for the establishment of the Most Great Peace and the one agency for the unification of the world, and the proclamation of the reign of righteousness and justice upon the earth."[48]

While Bahá'ís maintain that their Faith and its Administrative Order have an important role to play in the process of creating a united and peaceful world and they confidently work to establish the future World Order, they do not believe that the new Order will be brought into existence solely through their own efforts or the influence of their faith. In building for the future, they seek collaboration with peoples and organizations committed to the principle of the oneness of humankind and working to uphold human rights. Bahá'ís acknowledge the important steps taken by the League of Nations and the United Nations toward the emergence of a system of global governance based on justice; and they recognize that the achievement of such ends requires stages in the adjustment of national and international political attitudes, in the accepted and enforceable principles regulating the relationships between nations.

The Bahá'í teachings indicate that the unfoldment of World Order will occur in an evolutionary manner and will be associated with the gradual emergence of peace: First, progress toward the World Order will be marked by the establishment of the Lesser Peace, a form of political peace entered into by the nations by international agreement. The Bahá'í teachings envisage that the Lesser Peace will emerge from the suffering and social upheavals of the contemporary world. According to Hatcher and Martin, "The fundamental feature of the Lesser Peace is the establishment of international safeguards to prevent the recurrence of war among nations. These safeguards would be explicitly outlined in a formal agreement supported by all the nations of the earth, and based on the principle of 'collective security' according to which all the nations should arise collectively to suppress any aggressor nation."[49]

At a later stage, the Lesser Peace will evolve into the Most Great Peace. It is envisioned that the advent of the Most Great Peace will coincide with the emergence of the World Order of Bahá'u'lláh, and that the fruit of this great World Order will be the birth and efflorescence of a world civilization, described by Shoghi Effendi as "the child of the Most Great Peace and hallmark of the Golden Age of the Dispensation of Bahá'u'lláh." All these will come about as a result of the gradual recognition of Bahá'u'lláh's mission by the peoples of the world and by the acceptance and application of the principles contained in His Revelation. Anticipating the depth of such changes, Shoghi Effendi writes, "The Most Great Peace . . . as conceived by Bahá'u'lláh—a peace that must inevitably follow as the practical consequence of the spiritualization of the world and the fusion of all its races, creeds, classes and nations—can rest on no other basis, and can be preserved through no other agency, except the divinely appointed ordinances that are implicit in the World Order that stands associated with His Holy Name."[50]

The transformations necessary to build the World Order of Bahá'u'lláh will require centuries of dedicated effort, both on the individual and collective level. Its tasks are challenging and multifaceted—from understanding the vision of the oneness of the human family, trans-forming human values and systems of governance, and creating oppor-tunities for peace to emerge. Undeterred by the challenges involved, the members of the Bahá'í Faith are actively taking conscious steps to bring the vision closer to realization through developing the capac-ities of their administrative institutions to minister to the needs of humanity and through engaging in collaborative learning and sharing experiences with like-minded individuals and movements committed to rejuvenating the well-being and prosperity of humankind.

'Abdu'l-Bahá's call to fellowship, love, and unity, which forms the second of three interrelated conditions necessary to attain to the station of apostleship, provides an important component of the context in which such transformation takes place, and it sets in motion evolving processes that underpin actions undertaken by individuals, institutions, and communities to progressively involve and reshape mankind as a whole and the institutions of civil society. Confidence in the unfoldment of this vision is driven by the following considerations, namely

The conviction of the Bahá'í community that humanity, having passed through earlier stages of social evolution, stands at the threshold of its collective maturity; its belief that the principle of the oneness of humankind, the hallmark of the age of maturity, implies a change in the very structure of society; its dedication to a learning process that, animated by this principle, explores the workings of a new set of relationships among the individual, the community and the institutions of society, the three protagonists in the advancement of civilization; its confidence that a revised conception of power, freed from the notion of dominance with the accompanying ideas of contest, contention, division and superiority, underlies the desired set of relationships; its commitment to a vision of a world that, benefitting from humanity's rich cultural diversity, abides no lines of separation. . . .[51]

Commenting on the evolution of the World Order and the establishment of peace, the Universal House of Justice counsels that it should be viewed as "an organic process proceeding in accordance with the Divine Will and animated by a spiritual reality." To highlight the point, the House of Justice quotes the words of 'Abdu'l-Bahá: "The kingdom of peace, salvation, uprightness, and reconciliation is founded in the invisible world, and it will by degrees become manifest and apparent through the power of the Word of God!" And it offers the following assurance concerning the attainment of peace: "As a result of consecrated human endeavor over decades, and indeed centuries, this spiritual reality is gradually expressed in physical form."[52]

THE CHALLENGE OF UTOPIANISM

A cursory survey of the trends in modern society illustrates, among other things, a rising concern about the level of violence and conflict, the upsurge in religious fanaticism, the rise of authoritarian movements, and the corruption of institutions, including the highest levels of government. Associated with the intensifying turmoil and conflict in the contemporary world is a decline in idealism, a sense of bitter disappointment about the apparent inability to resolve the pressing issues facing humanity, and an increase in personal despair, suspicion, cynicism, and fear.

The evolution of the Bahá'í Faith and the implementation of its vision is not taking place in a vacuum. It is buffeted by the widespread social breakdown and intense suffering afflicting both individuals and existing social institutions in the contemporary world.[53]

As the Bahá'í Faith continues to grow in size and influence, as its evolving administrative institutions engage increasingly in the life of society, and as its community reflects a new pattern of life, more and more people become aware of the Faith's vision for the future of humanity. While many observers are likely to recognize the sincere efforts of the Bahá'í community to engage in activities aimed at progressively learning how to translate high ideals into action, others may well choose "to label the community's attempts to surmount these challenges 'idealistic.'" In addition, those who oppose the Faith and wish it ill may misconceive the "principle of unification with which it stands identified . . . as a shallow attempt at uniformity," and reject "the glory of its idealism . . . as mere utopia."[54]

DEFINING UTOPIA

In general, the terms *utopia* and *utopian thinking* relate either to the imaginary or the ideal or sometimes to both. The words are frequently used to refer to an imaginary and indefinitely remote place that existed in the distant past—such as the Garden of Eden—or that is projected to exist in the far future—an ideal place with perfect laws, a perfect government, and social conditions. *Utopia* is also used to describe communities that attempt to create an ideal society by systematic attempts to engineer a perfect society.

In addition, the terms may be used with decidedly negative connotations—such as, for example, to describe an impractical scheme for social improvement as unrealistic and even ultimately destructive, to discredit an idealistic proposal as being far-fetched or implausible, or to characterize utopian dreams that are not simply unrealistic but prone to violence and likely to breed political nightmares.[55]

Utopian communities frequently come into existence at a time of rapid social change or during periods of social, political, and economic turbulence. For instance, the utopian communities founded in the United States in the first half of the nineteenth century represented a variety of attempts to perfect society, to escape from the modern world, and to create greater social equality and a more simple way of life. Some focused on the perfection of the individual rather than the reform of the larger society. The twentieth century saw the formation of communes, the emergence of politically and ideologically based social experiments that in due course proved catastrophically destructive, and a number of religious groups driven by apocalyptic visions. In contemporary times, there are those who claim that "the idea of utopia has lost its ties with alluring visions of harmony and has turned into a threat."[56]

ISSUES ASSOCIATED WITH UTOPIAN THINKING

The opponents and proponents of the idea of utopia have different perspectives concerning the value of utopian thinking. Based on the past experience of utopian communities, opponents believe utopias fail because they are based on the unrealistic concept of human goodness. Their negative evaluation of utopia is confirmed by man's invariable failure to do good and his perceived inability to change. Further, those who are opposed to utopian thinking also make the point that any detailed blueprint that maps out the future in minute details rapidly becomes outdated because any vision of the future ultimately becomes static and tethered to the past. As a consequence, a utopian organizational structure becomes frozen, which often leads to the emergence of charismatic leadership and the imposition of authoritarian rule. There is no way to agree upon and accommodate change, and the community begins to fragment and eventually disperses.

Commenting on the thinking underlying challenges of utopian thinking, Fox observes that the "utopian label is often pinned on calls for comprehensive change as a means of dismissing them from serious consideration." And, citing earlier research on this subject, Fox notes, "However, utopia 'seems unrealizable only from the point of view of a given social order which is already in existence. . . .' Such social orders come and go, and those who indulge in utopian thinking may be more prepared for, and sympathetic to, the inevitability of widespread societal transformation."[57]

Historian Russell Jacoby, a supporter of the value of utopian thinking, stresses the importance of utopian dreams. He regards "a world without utopian longing" as "forlorn"—"For society as well as for the individual, it means to journey without a compass." For Jacoby, it is not necessary to choose between "reasonable proposals and an unreasonable utopianism." It is his view that "Utopian thinking does not undermine or discount real reforms. Indeed, it is almost the opposite: practical reforms depend on utopian dreaming—or at least utopian thinking drives incremental improvements." Given the complexity of the crises confronting present-day society, Jacoby holds that "utopianism demands boldness and audacity in dreaming." And, in the formulation of the utopian dream, he identifies the need for idealism and vision. The utopian thinker who dreams of another world is motivated by the pressing and intractable problems of contemporary life. Since the "utopian projects" "straddles two time zones—the one we inhabit now and the one that might exist in the future," it frees both the individual and society to contemplate visionary change.[58]

RESPONDING TO THE CHARGE OF UTOPIANISM

Given the level of pessimism in the world at large and the fragmentation of contemporary society, it is not surprising that, from time to time, charges of utopianism and impracticality may be raised against the Faith. Commenting on such perceptions, the Universal House of Justice states, "However idealistic the Bahá'í endeavor may appear to some, its deep-seated concern for the good of humankind cannot be ignored. And given that no current arrangement in the world seems capable of lifting humanity from the quagmire of conflict and contention and securing its felicity, why would any government object to the efforts of one group of people to deepen its understanding of the nature of those essential relationships inherent to the common future towards which the human race is being inexorably drawn? What harm is there in this?"[59]

While the Bahá'í vision of the future is unequivocally hopeful, it is far from being purely utopian. Centered round the implementation of the principle of the oneness of humankind, the teachings of Bahá'u'lláh illuminate an entirely new way of life for individuals and the institutions of society. "Above all," the Guardian's secretary writes, the Bahá'í Faith is

> a way of life. It is not a mere philosophical or social doctrine. It is a closely-knit and harmoniously functioning community, a world-wide spiritual fraternity which seeks to reform the world first and foremost by bringing about a deep inner spiritual change in the heart of individuals. To live the teachings of the Cause should be the paramount concern of every true believer, and the only way to do so is to commune both in spirit and through actual concrete means with the entire community of the faithful. The Bahá'í Cause encourages community life and makes it a duty for every one of its followers to become a living, a fully active and responsible member of the world-wide Bahá'í fellowship.[60]

There are a number of factors that distinguish the Bahá'í approach to social transformation from utopianism. These include the conception of the nature of man, the systematic development of individual and institutional capacity, the structure of the Bahá'í Administrative Order, an emerging culture of learning, and an understanding of the organic nature of growth and its relationship to evolutionary change.

Contrary to views concerning man's inherent evil and his inability to change, the Bahá'í conception of the nature of man recognizes that every human has both a spiritual and a material nature. His purpose is to subdue the material nature, which inclines him to evil and, with the aid of divine teachings, to develop his spiritual nature so that he can manifest commendable qualities worthy of the human station. Man has the power both to do good and to do evil. 'Abdu'l-Bahá links the fate of society to the choices made by man: "In short, man is endowed with two natures: one tendeth towards moral sublimity and intellectual perfection, while the other turneth to bestial degradation and carnal imperfections. If ye travel the countries of the globe ye shall observe on one side the remains of ruin and destruction, while on the other ye shall see the signs of civilization and development. Such desolation and ruin are the result of war, strife and quarrelling, while all development and progress are fruits of the lights of virtue, cooperation and concord."[61]

The Bahá'í view of the nature of man is more complete and more realistic. The Faith not only specifies the responsibility of each person to take steps to develop spiritually, it also links the path to spiritual transformation to upholding Bahá'í laws, and, beyond that, identifies the need to adopt systematic strategies to develop individual and institutional capacity to engage in society-building activities.

Another of the potential criticisms associated with utopias is the issue of the nature of the blueprint that underlies the utopian vision. Blueprints of the future, especially when prepared in minute detail, tend to stifle innovation and quickly become obsolete. Furthermore, the resulting inflexibilities give rise to disagreements over organizational structure and the means for effecting change.

Drawn from the writings of Bahá'u'lláh and 'Abdu'l-Bahá and the elucidations of Shoghi Effendi and the Universal House of Justice, the Bahá'í "blueprint" for the future envisages the achievement of the spiritual maturity and unity of humankind, the emergence of a World Order and universal peace, and the flowering of world civilization. It recognizes the organic nature of the evolutionary change required to achieve such visionary transformations, and rather than specifying a precise and detailed set of actions to accomplish this vision, it establishes a system of administration authorized to introduce new directions and strategies as circumstances change, and it sets in motion processes that project the influence of the religion into the future.

The master plan for the unfoldment of the Bahá'í vision is directly linked to 'Abdu'l-Bahá's Tablets of the Divine Plan. Styled by Shoghi

Effendi as the "Charter of the Master Plan," these historic letters describe in visionary terms the strategic systematic approach to promoting the influence of the Bahá'í Faith throughout the globe and also contain guidance calculated to exert a constructive influence on the advancement of the spiritual and social life of humankind.[62] They set in motion processes that, guided by the Head of the Faith, are modified over time as the strength of the Bahá'í community increases and the condition of society changes.

Though written almost one hundred years ago, these seminal Tablets constitute the continuing source of inspiration and guidance for the systematic plans, issued by Shoghi Effendi and later by the Universal House of Justice, for the expansion and consolidation of the Bahá'í Faith throughout the world. Indeed, these subsequent plans all form part of "the evolution of the Master Plan designed by 'Abdu'l-Bahá."[63]

The Tablets of the Divine Plan articulate an attitude toward change that is realistic, long-term, evolutionary, and flexible. Its mode of operation is organic, striving to achieve coherence between the spiritual and material aspects of life. Its emerging culture of learning gives emphasis to the progressive transformation of values at the level of the individual, the community, and the institutions, and the development of the skills and capacities necessary to tackle and resolve the issues confronting humankind as it continues to evolve toward its stage of maturity.

An understanding of the Bahá'í perspective of the state of the world and the historical process is critical to any response to the charge that the optimistic vision of the Bahá'í Faith is utopian. In brief, optimism concerning the advent of the coming of age of the human race is linked to belief in the operation of the Divine Will in human affairs— that God interacts with humanity on an individual and social level continually throughout history rather than only two thousand years ago. Therefore, the present and future condition of the world cannot be assessed without taking into account God and His will.

The Bahá'í model for understanding the historical process is progressive revelation—the advent of a series of Manifestations all prophesying the coming of the Promised One to terminate the Prophetic

Cycle and inaugurate the Cycle of Fulfillment distinguished by an evolving world civilization. The central feature of the Bahá'í view is that Bahá'u'lláh has come as the Promised One with teachings to give rise to world unity and world civilization. Describing "the supreme mission" of the Revelation of Bahá'u'lláh as "the achievement of this organic and spiritual unity of the whole body of nations," and that it should be regarded "as signalizing through its advent the coming of age of the entire human race," Shoghi Effendi highlights the uniqueness and scope of this transformation:

> It should be viewed not merely as yet another spiritual revival in the ever-changing fortunes of mankind, not only as a further stage in a chain of progressive Revelations, nor even as the culmination of one of a series of recurrent prophetic cycles, but rather as marking the last and highest stage in the stupendous evolution of man's collective life on this planet. The emergence of a world community, the consciousness of world citizenship, the founding of a world civilization and culture—all of which must synchronize with the initial stages in the unfoldment of the Golden Age of the Bahá'í Era—should, by their very nature, be regarded, as far as this planetary life is concerned, as the furthermost limits in the organization of human society, though man, as an individual, will, nay must indeed as a result of such a consummation, continue indefinitely to progress and develop.[64]

Note the reference to the concept of organic unity, to the organic nature of the world including human society. It suggests that all elements of human society are united, similar to how all parts of the human body are united by the human spirit. Therefore, as an organic unit, the future of the human race is to attain the stage of maturity. There may be setbacks, delays, and great suffering, but it will eventually occur. In considering the state of the world and its future it is, therefore, necessary to factor in the relationship between God and humanity.

While the Bahá'í community's optimism is based on its understanding of the operation of the Divine Will in the life of society and its conviction concerning the coming of age of the human race and the achievement of its maturity, it also understands the vital importance of individual effort in furthering the interests of the Faith and in transforming vision into reality. In describing the challenges associated with fostering "human existence and peace," and achieving "universal development and prosperity," 'Abdu'l-Bahá writes:

A few, unaware of the power latent in human endeavor, consider this matter as highly impracticable, nay even beyond the scope of man's utmost efforts. Such is not the case, however. On the contrary, thanks to the unfailing grace of God, the loving-kindness of His favored ones, the unrivaled endeavors of wise and capable souls, and the thoughts and ideas of the peerless leaders of this age, nothing whatsoever can be regarded as unattainable. Endeavor, ceaseless endeavor, is required. Nothing short of an indomitable determination can possibly achieve it. Many a cause which past ages have regarded as purely visionary, yet in this day has become most easy and practicable. Why should this most great and lofty Cause—the daystar of the firmament of true civilization and the cause of the glory, the advancement, the well-being and the success of all humanity—be regarded as impossible of achievement? Surely the day will come when its beauteous light shall shed illumination upon the assemblage of man.[65]

The Power of Deeds

The Tablets of the Divine Plan represent a call to action to create a peaceful world, one characterized by implementation of the principle of the oneness of humankind. 'Abdu'l-Bahá's identification of fellowship and love among believers as the second condition necessary for the attainment of the station of Apostleship of Bahá'u'lláh sets in motion processes that give impetus to the emergent culture of learning within the Bahá'í community and foster—within the individual, the community, and its institutions—the unfoldment of the transformative vision set out in the writings of the Faith. These processes highlight the spiritual nature of the enterprise and the efficacy of human effort in advancing the interests of the Faith.

The writings of the Faith underline the power of goodly deeds. Bahá'u'lláh, for example, stresses the impact of even "one righteous act." Such an act, He states, "is endowed with a potency that can so elevate the dust as to cause it to pass beyond the heaven of heavens. It can tear every bond asunder, and hath the power to restore the force that hath spent itself and vanished." And He offers the following counsel: "Whoso ariseth, in this Day, to aid Our Cause, and summoneth to his assistance the hosts of a praiseworthy character and upright conduct, the influence flowing from such an action will, most certainly, be diffused throughout the whole world."[66]

Likewise, Shoghi Effendi calls attention to the impact of noble deeds in vindicating the vision of the Faith's mission:

> It is primarily through the potency of noble deeds and character, rather than by the power of exposition and proofs, that the friends of God should demonstrate to the world that what has been promised by God is bound to happen, that it is already taking place and that the divine glad-tidings are clear, evident and complete. For unless some illustrious souls step forth into the arena of service and shine out resplendent in the assemblage of men, the task of vindicating the truth of this Cause before the eyes of enlightened people would be formidable indeed. However, if the friends become embodiments of virtue and good character, words and arguments will be superfluous. Their very deeds will well serve as eloquent testimony, and their noble conduct will ensure the preservation, integrity and glory of the Cause of God.[67]

Returning to the Tablets of the Divine Plan, it is interesting to note that 'Abdu'l-Bahá provides an early assessment of the progress that had been made in forging bonds of unity between nations. Addressing the American Bahá'ís, he describes the outcome of such spiritual endeavors:

Consider! The people of the East and the West were in the utmost strangeness. Now to what a high degree they are acquainted with each other and united together! How far are the inhabitants of Persia from the remotest countries of America! And now observe how great has been the influence of the heavenly power, for the distance of thousands of miles has become identical with one step! How various nations that have had no relations or similarity with each other are now united and agreed through this divine potency! Indeed to God belongs power in the past and in the future! And verily God is powerful over all things![68]

The Universal House of Justice employs an image from the story of creation to illustrate the significance of transformative processes set in motion by the Tablets of the Divine Plan and to foreshadow the amplification of such processes and their future contribution to the creation of world order. Their letter states:

We are told by Shoghi Effendi that two great processes are at work in the world: the great Plan of God, tumultuous in its progress, working through mankind as a whole, tearing down barriers to world unity and forging humankind into a unified body in the fires of suffering and experience. This process will produce in God's due time, the Lesser Peace, the political unification of the world. Mankind at that time can be likened to a body that is unified but without life. The second process, the task of breathing life into this unified body—of creating true unity and spirituality culminating in the Most Great Peace—is that of the Bahá'ís, who are laboring consciously, with detailed instructions and continuing divine guidance, to erect the fabric of the Kingdom of God on earth, into which they call their fellowmen, thus conferring upon them eternal life.[69]

8

The Third Condition of Apostleship

The Revelation of Bahá'u'lláh represents the inspired prescription of the Divine Physician for the progress of the world and the happiness of humankind. Describing the far-reaching impact of the Faith on the world, 'Abdu'l-Bahá states:

> The Faith of the Blessed Beauty is summoning mankind to safety and love, to amity and peace; it hath raised up its tabernacle on the heights of the earth, and directeth its call to all nations. Wherefore, O ye who are God's lovers, know ye the value of this precious Faith, obey its teachings, walk in this road that is drawn straight, and show ye this way to the people. Lift up your voices and sing out the song of the Kingdom. Spread far and wide the precepts and counsels of the loving Lord, so that this world will change into another world, and this darksome earth will be flooded with light, and the dead body of mankind will arise and live; so that every soul will ask for immortality, through the holy breaths of God.[1]

Given the life-giving, transformative potential of the Revelation, those who accept the Message incur the sacred duty of passing it on to their fellowman. "Teach ye the Cause of God, O people of Bahá,"

Bahá'u'lláh counsels His followers, "for God hath prescribed unto every one the duty of proclaiming His Message, and regardeth it as the most meritorious of all deeds." Indeed, one of the specific exhortations in Bahá'u'lláh's Book of Laws is "to teach and propagate the Faith after the ascension of its Founder." Likewise, in his Will and Testament 'Abdu'l-Bahá stresses the importance of teaching the Faith: "In these days," he states, "the most important of all things is the guidance of the nations and peoples of the world. Teaching the Cause is of utmost importance for it is the head corner-stone of the foundation itself."[2]

When setting out the third condition necessary to extend the influence of the Faith and to attain to the station of Apostleship of Bahá'u'lláh, 'Abdu'l-Bahá calls attention to the importance of teaching the Faith. He invokes the memory of the disciples of Christ and the example of their sacrificial behavior, and he describes specific tasks that need to be accomplished by the individual and how these tasks should be approached. He writes, "The third condition: Teachers must continually travel to all parts of the continent, nay, rather, to all parts of the world, but they must travel like 'Abdu'l-Bahá, who journeyed throughout the cities of America. He was sanctified and free from every attachment and in the utmost severance. Just as His Holiness Christ says: Shake off the very dust from your feet."[3]

In this chapter, we examine a number of themes and strategies set out in the Tablets of the Divine Plan, which have influenced and continue to influence the worldwide expansion of the Bahá'í Faith. "Every effort made by the friends to systematically propagate the divine teachings," the Universal House of Justice states, "traces its origins to the forces set in motion in the Divine Plan," and the teaching plans, to which it gave rise, have "successively set the worldwide Bahá'í community on the move," "broadened the boundaries of the Faith," and "summoned the followers of the Abhá Beauty to the spiritual conquest of the planet." The House of Justice also foreshadows that "These teaching plans will continue until the Golden Age."[4]

The subjects included for consideration in this chapter are the nature of teaching, the qualities of the teacher, the importance of arising to serve the Faith, the strategic emphasis on geographical place, the focus on minority populations, and the unique role of women in the promotion of the Faith.

The Teaching Enterprise

In relation to the importance of the work of teaching, 'Abdu'l-Bahá declares, "Of all the gifts of God the greatest is the gift of Teaching. It draweth unto us the Grace of God and is our first obligation." He asks, "Of such a gift how we can deprive ourselves?" And, his response highlights what must be the immediate, willing sacrifice of the teacher: "Nay, our lives, our goods, our comforts, our rest, we offer them all as a sacrifice for the Abhá Beauty and teach the Cause of God." Setting the tone for the exchange between the teacher and enquirer, he issues the following guidance: "Caution and prudence, however, must be observed even as recorded in the Book. The veil must in no wise be suddenly rent asunder." Linking the teaching work to spiritual development of the teacher, 'Abdu'l-Bahá indicates, this work should ". . . under all conditions be actively pursued by the believers because divine confirmations are dependent upon it. Should a Bahá'í refrain from being fully, vigorously and wholeheartedly involved in the teaching work he will undoubtedly be deprived of the blessings of the Abhá Kingdom."[5]

Not only does the teaching work have an impact on the teacher but also on the one taught. Describing teaching as "the food of the spirit," the Universal House of Justice explains, teaching, "brings life to unawakened souls and raises the new heaven and the new earth; it uplifts the banner of a unified world; it ensures the victory of the Covenant and brings those who give their lives to it the supernal happiness of attainment to the good pleasure of their Lord." The House of Justice underlines the importance of this activity and calls upon all members of the Bahá'í community to actively partake, writing, "Every individual believer—man, woman, youth and child—is summoned to this field of action; for it is on the initiative, the resolute will of the individual to teach and to serve, that the success of the entire community depends."[6]

So vital is the teaching work that from the inception of the first systematic teaching plan introduced by Shoghi Effendi in 1937, and continuing to the present day, emphasis has been placed on the universal participation of all the friends in the teaching enterprise. For example, when instructing the Bahá'ís to direct "their careful and sustained attention" to the "teaching requirements" of the plan, Shoghi Effendi writes, "The entire community must, as one man, arise to fulfill them." "All must participate, however humble their origin, however limited their experience, however restricted their means, however deficient their education, however pressing their cares and preoccupations, however unfavorable the environment in which they live."[7]

Teaching the Bahá'í Faith involves a number of different and increasingly interdependent processes and activities, including expansion and consolidation. While during the ministry of 'Abdu'l-Bahá the main focus was primarily on expansion and introducing the Faith to increasing numbers of countries, the teaching plans of Shoghi Effendi called for pioneers—those who moved to a new locality to teach the Faith—to remain at their post as long as possible to consolidate the newly opened community. As mentioned in chapter 4, the diverse efforts employed by the Bahá'í community to absorb and consolidate large numbers of new members did not prove adequate, and this learning eventually resulted in the establishment of the training institute. The current series of Plans of the Universal House of Justice aims at advancing the process of entry by troops, includes activities for teaching and community-building, and fosters progress on all levels through service so that expansion and consolidation are so intertwined that they become different ways to describe a single process. For example, when a training institute is well-established and constantly functioning, the core activities (study circles, devotional meetings, classes for children, and junior youth groups) multiply and begin to attract the participation of individuals from the wider community. This process then gives rise to new enrollments. The value of combining the core activities within the framework of clusters is that it has resulted in the emergence of "a model of coherence in lines of action," and the Universal House of Justice envisages that this approach "holds immense possibilities for the progress of the Cause in the years ahead."[8]

Since activities undertaken in pursuit of teaching the Faith are many and varied, so too are the approaches to teaching. While it is recognized that every situation is different, it is interesting to note that Bahá'u'lláh offers the following general guidance concerning "methods of teaching" to those contemplating engagement in the teaching work of the Faith:

> The sanctified souls should ponder and meditate in their hearts regarding the methods of teaching. From the texts of the wondrous, heavenly Scriptures they should memorize phrases and passages bearing on various instances, so that in the course of their speech they may recite divine verses whenever the occasion demandeth it, inasmuch as these holy verses are the most potent elixir, the greatest and mightiest talisman. So potent is their influence that the hearer will have no cause for vacillation. I swear by My life! This Revelation is endowed with such a power that it will act as the lodestone for all nations and kindreds of the earth. Should one pause to meditate attentively he would recognize that no place is there, nor can there be, for anyone to flee to.[9]

The overall aim in teaching the Bahá'í Faith, Shoghi Effendi indicates, is "to demonstrate, by words as well as by deeds, its indispensability, its potency, and universality."[10] In broad terms, teaching might be said to entail such processes as sharing information about the teachings and history of the Faith with inquirers, responding to questions, attracting the individual to the Person of Bahá'u'lláh and the spirit of the Faith, and gradually accompanying the individual as he or she becomes confirmed in their belief and an active participant in the life of the Bahá'í community. The specific activities undertaken by the Bahá'í community evolve in conformity with the needs and conditions of the time and the level of development of the community, its members, and its institutions.

Critical to the process of teaching is the manner in which it is carried out. Specifying "the fundamentals of teaching the Faith," 'Abdu'l-Bahá states, ". . . know thou that delivering the Message can be accomplished only through goodly deeds and spiritual attributes, an utterance that is crystal clear and the happiness reflected from the face of that one who is expounding the Teachings. It is essential that the deeds of the teacher should attest the truth of his words. Such is the state of whoso doth spread abroad the sweet savors of God and the quality of him who is sincere in his faith."[11]

Those who attain to the station of apostleship must be distinguished by their outstanding spiritual qualities. 'Abdu'l-Bahá links the spiritual qualities of the Apostles of Bahá'u'lláh to the "heavenly armies" of the "Lord of Hosts," Whom he identifies as Bahá'u'lláh. "By heavenly armies," 'Abdu'l-Bahá explains,

> those souls are intended who are entirely freed from the human world, transformed into celestial spirits and have become divine angels. Such souls are the rays of the Sun of Reality who will illumine all the continents. Each one is holding in his hand a trumpet, blowing the breath of life over all the regions. They are delivered from human qualities and the defects of the world of nature, are characterized with the characteristics of God, and are attracted with the fragrances of the Merciful. Like unto the apostles of Christ, who were filled with Him, these souls also have become filled with His Holiness Bahá'u'lláh; that is, the love of Bahá'u'lláh has so mastered every organ, part and limb of their bodies, as to leave no effect from the promptings of the human world.[12]

Emphasizing the power of such spiritual individuals, 'Abdu'l-Bahá attests, "These souls are the armies of God and the conquerors of the East and the West." Foreshadowing their station and the potential of their contribution, he affirms: "Any soul from among the believers of Bahá'u'lláh who attains to this station will become known as the Apostle of Bahá'u'lláh."[13]

UNDERSTANDING MILITARY IMAGERY

Given the focus of the teachings of Bahá'u'lláh on unity and peace, it is interesting to find that the writings of the Faith contain a number of military images and terms associated with battle, e.g., the army of God, the army of light, entry by troops, crusade, conquer, heroes, and the like. In light of the level of violence in contemporary society and the resurgence of fanatical religious fervor, it is essential to understand that Bahá'u'lláh condemns physical violence and stresses the importance of teaching His Faith with wisdom. "Know thou," Bahá'u'lláh states, "We have annulled the rule of the sword, as an aid to Our Cause, and substituted for it the power born of the utterance of men."[14] And, in one of his talks, 'Abdu'l-Bahá provides the following assessment of the destructive impact of religious wars. Taking, as an example, the Crusades, he asserts

Consider the record of religious warfare, the battles between nations, the bloodshed and destruction in the name of religion. One of the greatest religious wars, the Crusades, extended over a period of two hundred years. . . . During this period . . . the East and West were in a state of violence and commotion. Sometimes the crusaders were successful, killing, pillaging and taking captive the Muslim people; sometimes the Muslims were victorious, inflicting bloodshed, death and ruin in turn upon the invaders. So they continued for two centuries, alternately fighting with fury and relaxing from weakness, until the European religionists withdrew from the East, leaving ashes of desolation behind them and finding their own nations in a condition of turbulence and upheaval. Hundreds of thousands of human beings were killed and untold wealth wasted in this fruitless religious warfare. How many fathers mourned the loss of their sons! How many mothers and wives lamented the absence of their dear ones! Yet this was only one of the "holy" wars. Consider and reflect.[15]

Guiding His followers concerning the promotion of the Faith, Bahá'u'lláh counsels, "He that wisheth to promote the Cause of the one true God, let him promote it through his pen and tongue, rather than have recourse to sword or violence." And, "'Beware lest ye shed the blood of any one. Unsheathe the sword of your tongue from the scabbard of utterance for therewith ye can conquer the citadel of men's hearts.'" Likewise, 'Abdu'l-Bahá affirms: ". . . in this day and age the sword is not a suitable means for promulgating the Faith, for it would only fill peoples' hearts with revulsion and terror."[16]

It is important to note that the meaning and intent of military imagery contained in the Bahá'í writings has been redefined or it is simply used as an analogy or point of comparison. The following state- ment of 'Abdu'l-Bahá provides a valuable context for considering such usage: "O ye loved ones of God! In this, the Bahá'í dispensation, God's Cause is spirit unalloyed. His Cause belongeth not to the material world. It cometh neither for strife nor war, nor for acts of mischief or of shame; it is neither for quarrelling with other Faiths, nor for conflicts with the nations. Its only army is the love of God, its only joy the clear wine of His knowledge, its only battle the expounding of the Truth; its one crusade is against the insistent self, the evil promptings of the human heart. Its victory is to submit and yield, and to be selfless is its everlasting glory. In brief, it is spirit upon spirit."[17]

A further example of the redefinition of a term is the use of the word *crusade*, which formed part of the name of the Ten Year World Spiri- tual Crusade, the global plan for the expansion and consolidation of the Bahá'í community, introduced by the Guardian, Shoghi Effendi, in 1953. Clarifying the meaning and intention of the word, Shoghi Effendi states: "Let there be no mistake. The avowed, the primary aim of this Spiritual Crusade is none other than the conquest of the cita- dels of men's hearts."[18]

TEACHING VS. PROSELYTIZING

Every Bahá'í has the duty of teaching the Faith; however, Bahá'ís are not permitted to proselytize. The distinction between teaching and proselytizing is clarified by the Universal House of Justice: "Pro: proselytizing implies bringing undue pressure to bear upon someone to change his Faith. It is also usually understood to imply the making of threats or the offering of material benefits as an inducement to conversion. In some countries mission schools or hospitals, for all the good they do, are regarded with suspicion and even aversion by the local authorities because they are considered to be material inducements to conversion and hence instruments of proselytization."[19]

To assist the believers to understand the implications of the distinction between teaching and proselytizing, the House of Justice calls attention to the following passages from the writings of Bahá'u'lláh and letters of Shoghi Effendi:

> Bahá'u'lláh, in The Hidden Words, says, "O Son of Dust! The wise are they that speak not unless they obtain a hearing, even as the cup-bearer, who proffereth not his cup till he findeth a seeker, and the lover who crieth not out from the depths of his heart until he gazeth upon the beauty of his beloved. . . .", and on page 55 of *The Advent of Divine Justice*, a letter which is primarily directed towards exhorting the friends to fulfill their responsibilities in teaching the Faith, Shoghi Effendi writes: "Care, however, should, at all times, be exercised, lest in their eagerness to further the international interests of the Faith they frustrate their purpose, and turn away, through any act that might be misconstrued as an attempt to proselytize and bring undue pressure upon them, those whom they wish to win over to their Cause."[20]

Returning to the theme of personal responsibility and the sensitivity of the individual's approach to the task, the House of Justice writes:

> The responsibility of the Bahá'ís to teach the Faith is very great. The contraction of the world and the onward rush of events require us to seize every chance open to us to touch the hearts and minds of our fellowmen. . . . They should teach with enthusiasm, conviction, wisdom and courtesy, but without pressing their hearer, bearing in mind the words of Bahá'u'lláh: "Beware lest ye contend with any one, nay, strive to make him aware of the truth with kindly manner and most convincing exhortation. If your hearer respond, he will have responded to his own behoof, and if not, turn ye away from him, and set your faces towards God's sacred Court, the seat of resplendent holiness.[21]

Qualifications of the Teacher

As mentioned in an earlier chapter, there is no professional ecclesiastical class—priests, rabbis, mullahs, and the like, in the Bahá'í Faith. It follows that there are no special institutions such as seminaries, yeshiva, and other similar religious institutions for the formal training and certification of teachers, and teaching the Faith is not a paid career open to Bahá'í teachers. It is a voluntary act of love and service to humankind.

While there are no full-time paid clergy, it is interesting to note that, under certain circumstances, provisions exist within the Faith to provide temporary financial support to individuals engaged in assigned teaching projects and full-time service in the teaching field on behalf of the Faith. "Whoso is unable" to be personally engaged in "the propagation of the Faith," Bahá'u'lláh states, "it is his duty to appoint him who will, in his stead, proclaim this Revelation." In the Tablets of the Divine Plan, 'Abdu'l-Bahá makes a similar plea, "Either travel yourselves, personally," he counsels. "or choose others and send them, so that they may teach the souls." And, describing the conditions governing the giving and receiving of such financial assistance, 'Abdu'l-Bahá writes, "if a soul for the sake of God, voluntarily and out of his pure desire, wishes to offer a contribution (toward the expenses of a teacher) in order to make the contributor happy, the teacher may accept a small sum, but must live with the utmost contentment."[22]

In response to a request from a National Spiritual Assembly for clarification concerning the appropriateness of providing financial support to Bahá'ís who leave their homes or travel to teach the Faith, Shoghi Effendi's secretary wrote:

> . . . travelling teachers should be assisted financially to carry out the "projects" assigned to them. The friends should not for a moment confuse this type of support with the creation of a paid clergy. Any Bahá'í can, at the discretion of the N.S.A. [National Spiritual Assembly], receive this necessary assistance, and it is clearly understood it is temporary and only to carry out a specific plan. Bahá'u'lláh Himself has not only enjoined on every one the

duty of teaching His Faith, but stated if you cannot go yourself, to send someone in your stead. The National Assembly, through and with its National Teaching Committee, should take immediate steps to get pioneers out into the goal towns and teachers circulating about, to not only support and inaugurate the new work, but to stimulate the existing Assemblies and groups, and help them to expand.[23]

To hasten the systematic work of expanding the influence of the Bahá'í Faith throughout the globe, the Universal House of Justice formalized the means of providing temporary financial support to teachers through the establishment of an International Deputization Fund at the World Center of the Faith in 1965. Created to assist pioneers and travelling teachers who were ready to serve but unable to provide their own expenses, the Fund was later extended to support other projects within national communities. It is now also used for "assisting teaching projects and growth programs, for supporting the operations of training institutes," and for those who are engaged in full-time coordination of the training institutes and core activities. It is recognized that the provision of these resources enables the institution of the Faith to assist the believers "to respond to the exigencies of a dynamic and expanding community." All Bahá'ís, and particularly those who are unable to pioneer or travel to a new area are invited to support this Fund.[24]

Concerning the work of spreading the "Faith of God," 'Abdu'l-Bahá affirms that it "must be propagated through human perfections, through qualities that are excellent and pleasing, and spiritual behavior." At its heart, teaching the Bahá'í Faith is a spiritual enterprise. Nevertheless, to participate successfully in the teaching work, the teacher is called upon to develop and manifest not only spiritual qualities but also to acquire knowledge and develop other personal and administrative capacities as well. In the Tablets of the Divine Plan, 'Abdu'l-Bahá states, "The teachers of the Cause must be heavenly, lordly and radiant. They must be embodied spirit, personified intellect, and arise in service with the utmost firmness, steadfastness and self-sacrifice."[25]

The acquisition and practice of spiritual qualities by the teacher is a vital prerequisite to effecting individual transformation and social change. "The aim is this," writes 'Abdu'l-Bahá, "The intention of the teacher must be pure, his heart independent, his spirit attracted, his thought at peace, his resolution firm, his magnanimity exalted and in the love of God a shining torch. Should he become as such, his sanctified breath will even affect the rock; otherwise there will be no result whatsoever. As long as a soul is not perfected, how can he efface the defects of others? Unless he is detached from aught else save God, how can he teach severance to others?"[26]

As if to underline the importance of the motivation of the teacher and the spiritual nature of teaching, in the Tablets of the Divine Plan 'Abdu'l-Bahá includes a number of special prayers to inspire and sustain those arising to promulgate the Faith. For example, at the end of a Tablet addressed to the Bahá'ís of the Central States of the United States, 'Abdu'l-Bahá provides a special prayer for "the spreaders of the fragrances of God" to recite "every morning." The prayer begins with an expression of gratitude to God for the bounty of having recognized His Manifestation, then calls for divine assistance, and concludes with the following: "O Lord! I am weak, strengthen me with Thy power and potency. My tongue falters, suffer me to utter Thy commemoration and praise. I am lowly, honor me through admitting me into Thy kingdom. I am remote, cause me to approach the threshold of Thy mercifulness. O Lord! Make me a brilliant lamp, a shining star and a blessed tree, adorned with fruit, its branches overshadowing all these regions. Verily, Thou art the Mighty, the Powerful and Unconstrained."[27]

Each member of the community, as a party to the Covenant, has the privilege and duty to teach the Faith. Fulfillment of this obligation requires acquisition of knowledge of the teachings of the Faith in order to convey them more accurately to others. Bahá'u'lláh Himself calls for regular reading of the sacred scriptures. In the Kitáb-i-Aqdas, He instructs the believers to recite the "verses of God every morn and eventide." And He cautions, "Whoso faileth to recite them hath not been faithful to the Covenant of God and His Testament."[28]

'Abdu'l-Bahá specifically links systematic study of the Faith with preparation for teaching, and he broadens the process by calling on the Bahá'ís to "take hold of every means in the promulgation of the religion of God and the diffusion of the fragrances of God." Expanding on this guidance, he instructs the more seasoned members of the community to establish classes to help train those who are less experienced, and he suggests a course of study to be followed: "Amongst other things is the holding of the meetings for teaching so that blessed souls and the old ones from amongst the believers may gather together the youths of the love of God in schools of instruction and teach them all the divine proofs and irrefragable arguments, explain and elucidate the history of the Cause, and interpret also the prophecies and proofs which are recorded and are extant in the divine books and epistles regarding the manifestation of the Promised One, so that the young ones may go in perfect knowledge in all these degrees."[29]

The systematic teaching plans initiated by Shoghi Effendi amplified the processes of teaching and learning set in motion by 'Abdu'l-Bahá and took into consideration the capacity of the believers, the availability of Bahá'í literature, and the level of development of the community and its institutions. For example, at the time the first Seven Year Plan was introduced by Shoghi Effendi in 1937, he stressed the need for all participants in the Plan, both teachers and administrators, to acquire a detailed knowledge of the Faith and the Islamic context from which it emerged. He writes:

Those who participate in such a campaign, whether in an organizing capacity, or as workers to whose care the execution of the task itself has been committed, must, as an essential preliminary to the discharge of their duties, thoroughly familiarize themselves with the various aspects of the history and teachings of their Faith. In their efforts to achieve this purpose they must study for themselves, conscientiously and painstakingly, the literature of their Faith, delve into its teachings, assimilate its laws and principles, ponder its admonitions, tenets and purposes, commit to memory certain of its exhortations and prayers, master the essentials of its administration, and keep abreast of its current affairs and latest developments. They must strive to obtain, from sources that are authoritative and unbiased, a sound knowledge of the history and tenets of Islam—the source and background of their Faith—and approach reverently and with a mind purged from preconceived ideas the study of the Qur'án which, apart from the sacred scriptures of the Bábí and Bahá'í Revelations, constitutes the only Book which can be regarded as an absolutely authenticated Repository of the Word of God. They must devote special attention to the investigation of those institutions and circumstances that are directly connected with the origin and birth of their Faith, with the station claimed by its Forerunner, and with the laws revealed by its Author.[30]

Given the worldwide expansion of the Faith and the beginning of its emergence from obscurity the Universal House of Justice has, in more recent years, introduced a systematic framework for action involving a set of core activities. The core activities not only further the work of teaching the Faith and expand the size of the Bahá'í community, but beyond that, they are aimed at developing human resources by increasing the level of knowledge of all age groups within the Bahá'í community, and by building individual and administrative capacity for service both to the Bahá'í community and to the world at large. These activities, therefore, extend the scope of teaching to include engagement in processes associated with community-building, and other more direct forms of social action.

As the nature of the teaching enterprise continues to evolve and expand, so too does the nature of the educational process that must underpin it. Writing on this subject, the Universal House of Justice states, "Just as the habit of daily reading will remain an integral part of Bahá'í identity, so will these forms of study continue to hold a place in the collective life of the community. But understanding the implications of the Revelation, both in terms of individual growth and social progress, increases manifold when study and service are joined and carried out concurrently. There, in the field of service, knowledge is tested, questions arise out of practice, and new levels of understanding are achieved."[31]

In the estimation of the House of Justice, the current system of education established within the Bahá'í community, involving—among other things—a sequence of institute courses, has acquired "the capacity to enable thousands, nay millions, to study the writings in small groups with the explicit purpose of translating the Bahá'í teachings into reality, carrying the work of the Faith forward into its next stage: sustained large-scale expansion and consolidation." The "force necessary to propel change," the House of Justice states, depends to a large extent on the ability of the tutor to create "an environment conducive to the spiritual empowerment of individuals, who will come to see themselves as active agents of their own learning, as protagonists of a constant effort to apply knowledge to effect individual and collective transformation."[32] The interrelated processes of teaching and the acquisition of knowledge for the purpose of developing capacity for service will inevitably continue to evolve and increase in complexity as the Bahá'í community engages more and more in the life of society, collaborating with groups committed to shaping the movement toward unity, peace, and human prosperity.

Travel and Teaching

The third condition for becoming an Apostle of Bahá'u'lláh calls specifically for the teacher to "continually travel to all parts of the continent, nay, to all parts of the world."[33] During the ministry of 'Abdu'l-Bahá, the challenge of diffusing the light of Bahá'u'lláh's Revelation throughout the world had hardly begun. So pressing was this need that at the end of his life, 'Abdu'l-Bahá himself undertook a prolonged and arduous journey to the West for the purpose of promoting the teachings and vision of Bahá'u'lláh.

The movement of the teacher from place to place is associated with the birth of a new religion. The history of new religious movements is characterized by the activities of the early followers in diffusing the teachings of the Manifestation of God beyond the particular geographical location in which the message was first announced. For example, in the Tablets of the Divine Plan, 'Abdu'l-Bahá refers to the Gospel, where Christ is reported to have called upon His followers to shake the very dust from their feet and to travel to all parts of the world and give the glad tidings of the appearance of the Kingdom of God.[34]

Bahá'u'lláh not only refers to the process of traveling to teach the Faith, He also calls attention to the potency of the spiritual forces released by this activity, observing, "'The movement itself from place to place, when undertaken for the sake of God, hath always exerted, and can now exert, its influence in the world. In the Books of old the station of them that have voyaged far and near in order to guide the servants of God hath been set forth and written down.'"[35]

Beyond its potent influence in the world, traveling to teach the Faith has a profound impact on the teacher. Bahá'u'lláh praises those who have "forsaken their country" for the purpose of teaching His Cause, and assures them their actions will be strengthened by the power of God. Underlining the inestimable value of this form of service, Bahá'u'lláh exclaims, "How great the blessedness that awaiteth him that hath attained the honor of serving the Almighty! By My life! No act, however great, can compare with it, except such deeds as have been ordained by God, the All-Powerful, the Most Mighty. Such a service is, indeed, the prince of all goodly deeds, and the ornament of every goodly act. Thus hath it been ordained by Him Who is the Sovereign Revealer, the Ancient of Days."[36]

To those who wish to perform this matchless service, Bahá'u'lláh offers guidance concerning the importance of detachment, the motives of the teacher, and reliance on the power of divine assistance—all of which impact the outcome of the teacher's efforts:

Whoso ariseth to teach Our Cause must needs detach himself from all earthly things, and regard, at all times, the triumph of Our Faith as his supreme objective. This hath, verily, been decreed in the Guarded Tablet. And when he determineth to leave his home, for the sake of the Cause of his Lord, let him put his whole trust in God, as the best provision for his journey, and array himself with the robe of virtue. Thus hath it been decreed by God, the Almighty, the All-Praised.

If he be kindled with the fire of His love, if he forgoeth all created things, the words he uttereth shall set on fire them that hear him. Verily, thy Lord is the Omniscient, the All-Informed. Happy is the man that hath heard Our voice, and answered Our call. He, in truth, is of them that shall be brought nigh unto Us.[37]

Elaborating on this theme when addressing the "teachers of the Cause" in the Tablets of the Divine Plan, 'Abdu'l-Bahá sets the following priorities, advising that "In their journeys they must not be attached to food and clothing. They must concentrate their thoughts on the outpourings of the Kingdom of God and beg for the confirmations of the Holy Spirit. With a divine power, with an attraction of consciousness, with heavenly glad tidings and celestial holiness they must perfume the nostrils with the fragrances of the Paradise of Abhá."[38]

In light of the unique importance of arising to teach the Faith and the spiritual benefits accruing to the individual in bringing him or her close to God, 'Abdu'l-Bahá's poignant lament in the Tablets of the Divine Plan takes on additional meaning. "O that I could travel," he writes, "even though on foot and in the utmost poverty, to these regions, and, raising the call of 'Yá Bahá'u'l-Abhá' in cities, villages, mountains, deserts and oceans, promote the divine teachings! This, alas, I cannot do. How intensely I deplore it! Please God, ye may achieve it."[39] While regretting his own inability to take on this field of service, 'Abdu'l-Bahá offers heartfelt prayers that the believers will be able to avail themselves of this great opportunity.

NATURE OF TEACHING ACTIVITIES

As mentioned in earlier chapters, the nature of the activities undertaken by the Bahá'í community at different stages in the evolution of the Faith have evolved in accordance with the guidance of the Head of the Faith, the state of the world, and the condition of the Bahá'í community. It is therefore important to consider in a larger context the mandate linking teaching and travel set out in the third condition of apostleship

The types of activities traditionally associated with traveling to teach the Faith include pioneering and different forms of travel teaching. *Pioneering* is the term used to describe a Bahá'í leaving his or her native country or hometown to reside in another locality, either overseas or elsewhere on the home front, in order to serve the Faith. Typically, pioneers tend to make a longer term commitment to stay in a particular place. They seek to establish their residence and earn their livelihood in the new location and endeavor to become part of the new community. They initiate and support the development of the Bahá'í community in the new area. During the ministry of Shoghi Effendi, he set in motion systematic plans for the worldwide expansion of the Faith and the establishment of the framework of its administrative institutions. As part of this process, he called for pioneers to arise and settle in "virgin territories"—initially, countries where there were no resident Bahá'ís. These early pioneers laid the foundation for the Bahá'í community in the countries where they settled. John Henry Hyde Dunn, for example, who with his wife, Clara, forsook their home in California and settled as pioneers in Australia in 1921, thereby opening a new continent to the Cause. Through his work as a salesman, Hyde Dunn was able to "carry the Message to no less than seven hundred towns throughout that Commonwealth."[40]

In more recent years, following the introduction of the Bahá'í Faith into the vast majority of the countries of the world, the consolidation of its institutions, and the increasing self-sufficiency of national communities, the greatest need for pioneers has tended to be primarily on the home front—at the cluster and local levels, and in neighborhoods and villages. Furthermore, while long-term pioneers continue to be useful, there is also an important role for short-term pioneers with mature experience and particular skills who can spend time assisting a community to acquire or enhance capacity to take on a specific task or function.

Dating from the earliest days of the Faith, travel teaching has, over the years, assumed various forms, depending on the stage of development of the Faith. The first to respond to "the epoch-making summons" to travel-teach raised in the Tablets of the Divine Plan was Miss Martha

Root. Summarizing the exploits of this quintessential travel-teacher, Shoghi Effendi describes how she set out

> . . . with unswerving resolve and a spirit of sublime detachment, on her world journeys, covering an almost uninterrupted period of twenty years and carrying her four times round the globe, in the course of which she traveled four times to China and Japan and three times to India, visited every important city in South America, transmitted the message of the New Day to kings, queens, princes and princesses, presidents of republics, ministers and statesmen, publicists, professors, clergymen and poets, as well as a vast number of people in various walks of life, and contacted, both officially and informally, religious congresses, peace societies, Esperanto associations, socialist congresses, Theosophical societies, women's clubs and other kindred organizations . . .[41]

"This indomitable soul," Shoghi Effendi attests, "has, by virtue of the character of her exertions and the quality of the victories she has won, established a record that constitutes the nearest approach to the example set by 'Abdu'l-Bahá Himself to His disciples in the course of His journeys throughout the West."[42]

In response to 'Abdu'l-Bahá's call in the Tablets of the Divine Plan, legions of travel teachers have arisen to spread the society-building teachings of the Faith and to further the development of embryonic Bahá'í communities and their institutions. With the systematization of the organization of the teaching work under the direction of Spiritual Assemblies, teachers, traveling as individuals and in groups, have scattered to the four corners of the earth, traversed the length and breadth of their home countries, and made their way both to remote clusters and neighboring villages.

The present framework for action set in motion under the direction of the Universal House of Justice has seen the emergence of new forms of teaching, including the idea of a youth year of service. The youth year of service harnesses the energy and flexibility of youth and recognizes that, during their years of study, youth often have specific periods of time during which they can devote themselves to travel teaching or to serving the Bahá'í community in other ways. Travel teachers continue to be important in supporting intensive programs of growth within receptive neighborhoods of their home community and assisting the development of adjacent clusters.

SOCIETY-BUILDING IMPACT OF TRAVEL TEACHING

Pioneering and travel teaching, whether international, local, or at the level of the cluster, result in opening and consolidating new areas to the Faith. They support the emergence of an embryonic Bahá'í community in the new location, lay the foundation for the Faith's administrative structure in that area, and support programs of growth. In addition, pioneering and travel-teaching activities help foster and support the emergence of a distinctive social environment, which has the potential for effecting individual and social transformation. Indeed, the value of the "interchange of pioneers and travelling teachers," the Universal House of Justice indicates, is that it "contributes so importantly to the unity of the Bahá'í world and to a true understanding of the oneness of mankind."[43]

Transferring one's residence to a new country or different social milieu—an environment that potentially differs in language, culture, and traditions from one's own—or travel teaching in an unfamiliar location, at home or abroad, is likely to challenge personal assumptions and expectations. Travel teaching will often take one out of one's comfort zone, but it often will provide opportunities for personal and spiritual growth. Similarly, a local believer in his or her own home country may well be challenged when first encountering a foreign pioneer or travel teacher. The opportunity is there, however, for each party to engage in a learning process—to avoid immediately rejecting the perspective and way of life of the other, and to gain an appreciation of the fundamental oneness of the human family. Alluding to this process in the Tablets of the Divine Plan, 'Abdu'l-Bahá envisages the benefit that would derive if it were possible for "a commission composed of men and women, to travel together through China and

Japan." Were these journeys to take place, 'Abdu'l-Bahá expresses the hope "that this bond of love may become strengthened, and through this going and coming they may establish the oneness of the world of humanity, summon the people to the Kingdom of God and spread the teachings."[44]

To facilitate the interactions between traveling teacher and pioneer and the peoples they encountered in the field of service, Shoghi Effendi offered the following practical advice:

> Every laborer in those fields, whether as traveling teacher or set- tler, should, I feel, make it his chief and constant concern to mix, in a friendly manner, with all sections of the population, irrespective of class, creed, nationality, or color, to familiarize himself with their ideas, tastes, and habits, to study the approach best suited to them, to concentrate, patiently and tactfully, on a few who have shown marked capacity and receptivity, and to endeavor, with extreme kindness, to implant such love, zeal, and devotion in their hearts as to enable them to become in turn self-sufficient and independent promoters of the Faith in their respective localities. "Consort with all men, O people of Bahá," is Bahá'u'lláh's admonition, "in a spirit of friendliness and fellowship. If ye be aware of a certain truth, if ye possess a jewel, of which others are deprived, share it with them in a language of utmost kindliness and goodwill. If it be accepted, if it fulfill its purpose, your object is attained. If anyone should refuse it, leave him unto himself, and beseech God to guide him. Beware lest ye deal unkindly with him. A kindly tongue is the lodestone of the hearts of men. It is the bread of the spirit, it clotheth the words with meaning, it is the fountain of the light of wisdom and understanding."[45]

A critical element of the communication process is love. 'Abdu'l- Bahá, in his Will and Testament, set out what might be considered a number of general principles to guide social interactions and the resolution of certain challenges that tend to arise. He writes:

It is incumbent upon everyone to show the utmost love, rectitude of conduct, straightforwardness and sincere kindliness unto all the peoples and kindreds of the world, be they friends or strangers. So intense must be the spirit of love and loving kindness, that the stranger may find himself a friend, the enemy a true brother, no difference whatsoever existing between them. For universality is of God and all limitations earthly. . . . the affections and loving kindness of the servants of the One True God must be bountifully and universally extended to all mankind. Regarding this, restrictions and limitations are in no wise permitted.

Wherefore, O my loving friends! Consort with all the peoples, kindreds and religions of the world with the utmost truthfulness, uprightness, faithfulness, kindliness, good-will and friendliness, that all the world of being may be filled with the holy ecstasy of the grace of Bahá, that ignorance, enmity, hate and rancor may vanish from the world and the darkness of estrangement amidst the peoples and kindreds of the world may give way to the Light of Unity. Should other peoples and nations be unfaithful to you show your fidelity unto them, should they be unjust toward you show justice towards them, should they keep aloof from you attract them to yourselves, should they show their enmity be friendly towards them, should they poison your lives, sweeten their souls, should they inflict a wound upon you, be a salve to their sores. Such are the attributes of the sincere! Such are the attributes of the truthful.[46]

Beyond the importance of love to interpersonal relationships, love also has important implications for social cohesion and the ultimate attainment of peace. Beginning with the example of a family and generalizing his analysis to humanity itself, 'Abdu'l-Bahá states:

If love and agreement are manifest in a single family, that family will advance, become illumined and spiritual; but if enmity and hatred exist within it, destruction and dispersion are inevitable. This is, likewise, true of a city. If those who dwell within it manifest a spirit of accord and fellowship, it will progress steadily and human conditions become brighter, whereas through enmity and strife it will be degraded and its inhabitants scattered. In the same way, the people of a nation develop and advance toward civilization and enlightenment through love and accord and are disintegrated by war and strife. Finally, this is true of humanity itself in the aggregate. When love is realized and the ideal spiritual bonds unite the hearts of men, the whole human race will be uplifted, the world will continually grow more spiritual and radiant and the happiness and tranquillity of mankind be immeasurably increased. Warfare and strife will be uprooted, disagreement and dissension pass away and universal peace unite the nations and peoples of the world. All mankind will dwell together as one family, blend as the waves of one sea, shine as stars of one firmament and appear as fruits of the same tree. This is the happiness and felicity of humankind. This is the illumination of man, the eternal glory and everlasting life; this is the divine bestowal.[47]

In relation to the society-building implications of leaving one's home to serve the Faith, the movement from place to place has the potential to transcend cultural rigidity by opening the door to change. The Universal House of Justice calls attention to a number of the processes involved: "When the masses of mankind are awakened and enter the Faith of God, a new process is set in motion and the growth of a new civilization begins. Witness the emergence of Christianity and of Islam. These masses are the rank and file, steeped in traditions of their own, but receptive to the new Word of God, by which, when they truly respond to it, they become so influenced as to transform those who come in contact with them."[48] Contact with peoples from different cultural backgrounds provides opportunities for learning new ideas and examining alternative ways of doing things.

Concerning the contribution of the teacher who travels to promote the interests of the Faith, 'Abdu'l-Bahá observes that not only will he become "familiar with the geography of other lands; acquaint himself with their arts and wonders," an individual will, at a more fundamental level, "become informed of the customs, conduct, and character of their inhabitants; witness the civizilation and the advancement of the time; and be apprised of the manner of government, the capacity, and the receptivity of each country."[49] Such guidance is of continuing relevance in the present day; it pertains to identifying receptive populations and promotes enhanced understanding of the needs and condition of the society in which they have chosen to serve the Faith. It also increases capacity to share with like-minded groups the teachings and experience of the Faith that contribute to the amelioration of pressing issues confronting that society.

Teachers and pioneers contribute to the processes of social transformation by demonstrating the community-building power of the Faith. They teach the Faith "by words as well as by deeds," and through the power of example, they demonstrate "its indispensability, its potency, and universality."[50] Writing to the Bahá'ís in Iran in 1928, Shoghi Effendi stressed this twofold aspect of teaching:

> It is incumbent upon the Bahá'ís to seize the opportunities of the present hour and, with wisdom, firm resolve and cheerfulness, impress the verities of their Faith upon the attention of every reasonable-minded person in whom they find a willingness to listen, explaining to them its noble principles, its universal teachings, its basic tenets, and the fundamental laws of the new era inaugurated by Bahá'u'lláh. In like manner, they must clearly and convincingly demonstrate to their fellow-citizens, whether high or low, the necessity of accepting and recognizing the resplendent teachings of the Universal Manifestation of God; must show to the leaders of their country that the unity, the strength and spiritual vitality of the Bahá'í community are palpable and concrete realities; must eliminate and nullify the effects of prejudices, superstitions, misunderstandings and all fanciful and erroneous conceptions on the hearts of the pure and righteous people; and must attract to the community of the Greatest Name, through whatever channels and by whatever means, persons of capacity, experience and devotion who, joining the ranks of the believers,

severing themselves from every extraneous attachment, identifying themselves whole-heartedly with the organized community of
the Bahá'ís in the area, will labour heart and soul to consolidate
the foundations of Bahá'í belief and proclaim the tidings of the
Promised Day.[51]

Furthermore, the unity of the Bahá'í community and the distinctiveness of its administrative and decision-making processes not
only accelerate the expansion of the Faith but also provide a tangible
example of an alternative means for effecting and sustaining social
change. Stressing the importance of example, Shoghi Effendi's secretary conveyed his guidance to the Bahá'ís: "He longs to see a greater
degree of unity and love among the believers, for these are the spirit
which must animate their Community life. Until the people of the
world see a shining example set by us they will not embrace the Cause
in masses, because they require to see the teachings demonstrated in
a pattern of action." Likewise, the Universal House of Justice called
attention to the community-building implications of the manner in
which the Bahá'í community conducts its affairs, observing: "The
time has come for the Bahá'í community to become more involved
in the life of the society around it, without in the least supporting
any of the world's moribund and divisive concepts, or slackening its
direct teaching efforts, but rather, by association, exerting its influence
towards unity, demonstrating its ability to settle differences by consultation rather than by confrontation, violence or schism, and declaring
its faith in the divine purpose of human existence."[52]

Strategic Emphasis on Geographical Place

Through the revelation of the Tablets of the Divine Plan 'Abdu'l-
Bahá issued a mandate and outlined a plan that, in the years to come,
is destined to enable his followers "to diffuse the light, and erect the
administrative fabric, of the Faith throughout the five continents of
the globe."[53]

In what might well be considered a useful strategy for enabling the
Bahá'ís to grasp the vision of the universal character of the Faith and

the scope of their mission, 'Abdu'l-Bahá mentions by name over one hundred and twenty places in the Tablets of the Divine Plan, thereby clearly establishing the global nature of the spiritual enterprise to which his followers are called. 'Abdu'l-Bahá names continents, countries, island groups and individual islands, archipelagoes, states and provinces, and even a number of individual cities.

It is interesting to consider that many of the locations named by 'Abdu'l-Bahá were distant, even remote, from major centers of population and that their names were likely to have been unfamiliar to the general public. In addition, at the time the Tablets of the Divine Plan were written, many of the territories mentioned by 'Abdu'l-Bahá still formed part of large empires and had not achieved independent status. The rise of independence movements and the decline of empires were still several decades into the future. The majority of nations only achieved their independence after the Second World War.[54]

In addition to the potential strategic and educational value of naming so many geographical places to increase the Bahá'í community's understanding of the universal mission of the Faith, we can only wonder at the impact of the naming of places on individual and group identity. The concept of identity carries with it the weight of the need for a sense of who one is and where one belongs, a need that is likely to be intensified in times of rapid political and social change.[55] Consider, for example, the possible reaction of the inhabitants of remote islands and of forgotten and politically insignificant nations to the knowledge that their lands had not been overlooked in 'Abdu'l-Bahá's Divine Plan and that their peoples had a contribution to make to the spiritual regeneration of the planet. Might not the systematic naming of places be yet another affirmation of the principle of the oneness of humankind, an expression of respect and reassurance to the underappreciated peoples of the world?

Beyond the mere listing of places, 'Abdu'l-Bahá also establishes broad strategic priorities for the order in which the Faith was to be introduced into particular territories—calling for the Faith first to be introduced to a continent, then to a region within a continent, then to a specific country within a region; and even to a focus on a specific city with particular geographical or historical significance, such as Montreal (Quebec) and Bahia, Brazil. These priorities appear to have been governed partially by immediate practical considerations, including accessibility, and also by the requirements of his long-term vision for the regeneration of human society.

Drawing inspiration and direction from the Tablets of the Divine Plan, the plans introduced by Shoghi Effendi and the Universal House of Justice have followed the general pattern for the systematic unfoldment of the Faith set in place by 'Abdu'l-Bahá—namely, proceeding from general outlines to specific goals over the span of years, with increasing levels of decentralization and complexity. During the ministry of Shoghi Effendi (1921–1957), the Bahá'í Faith was introduced into the majority of the countries of the globe, the framework of its administrative structure was established, and attention was given to the diversification of the Faith's membership.

Since the establishment of the Universal House of Justice in 1963, the Faith has become a global religion, its institutions have continued to evolve and increase in maturity, and emphasis has increasingly been placed on decentralization in community functioning and the diversification of its membership. The following excerpt from an early letter of the Universal House of Justice serves to illustrate the evolving complexity of some of the processes involved in teaching the Faith:

> The paramount goal of the teaching work at the present time is to carry the message of Bahá'u'lláh to every stratum of human society and every walk of life. An eager response to the teachings will often be found in the most unexpected quarters, and any such response should be quickly followed up, for success in a fertile area awakens a response in those who were at first uninterested.
>
> The same presentation of the teachings will not appeal to everybody; the method of expression and the approach must be varied in accordance with the outlook and interests of the hearer. An approach which is designed to appeal to everybody will usually result in attracting the middle section, leaving both extremes untouched. No effort must be spared to ensure that the

healing Word of God reaches the rich and the poor, the learned and the illiterate, the old and the young, the devout and the atheist, the dweller in the remote hills and islands, the inhabitant of the teeming cities, the suburban businessman, the laborer in the slums, the nomadic tribesman, the farmer, the university student; all must be brought consciously within the teaching plans of the Bahá'í Community.[56]

CLUSTERS AND NEIGHBORHOODS

The world-embracing vision of the Bahá'í Faith anticipates that "Every nation and every group—indeed, every individual—will, to a greater or lesser degree, contribute to the emergence of the world civilization towards which humanity is irresistibly moving." While the Faith is now well-established throughout the world and its communities are increasingly well-distributed within national boundaries, the possibility now exists to narrow the focus to smaller geographic areas, to give attention to fostering intensive growth in neighborhoods and villages, and to increase the influence of the Faith in some of the remote areas of the globe. To facilitate the current stage in the unfoldment of the organic evolution of the Faith, the Universal House of Justice designated the cluster as the geographical area where expansion and consolidation of the Faith was to take place, and it called for the formulation of plans to promote systematic and intensive growth within these areas. Describing this new focus, the House of Justice writes, "There are many countries where increased institutional capacity, particularly at the level of the region, now makes it possible to focus attention on smaller geographic areas. Most of these will consist of a cluster of villages and towns, but, sometimes, a large city and its suburbs may constitute an area of this kind. Among the factors that determine the boundaries of a cluster are culture, language, patterns of transport, infrastructure, and the social and economic life of the inhabitants."[57]

As described in chapters 4 and 7, in recent years, the cluster has become the primary geographic area in which a broad range of Bahá'í activities are carried out. As the process of community-building set in motion by the core activities intensifies, a new level of decentral-ization becomes possible—namely, to focus on particular "receptive populations" so as to "find those souls longing to shed the lethargy imposed on them by society and work alongside one another in their neighborhoods and villages to begin a process of collective transforma-tion." The Universal House of Justice spells out the ultimate end of the work of teaching, encouraging the Bahá'ís to "press on and bring Bahá'u'lláh's message to waiting souls in every urban neighborhood, in every rural hamlet, in every corner of the globe, drawing them to His community, the community of the Greatest Name."[58]

As a result of the systematic approach to decentralization, Bahá'ís are finding themselves drawn more and more into the life of society. Commenting on the unfolding processes that accompany this stage of development, the Universal House of Justice writes:

A rich tapestry of community life begins to emerge in every cluster as acts of communal worship, interspersed with discus-sions undertaken in the intimate setting of the home, are woven together with activities that provide spiritual education to all members of the population—adults, youth and children. Social consciousness is heightened naturally as, for example, lively con-versations proliferate among parents regarding the aspirations of their children and service projects spring up at the initiative of junior youth. Once human resources in a cluster are in sufficient abundance, and the pattern of growth firmly established, the community's engagement with society can, and indeed must, increase.[59]

Anticipating future initiatives needed to expand the community-building contribution of the evolving Bahá'í community to the life of society, the House of Justice notes, "when so many clusters are nearing such a stage, it seems appropriate that the friends everywhere would reflect on the nature of the contributions which their growing, vibrant communities will make to the material and spiritual progress of society. In this respect, it will prove fruitful to think in terms of two interconnected, mutually reinforcing areas of activity: involvement in social action and participation in the prevalent discourses of society."[60]

Stressing the organic nature of the unfoldment of these new opportunities emerging at the level of the cluster for involvement in the life of society, the House of Justice calls attention to the fact that it will "proceed naturally," and that it is linked to an ongoing learning process involving "action, reflection, consultation and study." "Involvement in the life of society," the House of Justice states, "will flourish as the capacity of the community to promote its own growth and to maintain its vitality is gradually raised. It will achieve coherence with efforts to expand and consolidate the community to the extent that it draws on elements of the conceptual framework which governs the current series of global Plans. And it will contribute to the movement of populations towards Bahá'u'lláh's vision of a prosperous and peaceful world civilization to the degree that it employs these elements creatively in new areas of learning."[61]

Focus on Special Regions and Populations

In addition to outlining a methodical strategy for extending the influence of the Bahá'í Faith throughout the countries and territories of the world, in the Tablets of the Divine Plan, 'Abdu'l-Bahá foreshadows a special future for various regions such as Panama; the city of Bahia, Brazil; Greenland; and certain populations, including Native Americans and the Eskimo, or Inuit, peoples. Several of these special geographical spaces are described in the following sections.

BAHIA, BRAZIL

There are two references in the Tablets of the Divine Plan to the "city of Bahia." 'Abdu'l-Bahá encourages the Bahá'ís to visit "especially the city of Bahia, on the eastern shore of Brazil." The reason for the importance of Bahia, he explains is "Because in the past years this city was christened with the name, BAHIA, there is no doubt that it has been through the inspiration of the Holy Spirit." And, linking the naming of Bahia with its future, 'Abdu'l-Bahá predicts, "Because it is some time that it has become known by this name, its efficacy will be most potent."[62]

It is not possible to know what precisely 'Abdu'l-Bahá might have had in mind when he commented about the naming of Bahia. On the one hand, one can but speculate that the similarity of the word *Bahia* to the Arabic word *Bahá* might have struck a chord with 'Abdu'l-Bahá. The Arabic word *Bahá*, meaning *glory* or *splendor*, is integral to the name and titles of Bahá'u'lláh, the Manifestation of God for this age.

Furthermore, in relation to the naming of Bahia, it is also interesting to note that there are reports that suggest that when the Portuguese first sailed along the Atlantic coast of South America in 1500 and caught sight of a wide and beautiful bay dotted with islands, they claimed the land for Portugal and named their capital São Salvador da Bahia de Todos os Santos (Salvador of the Bay of all Saints). *Bahia* is an archaic spelling of the Portuguese word *baía*, meaning *bay*.

From 1549–1763, Salvador de Bahia served as the first capital of Brazil. In later years, one of the most populous Brazilian states was also named Bahia, and its capital city became known simply as Salvador. Bahia was a prime area for its sugar plantations and industry, attracting to an enormous influx of people, including African slaves.

From 1558 onward, Salvador de Bahia became the first slave market in the New World, with slaves arriving to work on the sugar plantations. More than 37% of all slaves taken from Africa were sent to Brazil, mostly to be processed in Bahia before being sent to work in plantations elsewhere in the country. Bahia was also the site in 1835 of one of the most important urban slave rebellions in the Americas, which is of particular note because it was the only predominantly Muslim slave revolt in the history of the New World.

Ethnically and culturally, Salvador de Bahia has a most interesting background. It witnessed the blending of European, African, and Amerindian cultures. And as the chief locus of the early Brazilian slave trade, Bahia is considered to possess the greatest and most distinctive African imprint, in terms of culture and customs, in Brazil. Bahia is also the birthplace of many noted Brazilian artists, writers, and musicians. For example, during the nineteenth century, the outstanding

Bahian abolitionist poet and playwright Castro Alves wrote his famous poem "Navio negreiro," about slavery; the poem is considered a masterpiece of Brazilian Romanticism and an important contribution to anti-slavery literature.[63]

As to 'Abdu'l-Bahá's comments concerning the future of Bahia, apart from the spiritual connection to which he alludes, it is not possible to know for sure what he might have intended. However, given the forthrightness of his guidance and taking into consideration the historical background of Bahia—the suffering and dislocation associated with the experience of slavery, the inevitable economic and social inequality, the challenge of racial and cultural diversity—one might well ask whether such conditions potentially provide an environment ripe for social change and receptive to the message of peace and unity embodied in the teachings of Bahá'u'lláh.

The first Bahá'í to visit Bahia was Martha Root. Conscious of 'Abdu'l-Bahá's encouragement to visit Bahia, she stopped off for six days during her 1919 voyage along the coast of South America. Arriving in Bahia during a violent rainstorm and at a time when yellow fever was raging in the area, she immediately set about placing Bahá'í books in libraries and arranging for the publication of articles about the Faith in local newspapers. Martha's presence and the information about the Faith she shared attracted a great deal of interest. People offered to assist her—to act as her interpreter, to translate her articles into Portuguese, and to introduce her to prominent people. In addition, for the information of 'Abdu'l-Bahá and the benefit of future Bahá'í teachers, Martha compiled a detailed report concerning the region. The report included comments about trade and commerce, religious views and tendencies, intellectual pursuits, level of illiteracy among the indigenous populations, and the availability of medical facilities.[64]

In 1921, two years after the extensive travels of Martha Root in South America, another American woman, Leonora Holsapple Armstrong, became "one of a handful of valiant souls who arose in response to 'Abdu'l-Bahá's call during His Own lifetime, and the first Bahá'í pioneer to settle permanently in Latin America." Addressed by 'Abdu'l-Bahá as a "Herald of the Kingdom," and styled by the Universal House of

Justice as both the "mother of the Bahá'ís of Brazil" and the "spiritual mother of Latin America," Leonora settled in Bahia and subsequently resided in other cities during the course of the more than sixty years she spent in Latin America. During the course of her life, she made a significant contribution to the progress of the Faith and the establishment of its administrative system not only in Bahia but throughout the continent, traveling widely and undertaking extensive translations of Bahá'í literature into Portuguese and Spanish.[65]

The history of the Bahá'í Faith in Brazil is still unfolding. Suffice it to say, the first National Spiritual Assembly of Brazil was established in 1961. Considerable progress has been achieved in many fields of service throughout the South American Bahá'í community, particularly in attracting to the Cause large numbers of its indigenous peoples and in developing capacity to interact with society at large. In a letter addressed to the Bahá'ís in Latin America and the Caribbean, the Universal House of Justice comments on some of these developments and their implications for the future work of the Faith in the region:

> While paying close attention to areas of large-scale expansion, you should not lose sight of the fact that your nations have undergone profound change over the past decades, resulting in increased receptivity to the Faith in many sectors of society. You have, in each of your national communities, developed remarkable capacity to interact with society at large. Through your extensive work in social and economic development, especially in the area of education, through your discourse on issues such as the preservation of the environment and the organization of social action, through your substantive interactions with leaders of thought, you are developing a keen understanding of the needs and aspirations of your peoples which enhances your ability to present the Faith to a wide range of interests.[66]

The contribution of the Bahá'í Faith to the spiritual and social transformation of Latin America is ongoing. Much more will be accomplished in the future. 'Abdu'l-Bahá's focus on the city of Bahia led the way to the opening of South America to the message of Bahá'u'lláh. The arrival of the initial travel teacher and the first Bahá'í pioneer set in motion creative society-building processes that will continue to unfold and become more complex, and as the Bahá'í community continues to increase in size and in its capacity to minister to the needs of society, so too will its ability to collaborate with others to reshape society and its institutions be enhanced.

PANAMA

In the Tablets of the Divine Plan, 'Abdu'l-Bahá stresses the importance of the Republic of Panama as a crossroads between East and West and as a place of future potential influence. Singling out Panama from among the Republics of Central America, 'Abdu'l-Bahá states, "All the above countries have importance, but especially the Republic of Panama, wherein the Atlantic and Pacific Oceans come together through the Panama Canal. It is a center for travel and passage from America to other continents of the world, and in the future it will gain most great importance."[67]

Historically, geographic crossroads and places of travel tend to be centers not only of commerce but, given the movement of peoples, also of opportunities for the exchange of new ideas, the flowering of creativity, and the openness for change. Highlighting the potential for change, 'Abdu'l-Bahá advises, ". . . ye must give great attention to the Republic of Panama, for in that point the Occident and the Orient find each other united through the Panama Canal, and it is also situated between the two great oceans. That place will become very important in the future. The teachings, once established there, will unite the East and the West, the North and the South."[68] The geographical location of Panama may well symbolize a uniting world. It is the locus of the physical unity of the globe, and as the region embraces the teachings of Bahá'u'lláh, it will acquire the capacity to serve as a force for social unity.

The intrepid Martha Root was the first Bahá'í to visit Panama. Inspired by 'Abdu'l-Bahá's statements, Martha was determined to find a way to get to Panama. Braving high altitude, freezing weather, and hazardous conditions, she crossed the Andes on muleback during the first leg of her journey. She then caught a train to Valparaiso, with its tropical climate, and boarded a ship to Panama, arriving on October 25, 1919.[69] She immediately set about visiting newspapers, writing articles about the Faith, and finding other ways to promote its ideas.

When mobilizing the support of the American Bahá'í community for the systematic achievement of the goals of the first Seven Year Plan (1937–1944), Shoghi Effendi called attention to the practical and strategic importance of Panama, such as the fact that it was closer and more accessible to the American community than some of the more distant goal countries. Shoghi Effendi refers to the "special position enjoyed by the Republic of Panama, both in view of its relative proximity to the heart and center of the Faith in North America, and of its geographical position as the link between two continents."[70]

In 1939, the first Bahá'í pioneers arrived in Panama. Initially, the teaching work proceeded slowly, and it was not until 1945 that the first Local Spiritual Assembly was formed. As the community expanded, its administrative structure emerged, with the National Spiritual Assembly of Panama being established in 1961. Furthermore, in anticipation of the development of the Bahá'í community in Panama and the increasing complexity of its functioning, in 1953, Shoghi Effendi called for the purchase of land for "the eventual establishment of a Bahá'í House of Worship in the City of Panama, specially mentioned by 'Abdu'l-Bahá, situated in the heart of the Western Hemisphere," thereby initiating processes that, in later years, resulted in the erection of this edifice on a "mountaintop between the two greatest oceans and the two American continents," and its official dedication in 1972.[71]

The Bahá'í House of Worship in Panama, the first House of Worship in Latin America, is described by the Universal House of Justice as "the Mother Temple of Latin America, an edifice which glorifies the Cause of Bahá'u'lláh at that point where, the beloved Master asserted, 'the Occident and the Orient find each other united through the Panama Canal.'" In its message addressed to the conference called on the occasion of the dedication of the Temple, the House of Justice describes the long-term significance of the completion of this "glorious Silent Teacher," in these words:[72]

> A crown to the labors of all those who have striven to establish the Faith of Bahá'u'lláh in Latin America, this Mashriqu'l-Adhkár, the rallying point for the Bahá'ís of those lands, whether they are of the blessed Indian peoples or represent the other races whose diversity enriches the nations of that hemisphere, will be a fountainhead of spiritual confirmations, and this mighty achievement will endow the Bahá'í Community with new and greater capacities, enabling the friends in Latin America, and particularly in this privileged land of Panama, to win victories that will eclipse all their past achievements.[72]

The processes set in motion by the focus on Panama in the Tablets of the Divine have yet to run their course. A brief snapshot highlights an evolving reality. As the Bahá'í community in Panama continues to evolve, its membership reflects more closely the diversity of the national population, and as the community increases in size and builds individual and administrative capacity, it engages progressively in more complex activities associated with social and economic development. For example, in 1987, a Bahá'í cultural center in the Chiriqui Province of Panama was constructed. It was an educational complex operated by and for the Guaymi people who are Central American Indians.[73]

The educational programs implemented under the auspices of the cultural center are disseminated through a system of decentralized learning centers. These learning centers are focused on the development of human resources for the spiritual, social, and cultural development of the Guaymi people, and they are designed to enable the Guaymi people to serve as members of regional and local councils, as teachers, as community helpers, and as staff for the Bahá'í radio station established in 1986.[74] It should be noted that while in some development settings, radio is regarded as a high-technology instrument of cultural domination, the Guaymis have transformed its use into a means of affirming and strengthening their culture. It reinforces literacy and child education programs in the learning centers, and it broadcasts news, folklore, legends, and music in the Guaymi language.[74]

In the Tablets of the Divine Plan, 'Abdu'l-Bahá focuses special attention on Greenland and predicts the spiritual transformation of the region. Why does Greenland merit special attention? Might an answer be found in Greenland's unique geographical position, and in the fact that its population shares a cultural link with the indigenous peoples inhabiting the Arctic regions of the globe?

Concerning its geographical position, Greenland is the world's largest island. Located in the remote and inhospitable regions of the far north, between the Arctic and Atlantic Oceans, east of the Canadian Arctic Archipelago, Greenland forms part of the continent of North America. Straddling the Arctic Circle, Greenland's climate is extreme. Over three-quarters of the surface of Greenland is covered by a permanent, thick ice-sheet. Formerly a province of Denmark, Greenland gained the status of an autonomous Danish dependent territory with limited self-government as well as its own parliament in 1979.

As to Greenland's population, it is small, with fewer than sixty thousand inhabitants, who are largely confined to the coastal areas and who consist predominately of the indigenous people, the Eskimos. Eskimos constitute the chief element in the indigenous population of the Arctic and subarctic regions of Greenland, Canada, the United States, and far eastern Russia. While the name *Eskimo* has been applied to Arctic peoples by Europeans and others since the sixteenth century, in contemporary times, Greenlanders (and indigenous Canadians) prefer to be known by the name Inuit. The Greenlandic Inuit are the descendants of migrations from Canada.[75]

In two of his Tablets addressed to the Bahá'ís of Canada and Greenland, included in the Tablets of the Divine Plan, 'Abdu'l-Bahá calls for the Faith to be taught in all the provinces of Canada, including those in the remote Arctic areas. He also calls for the dispatch of teachers "to Greenland and the home of the Eskimos."[76]

'Abdu'l-Bahá expresses the hope that "the call of the Kingdom may reach the ears of the Eskimos, the inhabitants of the Islands of Franklin in the north of Canada, as well as Greenland," and he discloses an inspiring vision of what is likely to occur if "the fire of the love of God be kindled in Greenland." He writes,". . . all the ice of that country will be melted, and its cold weather become temperate—that is, if the hearts be touched with the heat of the love of God, that territory will become a divine rose garden and a heavenly paradise, and the souls, even as fruitful trees, will acquire the utmost freshness and beauty." 'Abdu'l-Bahá cautions that the transformation he envisions requires "the utmost effort" on the part of the Bahá'ís, and he assures them, that should they "display an effort, so that the fragrances of God may be diffused among the Eskimos, its effect will be very great and far-reaching." 'Abdu'l-Bahá then goes on to explain the nature of the effect and its global impact: "God says in the great Qur'án: A day will come wherein the lights of unity will enlighten all the world. 'The earth will be irradiated with the light of its Lord.' In other words, the earth will become illumined with the light of God. That light is the light of unity. 'There is no God but God.' The continent and the islands of Eskimos are also parts of this earth. They must similarly receive a portion of the bestowals of the Most Great Guidance."[77]

The introduction of the Faith to the peoples, including Native Americans and "the Eskimos of Greenland and Alaska," who are scattered throughout the remote areas of the globe, is an expression of the oneness of mankind, of acceptance of and respect for human diversity. All of these areas are important, representing as they do "earthly symbols of Bahá'u'lláh's unearthly Sovereignty."[78]

Shoghi Effendi actively encouraged the intensification of the teaching work among the various indigenous peoples of North America and the Arctic region. Writing to the Canadian Bahá'ís, for example, he called for the establishment of special committees to give close attention to this work and to set in motion systematic activities not only to increase the number of minority adherents of the Faith, but also to foster "their active participation in both the teaching and administrative spheres of Bahá'í activity." In response to this call, a succession of homefront pioneers settled and opened the four corners of their land, while North American and European pioneers brought the light of the Faith to the fringes of Greenland. Summarizing the outcome of these activities, the Universal House of Justice writes:

> As a result of these movements and organized activities, the call of the Kingdom reached "the ears of the Eskimos," and the divine spark was struck in their lands. . . . The teaching work among the Indians of the northern lands of the Western Hemisphere has likewise borne rich fruit, as tribe upon tribe has been enlisted under the banner of Bahá'u'lláh. Whether in Alaska's south-eastern islands and rugged mountains, or in Canada's huge Indian reserves from the west to the east, many Amerindian believers have arisen to serve the Cause, and through their joint efforts, their sacrificial endeavors and distinctive talents they bid fair to accelerate the dawn of the day when they will be so "illumined as to enlighten the whole world."[79]

The ongoing diversification of the membership of the Bahá'í community and its ability to remain united are critical to the Faith's ability to demonstrate ever more effectively the unifying power of Bahá'u'lláh's Faith to achieve its primary society-building principle, the oneness of humankind. Writing on this theme to the North American Bahá'ís, the Universal House of Justice states:

> The calls of the Master and the Guardian plainly summon the Bahá'ís of the Americas to prodigies of proclamation, of teaching and of service. The American melting pot of peoples needs the unifying power of the new Faith of God to achieve its fusion. The representative character of the Bahá'í community should therefore be reinforced through the attraction, conversion and support of an ever-growing number of new believers from the diverse elements constituting the population of that vast mainland and particularly from among Indians and Eskimos about whose future the Master wrote in such glowing terms.[80]

The introduction of the Bahá'í Faith to Greenland proved challenging given such factors as visa requirements and lack of employment opportunities. Shoghi Effendi assigned the responsibility to the Canadian Bahá'ís following the establishment of the National Spiritual Assembly of Canada in 1948. After attempts by several Canadian Bahá'ís proved unsuccessful, in 1951, a Danish believer, Mr. Palle Bischoff, offered to fill the goal and succeeded in becoming the first pioneer to Greenland. He remained at his post until 1954.[81]

During World War II (1939–1945) a number of American air force bases were established in Greenland, and they continue to operate in the present day. These bases provided opportunities for several Bahá'ís, including the Canadian pioneer, Bill Carr, to live in Greenland for extended periods of time. Bill Carr served at Thule Air Base from 1955 until 1972. On receiving news of Carr's arrival, Shoghi Effendi announced to the Bahá'í world that "The northernmost outpost of the Faith has now been pushed far beyond the Arctic Circle, as far as 76 degrees latitude, in consequence of the arrival of William Carr, a Canadian believer, in Thule, Greenland."[82]

Beyond the difficulty of gaining entry to Greenland, Shoghi Effendi's secretary describes the challenges associated with the social isolation and lack of response to Bahá'u'lláh's message experienced by lone pioneers in "infertile" teaching fields, including Greenland: "It is hard for the friends to appreciate, when they are isolated in one of these goal territories, and see that they are making no progress in teaching others, are living in inhospitable climes for the most part, and are lonesome for Bahá'í companionship and activity, that they represent a force for good, that they are like a light-house of Bahá'u'lláh shining at a strategic point and casting its beam out into the darkness. This is why he so consistently urges these pioneers not to abandon their posts."[83]

Gradually the Bahá'í community took root in Greenland with the acceptance of the Faith by a number of local residents. The first Local Spiritual Assembly was formed in the capital in 1979, and the National Spiritual Assembly was established in 1992. Anticipating the further unfoldment of these processes and the impact of the Faith on the nation, the Universal House of Justice wrote, ". . . the Bahá'í community of Greenland, whose staunchness of faith and dogged perseverance have won our admiration and praise, and have resulted in the Faith's becoming firmly established in that distant land. Inspired by the promise set out in the Tablets of the Divine Plan that 'if the hearts be touched with the heat of the love of God, that territory will become a divine rose-garden and a heavenly paradise, and the souls, even as fruitful trees, will acquire the utmost freshness and beauty,' let them now go forth to claim new victories on the home front and to transform their nation through the power of the Divine Teachings."[84]

INDIGENOUS POPULATIONS

As mentioned earlier, 'Abdu'l-Bahá places particular importance on teaching the Faith to indigenous peoples and on their spiritual regeneration and education. He confidently anticipates a great future for the Native Americans of the American continent as they accept and become enlightened by the teachings of Bahá'u'lláh. Stressing the potential for collective transformation this affords, Shoghi Effendi states, "To believe in the Mouthpiece of God in His Day confers very great blessings, not only on individuals, but on races . . ."[85]

In the Tablets of the Divine Plan, 'Abdu'l-Bahá likens the "indigenous population of America" to the "ancient inhabitants of the Arabian Peninsula," and commenting on their shared capacity to contribute to the spiritual enlightenment of the world, affirms, "When the light of Muḥammad shone forth in their midst . . . they became so radiant as to illumine the world. Likewise, these Indians, should they be educated and guided, there can be no doubt that they will become so illumined as to enlighten the whole world." Elaborating on the statement of 'Abdu'l-Bahá, Shoghi Effendi, in a letter addressed to the Bahá'ís in Central America and Mexico, underlined the potential contribution of the indigenous peoples to the development of an enlightened society:

If the light of Divine Guidance enters properly into the lives of the Indians, it will be found that they will arise with a great power and will become an example of spirituality and culture to all of the people in these countries.

275

The Master has likened the Indians in your Countries to the early Arabian Nomads at the time of the appearance of Muhammad. Within a short period of time they became the outstanding examples of education, of culture and of civilization for the entire world. The Master feels that similar wonders will occur today if the Indians are properly taught and if the power of the Spirit properly enters into their living.[86]

During the ministry of Shoghi Effendi and in the time of the Universal House of Justice, emphasis was given to expanding the number of tribes represented within the Bahá'í community and to increasing their knowledge and capacity for undertaking the work of teaching and for serving on Bahá'í administrative agencies. It was anticipated that indigenous peoples would have an expanding role to play, not only within the Bahá'í community but also among the wider society, by offering an example to ethnic groups and developing approaches to change. In a letter addressed to the North American Bahá'ís, the Universal House of Justice states:

> In the Divine Plan bequeathed to you by 'Abdu'l-Bahá is disclosed the glorious destiny of those who are the descendants of the early inhabitants of your continent. We call upon the indigenous believers who are firmly rooted in the Bahá'í Teachings to aid, through both deed and word, those who have not yet attained that level of understanding. Progress along the path to their destiny requires that they refuse to be drawn into the divisiveness and militancy around them, and that they strive to make their own distinctive contribution to the pursuit of the goals of the . . . Plan, both beyond the confines of North America and at home. They should be ever mindful of the vital contribution they can make to the work of the Faith throughout the American continent, in the circumpolar areas and in the Asian region of the Russian Federation.[87]

'Abdu'l-Bahá's inspiring vision has yet to be fully realized. Nevertheless, from the record of the global Bahá'í community, there is increasing evidence to suggest that the transformative processes set in motion in response to his visionary guidance are progressively building capacity in individuals and communities, thus auguring well for the continuing evolution of indigenous peoples and for their contribution to the emergence of an enlightened world.

In a recent letter, the Universal House of Justice comments on the importance of the emergence of receptivity to the Faith "within distinct populations who represent a particular ethnic, tribal, or other group," and it outlines the potential this has for the processes of growth. It writes:

> There is much to be learned about the dynamics involved when a population of this kind embraces the Faith and is galvanized through its edifying influence. We stress the importance of this work for advancing the Cause of God: every people has a share in the World Order of Bahá'u'lláh, and all must be gathered together under the banner of the oneness of humanity. In its early stages, the systematic effort to reach out to a population and fos- ter its participation in the process of capacity building accelerates markedly when members of that population are themselves in the vanguard of such an effort. These individuals will have special insight into those forces and structures in their societies that can, in various ways, reinforce the endeavors under way.[88]

WOMEN AS TEACHERS

At the outset, it is important to note that all members of the Bahá'í community—men, women, young, and old—are called upon to teach the Faith of Bahá'u'lláh. 'Abdu'l-Bahá's mandate is all-inclusive. "In this day," he attests, "the duty of everyone, whether man or woman, is to teach the Cause."[89]

The call to apostleship set out in the Tablets of the Divine Plan is not confined to any one segment of the population. In fact, a number of these Tablets are specifically addressed both to men and women, and in another Tablet, 'Abdu'l-Bahá expresses pleasure at the prospect of "a commission composed of men and women" traveling together to promote the oneness of humanity and to teach the Faith, suggesting that he might well favor collaboration between women and men in the field of teaching.[90]

Furthermore, while the responsibility to teach the Faith is shared by all, it is interesting to observe that in the Tablets of the Divine Plan 'Abdu'l-Bahá makes special mention of the outstanding contribution of a number of women to the promotion of their Faith. In particular, he names two biblical figures, "Mary Magdalene and Mary the mother of John," as well as several Bahá'í women—Agnes Alexander, Alma Knobloch, May Maxwell—and he refers to an unnamed maidservant, who was "serving in the public library" in Alaska.[91]

Elsewhere in his writings, 'Abdu'l-Bahá comments on the part played by women in promoting the Faith in the West. He observes that "women have outdone the men in this regard and have taken the lead in this field. They strive harder in guiding the peoples of the world, and their endeavors are greater. They are confirmed by divine bestowals and blessings." He expresses the hope that "in the East the handmaids of the Merciful will also exert such effort, reveal their powers, and manifest their capacities."[92]

Reflecting on the contribution of Western Bahá'í women to the worldwide expansion of the Faith, Shoghi Effendi cites a statement of 'Abdu'l-Bahá concerning the unique role played by women in the establishment of the Faith; he pays his own tribute to their exemplary accomplishments, and calls for even greater deeds in the future:

> I am moved, at this juncture, as I am reminded of the share which, ever since the inception of the Faith in the West, the handmaidens of Bahá'u'lláh, as distinguished from the men, have had in opening up, singlehanded, so many, such diversified, and widely scattered countries over the whole surface of the globe, not only to pay a tribute to such apostolic fervor as is truly reminiscent of those heroic men who were responsible for the birth of the Faith of Bahá'u'lláh, but also to stress the significance of such a preponderating share which the women of the West have had and are having in the establishment of His Faith throughout the

whole world. "Among the miracles," 'Abdu'l-Bahá Himself has testified, "which distinguish this sacred Dispensation is this, that women have evinced a greater boldness than men when enlisted in the ranks of the Faith." So great and splendid a testimony applies in particular to the West, and though it has received thus far abundant and convincing confirmation must, as the years roll away, be further reinforced, as the American believers usher in the most glorious phase of their teaching activities under the Seven Year Plan. The "boldness" which, in the words of 'Abdu'l-Bahá, has characterized their accomplishments in the past must suffer no eclipse as they stand on the threshold of still greater and nobler accomplishments. Nay rather, it must, in the course of time and throughout the length and breadth of the vast and virgin territories of Latin America, be more convincingly demonstrated, and win for the beloved Cause victories more stirring than any it has as yet achieved.[93]

As described in chapter 6, one of the important principles of Bahá'u'lláh is the principle of the equality of women and men. It is integral to the achievement of the oneness of humankind and a prerequisite to the establishment of global peace. From the earliest days of the Faith, emphasis has been placed on building the capacity of women not only to teach the Faith but also to participate fully within the Bahá'í community and society at large, through creating educational experiences and administrative structures to promote the advancement of women. Shoghi Effendi, for example, when outlining the functions of Spiritual Assemblies in a letter addressed to the Persian Bahá'ís in 1926, included among the list, "to promote the emancipation and advancement of women and support the compulsory education of both sexes."[94]

Bahá'ís are committed to the practice of equality even in those parts of the world where gender equality is not in accord with traditional cultural practices. Assessing the condition of the worldwide Bahá'í community in 1984, the Universal House of Justice wrote, "The equality of men and women is not, at the present time, universally applied. In those areas where traditional inequality still hampers its progress we must take the lead in practicing this Bahá'í principle. Bahá'í women and girls must be encouraged to take part in the social, spiritual and administrative activities of their communities." To remedy this situation, the Universal House of Justice has, in the past, set specific goals for certain National Spiritual Assemblies concerning the promotion of "the full and equal participation of women in all aspects of Bahá'í community life." It continues to monitor the state of women's development, providing guidance, as needed, to particular Bahá'í communities in different regions of the world. For example, Bahá'í communities in Western Asia were called upon "to give special attention to the advancement of women." Explaining the need for such action, the House of Justice wrote, "In almost all of your region, women have traditionally played a secondary role in the life of society, a condition which is still reflected in many Bahá'í communities. Effective measures have to be adopted to help women take their rightful place in the teaching and administrative fields. By teaching entire families, you can ensure that increasing numbers of women enter the Faith, thereby improving the balance in the composition of your communities and beginning in each family, from the moment of acceptance, a process through which the fundamental principle of the equality between men and women can be realized."[95]

The Bahá'í endeavors to promote the equality of women and men extend beyond the Bahá'í community. For many years, leadership was provided by the Bahá'í International Community Office at the United Nations. As a reflection of the growth and increasing capacity of the global Bahá'í community to engage with the pressing issues in the wider society, in 1992, the Universal House of Justice established an Office for the Advancement of Women, located at the United Nations. Describing this new Office, the House of Justice indicated that "as an agency of the Bahá'í International Community, [it] will promote the principles of the Faith through its interaction with international entities concerned with matters affecting the rights, status and well-being of women. It will also advise National Spiritual Assemblies regarding programs and projects in which the involvement of the community can encourage efforts towards the realization of the equality of men and women."[96]

Concluding Comments

'Abdu'l-Bahá's historic travels in North America and Europe in the later years of his life "opened the door of teaching." He compares his teaching activities to the work of a farmer "who comes into possession of a piece of pure and virgin soil," and immediately proceeds in an orderly and systematic manner to bring the land under cultivation by preparing the fields and sowing seeds.[97]

In the Tablets of the Divine Plan, 'Abdu'l-Bahá calls upon the believers to follow in his footsteps, to become "heavenly farmers," and to "scatter pure seeds in the prepared soil." Continuing with this farming analogy, he sets out the role of "the believers of God and the maidservants of the Merciful," namely, they "must irrigate these fields and with the utmost power engage themselves in the cultivation of these heavenly plantations so that the seeds may grow and develop, prosperity and blessing be realized and many rich and great harvests be gathered in." He counsels the believers to appreciate "the value of this time," and to be "engaged in the sowing of the seeds," so that they may be the recipients of "the heavenly blessings and the lordly bestowals."[98]

Anticipating the advent of the bountiful harvest season, 'Abdu'l-Bahá offers the following encouragement to those who are striving to be faithful to his mandate:

Throughout the coming centuries and cycles many harvests will be gathered. Consider the work of former generations. During the lifetime of Jesus Christ the believing, firm souls were few and numbered, but the heavenly blessings descended so plentifully that in a number of years countless souls entered beneath the shadow of the Gospel. God has said in the Qur'án: "One grain will bring forth seven sheaves, and every sheaf shall contain one hundred grains." In other words, one grain will become seven hundred; and if God so wills He will double these also. It has often happened that one blessed soul has become the cause of the guidance of a nation. Now we must not consider our ability and capacity, nay, rather, we must fix our gaze upon the favors and bounties of God, in these days, Who has made of the drop a sea, and of the atom a sun.[99]

Given the evolutionary nature of the organic processes involved in the unfoldment of the Faith, 'Abdu'l-Bahá in his writings calls upon the believers to adopt a long-term perspective. "Look ye not upon the present," he advises. "Fix your gaze upon the times to come. In the beginning, how small is the seed, yet in the end it is a mighty tree. Look ye not upon the seed, look ye upon the tree, and its blossoms, and its leaves and its fruits."[100] In elaboration of this theme, 'Abdu'l-Bahá refers to the remarkable growth that transpired at the time of Christ; he foreshadows the glorious consummation of the Dispensation of Bahá'u'lláh; and he calls upon the "loved ones of God" to truly appreciate the great bounties they have received in being participants in this mighty enterprise:

Consider the days of Christ, when none but a small band followed Him; then observe what a mighty tree that seed became, behold ye its fruitage. And now shall come to pass even greater things than these, for this is the summons of the Lord of Hosts, this is the trumpet-call of the living Lord, this is the anthem of world peace, this is the standard of righteousness and trust and understanding raised up among all the variegated peoples of the globe; this is the splendor of the Sun of Truth, this is the holiness of the spirit of God Himself. This most powerful of dispensations will encompass all the earth, and beneath its banner will all peoples gather and be sheltered together. Know then the vital import of this tiny seed that the true Husbandman hath, with the hands of His mercy, sown in the ploughed fields of the Lord, and watered with the rain of bestowals and bounties and is now nurturing in the heat and light of the Daystar of Truth.

Wherefore, O ye loved ones of God, offer up thanks unto Him, since He hath made you the object of such bounties, and the recipients of such gifts. Blessed are ye, glad tidings to you, for this abounding grace.[101]

9

Responding to the Call to Apostleship

Written one hundred years ago during the darkest period of the First World War, 'Abdu'l-Bahá's Tablets of the Divine Plan offered an alternative vision of the world, a vision that held the tantalizing promise of "a day when the light of His Father's Revelation would illuminate every corner of the world."[1] These historic letters did more than simply describe a vision. They laid out the charter for diffusing the teachings of the Bahá'í Faith throughout the planet, assigned certain responsibilities to the believers, and set out strategies, guiding principles, and unchanging spiritual requisites for achieving this objective in the long term.

The Divine Plan of 'Abdu'l-Bahá and its implementation have continued to unfold over the decades as the individual and collective capacity of Bahá'u'lláh's followers has grown, enabling them to take on progressively more complex functions, and ever-greater challenges. The initial response of the Bahá'í community to the mandate contained in the Tablets of the Divine Plan has been described in chapter 4. Particular emphasis has also been given to the growth that has occurred under the direction of the Universal House of Justice, especially during the period beginning in 1996, where the primary emphasis of the Plan has been directed toward advancing the process of entry by troops.

Advancing the process of entry by troops is critical to accelerating not only the growth of the Bahá'í community but also to increasing the capacity of the community to engage in social action and to collaborate with like-minded groups to address the pressing issues of the day and to influence the forces for social change, thereby contributing to the spiritual regeneration of the planet. Writing about the outcome of the growth of the Faith, the Universal House of Justice observes:

> When the reach of activity is extensive, the societal impact of the Faith becomes more evident. The Bahá'í community is afforded higher standing as a distinctive moral voice in the life of a people and is able to contribute an informed perspective to the discourses around it, on, say, the development of the younger generations. Figures of authority from the wider society start to draw on the insight and experience arising from initiatives of social action inspired by Bahá'u'lláh's teachings. Conversations influenced by those teachings, concerned with the common weal, permeate an ever-broader cross section of the population, to the point where an effect on the general discourse in a locality can be perceived.[2]

The processes associated with advancing the movement toward entry by troops derive their inspiration from the writings of the Bahá'í Faith, and they are driven by an approach to learning that involves action and learning from experience. The aim is to assist growing numbers of individuals and Bahá'í administrative agencies to develop the capacity to engage in community-building, empowering individuals and communities to assume responsibility for their own social, spiritual, and intellectual growth. This community-building process is open to all who wish to participate, whether Bahá'í or not. The framework for action introduced by the Universal House of Justice comprises, among other things, the work of the training institute—study circles where participants progress through a sequence of courses to acquire knowledge and capacities for service, participate in devotional gatherings and home visits, and learn to plan and conduct increasingly diverse and complex activities associated with the systematic expansion and consolidation of the Faith within the cluster area. A number of these processes have been described in detail in chapters 6, 7, and 8.

The society-building processes set in motion by the Tablets of the Divine Plan are flexible and amenable to modification in light of the assessment of the current needs of a given community or cluster; and as the influence of the Faith grows, these processes are assuming greater importance. Given the organic nature of the process of growth, and in light of the orientation toward learning and the systematic mode of operation adopted by the Bahá'í community, the community has, with the passage of time and as a result of recent experience, acquired a clearer understanding of the complexity both of the task itself and of the system of multiple interacting factors that impact the work of diffusing the Light of Bahá'u'lláh to the four corners of the world.

Standing on the threshold of a new Five Year Plan (2016–2021), to be launched at Riḍván 2016 by the Universal House of Justice, it is useful to consider the broad action priorities outlined in the new plan. The provisions of the new plan set out the immediate tasks to which the present-day Apostles of Bahá'u'lláh are summoned.

The Five Year Plan (2016–2021) calls for the number of clusters where a program of growth has become intensive to be raised to five thousand by Riḍván 2021. Commenting on the challenge this poses for the Bahá'í community, the Universal House of Justice writes: "We set this objective before the Bahá'í world conscious that it is truly formidable; that a herculean labour will be required; that many sacrifices will have to be made. But faced with the plight of a world that suffers more each day bereft of Bahá'u'lláh's elixir, we cannot, in conscience, ask anything less of His devoted followers. God willing, their exertions will prove worthy to crown a hundred years of toil and set the stage for exploits as yet unimagined that must adorn the second century of the Formative Age."[3]

While the task is immense and extremely challenging, the House of Justice reassures the Bahá'ís that the "essential elements of the coming Plan, like those that came before it, are straightforward." Nevertheless, at the same time it cautions against both underestimating the challenging requirements of the new plan and failing to take into consideration the complexity of the interacting processes associated with growth. Given the emphasis in the new Plan on the acceleration of growth in all clusters where it has begun, the House of Justice calls attention to the learning that is essential for the successful implementation of the Plan. What is required, the House of Justice states, is "a profound understanding of its [the Plan's] various facets;" and it affirms that this understanding "requires an appreciation of the sophisticated set of operations through which a cluster develops." Elaborating on the way forward, the Universal House of Justice writes:

> The coming global endeavor to which the friends will be summoned calls for the application of proven strategies, systematic action, informed analysis, and keen insight. Yet above all, it is a spiritual enterprise, and its true character should never be obscured. The urgency to act is impelled by the world's desperate condition. All that the followers of Bahá'u'lláh have learned in the last twenty years must culminate in the accomplishments of the next five. The scale of what is being asked of them brings to mind one of His Tablets in which He describes, in striking terms, the challenge entailed in spreading His Cause:

>> "How many the lands that remained untilled and uncultivated; and how many the lands that were tilled and cultivated, and yet remained without water; and how many the lands which, when the harvest time arrived, no harvester came forth to reap! However, through the wonders of God's favour and the revelations of His loving-kindness. We cherish the hope that souls may appear who are the embodiments of heavenly virtue and who will occupy themselves with teaching the Cause of God and training all that dwell on earth."

> The systematic efforts of His loved ones throughout the world aim at the fulfilment of the hope thus expressed by the Blessed Perfection. May He Himself reinforce them at every turn.[4]

The Urgency to Act

The present stage of the evolution of the Divine Plan for the spiritual regeneration and well-being of the planet coincides with a time when the level of suffering and the issues confronting humankind demand urgent action, and when the Bahá'í community has acquired the necessary experience and community-building capacities to enable the community to engage systematically and more directly in social action and in promoting the forces for change in the wider community.

Implicit in the "urgency to act," identified by the Universal House of Justice, is a renewed call to apostleship. What is the present-day apostle called upon to do in shouldering his or her share of the "herculean labor" that is required to achieve the objective of the new Plan? What steps can individuals take to enhance their capacity to attain to the station of "Apostle of Bahá'u'lláh?" In this regard, we take up 'Abdu'l-Bahá's invitation in the Tablets of the Divine Plan to learn from the example of his actions. In outlining the third of the three interrelated conditions for the attainment to the station of apostleship, 'Abdu'l-Bahá offers as an illustration, a description of how he approached the task of teaching: "Teachers must continually travel to all parts of the continent, nay, rather, to all parts of the world, but they must travel like 'Abdu'l-Bahá, who journeyed throughout the cities of America. He was sanctified and free from every attachment and in the utmost severance. Just as His Holiness Christ says: Shake off the very dust from your feet."[5]

This final chapter explores a number of insights gained from reflection on the example of the life of 'Abdu'l-Bahá as it relates to the attainment of the three conditions of apostleship: firmness in the Covenant, fellowship and love among the believers, and arising to teach the Faith.

The Station and Functions of 'Abdu'l-Bahá

As a context within which to consider the actions of 'Abdu'l-Bahá, it is useful to consider briefly his station and major functions. Bahá'u'lláh in His writings confers upon His eldest son, 'Abdu'l-Bahá, a unique station. Appointed to succeed Bahá'u'lláh after His passing, 'Abdu'l-Bahá is at once the Exemplar of the pattern of life taught by his Father, the divinely inspired authoritative Interpreter of His teachings and the center and pivot of the Covenant that the Author of the Bahá'í Revelation, Bahá'u'lláh, made with all who recognize Him. Shoghi Effendi affirms that 'Abdu'l-Bahá fulfills "a unique function," "not only in the Dispensation of Bahá'u'lláh but in the entire field of religious history."[6]

'Abdu'l-Bahá is the bearer of many high and inspiring titles. However, he himself attests that the one he most prizes is that of the "Servant of Bahá" ('Abdu'l-Bahá). "My name is 'Abdu'l-Bahá," he announces. "My qualification is 'Abdu'l-Bahá. My reality is 'Abdu'l-Bahá. My praise is 'Abdu'l-Bahá. Thraldom to the Blessed Perfection is my glorious and refulgent diadem, and servitude to all the human race my perpetual religion . . . No name, no title, no mention, no commendation have I, nor will ever have, except 'Abdu'l-Bahá. This is my longing. This is my greatest yearning. This is my eternal life. This is my everlasting glory."[7]

While a detailed treatment of the functions of 'Abdu'l-Bahá is beyond the scope of the present chapter, it is interesting to note the elucidation concerning the significance of 'Abdu'l-Bahá's primary functions provided by the Universal House of Justice. Citing Shoghi Effendi, the Universal House of Justice explains that as the "perfect Exemplar" of the teachings, the "unerring Interpreter of His Word," the "embodiment of every Bahá'í ideal," and the "incarnation of every Bahá'í virtue," 'Abdu'l-Bahá's life and work exemplify "the meaning of the Word, both in theory and practice."[8]

'Abdu'l-Bahá not only elaborated and promoted the Bahá'í teachings in his writings and talks, but as the perfect Exemplar of the pattern of life taught by his Father, his every action is significant since it represents a full expression of the Faith applied in the world. Bahá'ís, as parties to the Covenant, are therefore encouraged to study the approach of 'Abdu'l-Bahá and to follow his example as a means of attaining a more concrete understanding of the Bahá'í way of life.

The example set by 'Abdu'l-Bahá translates abstract spiritual principles into visible reality and demonstrates their application, thereby making it possible for the individual to strive to emulate his actions. 'Abdu'l-Bahá is a recent historical figure who lived and traveled in the East and the West during his later years. His life is well-documented and available to all for scrutiny. Examination of his writings, the events in his life, and the nature of his relationships with people from diverse backgrounds and cultures illustrate the relevance of his attitudes and behavior to contemporary life. His interactions readily demonstrate that his behavior was not bound by culture, and his example transcends traditional limitations and stereotypes. He defines and models a way of life that is appropriate in both the East and the West.

Enhancing Capacity to Respond to the Call to Apostleship

In the remainder of this chapter, we will reflect on aspects of the life of 'Abdu'l-Bahá pertaining to the application of the three conditions specified by 'Abdu'l-Bahá for attainment to the rank of Apostle of Bahá'u'lláh. The aim of the discussion is to enhance understanding of the practice of the transformative processes involved, to encourage the application of these processes by the members of the Bahá'í community throughout the world, and to increase individual and collective capacity for the systematic execution of 'Abdu'l-Bahá's grand design for the spiritual conquest of the planet as set out in the Tablets of the Divine Plan.

FIRMNESS IN THE COVENANT—THE FIRST CONDITION

Firmness in the Covenant calls for the individual believers, the Bahá'í community, and the Bahá'í institutions to be aware of the guidance set out in the Bahá'í writings and the messages of the Universal House of Justice, to strive to implement this guidance, and to demonstrate a high standard of behavior, a standard that exemplifies a way of life embodied in the Bahá'í teachings and which promotes the oneness of humankind. Adherence to these teachings sets in motion transformative processes that will impact individual and social change on the part of the believer and the Bahá'í community alike.

Shoghi Effendi underlines some of the enormous challenges involved in effecting fundamental change in individual and collective behavior, and he relates the fulfillment of such transformation to "the strictest adherence" to the example of 'Abdu'l-Bahá:

> Not by merely imitating the excesses and laxity of the extravagant age they live in; not by the idle neglect of the sacred

responsibilities it is their privilege to shoulder; not by the silent compromise of the principles dearly cherished by 'Abdu'l-Bahá; not by their fear of unpopularity or their dread of censure can they hope to rouse society from its spiritual lethargy, and serve as a model to a civilization the foundations of which the corrosion of prejudice has well-nigh undermined. By the sublimity of their principles, the warmth of their love, the spotless purity of their character, and the depth of their devoutness and piety, let them demonstrate to their fellow-countrymen the ennobling reality of a power that shall weld a disrupted world.

We can prove ourselves worthy of our Cause only if in our individual conduct and corporate life we sedulously imitate the example of our beloved Master, Whom the terrors of tyranny, the storms of incessant abuse, the oppressiveness of humiliation, never caused to deviate a hair's breadth from the revealed Law of Bahá'u'lláh.

Such is the path of servitude, such is the way of holiness He chose to tread to the very end of His life. Nothing short of the strictest adherence to His glorious example can safely steer our course amid the pitfalls of this perilous age, and lead us on to fulfill our high destiny.[9]

As to what can be learned from examining the life of 'Abdu'l-Bahá, as the "True Exemplar of the Bahá'í Cause," in his Will and Testament, the Master attests to his wholehearted commitment to fulfilling the duty prescribed by Bahá'u'lláh for the people of Bahá to proclaim the Cause of God.[10] Calling attention to the importance of teaching, for example, 'Abdu'l-Bahá explains what actions he himself has taken in this regard, and he calls upon the believers to follow his example:

In these days, the most important of all things is the guidance of the nations and peoples of the world. Teaching the Cause is of utmost importance for it is the head corner-stone of the foundation itself. This wronged servant has spent his days and nights in promoting the Cause and urging the peoples to service. He rested not a moment, till the fame of the Cause of God was noised abroad in the world and the celestial strains from the Abhá Kingdom roused the East and the West. The beloved of God must also follow the same example. This is the secret of faithfulness, this is the requirement of servitude to the Threshold of Bahá![11]

In every age and every generation, each individual believer is challenged to assess the particular needs and the specific tasks confronting the Bahá'í community and to decide where the duty of the individual lies. Shoghi Effendi provides the following useful guidelines and suggests what can be learned from examining the example of 'Abdu'l-Bahá:

The individual alone must assess its character [the duty of the individual], consult his conscience, prayerfully consider all its aspects, manfully struggle against the natural inertia that weighs him down in his effort to arise, shed, heroically and irrevocably, the trivial and superfluous attachments which hold him back, empty himself of every thought that may tend to obstruct his path, mix, in obedience to the counsels of the Author of His Faith, and in imitation of the One Who is its true Exemplar, with men and women, in all walks of life, seek to touch their hearts, through the distinction which characterizes his thoughts, his words and his acts, and win them over tactfully, lovingly, prayerfully and persistently, to the Faith he himself has espoused.[12]

In the present-day, those embarking on the new Five Year Plan and committed to striving to attain to the station of apostleship are challenged, among other things, to make a deep study of the current guidance of the Universal House of Justice; to acquire a clear understanding of the increasingly complex present-day goals and priorities for the achievement of the major objective of the Faith, advancing the process of entry by troops; to act within the framework of the current plan; to give priority to the core activities; to adopt an ongoing systematic mode of learning and planning based on action, reflection, and study; and to appreciate the long-term nature of the society-building enterprise in which they are engaged.

Clearly there are many different kinds of activities an individual might undertake in service to the needs of the Plan, depending on local conditions and the stage of development of a particular cluster. However, all such activities must be governed by a devotional attitude, the practice of spiritual qualities, a humble orientation toward service, a willingness to continue to learn and adapt to change, and a realistic, long-term perspective concerning the complexity of the process of growth and change.

In light of the breadth of the individual and collective transformations required for the spiritual regeneration of the planet envisioned in the Revelation of Bahá'u'lláh, and the evolutionary nature of such fundamental change, one of the challenges confronting the individual is to retain a clear understanding of how the present goals of the Faith relate to its vision of the future and to sustain motivation for action, especially in times of difficulties and tests, and to continue to make a sincere effort to follow the guidance in the teachings of the Faith as well as the directives of the institutions of the Bahá'í Administrative Order.

In the Tablets of the Divine Plan, 'Abdu'l-Bahá points to the connection between sacrificial effort and attracting divine assistance. He encourages the Bahá'ís to extend the "scope" of their "exertions," explaining that, "The wider its range, the more striking will be the evidence of divine assistance."[13] To illustrate the dynamic connection between the power of divine assistance and motivation to serve, 'Abdu'l-Bahá makes reference to what happened during his travels in the West:

> You have observed that while 'Abdu'l-Bahá was in the utmost bodily weakness and feebleness, while he was indisposed, and had not the power to move—notwithstanding this physical state he traveled through many countries, in Europe and America, and in churches, meetings and conventions was occupied with the promotion of the divine principles and summoned the people to the

manifestation of the Kingdom of Abhá. You have also observed how the confirmations of the Blessed Perfection encompassed all. What result is forthcoming from material rest, tranquillity, luxury and attachment to this corporeal world? It is evident that the man who pursues these things will in the end become afflicted with regret and loss.[14]

The life of 'Abdu'l-Bahá exemplifies his willingness to accept responsibility for the work of the Cause. The Guardian's secretary, writing on his behalf, comments on the general importance of this quality and its impact on the believer, affirming: "God will . . . assist us if we do our share and sacrifice in the path of the progress of His Faith. We have to feel the responsibility laid upon our shoulders, arise to carry it out, and then expect divine grace to be showered upon us."[15]

Similarly, perseverance in service to the Cause is critical to implementation of the Divine Plan. Shoghi Effendi in his letters stresses the role of sustained sacrificial effort in attracting the power of divine assistance. In one such letter, for example, he counseled the Bahá'ís not to feel discouraged if their efforts "do not always yield an abundant fruitage," explaining that

. . . a quick and rapidly-won success is not always the best and the most lasting. The harder you strive to attain your goal, the greater will be the confirmations of Bahá'u'lláh, and the more certain you can feel to attain success. Be cheerful, therefore, and exert yourself with full faith and confidence. For Bahá'u'lláh has promised His Divine assistance to every one who arises with a pure and detached heart to spread His Holy Word, even though he may be bereft of every human knowledge and capacity, and notwithstanding the forces of darkness and of opposition which may be arrayed against him. The goal is clear, the path safe and certain, and the assurances of Bahá'u'lláh as to the eventual success of our efforts quite emphatic. Let us keep firm, and whole-heartedly carry on the great work which He has entrusted into our hands.[16]

Given the evolutionary nature of the transformative processes set in train by the teachings of Bahá'u'lláh for the spiritual regeneration of the planet, it is important not only to be optimistic but also to have a realistic understanding of the pace at which the necessary transformations in individual and collective life are likely to unfold. Conceptualizing this evolutionary process as a journey, Shoghi Effendi calls attention to the nature of the preparation required and anticipates a positive outcome: "Putting on the armor of His love, firmly buckling on the shield of His mighty Covenant, mounted on the steed of steadfastness, holding aloft the lance of the Word of the Lord of Hosts, and with unquestioning reliance on His promises as the best provision for their journey, let them set their faces towards those fields that still remain unexplored and direct their steps to those goals that are as yet unattained, assured that He . . . will continue to assist them . . . to a degree that no finite mind can imagine or human heart perceive." And, stressing the adoption of an evolutionary perspective, the Universal House of Justice offers the following guidance to the believers: "Above all, in every aspect of teaching the Message, the friends should have confidence in the regenerative power of the Word of God, seek strength from the hosts of divine assistance, and anticipate the bounties that will continually be showered upon them. To build a new world is no easy task. The road is stony and filled with obstacles, but the journey is infinitely rewarding."[17]

From the foregoing it is suggested that firmness in the Covenant provides the spiritual foundation for activities undertaken in pursuit of the "wondrous vision" set out in the Tablets of the Divine Plan.[18] It ensures clarity of focus on the evolving task, promotes cooperation between the individual, the institutions, and the community, and is critical to sustaining motivation to learn and to serve.

FELLOWSHIP AND LOVE AMONG THE BELIEVERS—
THE SECOND CONDITION

The hallmark of Bahá'u'lláh's vision for the spiritual regeneration of the planet is the acceptance and application of the principle of the oneness of humankind. Referring to the relative importance of this spiritual principle in religious history, 'Abdu'l-Bahá observes, "In every dispensation, there hath been the commandment of fellowship and love, but it was a commandment limited to the community of those in mutual agreement, not to the dissident foe. In this wondrous age, however, praised be God, the commandments of God are not delimited, not restricted to any one group of people, rather have all the friends been commanded to show forth fellowship and love, consideration and generosity and loving-kindness to every community on earth." Addressing the believers and stressing the urgency of their response, 'Abdu'l-Bahá states: "O ye loved ones of the Lord! This is the hour when ye must associate with all the earth's peoples in extreme kindliness and love, and be to them the signs and tokens of God's great mercy. Ye must become the very soul of the world, the living spirit in the body of the children of men." And repeating his appeal, "Now is the time for the lovers of God to raise high the banners of unity, to intone, in the assemblages of the world, the verses of friendship and love and to demonstrate to all that the grace of God is one. Thus will the tabernacles of holiness be upraised on the summits of the earth, gathering all peoples into the protective shadow of the Word of Oneness. This great bounty will dawn over the world at the time when the lovers of God shall arise to carry out His Teachings, and to scatter far and wide the fresh, sweet scents of universal love."[19]

Foreshadowing the transformative impact of the Bahá'í Revelation on the state of the world, 'Abdu'l-Bahá in the Tablets of the Divine Plan calls the believers to demonstrate a high standard of unity. He specifies achievement of fellowship and love among the believers as the second condition for attainment to the station of Apostle of Bahá'u'lláh. "O ye friends," he writes, "Fellowship, fellowship! Love, love! Unity, unity!—so that the power of the Bahá'í Cause may appear and become manifest in the world of existence." And again he observes, "When the most great bestowal reveals itself in the hearts of the believers, the world of nature will be transformed, the darkness of the contingent being will vanish, and heavenly illumination will be obtained. Then the whole world will become the Paradise of Abhá, every one of the believers of God will become a blessed tree, producing wonderful fruits."[20]

"Fellowship and love amongst the believers," the "second condition" established by 'Abdu'l-Bahá for attaining to the station of apostleship, sets a very high standard of conduct for the Bahá'ís. "The divine friends," 'Abdu'l-Bahá states, "must be attracted to and enamored of each other and ever be ready and willing to sacrifice their own lives for each other. Should one soul from amongst the believers meet another, it must be as though a thirsty one with parched lips has reached to the fountain of the water of life, or a lover has met his true beloved."[21]

The current Plans of the Universal House of Justice provide Bahá'ís, eager to attain to the station of apostleship, with many opportunities to practice fellowship and love and to promote unity. The importance of fellowship and love for individual conduct become apparent as the process of entry by troops continues to advance, as the Faith is established in increasing numbers of neighborhoods and villages, as it reaches out to more and diverse receptive populations, and as the community-building functions of the Bahá'í community impact the wider society. These qualities have relevance, for example, to social action, and they give direction to the processes involved in remolding the complex relationships that bind the individual, the community, and the institutions of society.

How to achieve such a high standard of love and unity? While there are, no doubt, many strategies that might be adopted, Shoghi Effendi, in a letter written on his behalf, offers the following general guidance: ". . . if we are ever in any doubt as to how we should conduct ourselves as Bahá'ís we should think of 'Abdu'l-Bahá and study His life and ask ourselves what would He have done, for He is our perfect example in every way."[22]

'Abdu'l-Bahá's extended travels in the West provided the Bahá'ís with the opportunity not only to listen to his admonitions but also to observe firsthand the nature of his interactions with the many different kinds of people he encountered along the way. Shoghi Effendi provides a fascinating glimpse into the breadth of 'Abdu'l-Bahá's interactions with people from all classes of society and different cultural backgrounds. He sheds light on how the Master, as "the incarnation of every Bahá'í virtue and the embodiment of every Bahá'í ideal," related to those he encountered. Shoghi Effendi explains that while pursuing the task of promulgating the Message of Bahá'u'lláh with "a vitality, a courage, [and] a single-mindedness," 'Abdu'l-Bahá was at the same time

> unfailing in His solicitude for the sick, the sorrowful and the down-trodden; uncompromising in His championship of the underprivileged races and classes; bountiful as the rain in His generosity to the poor; contemptuous of the attacks launched against Him by vigilant and fanatical exponents of orthodoxy and sectarianism; marvelous in His frankness while demonstrating, from platform and pulpit, the prophetic Mission of Jesus Christ to the Jews, of the Divine origin of Islám in churches and synagogues, or the truth of Divine Revelation and the necessity of religion to materialists, atheists or agnostics; unequivocal in His glorification of Bahá'u'lláh at all times and within the sanctuaries of divers sects and denominations; adamant in His refusal, on several occasions, to curry the favor of people of title and wealth both in England and in the United States; and last but not least incomparable in the spontaneity, the genuineness and warmth of His sympathy and loving-kindness shown to friend and stranger alike, believer and unbeliever, rich and poor, high and low, whom He met, either intimately or casually, whether on board ship, or whilst pacing the streets, in parks or public squares, at receptions or banquets, in slums or mansions, in the gatherings of His followers or the assemblage of the learned. . .[23]

The passage quoted above brings to life 'Abdu'l-Bahá's great sensitivity and his all-embracing acceptance of and concern for the common weal.

Detailed accounts of the events that transpired during 'Abdu'l-Bahá's historic journeys in the West have already been written.[24] Rather than recount particular episodes, we will refer instead to a number of Shoghi Effendi's descriptions of 'Abdu'l-Baha's interactions with different people, including representatives of minority groups and those on the margins of society. These descriptions highlight the example of 'Abdu'l-Bahá and offer useful insights into the practice of the oneness of humankind.

One of the outstanding features of 'Abdu'l-Bahá's interactions with people, to which Shoghi Effendi referred in the passage above, is his "uncompromising . . . championship of the underprivileged races and classes." To take but one example, the Guardian affirms that the "representatives of the pure-hearted and the spiritually receptive Negro race," were "dearly loved" by 'Abdu'l-Bahá, that he yearned for their conversion to his Father's Faith, and he "ardently championed" their interests "in the course of His memorable visit to the North American continent." It is, therefore, useful to examine in more detail the example of 'Abdu'l-Bahá's relationship with people of different races.[25]

At the outset, it must be noted that racial prejudice, which is antithetical to the principle of the oneness of humankind, has long been an unresolved issue in American society, as well as in other parts of the world. In a letter written on his behalf in response to a question concerning the Bahá'í attitude toward people of color, Shoghi Effendi replied, "It is only evident that the principle of the oneness of Mankind—which is the main pivot round which all the Teachings of Bahá'u'lláh revolves—precludes the possibility of considering race as a bar to any intercourse, be it social or otherwise. The Faith, indeed, by its very nature and purpose transcend all racial limitations and differences, and proclaims the basic essential unity of the entire human race. Racial prejudice, of whatever nature and character, is therefore severely condemned, and as such should be wiped out by the friends in all their relations, whether private or social."[26]

Writing to the North American Bahá'ís in 1937, when launching the first of the systematic teaching plans inspired by 'Abdu'l-Bahá's Divine Plan, Shoghi Effendi characterized racial prejudice as "the most vital and challenging issue confronting the Bahá'í community" and he called for the urgent solution of this longstanding situation through the "ceaseless exertions" of all members of the community, "whether colored or noncolored," in the "common task of fulfilling the instruc-

tions, realizing the hopes, and following the example of 'Abdu'l-Bahá."
Shoghi Effendi makes it clear that "neither race has the right, or can
conscientiously claim, to be regarded as absolved from such an obligation, as having realized such hopes, or having faithfully followed such
an example."[27]

To encourage the Bahá'ís in their endeavors, Shoghi Effendi directs
the friends "fearlessly and determinedly" not only to act on 'Abdu'l-
Bahá's "instructions" concerning relationships between the races,
but also to call to mind how he himself acted "while in their midst."
'Abdu'l-Bahá's "instructions" and "hopes" highlight his vision for a
united and harmonious world, a world that gives full expression to the
oneness of humankind, and his example demonstrates practical steps
that can be taken to support evolution toward individual and collective
spiritual transformation.[28]

To help the believers recapture recollections of how 'Abdu'l-Bahá
had acted while he was in North America, Shoghi Effendi offered the
following prompts:

> Let them remember, His courage, His genuine love, His infor-
> mal and indiscriminating fellowship, His contempt for and
> impatience of criticism, tempered by His tact and wisdom. Let
> them revive and perpetuate the memory of those unforgettable
> and historic episodes and occasions on which He so strikingly
> demonstrated His keen sense of justice, His spontaneous sympa-
> thy for the downtrodden, His ever-abiding sense of the oneness
> of the human race, His overflowing love for its members, and His
> displeasure with those who dared to flout His wishes, to deride
> His methods, to challenge His principles, or to nullify His acts."[28]

Shoghi Effendi called attention to the impact of prejudice on the
community and its structures. For example, in the following passage
he identifies some of the pernicious and socially destructive attitudes
underlying racial discrimination, and contrasts them with the Bahá'í
standard:

To discriminate against any race, on the ground of its being socially backward, politically immature, and numerically in a minority, is a flagrant violation of the spirit that animates the Faith of Bahá'u'lláh. The consciousness of any division or cleavage in its ranks is alien to its very purpose, principles, and ideals. Once its members have fully recognized the claim of its Author, and, by identifying themselves with its Administrative Order, accepted unreservedly the principles and laws embodied in its teachings, every differentiation of class, creed, or color must automatically be obliterated, and never be allowed, under any pretext, and however great the pressure of events or of public opinion, to reassert itself.[29]

Highlighting the uniqueness of the Bahá'í approach to minority groups, Shoghi Effendi observes:

Unlike the nations and peoples of the earth, be they of the East or of the West, democratic or authoritarian, communist or capitalist, whether belonging to the Old World or the New, who either ignore, trample upon, or extirpate, the racial, religious, or political minorities within the sphere of their jurisdiction, every organized community enlisted under the banner of Bahá'u'lláh should feel it to be its first and inescapable obligation to nurture, encourage, and safeguard every minority belonging to any faith, race, class, or nation within it. So great and vital is this principle that in such circumstances, as when an equal number of ballots have been cast in an election, or where the qualifications for any office are balanced as between the various races, faiths or nationalities within the community, priority should unhesitatingly be accorded the party representing the minority, and this for no other reason except to stimulate and encourage it, and afford it an opportunity to further the interests of the community.[30]

In addition to the development of capacity within the particular minority group, Shoghi Effendi also calls attention to the long-term society-building implications of the Bahá'í approach to upholding the principle of the oneness of humankind, a principle clearly exemplified by 'Abdu'l-Bahá in his interactions with the diverse peoples he encountered. The Guardian writes, "The adoption of such a course, and faithful adherence to it, would not only be a source of inspiration and encouragement to those elements that are numerically small and inadequately represented, but would demonstrate to the world at large the universality and representative character of the Faith of Bahá'u'lláh, and the freedom of His followers from the taint of those prejudices which have already wrought such havoc in the domestic affairs, as well as the foreign relationships, of the nations."[31]

The degree of individual and community transformation called for by the practice of fellowship and love is very demanding. A tremendous effort is required to eliminate prejudice, to tear down barriers between people, and to remold the outlook, manners, and conduct of the masses and the institutions of society to reflect ever more closely the spirit and teachings of the Faith of Bahá'u'lláh. Reflection on the example of 'Abdu'l-Bahá is an important tool in enhancing and inspiring sustained effort to attain to the level of fellowship, unity, and love that gives expression to the oneness of humankind and promotes unity in diversity.

TRAVELING TO TEACH—THE THIRD CONDITION

Diffusing the Light of the Revelation of Bahá'u'lláh is a privilege and fundamental spiritual duty for all believers. Indeed, Shoghi Effendi designates teaching as "the paramount and most urgent duty of every Bahá'í," and calls for it to become "the dominating passion of our life."[32] As described in chapters 4 and 8, the scope of the activities associated with the work of teaching the Faith has, under the direction of the Head of the Faith, broadened and become more complex with the passage of time.

The individual aspiring to attain to the station of apostleship has much to learn from following the example of 'Abdu'l-Bahá. As noted above, in his Will and Testament, 'Abdu'l-Bahá himself stresses the supreme importance of teaching the Faith. He describes his own ceaseless endeavors in promoting the message of Bahá'u'lláh and calls upon the believers to follow his example, asserting, "this is the requirement of servitude to the Threshold of Bahá."[33]

Stressing the level of sustained effort that is required of those who "stand fast in the Covenant," 'Abdu'l-Bahá states, "It behooveth them not to rest for a moment, neither to seek repose. They must disperse themselves in every land, pass by every clime, and travel throughout all regions. Bestirred, without rest, and steadfast to the end, they must raise in every land the triumphal cry 'Yá Bahá'u'l-Abhá!' (O Thou the Glory of Glories). . . ." And he invokes the eternal memory of the sacrificial services of the disciples: "The disciples of Christ forgot themselves and all earthly things, forsook all their cares and belongings, purged themselves of self and passion, and with absolute detachment scattered far and wide and engaged in calling the peoples of the world to the divine guidance; till at last they made the world another world, illumined the surface of the earth, and even to their last hour proved self-sacrificing in the pathway of that beloved One of God. Finally in various lands they suffered glorious martyrdom. Let them that are men of action follow in their footsteps!"[34]

The letters of Shoghi Effendi contain a number of passages illustrating 'Abdu'l-Bahá's sensitive approach to teaching the Faith. Reflection on these descriptions will, likely, prove a valuable resource in suggesting ways to refine individual and collective responses to the duty of teaching, and they will enable fulfillment of the third condition associated with attaining the station of Apostle of Bahá'u'lláh. Drawing attention to the general approach adopted by 'Abdu'l-Bahá in His presentation of the Faith, the Guardian advises, "Let us . . . bear in mind the example which our beloved Master has clearly set before us. Wise and tactful in His approach, wakeful and attentive in His early intercourse, broad and liberal in all His public utterances, cautious and gradual in the unfolding of the essential verities of the Cause, passionate in His appeal yet sober in argument, confident in tone, unswerving in conviction, dignified in His manners—such were the distinguishing features of our Beloved's noble presentation of the Cause of Bahá'u'lláh."[35]

In another letter on this general subject, the Guardian, in a letter written on his behalf, offered the following general advice: "We must be careful not to teach in a fanatical way. We should teach as the Master taught. He was the perfect Exemplar of the Teachings. He proclaimed the universal truths, and, through love and wise demonstration of the universal verities of the Faith, attracted the hearts and the minds." Turning to the example of 'Abdu'l-Bahá's wisdom, sensitivity, and understanding of people, within the context of teaching the Faith, Shoghi Effendi comments, "It was He, our beloved 'Abdu'l-Bahá, our true and shining Exemplar, who with infinite tact and patience, whether in His public utterances or in private converse, adapted the presentation of the fundamentals of the Cause to the varying capacities and the spiritual receptiveness of His hearers. He never hesitated, however, to tear the veil asunder and reveal to the spiritually ripened those challenging verities that set forth in its true light the relationship of this Supreme Revelation with the Dispensations of the past."[36]

To those who are taking tentative steps in the field of teaching the Cause, Shoghi Effendi holds up 'Abdu'l-Bahá as an example and explains how to get started. He calls upon the believer to mix with men and women in all walks of life and "seek to touch their hearts, through the distinction which characterizes his thoughts, his words and his acts, and win them over tactfully, lovingly, prayerfully and persistently, to the Faith he himself has espoused."[37] In yet another letter, Shoghi Effendi provides insights into 'Abdu'l-Bahá's approach to the seeker. In addition, in the passage cited below, he captures the quality of the interaction and describes the important role of the individual in accompanying the new believer so as to build capacity for service, ensuring that he or she becomes a mature and active member of the Bahá'í community, thus linking the teaching process to community-building:

Let him remember the example set by 'Abdu'l-Bahá, and His constant admonition to shower such kindness upon the seeker, and exemplify to such a degree the spirit of the teachings he hopes to instill into him, that the recipient will be spontaneously impelled to identify himself with the Cause embodying such teachings.

Let him refrain, at the outset, from insisting on such laws and observances as might impose too severe a strain on the seeker's newly awakened faith, and endeavor to nurse him, patiently, tactfully, and yet determinedly, into full maturity, and aid him to proclaim his unqualified acceptance of whatever has been ordained by Bahá'u'lláh. Let him, as soon as that stage has been attained, introduce him to the body of his fellow-believers, and seek, through constant fellowship and active participation in the local activities of his community, to enable him to contribute his share to the enrichment of its life, the furtherance of its tasks, the consolidations of its interests, and the coordination of its activities with those of its sister communities. Let him not be content until he has infused into his spiritual child so deep a longing as to impel him to arise independently, in his turn, and devote his energies to the quickening of other souls, and the upholding of the laws and principles laid down by his newly adopted Faith.[38]

Education and capacity-building are vital to the preparation of teachers. Here again, the example of 'Abdu'l-Bahá is relevant. Shoghi Effendi includes, among his list of useful tools, examination of the public talks of 'Abdu'l-Bahá. While the following extract focuses specifically on the training of youth, it is suggested Shoghi Effendi's guidance bears more general consideration. The letter states, "The Bahá'í youth must be taught how to teach the Cause of God. Their knowledge of the fundamentals of the Faith must be deepened and the standard of their education in science and literature enhanced. They must become thoroughly familiar with the language used and the example set by 'Abdu'l-Bahá in His public addresses throughout the West. They must also be acquainted with those essential prerequisites of teaching as recorded in the Holy Books and Tablets."[39]

Further, in relation to the importance of acquiring knowledge about the Faith in preparation for the work of teaching, Shoghi Effendi reiterated the value of studying the talks of 'Abdu'l-Bahá and explained the vital connection between knowledge of the Faith and being able to relate its teaching to the resolution of the current problems confronting humanity. The letter written on his behalf states:

> The Cause needs more Bahá'í scholars, people who not only are devoted to it and believe in it and are anxious to tell others about it, but also who have a deep grasp of the Teachings and their significance, and who can correlate its beliefs with the current thoughts and problems of the people of the world.
>
> The Cause has the remedy for all the world's ills. The reason why more people don't accept it is because the Bahá'ís are not always capable of presenting it to them in a way that meets the immediate needs of their minds. Young Bahá'ís like yourself must prepare themselves to really bring the Message to their generation, who need it so desperately and who can understand the language it speaks so well. He would advise you among other books to study the Talks of 'Abdu'l-Bahá, as His method of approaching the mind of the public cannot be surpassed . . .[40]

The example of 'Abdu'l-Bahá's attitude to the seeker and his approach to the process of teaching described in the letters of Shoghi Effendi has particular relevance to enhancing capacity to engage in meaningful and elevated conversations with a wide range of people called for in the current Plans of the Universal House of Justice. Likewise, the emphasis on the important role of preparation for teaching through learning resonates with current activities for the study of the sacred texts, engagement in social action, and participation in the prevalent discourses of society.

DEALING WITH CHALLENGES

As with all forms of service, over time, challenges may well arise that test the resolve of the believer to persist in his or her activity. The travels of 'Abdu'l-Bahá in the West provide an inspiring and thought-provoking example of his response to difficult situations. For example, determined to take advantage of the opportunities that came about as a result of the sudden change in regime in the Ottoman domains, 'Abdu'l-Bahá embarked immediately on his historic journeys through the West. Though he had reached an advanced age and was failing in health, he arose "without thought of comfort, undeterred by the risks involved, and utterly reliant upon divine assistance, to champion the Cause of God."[41]

In the Tablets of the Divine Plan, 'Abdu'l-Bahá refers to the poor state of his health during his travels, and he observes that although he was weak and indisposed, he continued to travel and to be occupied with promoting the Faith.[42] He also comments on his health in a number of public talks he delivered in the course of his travels, and in each instance, his remarks are not only instructive but also provide insight into why he chose to attend a particular event. For example, while in Europe, at the end of a presentation on the subject of universal love, 'Abdu'l-Bahá refers to the importance of invoking divine assistance and having positive expectations about the outcome of such a venture. "Remember not your own limitations," he advises. "The help of God will come to you. Forget yourself. God's help will surely come! When you call on the Mercy of God waiting to reinforce you, your strength will be tenfold." He illustrates his point by describing his own situation:

> Look at me: I am so feeble, yet I have had the strength given me to come amongst you: a poor servant of God, who has been enabled to give you this message! I shall not be with you long! One must never consider one's own feebleness, it is the strength of the Holy Spirit of Love, which gives the power to teach. The thought of our own weakness could only bring despair. We must look higher than all earthly thoughts; detach ourselves from every material idea, crave for the things of the spirit; fix our eyes on the everlasting bountiful Mercy of the Almighty, who will fill our souls with the gladness of joyful service to His command "Love One Another."[43]

Additional examples are to be found in the accounts of 'Abdu'l-Bahá's sojourn in North America. When addressing a gathering at a reception hosted by the New York Peace Society, for example, 'Abdu'l-Bahá stated:

> Although I felt indisposed this afternoon, yet because I attach great importance to this assembly and was longing to see your faces, I have come. The expression of kindly feelings and the spirit of hospitality manifested by the former speakers are most grateful. I am thankful for the susceptibilities of your hearts, for it is an evidence that your greatest desire is the establishment of international peace. You are lovers of the oneness of humanity, seekers after the good pleasure of the Lord, investigators of the foundations of the divine religions.
>
> Today there is no greater glory for man than that of service in the cause of the Most Great Peace.[44]

Likewise, in his opening remarks during a presentation to an Open Forum in San Francisco, 'Abdu'l-Bahá is reported to have explained: "Although I was feeling indisposed this evening, yet owing to the love I entertain for you I have attended this meeting. For I have heard that this is an open forum, investigating reality; that you are free from blind imitations, desiring to arrive at the truth of things, and that your endeavors are lofty."[45]

In the above instances, 'Abdu'l-Bahá made a conscious choice. He closed his eyes to thoughts of the material world and refused to focus only on the needs of the physical body. In the Tablets of the Divine Plan, he comments on the significance of his actions, calling attention to "how the confirmations of the Blessed Perfection encompassed all." Underlining the importance of making a considered choice, he asks, "What result is forthcoming from material rest, tranquility, luxury and attachment to this corporeal world?" His sobering response to this rhetorical question makes it clear that there are consequences associated with choice. "It is evident," he thus attests," that the man who pursues these things will in the end become afflicted with regret and loss."[46]

'Abdu'l-Bahá stresses the importance of recognizing opportunities and seizing the moment for action. Indeed, the eagerness with which he seized the opportunity to embark on his travels to the West after having been providentially released from captivity is an example to all Bahá'ís. Commenting on the immediate action taken by 'Abdu'l-Bahá following the unexpected change in the circumstances of his life, Shoghi Effendi attests that the Master was "Inflexibly resolved to undertake this arduous voyage, at whatever cost to His strength, at whatever risk to His life."[47] Such was his determination to take full and immediate advantage of this God-sent opportunity.

During the course of the evolution of the Bahá'í community throughout the world, there have been, and will continue to be, not only unexpected opportunities for the promotion of the interests of the Faith, but also periods of crisis and challenge that require extraordinary actions on the part of its members in order to sustain momentum for growth. The challenge is to recognize and embrace opportunities for service that are critical to the promotion of the Faith's current level of development and that will propel it to the next stage in its organic growth. The guidance of the Universal House of Justice and the institutions of the Faith reiterate the vision set out in the Divine Plan, establish the major priorities, and define the way forward. A timely response to this guidance is the challenge confronting anyone who wishes to reach the station of apostleship.

Conclusion

By reflecting on the life of 'Abdu'l-Bahá, those striving to attain the station of Apostle of Bahá'u'lláh can greatly expand their vision. Mention has been made of the Master's unique role in the Covenant, of his complete identification with his Father's teachings—illustrated, among other things, by his wholehearted response to Bahá'u'lláh's call for teaching the Cause and his all-embracing love and concern for humankind.

'Abdu'l-Bahá's understanding of human nature, his sensitive interactions with people from different backgrounds, races, and classes, his willingness to engage with men and women from diverse cultures, to transcend traditional cultural barriers that promoted separation between the races and constituted a source of disunity, offer useful insights into the promotion of fellowship, love, and unity, and have implications for the practice of the principle of the oneness of mankind by the individual, the community, and the institutions of the Faith, as well as the wider society.

Much too, can be learned from 'Abdu'l-Bahá's approach to service, as it relates to teaching the Faith. His approach was systematic, and his perspective reached far into the future. He immediately recognized opportunities for service that presented themselves; he understood what action was required in each new circumstance; and he established priorities, often specifying the sequence and the manner in which tasks were to be completed. Furthermore, he willingly sacrificed his personal comfort and pushed himself to the limit physically for the advancement of the Cause. Confident in the power of divine assistance, he persevered in serving until the task was completed. Insights such as these are pertinent both to the role of the teacher and the means of sustaining the processes of growth and transformation over time.

The tasks the Bahá'í community will be called upon to undertake in the years ahead, as a result of the operation of 'Abdu'l-Bahá's Divine Plan, will doubtless evolve and increase in complexity and scale. So too, will the opportunity afforded the individual believer, as an Apostle of Bahá'u'lláh, to make his or her contribution to the spiritual regeneration of the planet. To this end, 'Abdu'l-Bahá, the Servant of God, invites the "friends of God" to "follow the pathway of service":

> Wherefore, O ye friends of God, redouble your efforts, strain every nerve, till ye triumph in your servitude to the Ancient Beauty, the Manifest Light, and become the cause of spreading far and wide the rays of the Daystar of Truth. Breathe ye into the world's worn and wasted body the fresh breath of life, and in the furrows of every region sow ye holy seed. Rise up to champion this Cause; open your lips and teach. In the meeting place of life be ye a guiding candle; in the skies of this world be dazzling stars; in the gardens of unity be birds of the spirit, singing of inner truths and mysteries.
>
> Expend your every breath of life in this great Cause and dedicate all your days to the service of Bahá, so that in the end, safe

from loss and deprivation, ye will inherit the heaped-up treasures of the realms above. For the days of a man are full of peril and he cannot rely on so much as a moment more of life . . .

Wherefore, rest ye neither day nor night and seek no ease. Tell ye the secrets of servitude, follow the pathway of service, till ye attain the promised succor that cometh from the realms of God.[48]

Notes

Introduction

1. Shoghi Effendi, *Citadel of Faith*, p. 5.
2. Shoghi Effendi, *The World Order of Bahá'u'lláh*, p. 41; 'Abdu'l-Bahá, cited in Shoghi Effendi, *The World Order of Bahá'u'lláh*, p. 169.
3. 'Abdu'l-Bahá, *Tablets of the Divine Plan*, ¶8.1.
4. Ibid., ¶8.9; the Universal House of Justice, letter dated March 2, 2013 to the Bahá'ís of Iran, ¶9.
5. 'Abdu'l-Bahá, *Tablets of the Divine Plan*, ¶14.3.

1 / Seminal Documents

1. Philip Hammond MP, cited in "Magna Carta ripples are still spreading," *Surrey Herald*, 18 November 2010. From Web site http://www.surreyherald.co.uk/surrey-news-columnists/2010/11/18 as of November 19, 2010.
2. Frederic Jessup Stimson, *The Law of the Federal and State Constitutions of the United States: Book One, Origin and Growth of the American Constitutions*. See citation in http://en.wikipedia.org/wiki/Magna_Carta, as of November 19, 2010.
3. "Constitution of the United States of America," *Encyclopedia Britannica, Micropaedia,* vol. III, p. 106.
4. "United States (U.S.) Constitution and Amendments," http://www.constitutionfacts.com, as of 19 November 2010.

5. For a detailed description of the framing of the Declaration, please refer to material prepared by the United Nations, Office of the High Commissioner of Human Rights, at http://www.ohchr.org/EN/Pages/WelcomePage.aspx.

6. Ibid.

7. Ibid.; Bahá'í International Community, "60th Anniversary of the Universal Declaration of Human Rights," February, 2008. See http://www.bic.org/statements-abd-reports/bic-statements/08-0206.htm.

8. Shoghi Effendi, *Messages to the Bahá'í World 1950–1957*, pp. 84–85.

9. Shoghi Effendi, *God Passes By*, p. 631; 'Abdu'l-Bahá, *Tablets of the Divine Plan*, ¶11.11, ¶7.5.

10. Cited in *'Abdu'l-Bahá in Canada*, p. 51.

11. 'Abdu'l-Bahá, *Tablets of the Divine Plan*, ¶4.5; 'Abdu'l-Bahá, *The Promulgation of Universal Peace*, p. 512.

12. For a concise history of World War I refer to A. J. P. Taylor, *A History of the First World War* and "World Wars," *Encyclopedia Britannica, Micropaedia*, vol. X, p. 752.

13. Henry Kissinger, *World Order*, p. 82.

14. Wells, *A Short History of the World*, p. 307.

15. For details, refer to A. W. Palmer, *A Dictionary of Modern History 1789–1945*, p. 354.

16. Wells, *A Short History of the World*, p. 307.

17. For additional details, see *Century of Light*, pp. 33–35.

18. Hobsbawm, "Barbarism: A User's Guide," in *On History*, pp. 256–257.

19. Shoghi Effendi, *God Passes By*, p. 482. For a detailed description refer to H. M. Balyuzi, *'Abdu'l-Bahá, The Centre of the Covenant*, ch. 22 and Lady Blomfield, *The Chosen Highway*, Part III, ch. 4.

20. H. M. Balyuzi, *'Abdu'l-Bahá, The Centre of the Covenant*, p. 443; for details see also ch. 22.

21. Shoghi Effendi, *God Passes By*, pp. 483.

22. Amin Banani, Foreword to 1977 Edition, *Tablets of the Divine Plan*, p. xix.

23. Ibid.

24. Taylor, *A History of the First World War*, pp. 74–75, 76–79.

25. 'Abdu'l-Bahá, *Tablets of the Divine Plan*, ¶7.4.

26. Ibid., ¶7.5, ¶8.1–¶8.11, ¶8.21. For additional references, see also Tablets 4 and 7.

27. Taylor, *A History of the First World War*, pp. 83–86.

28. For brief details, refer to A. W. Palmer, *A Dictionary of Modern History 1789–1945*, p. 171.

29. Taylor, *A History of the First World War*, pp. 109, 110, 113–14.

30. 'Abdu'l-Bahá, *Tablets of the Divine Plan*, ¶14.1–¶14.11, ¶11.10. See also ¶12.5.

31. Shoghi Effendi, *God Passes By*, pp. 630–31.

32. Ibid., p. 513.

33. Shoghi Effendi, *Citadel of Faith*, p. 123; Shoghi Effendi, *Messages to the Bahá'í World 1950–1957*, p. 144.

34. 'Abdu'l-Bahá, *Tablets of the Divine Plan*, ¶7.14, ¶7.15.

35. 'Abdu'l-Bahá, *The Secret of Divine Civilization*, ¶173.

36. 'Abdu'l-Bahá, *Tablets of the Divine Plan*, ¶14.10.

37. Ibid., ¶14.10 and ¶14.11.

38. Shoghi Effendi, "The Faith of Bahá'u'lláh, A World Religion," *World Order*, vol. XIII, no. 7, p. 2.

39. The Universal House of Justice, Riḍván 2010 letter to the Bahá'ís of the world, ¶26.

40. Shoghi Effendi, "The Faith of Bahá'u'lláh, A World Religion," *World Order*, vol. XIII, no. 7, p. 2; 'Abdu'l-Bahá, *Tablets of the Divine Plan*, ¶8.20, ¶8.27, ¶8.20, ¶8.27, and ¶11.14.

41. Bahá'u'lláh, *Gleanings from the Writings of Bahá'u'lláh*, ¶110.1, ¶131.2.

42. For a detailed discussion of this subject, please refer to William S. Hatcher and J. Douglas Martin, *The Bahá'í Faith, The Emerging Global Religion*, ch. 5.

43. The Universal House of Justice, *Messages from the Universal*

House of Justice 1979–1986, ¶379.2; Shoghi Effendi, *The World Order of Bahá'u'lláh,* pp. 42–43.

44. For a detailed discussion of the implications of the age of maturity and its impact on the evolution of society, please refer to Shoghi Effendi, *The World Order of Bahá'u'lláh,* pp. 161–206; and William S. Hatcher and J. Douglas Martin, *The Bahá'í Faith: The Emerging Global Religion,* ch. 7.

45. Shoghi Effendi, from a letter dated March 11, 1936, published in *The World Order of Bahá'u'lláh,* p. 202.

46. The Universal House of Justice, *Messages from the Universal House of Justice 1979–1986,* ¶379.2; 'Abdu'l-Bahá, *Tablets of the Divine Plan,* ¶14.3.

47. 'Abdu'l-Bahá, *Tablets of the Divine Plan,* ¶14.3.

48. Bahá'u'lláh, The Kitáb-i-Íqán, ¶270.

49. The Universal House of Justice, Riḍván 2010 letter to the Bahá'ís of the world, ¶25.

50. 'Abdu'l-Bahá, *Tablets of the Divine Plan,* ¶12.5, ¶6.11, ¶6.4, and ¶6.7.

51. Ibid., ¶10.9.

52. Ibid., ¶1.3.

53. Ibid., ¶3.3.

54. Shoghi Effendi, *Messages to the Bahá'í World 1950–1957,* p. 153; 'Abdu'l-Bahá, *Tablets of the Divine Plan,* ¶7.16 and ¶7.4.

55. Bahá'u'lláh, *Gleanings from the Writings of Bahá'u'lláh,* ¶101.1, ¶156.1, ¶128.6, ¶128.10.

56. 'Abdu'l-Bahá, *Tablets of the Divine Plan,* ¶12.10.

57. Ibid., ¶8.15; ¶12.9; and ¶8.16–17.

58. Ibid., ¶11.9 and ¶11.8.

59. Ibid., ¶6.5.

60. Ibid., ¶8.7, ¶8.4, ¶8.8–8.11.

61. Ibid., ¶8.8.

62. Ibid., ¶8.11, ¶8.11–13.

2 / Call to the Nations

1. *The Summons of the Lord of Hosts: Tablets of Bahá'u'lláh* (Wilmette, IL: Bahá'í Publishing, 2006).
2. Bahá'u'lláh, *Gleanings from the Writings of Bahá'u'lláh*, ¶4.2, ¶110.1.
3. Bahá'u'lláh, The Kitáb-i-Aqdas, ¶83.
4. Shoghi Effendi, *God Passes By*, p. 326; Shoghi Effendi, *The Promised Day is Come*, ¶36.
5. Shoghi Effendi, *God Passes By*, p. 335.
6. Bahá'u'lláh, cited in ibid., p. 336.
7. Detailed historical treatments of these subjects are found in such works as Shoghi Effendi, *God Passes By*, ch. 10 and ch. 12; Adib Taherzadeh, *The Revelation of Bahá'u'lláh*, vol. 2, ch. 15 and Adib Taherzadeh, *The Revelation of Bahá'u'lláh*, vol. 3, chs. 6–9; Peter J. Khan, *The Promised Day is Come, Study Guide*.
8. Shoghi Effendi, *The Promised Day is Come*, ¶12.
9. Geoffrey Nash, *The Phoenix and the Ashes: The Bahá'í Faith and the Modern Apocalypse*, p. 141.
10. David M. Earle, "A Turning Point in History," *World Order* vol. 2, no. 1 (Fall 1967): 8.
11. Ibid., p. 9.
12. Bahá'u'lláh, The Kitáb-i-Aqdas, ¶88.
13. The Báb, quoted in Shoghi Effendi, *God Passes By*, p. 399.
14. Shoghi Effendi, *This Decisive Hour*, ¶158.3.
15. Bahá'u'lláh cited in Shoghi Effendi, *The World Order of Bahá'u'lláh*, p. 78.
16. 'Abdu'l-Bahá, cited in Shoghi Effendi, *God Passes By*, p. 400.
17. Shoghi Effendi, *God Passes By*, p. 354; Shoghi Effendi, *This Decisive Hour*, ¶94.1.
18. Shoghi Effendi, *This Decisive Hour*, ¶158.4.
19. Ibid., ¶73.
20. 'Abdu'l-Bahá, *Tablets of the Divine Plan*, ¶9.3.

21. Ibid., ¶8.6.
22. Ibid., ¶7.2.
23. Ibid., ¶7.5.
24. Shoghi Effendi, *The Advent of Divine Justice*, ¶33, ¶16.
25. Ibid., ¶32.
26. Bahá'u'lláh, *The Summons of the Lord of Hosts*, "Súriy-i-Mulúk," ¶2.
27. Ibid., "Súriy-i-Haykal," ¶145.
28. Bahá'u'lláh, *Gleanings from the Writings of Bahá'u'lláh*, ¶84.1; Bahá'u'lláh, *Epistle to the Son of the Wolf*, p. 115.
29. Shoghi Effendi, *Messages to the Bahá'í World, 1950–1957*, p. 35.
30. Shoghi Effendi, *The Advent of Divine Justice*, ¶16; Shoghi Effendi, *The World Order of Bahá'u'lláh*, p. 72.
31. 'Abdu'l-Bahá, *Tablets of the Divine Plan*, ¶14.3.
32. Ibid., ¶11.10.
33. Shoghi Effendi, *This Decisive Hour*, ¶158.6.
34. Shoghi Effendi, *Citadel of Faith*, p. 32; Shoghi Effendi, *This Decisive Hour*, ¶140.1.
35. Shoghi Effendi, *This Decisive Hour*, ¶82.6.

3 / An Epoch-making Gathering

1. *Star of the West*, vol. IX, no. 12 (October 16, 1918): 132.
2. Cited in *Star of the West*, vol. IX, no. 12 (November 4, 1918): 142.
3. *Star of the West*, vol. IX, no. 17 (January 19, 1919): 188.
4. *Star of the West*, vol. X, no. 2 (April 9, 1919): 21.
5. Ibid., pp. 20–21.
6. *Star of the West*, vol. X, no. 4 (May 17, 1919): 55.
7. Henry Kissinger, *World Order*, pp. 84, 85.
8. Wright, *The History of the World: The Last Five Hundred Years*, p. 584.
9. *Century of Light*, p. 35.
10. *Star of the West*, vol. X, no. 4 (May 17, 1919): 54.
11. Ibid., pp. 65–66.

12. Sohrab, Ahmad. *Unveiling of the Divine Plan: Tablets, Instructions, and Words of Explanation*, p. 2.

13. *Star of the West*, vol. X, no. 4 (May 17, 1919): 61.

14. *Star of the West*, vol. X, no. 11 (September 27, 1919): 213.

15. *Star of the West*, vol. X, no. 4 (May 17, 1919): 67.

16. *Star of the West*, vol. X, no. 9 (August 20, 1919): 182.

17. *Star of the West*, vol. X, no. 5 (June 5, 1919): 91.

18. 'Abdu'l-Bahá, *Tablets of the Divine Plan*, ¶7.5.

19. *Star of the West*, vol. X, no. 7 (July 13, 1919): 118–19.

20. *Star of the West*, vol. X, no. 10 (September 8, 1919): 197.

21. *Star of the West*, vol. X, no. 4 (May 17, 1919): 72.

22. *Star of the West*, vol. XI, no. 3 (April 28, 1920): 43.

23. Ibid., p. 43.

24. Ibid., p. 44.

25. Peter Smith, *A Short History of the Bahá'í Faith*, p. 88.

26. Shoghi Effendi, *God Passes By*, pp. 404–405.

27. Words of Bahá'u'lláh reported by Professor E. G. Browne, cited in H. M. Balyuzi, *'Abdu'l-Bahá: The Centre of the Covenant*, p. 64.

28. Shoghi Effendi, *The World Order of Bahá'u'lláh*, p. 71.

29. For details of the early history of the Bahá'í Faith in North America, see Robert H. Stockman, *The Bahá'í Faith in America: Origins 1892–1900*, vol. 1, *The Bahá'í Faith in America: Early Expansion 1900–1912*, vol. 2, and *Thornton Chase: The First American Bahá'í*.

30. For a detailed account of the first group of pilgrims to visit 'Abdu'l-Bahá, see Kathryn Jewett Hogenson, *Lighting the Western Sky: The Hearst Pilgrimage and the Establishment of the Bahá'í Faith in the West*; Shoghi Effendi, *The World Order of Bahá'u'lláh*, p. 81.

31. Shoghi Effendi, *The World Order of Bahá'u'lláh*, p. 82.

32. For detailed information about the groups addressed by 'Abdu'l-Bahá and the subjects of his talks, refer to *The Promulgation of Universal Peace: Talks Delivered by 'Abdu'l-Bahá during His Visit to the United States and Canada in 1912*, rev. ed..

33. For details concerning the embryonic administrative institutions that existed in the last years of the Heroic Age, refer to Robert. H. Stockman, *The Bahá'í Faith in America: Origins 1892–1900*, vol. 1, *The Bahá'í Faith in America: Early Expansion 1900–1912*, vol. 2.

34. Shoghi Effendi, *The World Order of Bahá'u'lláh*, p. 72; Shoghi Effendi, *Bahá'í Administration*, p. 105.

35. Shoghi Effendi, *Citadel of Faith*, p. 34.

36. *Star of the West*, vol. XI, no. 6 (June 24, 1920): 99–101.

37. Ibid., p. 100.

38. *Star of the West*, vol. X, no. 5 (June 5, 1919): 88–89. For details of the services of Louis Gregory and Dorothy Baker in the South see, Gayle Morrison, *To Move the World*; concerning Mrs. Parsons, see Richard Hollinger, ed., *'Abdu'l-Bahá in America: Agnes Parsons' Diary*. Louis Gregory, "Inter-Racial Amity," *The Bahá'í World, 1926–1928*, vol. II, p. 281. Horace Holley, "Survey of Current Bahá'í Activities in the East and West," *The Bahá'í World, 1926–1928*, vol. II, p. 22.

39. Shoghi Effendi, *The World Order of Bahá'u'lláh*, p. 87.

40. For details of Miss Root's life and exploits, see Mabel R. Garis, *Martha Root: Lioness of the Threshold*. The Universal House of Justice, *Messages from the Universal House of Justice, 1963–1986*, ¶185.3.

41. Shoghi Effendi, *God Passes By*, p. 488. Report in *The Bahá'í World*, vol. 2 (New York City: Bahá'í Publishing Committee, 1928), p. 40.

42. Shoghi Effendi, *The World Order of Bahá'u'lláh*, pp. 87–88.

43. Shoghi Effendi, *This Decisive Hour*, ¶94.1, 20.1, 25.1.

44. Ibid., ¶82.6.

4 / Diffusing the Light

1. Shoghi Effendi, *God Passes By*, p. 513.

2. The Báb, *Selections from the Writings of the Báb*, 3:12:2.

3. Shoghi Effendi, *The Promised Day is Come*, p. v.

4. Bahá'u'lláh, *Gleanings from the Writings of Bahá'u'lláh*, ¶106.1.

5. Ibid., no. 106.3, 25.1, the Báb, *Selections from the Writings of the Báb*, 3:38:1.
6. Bahá'u'lláh, *Gleanings from the Writings of Bahá'u'lláh*, ¶52.2.
7. Ibid., ¶5.4.
8. Bahá'u'lláh, *Tablets of Bahá'u'lláh*, p. 181.
9. Bahá'u'lláh, *Gleanings from the Writings of Bahá'u'lláh*, ¶5.3.
10. Bahá'u'lláh, *The Hidden Words*, Persian no. 36.
11. 'Abdu'l-Bahá, *The Promulgation of Universal Peace*, p. 523.
12. Matthew 28:19.
13. 'Abdu'l-Bahá, *Selections from the Writings of 'Abdu'l-Bahá*, ¶196.2.
14. "Christianity," in Mircea Eliade, ed., *The Encyclopedia of Religion*, vol. 3, p. 349.
15. Stephen C. Neill, "Christian Missions," in Mircea Eliade, ed., *The Encyclopedia of Religion*, vol. 9, p. 573.
16. John A. Noss, *Man's Religions*, p. 589.
17. "Bartholomew, Saint." *The New Encyclopaedia Britannica*, Micropaedia, vol. 1, p. 844; 'Abdu'l-Bahá, *Tablets of the Divine Plan*, ¶10.9.
18. Stephen C. Neill, "Christian Missions," in Mircea Eliade, *The Encyclopedia of Religion*, vol. 9, pp. 573–74.
19. Shoghi Effendi, *The World Order of Bahá'u'lláh*, p. 20.
20. Robert S. Paul, "Ministry," in Mircea Eliade, ed., *The Encyclopedia of Religion*, vol. 11, p. 539.
21. Robert L. Montgomery, *The Lopsided Spread of Christianity: Toward an Understanding of the Diffusion of Religions*, p. 141.
22. 'Abdu'l-Bahá, *The Secret of Divine Civilization*, ¶154
23. Robert L. Montgomery, *The Lopsided Spread of Christianity: Toward an Understanding of the Diffusion of Religions*, pp. 2, 37.
24. Shoghi Effendi, *God Passes By*, p. 86.
25. The Universal House of Justice, Riḍván 2010 letter, p. 8; Shoghi Effendi, *The World Order of Bahá'u'lláh*, p. 163.
26. The Universal House of Justice, Riḍván 2010 letter to the Bahá'ís of the world, ¶25.
27. The Universal House of Justice, "Introduction," in Bahá'u'lláh, The Kitáb-i-Aqdas, p. 3.

28. For additional information, refer to Shoghi Effendi, *Citadel of Faith*, p. 7.
29. Ibid.
30. Shoghi Effendi, *God Passes By*, p. 9.
31. H. M. Balyuzi, *The Báb: The Herald of the Day of Days*, ch. 1.
32. Ibid., p. 17.
33. Ibid., p. 19.
34. Ibid., p. 20.
35. Ibid., p. 21.
36. Shoghi Effendi, *God Passes By*, p. 10.
37. Nabíl-i-Aʿzam, *The Dawn-Breakers*, p. 92.
38. Ibid., p. 93.
39. Ibid., p. 94.
40. Shoghi Effendi, *God Passes By*, p. 17.
41. Ibid., p. 4.
42. Adib Taherzadeh, *The Revelation of Baháʾuʾlláh*, vol. 4, ch. 18.
43. The Universal House of Justice, December 28, 2010 letter, ¶12.
44. Adib Taherzadeh, *The Revelation of Baháʾuʾlláh*, vol. 4, ch. 12.
45. Ibid., p. 182.
46. Shoghi Effendi, *God Passes By*, pp. 479–80.
47. The Universal House of Justice, December 28, 2010 letter, ¶12.
48. Shoghi Effendi, *God Passes By*, p. 513.
49. Shoghi Effendi, *The World Order of Baháʾuʾlláh*, pp. 87–88.
50. The Universal House of Justice, *The Constitution of the Universal House of Justice*, pp. 3–4.
51. Shoghi Effendi, *God Passes By*, p. xxvi.
52. ʿAbduʾl-Bahá, cited in Shoghi Effendi, *God Passes By*, p. 375; the Universal House of Justice, *Messages from the Universal House of Justice,1986–2001*, ¶145.16.
53. Baháʾuʾlláh, *Gleanings from the Writings of Baháʾuʾlláh*, ¶38.1.
54. Baháʾuʾlláh, cited in a letter dated May 31, 1988 from the Universal House of Justice, *Messages from the Universal House of Justice, 1986–2001*, ¶52.7a.

55. The Universal House of Justice, *Messages from the Universal House of Justice, 1986–2001*, ¶145.13.

56. Ibid.

57. Ibid.

58. Shoghi Effendi, *The World Order of Bahá'u'lláh*, p. 20; *Messages from the Universal House of Justice, 1963–1986*, ¶23.20, ¶75.15; Shoghi Effendi, *The World Order of Bahá'u'lláh*, p. 23.

59. Shoghi Effendi, *The World Order of Bahá'u'lláh*, p. 153; *Messages from the Universal House of Justice, 1963–1986*, ¶23.20, ¶75.15; Shoghi Effendi, *The World Order of Bahá'u'lláh*, p. 23.

60. The Universal House of Justice, *Messages from the Universal House of Justice, 1963–1986*, ¶35.7a.

61. Ibid., ¶308.18.

62. The Universal House of Justice, *Messages from the Universal House of Justice, 1963–1986*, ¶141.12.

63. Bahá'í International Community, Office of Public Information, *Who is Writing the Future?* Part II, p. 5.

64. For details about the epochs of the Formative Age, refer to *Messages of the Universal House of Justice 1963–1986*, no. 451, and *Messages of the Universal House of Justice 1986–2001*, pp. xxix–xxx.

65. From a letter dated July 6, 1942, written on behalf of Shoghi Effendi to an individual, in Helen Hornby, comp., *Lights of Guidance*, no. 250.

66. For details, refer to Statement on the Epochs of the Formative Age, in The Universal House of Justice, *Messages of the Universal House of Justice 1963–1986*, ¶451.

67. For information concerning the role of pioneers, see, for example Janet A. Khan, *Heritage of Light, The Spiritual Destiny of America*, ch. 7.

68. Shoghi Effendi, *The World Order of Bahá'u'lláh*, p. 195.

69. Ibid., pp. 197–98.

70. Shoghi Effendi, *God Passes By*, p. xxvi.

71. Shoghi Effendi, *The World Order of Bahá'u'lláh*, p. 195.

72. Shoghi Effendi, *Messages to the Bahá'í World, 1950–1957*, p. 155.

73. The Universal House of Justice, *Messages from the Universal House of Justice 1963–1986*, ¶427.1; the Universal House of Justice, *Messages from the Universal House of Justice, 1986–2001*, ¶331.6.
74. The Universal House of Justice, letter dated December 28, 2010, p. 5.
75. Preface, *Turning Point: Selected Messages of the Universal House of Justice and Supplementary Material 1996–2006*, p. vi.
76. The Universal House of Justice, letter dated December 28, 2010, ¶12.
77. The Universal House of Justice, *Messages from the Universal House of Justice, 1986–2001*, ¶216.17–¶216.18.
78. Ibid.
79. The Universal House of Justice, Riḍván 2010 letter to the Bahá'ís of the world, ¶9.
80. The Universal House of Justice, *Turning Point: Selected Messages of the Universal House of Justice and Supplementary Material 1996–2006*, ¶35.2.
81. The Universal House of Justice, letter dated December 28, 2010, ¶11.
82. The Universal House of Justice, *Turning Point: Selected Messages of the Universal House of Justice and Supplementary Material 1996–2006*, ¶38.9.
83. The Universal House of Justice, letter dated December 28, 2010, ¶40.
84. Ibid.
85. The Universal House of Justice, Riḍván 2010 letter to the Bahá'ís of the world, ¶10.

5 / Fostering the Spiritual Regeneration of the Planet
1. 'Abdu'l-Bahá, *Selections from the Writings of 'Abdu'l-Bahá*, ¶220.1.
2. 'Abdu'l-Bahá, *Tablets of the Divine Plan*, ¶14.11.
3. 'Abdu'l-Bahá, *Will and Testament of 'Abdu'l-Bahá*, p. 13.

4. Letter dated February 20, 1932 written on behalf of Shoghi Effendi, *Compilation of Compilations*, vol. II, no. 1275.

5. Shoghi Effendi, letter dated June 20, 1954, *Compilation of Compilations*, vol. I, no. 1333.

6. 'Abdu'l-Bahá, *Tablets of the Divine Plan*, ¶8.1, ¶6.5.

7. Ibid., ¶8.2, ¶8.4.

8. Ibid., ¶8.4, ¶8.7, ¶8.8–8.11.

9. 'Abdu'l-Bahá, *The Secret of Divine Civilization*, ¶143; 'Abdu'l-Bahá, *The Promulgation of Universal Peace*, p. 452.

10. "Eremitism," *The Encyclopedia of Religion*, vol. 5, pp. 137–46.

11. Bahá'u'lláh, cited in The Kitáb-i-Aqdas, note 61.

12. 'Abdu'l-Bahá, *The Secret of Divine Civilization*, ¶170.

13. 'Abdu'l-Bahá, *Selections from the Writings of 'Abdu'l-Bahá*, ¶201.2.

14. Shoghi Effendi, from a letter written on his behalf dated December 8, 1935, in *Compilation of Compilations*, vol. II, no. 1762.

15. The Universal House of Justice, letter dated February 6, 1973, in *Compilation of Compilations*, vol. I, no. 117.

16. The Universal House of Justice, *Messages from the Universal House of Justice, 1986–2001*, ¶315.7.

17. Shoghi Effendi, letter dated October 14, 1941, written on his behalf, in *Compilation of Compilations*, vol. II, no. 1405.

18. The Universal House of Justice, *Messages from the Universal House of Justice, 1986–2001*, ¶183.33.

19. Shoghi Effendi, letter dated November 2, 1933, written on his behalf, in *Compilation of Compilations*, vol. II, no. 2259, pp. 424–25.

20. Shoghi Effendi, letter dated March 1, 1951 to a National Spiritual Assembly, in *Compilation of Compilations*, vol. I, no. 444.

21. The Universal House of Justice, Riḍván 2010 letter, ¶9, ¶10.

22. 'Abdu'l-Bahá, *Tablets of the Divine Plan*, ¶8.7, ¶8.4, ¶8.8–8.11.

23. Ibid., ¶8.8.

24. 'Abdu'l-Bahá, cited in Shoghi Effendi, *God Passes By*, p. 238; 'Abdu'l-Bahá, *Tablets of the Divine Plan*, ¶8.8.

25. 'Abdu'l-Bahá, *The Importance of Obligatory Prayer and Fasting,* section V.
26. 'Abdu'l-Bahá, *Selections from the Writings of 'Abdu'l-Bahá,* ¶184.2.
27. 'Abdu'l-Bahá, *Paris Talks,* ¶51.7; 'Abdu'l-Bahá, *Tablets of the Divine Plan,* ¶10.13.
28. 'Abdu'l-Bahá, *Some Answered Questions,* ¶25.2, ¶36.7, ¶36.8–36.9.
29. Ibid., ¶24.3–24.4.
30. The Universal House of Justice, *Messages from the Universal House of Justice, 1986–2001,* ¶48.10; letter written on behalf of Shoghi Effendi, dated July 12, 1952, *Lights of Guidance,* no. 405.
31. Letter dated December 18, 1953, written on behalf of Shoghi Effendi in *Compilation of Compilations,* vol. II, no. 1984.
32. The Universal House of Justice, *Messages from the Universal House of Justice, 1986–2001,* ¶248.5.
33. 'Abdu'l-Bahá, *Compilation of Compilations,* vol. I, no. 251; 'Abdu'l-Bahá, *Selections from the Writings of 'Abdu'l-Bahá,* ¶68.5.
34. Ibid., ¶71.1.
35. 'Abdu'l-Bahá, *Selections from the Writings of 'Abdu'l-Bahá,* ¶220.1; 'Abdu'l-Bahá, *Tablets of the Divine Plan,* ¶12.10.

6 / The First Condition of Apostleship

1. 'Abdu'l-Bahá, *Tablets of the Divine Plan,* ¶8.7, ¶8.4, ¶8.7, ¶8.8, ¶8.9, ¶8.11.
2. Ibid., ¶8.8.
3. The Universal House of Justice, *Messages of the Universal House of Justice 1986–2001,* ¶220.4.
4. 'Abdu'l-Bahá, *The Promulgation of Universal Peace,* pp. 640, 642.
5. 'Abdu'l-Bahá, *Tablets of the Divine Plan,* ¶8.8, ¶8.7.
6. The Universal House of Justice, *Messages of the Universal House of Justice 1986–2001,* ¶64.11.

7. Bahá'u'lláh, *Gleanings*, ¶90.2, ¶109.2; Bahá'u'lláh, The Kitáb-i-Aqdas ¶1; the Universal House of Justice, *Messages of the Universal House of Justice 1986–2001*, ¶145.12.
8. 'Abdu'l-Bahá, *The Promulgation of Universal Peace*, p. 406; the Universal House of Justice, letter written on its behalf dated April 19, 2013, cited in *The Covenant of Bahá'u'lláh*, Book 8, Unit 3, p. 66.
9. See Bahá'u'lláh, The Kitáb-i-Aqdas, p. 163.
10. 'Abdu'l-Bahá, *The Secret of Divine Civilization*, ¶130.
11. Shoghi Effendi, from a letter dated January 5, 1934, written on his behalf, in Helen Hornby, comp., *Lights of Guidance*, no. 1563.
12. Adib Taherzadeh, *Child of the Covenant* pp. 403–404; Adib Taherzadeh, *The Revelation of Bahá'u'lláh*, vol. 3, pp. 292–93.
13. The Universal House of Justice, *Messages of the Universal House of Justice 1986–2001*, ¶60.12.
14. Bahá'u'lláh, The Kitáb-i-Aqdas, ¶5.
15. Ibid., ¶125.
16. The Universal House of Justice, *Messages of the Universal House of Justice 1986–2001*, ¶60.53–55.
17. 'Abdu'l-Bahá, *Selections from the Writings of 'Abdu'l-Bahá*, ¶227.27; the Universal House of Justice, *Messages of the Universal House of Justice 1986–2001*, ¶60.16.
18. The Universal House of Justice, *Messages of the Universal House of Justice 1986–2001*, ¶60.18, ¶60.50.
19. The Universal House of Justice, *Messages of the Universal House of Justice 1986–2001*, ¶64.11.
20. Bahá'u'lláh, cited in Shoghi Effendi, *The World Order of Bahá'u'lláh*, p. 25.
21. The Universal House of Justice, Riḍván 2010 letter to the Bahá'ís of the world, ¶25.
22. Shoghi Effendi, letter dated October 6, 1954 written on his behalf, in Helen Hornby, comp., *Lights of Guidance*, no. 247.
23. The Universal House of Justice, from a letter dated July 13, 1964, in Helen Hornby, comp., *Lights of Guidance*, no. 257.

24. The Universal House of Justice, letter dated December 28, 2010 to Bahá'ís of the world, ¶36; the Universal House of Justice, letter written on its behalf dated April 19, 2013, cited in *The Covenant of Bahá'u'lláh,* Book 8, Unit 3, p. 66.

25. The Universal House of Justice, *Messages of the Universal House of Justice 1963–1986,* ¶397.3.

26. The Universal House of Justice, Riḍván 2010 letter, ¶5.

27. The Universal House of Justice, Riḍván 2010 letter, ¶9; the Universal House of Justice, Riḍván 2008 letter, ¶1.

28. The Universal House of Justice, Riḍván 2010 letter, ¶9.

29. The Universal House of Justice, Riḍván 2010 letter, ¶11.

30. The Universal House of Justice, Riḍván 2010 letter, ¶21.

31. The Universal House of Justice, letter dated December 29, 2015, ¶13.

32. The Universal House of Justice, Riḍván 2010 letter, ¶29.

33. Ibid.

34. The Universal House of Justice, Riḍván 2010 letter, ¶26

35. The Universal House of Justice, Riḍván 2010 letter, ¶25.

36. The Universal House of Justice, Riḍván 2010 letter, ¶10.

37. The Universal House of Justice, Riḍván 2010 letter, ¶21.

38. The Universal House of Justice, Riḍván 2010 letter, ¶19.

39. The Universal House of Justice, Riḍván 2010 letter, ¶20.

40. The Universal House of Justice, Riḍván 2010 letter, ¶19.

41. The Universal House of Justice, Riḍván 2010 letter, ¶10.

42. The Universal House of Justice, December 28, 2010 letter to Bahá'ís of the world, ¶28.

43. Ibid., ¶38.

44. The Universal House of Justice, letter dated March 2, 2013 to the Bahá'ís of Iran, ¶7.

45. The Universal House of Justice, letter dated March 2, 2013 to the Bahá'ís of Iran, ¶8, ¶9.

46. The Universal House of Justice, *Messages of the Universal House of Justice 1963–1986,* ¶358.8.

47. 'Abdu'l-Bahá, *Tablets of the Divine Plan,* ¶9.6.

48. Shoghi Effendi, *The World Order of Bahá'u'lláh*, p. 37; the Universal House of Justice, letter dated November 26, 2003 to the Bahá'ís of Iran, ¶2, ¶9.

49. For details, see, for example, *The Bahá'í Question, Iran's Secret Blueprint for the Destruction of a Religious Community, An Examination of the Persecution of the Bahá'ís of Iran* (New York: Bahá'í International Community, 1999), prepared by the Bahá'í International Community United Nations' Office for distribution to members of the United Nations Human Rights Commission.

50. The Universal House of Justice, letter dated June 20, 2008 to the believers in the Cradle of the Faith, ¶1.

51. Ibid., ¶1.

52. Ibid., ¶2.

53. See Janet A. Khan and Peter J. Khan, *Advancement of Women: A Bahá'í Perspective,* chs. 5 and 6. The Universal House of Justice, letter dated June 20, 2008 to the believers in the Cradle of the Faith, ¶3.

54. See 'Abdu'l-Bahá, *Memorials of the Faithful,* pp. 188–200.

55. For details see Soli Shahvar, *The Forgotten Schools* and Janet A. Khan and Peter J. Khan, *Advancement of Women: A Bahá'í Perspective,* ch. 5.

56. See for example, Janet A. Khan and Peter J. Khan, *Advancement of Women: A Bahá'í Perspective*, ch. 5.

57. Shoghi Effendi, *Messages to the Bahá'í World,* p. 65.

58. The Universal House of Justice, letter dated June 20, 2008 to the believers in the Cradle of the Faith, ¶5.

59. Ibid., ¶4.

60. Ibid., ¶4, ¶5.

61. The Universal House of Justice, *The Promise of World Peace,* ¶36, 37.

62. 'Abdu'l-Bahá, *The Secret of Divine Civilization,* ¶122.

63. The Universal House of Justice, Riḍván 2010 letter to the Bahá'ís of the world, ¶11.

64. The Universal House of Justice, letter dated March 2, 2013 to the Bahá'ís of Iran, ¶9.
65. The Universal House of Justice, *Messages of the Universal House of Justice 1986–2001*, ¶145.7; *Century of Light*, ¶9.33–¶9.34.
66. The Universal House of Justice, Riḍván 2010 letter to the Bahá'ís of the world, ¶26.
67. Ibid., ¶25.

7 / The Second Condition of Apostleship

1. Bahá'u'lláh, *Gleanings from the Writings of Bahá'u'lláh*, ¶131.3.
2. Shoghi Effendi, *God Passes By*, pp. 343–44.
3. Shoghi Effendi, *The World Order of Bahá'u'lláh*, pp. 42–43.
4. The Universal House of Justice, *The Promise of World Peace*, ¶40-41.
5. 'Abdu'l-Bahá, cited in Shoghi Effendi, *God Passes By*, p. 375; 'Abdu'l-Bahá, *Tablets of the Divine Plan*, ¶8.8.
6. The Universal House of Justice, *The Institution of the Counsellors*, p. 15.
7. 'Abdu'l-Bahá, *Tablets of the Divine Plan*, ¶8.9; ¶8.9–8.10.
8. Ibid., ¶11.11 and ¶11.13.
9. Ibid., ¶11.11.
10. Ibid., ¶14.3.
11. Ibid.
12. Ibid.
13. Ibid.; 'Abdu'l-Bahá, cited in Shoghi Effendi, *God Passes By*, p. 376.
14. The Universal House of Justice, *The Institution of the Counsellors*, p. 15; 'Abdu'l-Bahá, *Tablets of the Divine Plan*, ¶ 14.3.
15. Bahá'u'lláh, The Kitáb-i-Íqán, ¶270.
16. 'Abdu'l-Bahá, *Tablets of the Divine Plan*, ¶14.3; The Universal House of Justice, *The Promise of World Peace*, ¶39; 'Abdu'l-Bahá, *Tablets of the Divine Plan*, ¶14.3; The Universal House of Justice, *The Promise of World Peace*, ¶40.
17. The Universal House of Justice, letter dated March 2, 2013 to the Bahá'ís of Iran, ¶6.
18. Ibid., ¶7.

19. 'Abdu'l-Bahá, *The Promulgation of Universal Peace*, pp. 215–16.
20. 'Abdu'l-Bahá, *Tablets of the Divine Plan*, ¶14.11.
21. The Universal House of Justice, letter dated March 2, 2013 to the Bahá'ís of Iran, ¶9.
22. Ibid.
23. Ibid.
24. 'Abdu'l-Bahá, *Tablets of the Divine Plan*, ¶14.10, ¶14.11.
25. Ibid., ¶14.5.
26. Shoghi Effendi, *The World Order of Bahá'u'lláh*, pp. 41–42.
27. The Universal House of Justice, *Messages of the Universal House of Justice 1986–2001*, ¶55.3
28. The Universal House of Justice, *Messages of the Universal House of Justice, 1986–2001*, ¶221.8.
29. The Universal House of Justice, letter dated February 13, 1996, written on its behalf in compilation on *Traditional Practices in Africa*, extract 7.
30. 'Abdu'l-Bahá, *The Secret of Divine Civilization*, ¶135.
31. 'Abdu'l-Bahá, *Tablets of the Divine Plan*, ¶14.3.
32. The Universal House of Justice, letter dated December 28, 2010 to the Bahá'ís of the world, ¶40.
33. The Universal House of Justice, letter dated December 28, 2010 to the Bahá'ís of the world, ¶40.
34. Shoghi Effendi, letter dated November 20, 1946 written on his behalf, *The Unfolding Destiny of the British Bahá'í Community*, p. 444.
35. The Universal House of Justice, *Turning Point: Selected Messages of the Universal House of Justice and Supplementary Material 1996–2006*, ¶30.7, ¶30.8.
36. The Universal House of Justice, letter dated December 29, 2015 to the meeting of the Continental Board of Counselors, ¶14.
37. The Universal House of Justice, letter dated April 10, 2011, written on behalf of the Universal House of Justice, ¶4.
38. The Universal House of Justice, letter dated March 2, 2013 to the Bahá'ís of Iran, ¶12.

39. The Universal House of Justice, letter dated March 2, 2013 to the Bahá'ís of Iran, ¶14.

40. Shoghi Effendi, *The World Order of Bahá'u'lláh*, p. 144.

41. The Universal House of Justice, *Messages from the Universal House of Justice, 1963–1986*, ¶141.13–¶141.14; ¶141.16–¶141.17.

42. The Universal House of Justice, *Messages from the Universal House of Justice, 1986–2001*, ¶183.33.

43. 'Abdu'l-Bahá, *The Promulgation of Universal Peace*, pp. 478–79.

44. The Universal House of Justice, *Messages from the Universal House of Justice, 1963–1986*, ¶63.5.

45. Ibid., ¶183.35.

46. The Universal House of Justice, *The Promise of World Peace*, ¶56.

47. 'Abdu'l-Bahá, *Tablets of the Divine Plan*, ¶8.20, ¶14.3; the Universal House of Justice, letter dated March 2, 2013 to the Bahá'ís of Iran, ¶16.

48. For a summary of Bahá'u'lláh's vision of the future World Order, see an extract from a letter dated March 11, 1936, written by Shoghi Effendi in *The World Order of Bahá'u'lláh*, pp. 203–204; Shoghi Effendi, *The World Order of Bahá'u'lláh*, pp. 144, 19.

49. William S. Hatcher & J. Douglas Martin, *The Bahá'í Faith: The Emerging Global Religion*, pp. 142–43.

50. Shoghi Effendi, *Citadel of Faith*, p. 38; Shoghi Effendi, *The World Order of Bahá'u'lláh*, pp. 162–63.

51. The Universal House of Justice, letter dated March 2, 2013 to the Bahá'ís of Iran, ¶17.

52. The Universal House of Justice, *Messages from the Universal House of Justice, 1986–2001*, ¶356.4.

53. For a discussion of this subject, please refer to Shoghi Effendi's analysis in *The Promised Day Is Come*.

54. The Universal House of Justice, letter dated March 2, 2013 to the Bahá'ís of Iran, ¶14; Shoghi Effendi, *The World Order of Bahá'u'lláh*, p. 73.

55. Paul Edwards, ed., *The Encyclopedia of Philosophy*, vol. 8, pp. 212–15; Mircea Eliade, *The Encyclopedia of Religion*, vol. 15, pp. 159–62.

56. *U.S. History Encyclopedia*, "Utopian Communities," http:/www.answers.com/topic/utopian-communities; Russell Jacoby, *Picture Imperfect: Utopian thought for an Anti-Utopian Age*, p. 81.

57. Dennis R. Fox, "Psychology, Ideology, Utopia, and the Commons," *American Psychologist*, vol. 40, no. 1, p. 55.

58. Russell Jacoby, *Picture Imperfect: Utopian thought for an Anti-Utopian Age*, pp. 143, 1, 146–49.

59. The Universal House of Justice, letter dated March 2, 2013 to the Bahá'ís of Iran, ¶14.

60. Shoghi Effendi, in Helen Hornby, comp., *Lights of Guidance*, no. 1570.

61. 'Abdu'l-Bahá, *Selections from the Writings of 'Abdu'l-Bahá*, ¶225.15.

62. Shoghi Effendi, *Citadel of Faith*, p. 112.

63. Ibid., p. 104.

64. Shoghi Effendi, *The World Order of Bahá'u'lláh*, p. 163.

65. 'Abdu'l-Bahá, *The Secret of Divine Civilization*, ¶122.

66. Bahá'u'lláh, *Gleanings from the Writings of Bahá'u'lláh*, ¶131.3, ¶131.4.

67. Shoghi Effendi, from a letter dated December 19, 1923, in *The Compilation of Compilations*, vol. II, no. 1267.

68. 'Abdu'l-Bahá, *Tablets of the Divine Plan*, ¶14.4.

69. The Universal House of Justice, *Messages from the Universal House of Justice, 1963–1986*, ¶55.5.

8 / The Third Condition of Apostleship

1. 'Abdu'l-Bahá, *Selections from the Writings of 'Abdu'l-Bahá*, ¶1.6.

2. Bahá'u'lláh, *Gleanings from the Writings of Bahá'u'lláh*, ¶128.10; Bahá'u'lláh, The Kitáb-i-Aqdas, p. 159; 'Abdu'l-Bahá, *Will and Testament of 'Abdu'l-Bahá*, p. 10.

3. 'Abdu'l-Bahá, *Tablets of the Divine Plan*, ¶8.11.

4. The Universal House of Justice, December 29, 2015, ¶51; the Universal House of Justice, *Messages from the Universal House of Justice, 1986–2001*, ¶248.2.

5. 'Abdu'l-Bahá, *Will and Testament of 'Abdu'l-Bahá*, p. 25; 'Abdu'l-Bahá, *Selections from the Writings of 'Abdu'l-Bahá*, ¶213.1.

6. The Universal House of Justice, *Messages from the Universal House of Justice, 1986–2001*, ¶48. ¶9, ¶48.9–¶48.10.

7. Shoghi Effendi, *The Advent of Divine Justice*, ¶66.

8. The Universal House of Justice, *Turning Point: Selected Messages of the Universal House of Justice and Supplementary Material 1996–2006*, ¶29.4.

9. Bahá'u'lláh, *Tablets of Bahá'u'lláh*, p. 200.

10. Shoghi Effendi, *The Advent of Divine Justice*, ¶66.

11. 'Abdu'l-Bahá, *Selections from the Writings of 'Abdu'l-Bahá*, ¶146.12.

12. 'Abdu'l-Bahá, *Tablets of the Divine Plan*, ¶8.2.

13. Ibid., ¶8.3–¶8.4.

14. Bahá'u'lláh, *Gleanings from the Writings of Bahá'u'lláh*, ¶139.5.

15. 'Abdu'l-Bahá, *The Promulgation of Universal Peace*, pp. 370–71.

16. Bahá'u'lláh, *Gleanings from the Writings of Bahá'u'lláh*, ¶154.1; Bahá'u'lláh, *Epistle to the Son of the Wolf*, p. 25; 'Abdu'l-Bahá, *The Secret of Divine Civilization*, ¶80.

17. 'Abdu'l-Bahá, *Selections from the Writings of 'Abdu'l-Bahá*, ¶206.9.

18. Shoghi Effendi, *Messages to the Bahá'í World*, p. 152.

19. The Universal House of Justice, *Messages from the Universal House of Justice, 1963–1986*, ¶308.3.

20. Bahá'u'lláh and Shoghi Effendi, quoted in the Universal House of Justice, *Messages from the Universal House of Justice, 1963–1986*, ¶308.4.

21. The Universal House of Justice, *Messages from the Universal House of Justice, 1963–1986*, ¶308.3–¶308.5.

22. Bahá'u'lláh, *Gleanings from the Writings of Bahá'u'lláh*, ¶96.3; 'Abdu'l-Bahá, *Tablets of the Divine Plan*, ¶4.2, ¶8.12.

23. Shoghi Effendi, in Helen Hornby comp., *Lights of Guidance*, no. 1992.

24. The Universal House of Justice, *Messages from the Universal House of Justice, 1963–1986*, ¶24.11; the Universal House of Justice, *The Institution of the Counsellors*, January 1, 2001, p. 16; the Universal House of Justice, *Messages from the Universal House of Justice, 1963–1986*, ¶24.11.

25. 'Abdu'l-Bahá, *The Secret of Divine Civilization*, ¶82; 'Abdu'l-Bahá, *Tablets of the Divine Plan*, ¶12.10.

26. 'Abdu'l-Bahá, *Tablets of the Divine Plan*, ¶8.13.

27. Ibid., ¶11.15, ¶11.18.

28. Bahá'u'lláh, The Kitáb-i-Aqdas, ¶149.

29. 'Abdu'l-Bahá, *Tablets of the Divine Plan*, ¶8.14, ¶8.15.

30. Shoghi Effendi, *The Advent of Divine Justice*, ¶75.

31. The Universal House of Justice, Riḍván 2010 letter to the Bahá'ís of the world, ¶9.

32. Ibid., ¶11.

33. 'Abdu'l-Bahá, *Tablets of the Divine Plan*, ¶8.11.

34. See 'Abdu'l-Bahá, *Tablets of the Divine Plan*, ¶8.11 and ¶2.3.

35. Bahá'u'lláh, cited in Shoghi Effendi, *The Advent of Divine Justice*, ¶114.

36. Bahá'u'lláh, *Gleanings from the Writings of Bahá'u'lláh*, ¶157.1.

37. Ibid., ¶157.2–157.3.

38. 'Abdu'l-Bahá, *Tablets of the Divine Plan*, ¶12.10.

39. Ibid., ¶7.8.

40. Shoghi Effendi, *God Passes By*, p. 488.

41. Ibid., p. 614.

42. Ibid., pp. 614–15.

43. The Universal House of Justice, *Messages from the Universal House of Justice, 1963–1986*, ¶221.13f.

44. 'Abdu'l-Bahá, *Tablets of the Divine Plan*, ¶7.10.

45. Shoghi Effendi, *The Advent of Divine Justice*, ¶95.

46. 'Abdu'l-Bahá, *Will and Testament of 'Abdu'l-Bahá*, pp. 13–14.

47. 'Abdu'l-Bahá, *The Promulgation of Universal Peace*, pp. 200–201.

48. The Universal House of Justice, *Messages from the Universal House of Justice, 1963–1986*, ¶18.1.
49. 'Abdu'l-Bahá, *Some Answered Questions*, ¶52.2.
50. Shoghi Effendi, *The Advent of Divine Justice*, ¶66.
51. Shoghi Effendi, from a letter dated November 2, 1928, in *Compilation of Compilations*, vol. II, no. 1825.
52. Shoghi Effendi, from a letter dated March 13, 1944 written on his behalf, in *Promoting Entry by Troops*, no. 9; the Universal House of Justice, *Messages from the Universal House of Justice, 1963–1986*, ¶427.4.
53. Shoghi Effendi, *God Passes By*, p. 513.
54. The Universal House of Justice, *The Promise of World Peace*, ¶3.
55. Judith A. Howard, "Social Psychology of Identities," *Annual Review of Sociology*, 2000, 26, pp. 367–93.
56. The Universal House of Justice, *Messages from the Universal House of Justice, 1963–1986*, ¶52.2–¶52.3.
57. The Universal House of Justice, letter dated March 2, 2013 to the Bahá'ís of Iran, ¶7; the Universal House of Justice, *Messages from the Universal House of Justice, 1986–2001*, ¶348.11.
58. The Universal House of Justice, Riḍván 2010 letter to the Bahá'ís of the world, ¶6, ¶33.
59. Ibid., ¶27.
60. Ibid.
61. Ibid., ¶32.
62. 'Abdu'l-Bahá, *Tablets of the Divine Plan*, ¶14.7, ¶6.11.
63. Article "Bahia" in https://en.wikipedia.org/wiki/Bahia. Accessed 08/07/15.
64. M.R. Garis, *Martha Root: Lioness at the Threshold*, pp. 93–98.
65. For details of her life, refer to "In Memoriam," *The Bahá'í World*, vol. XVIII, pp. 733–38, p. 734; 'Abdu'l-Bahá, cited in the Universal House of Justice, *Messages from the Universal House of Justice, 1963–1986*, ¶265; the Universal House of Justice, *Messages from the Universal House of Justice, 1963–1986*, ¶185.3; the Universal House of Justice, cited in "In Memoriam," *The Bahá'í World*, vol. XVIII, p. 738.

66. The Universal House of Justice, *Messages of the Universal House of Justice, 1986–2001*, ¶217.6.

67. 'Abdu'l-Bahá, *Tablets of the Divine Plan*, ¶6.9.

68. Ibid., ¶14.8.

69. M. R. Garis, *Martha Root: Lioness at the Threshold*, pp. 106–107.

70. Shoghi Effendi, *The Advent of Divine Justice*, p. 70.

71. Janet A. Khan, *Heritage of Light: The Spiritual Destiny of America*, pp. 169–70; Glen Cameron and Wendi Momen, *A Basic Bahá'í Chronology*, p. 351; Shoghi Effendi, *Messages to the Bahá'í World*, p. 156; the Universal House of Justice, *Messages from the Universal House of Justice, 1963–1986*, ¶97.1.

72. The Universal House of Justice, *Messages from the Universal House of Justice, 1963–1986*, ¶108.1–¶108.2.

73. The Universal House of Justice, Riḍván 2000 letter to the Bahá'ís of the world, ¶14; Glen Cameron and Wendi Momen, *A Basic Bahá'í Chronology*, p. 453.

74. The Universal House of Justice, *Messages from the Universal House of Justice, 1963–1986*, ¶450.1; Janet A. Khan, "New Vision, new values, the emergence of a new world order," *Dialogue and Universalism*, vol. VI, no. 11–12, 1996.

75. http://www.britannica.com/topic/Eskimo-people/, accessed 8/16/15; https://en.wikipedia.org/wiki/Inuit, accessed 8/16/15.

76. 'Abdu'l-Baha, *Tablets of the Divine Plan*, ¶13.6.

77. Ibid., ¶5.2.

78. Shoghi Effendi, *Messages to the Bahá'í World*, p. 44.

79. Shoghi Effendi, *Messages to Canada*, pp. 64, 60; the Universal House of Justice, *Messages from the Universal House of Justice, 1963–1986*, ¶172.3.

80. The Universal House of Justice, *Messages from the Universal House of Justice, 1963–1986*, ¶340.3.

81. See reference notes 7 and 14 in Shoghi Effendi, *Messages to Canada*, pp. 73–74.

82. Shoghi Effendi, *Messages to the Bahá'í World*, p. 106.

83. Shoghi Effendi, *Messages to Canada*, pp. 67–68.

84. Glen Cameron and Wendi Momen, *A Basic Bahá'í Chronology*,

pp. 419, 481; the Universal House of Justice, *Messages from the Universal House of Justice, 1986–2001*, ¶220.13.

85. Shoghi Effendi, *Lights of Guidance*, no. 1802.
86. 'Abdu'l-Bahá, *Tablets of the Divine Plan*, ¶6.8; Shoghi Effendi, in Helen Hornby, comp., *Lights of Guidance*, no. 2029.
87. The Universal House of Justice, *Messages from the Universal House of Justice, 1986–2001*, ¶220.8.
88. The Universal House of Justice, letter dated December 29, 2015 to the Conference of the Continental Boards of Counselors, ¶25.
89. 'Abdu'l-Bahá, translated from the Persian, in *Compilation of Compilations*, vol. II, no. 2191.
90. 'Abdu'l-Bahá, *Tablets of the Divine Plan*, ¶7.10–¶7.11.
91. For details see, 'Abdu'l-Bahá, *Tablets of the Divine Plan*, ¶7.3, ¶7.6 and ¶7.9, ¶7.7, ¶13.4, and ¶6.4.
92. 'Abdu'l-Bahá, translated from the Persian, in *Compilation of Compilations*, vol. II, no. 2191.
93. Shoghi Effendi, *The Advent of Divine Justice*, ¶100.
94. For a detailed treatment of this subject, refer to Janet A. Khan and Peter J. Khan, *Advancement of Women: A Bahá'í Perspective*; Shoghi Effendi, letter dated January 30, 1926, translated from Persian, in *Compilation of Compilations*, vol. II, no. 2079.
95. The Universal House of Justice, *Messages from the Universal House of Justice, 1963–1986*, ¶394.7, ¶162.32, ¶11.
96. The Universal House of Justice, *Messages from the Universal House of Justice, 1986–2001*, ¶147.1.
97. 'Abdu'l-Bahá, *Tablets of the Divine Plan*, ¶9.5, ¶ 9.7.
98. Ibid., ¶1.3, ¶9.6, ¶2.5.
99. Ibid., ¶1.3.
100. 'Abdu'l-Bahá, *Selections from the Writings of 'Abdu'l-Bahá*, ¶40.3.
101. Ibid., ¶40.3–40.4.

9 / Responding to the Call to Apostleship

1. The Universal House of Justice, letter dated December 29, 2015 to the Conference of the Continental Boards of Counselors, ¶51.

2. Ibid., ¶32.

3. Ibid., ¶19, ¶20.

4. Ibid., ¶19, ¶48, ¶52.

5. Ibid., ¶52, ¶20; Abdu'l-Bahá, *Tablets of the Divine Plan*, ¶8.11.

6. Shoghi Effendi, *The World Order of Bahá'u'lláh*, pp. 131–32.

7. 'Abdu'l-Bahá, cited in Shoghi Effendi, *The World Order of Bahá'u'lláh*, p. 139.

8. Shoghi Effendi, *The World Order of Bahá'u'lláh*, p. 134; the Universal House of Justice, *Messages from the Universal House of Justice 1986–2001*, ¶60.6.

9. Shoghi Effendi, *Bahá'í Administration*, pp. 131–32.

10. Ibid., p. 90.

11. 'Abdu'l-Bahá, *Will and Testament of 'Abdu'l-Bahá*, p. 10.

12. Shoghi Effendi, *Citadel of Faith*, p. 148.

13. 'Abdu'l-Bahá, *Tablets of the Divine Plan*, ¶7.16.

14. Ibid., ¶7.17.

15. Shoghi Effendi, in *Promoting Entry by Troops*, Compilation, no. 3.

16. Shoghi Effendi, *Unfolding Destiny: The Messages from the Guardian of the Bahá'í Faith to the Bahá'í Community of the British Isles*, p. 436.

17. Shoghi Effendi, *Messages to the Bahá'í World, 1950–1957*, p. 102; the Universal House of Justice, *Messages from the Universal House of Justice, 1986–2001*, ¶172.4.

18. The Universal House of Justice, letter dated December 29, 2015 to the Conference of the Continental Boards of Counselors, ¶51.

19. 'Abdu'l-Bahá, *Selection from the Writings of 'Abdu'l-Bahá*, ¶7.4, ¶7.2, ¶7.3.

20. 'Abdu'l-Bahá, *Tablets of the Divine Plan*, ¶8.9.

21. Ibid.

22. Shoghi Effendi, *The Compilation of Compilations,* vol. I, no. 886.

23. Shoghi Effendi, *God Passes By*, pp. 446–47.

24. See for example, Kathryn Jewett Hogenson, *Lighting the Western Sky: The Hearst Pilgrimage and the Establishment of the Bahá'í Faith in the West;* Gayle Morrison, *To Move the World: Louis G. Gregory and the Advancement of Racial Unity in America,* Robert H. Stockman, *'Abdu'l-Bahá in America.*

25. Shoghi Effendi, *God Passes By,* p. 447; Shoghi Effendi, *Messages to the Bahá'í World,* pp. 135–36.

26. Shoghi Effendi, in Helen Hornby, comp., *Lights of Guidance,* no. 788.

27. Shoghi Effendi, *The Advent of Divine Justice,* ¶51.

28. Ibid., ¶51, ¶52.

29. Ibid., ¶52.

30. Ibid., ¶53.

31. Shoghi Effendi, *The Advent of Divine Justice,* ¶53.

32. Shoghi Effendi, *Bahá'í Administration,* p. 69.

33. 'Abdu'l-Bahá, *Will and Testament of 'Abdu'l-Bahá,* p. 10.

34. Ibid., pp. 10–11.

35. Shoghi Effendi, *Bahá'í Administration,* pp. 69–70.

36. Shoghi Effendi, *The Compilation of Compilations,* vol. II, no. 2002; Shoghi Effendi, *Bahá'í Administration,* p. 125.

37. Shoghi Effendi, *Citadel of Faith,* p. 148.

38. Shoghi Effendi, *The Advent of Divine Justice,* ¶78.

39. Shoghi Effendi, *The Compilation of Compilations,* vol. II, no. 2237.

40. Ibid., no. 2273.

41. The Universal House of Justice, letter dated August 29, 2010, ¶2.

42. 'Abdu'l-Bahá, *Tablets of the Divine Plan,* ¶7.16–¶7.17.

43. 'Abdu'l-Bahá, *Paris Talks,* ¶9.26.

44. 'Abdu'l-Bahá, *The Promulgation of Universal Peace,* p. 170.

45. Ibid., p. 502.

46. 'Abdu'l-Bahá, *Tablets of the Divine Plan,* ¶7.16.

47. Shoghi Effendi, *God Passes By*, p. 443.
48. 'Abdu'l-Bahá, *Selection from the Writings of 'Abdu'l-Bahá*, ¶218.5–7.

Selected Bibliography

Works of Bahá'u'lláh

Epistle to the Son of the Wolf. Translated by Shoghi Effendi. 1st pocket-sized ed. Wilmette, IL: Bahá'í Publishing Trust, 1988.

Gleanings from the Writings of Bahá'u'lláh. Translated by Shoghi Effendi. New ed. Wilmette, IL: Bahá'í Publishing, 2005.

Tablets of Bahá'u'lláh Revealed after the Kitáb-i-Aqdas. Compiled by the Research Department of the Universal House of Justice and translated by Habib Taherzadeh with the assistance of a Committee at the Bahá'í World Center. Wilmette, IL: Bahá'í Publishing Trust, 1988.

The Hidden Words of Bahá'u'lláh. Translated by Shoghi Effendi. Wilmette, IL: Bahá'í Publishing, 2002.

The Kitáb-i-Aqdas: The Most Holy Book. 1st pocket-sized ed. Wilmette, IL: Bahá'í Publishing Trust, 1993.

The Kitáb-i-Íqán: The Book of Certitude. Translated by Shoghi Effendi. Wilmette, IL: Bahá'í Publishing, 2003.

The Summons of the Lord of Hosts: Tablets of Bahá'u'lláh. Wilmette, IL: Bahá'í Publishing, 2006.

Works of the Báb

Selections from the Writings of the Báb. Compiled by the Research Department of the Universal House of Justice. Translated by Habib Taherzadeh et al. 1st pocket-sized ed. Wilmette, IL: Bahá'í Publishing Trust, 2006.

Works of 'Abdu'l-Bahá

Memorials of the Faithful. New ed. Translated by Marzieh Gail. Wilmette, IL: Bahá'í Publishing Trust, 1996.

Paris Talks: Addresses Given by 'Abdu'l-Bahá in Paris in 1911. Wilmette, IL: Bahá'í Publishing, 2006.

Selections from the Writings of 'Abdu'l-Bahá. Wilmette, IL: Bahá'í Publishing, 2010.

Some Answered Questions. Compiled and translated from the Persian by Laura Clifford Barney. Newly Revised by a Committee at the Bahá'í World Center. Reprinted with the permission of the Bahá'í World Center. Wilmette, IL: Bahá'í Publishing, 2014.

Tablets of the Divine Plan: Revealed by 'Abdu'l-Bahá to the North American Bahá'ís. 1st pocket-sized ed. Wilmette, IL: Bahá'í Publishing Trust, 1993.

The Promulgation of Universal Peace: Talks Delivered by 'Abdu'l-Bahá during His Visit to the United States and Canada in 1912. New ed. Wilmette: Bahá'í Publishing Trust, 2007.

The Secret of Divine Civilization. Wilmette, IL: Bahá'í Publishing, 2007.

Will and Testament of 'Abdu'l-Bahá. Wilmette: Bahá'í Publishing Trust, 1991.

Works of Shoghi Effendi

Bahá'í Administration, Selected Messages, 1922–1932. 7th ed. Wilmette, IL: Bahá'í Publishing Trust, 1974.

Citadel of Faith: Messages to America, 1947–1957. Wilmette, IL: Bahá'í Publishing Trust, 1965.

God Passes By. Eighth printing. Wilmette, IL: Bahá'í Publishing Trust, 2012.

Messages to the Bahá'í World, 1950–1957. Wilmette, IL: Bahá'í Publishing Trust, 1971.

Messages to Canada. National Spiritual Assembly of the Bahá'ís of Canada, 1965.

"The Faith of Bahá'u'lláh, A World Religion," *World Order Magazine*, volume XIII, no. 7, October 1947.

The Advent of Divine Justice. New ed. Wilmette, IL: Bahá'í Publishing Trust, 2006.

The Promised Day is Come. 1st pocket-sized ed. Wilmette, IL: Bahá'í Publishing Trust, 1996.

The World Order of Bahá'u'lláh. First pocket-sized edition. Wilmette, IL: Bahá'í Publishing Trust, 1991.

The Unfolding Destiny of the British Bahá'í Community: The Messages from the Guardian of the Bahá'í Faith to the Bahá'ís of the British Isles. London: Bahá'í Publishing Trust, 1981.

This Decisive Hour: Messages from Shoghi Effendi to the North American Bahá'ís, 1932–1946. Wilmette, IL: Bahá'í Publishing Trust, 2002.

Works of the Universal House of Justice

Century of Light. Commissioned by the Universal House of Justice. Haifa, Israel: Bahá'í World Center, 2001.

Messages from the Universal House of Justice 1963–1986: The Third Epoch of the Formative Age. Compiled by Geoffry Marks. Wilmette, IL: Bahá'í Publishing Trust, 1996.

Messages from the Universal House of Justice 1986–2001: The Fourth Epoch of the Formative Age. Wilmette, IL: Bahá'í Publishing, 2010.

The Constitution of the Universal House of Justice. Haifa, Israel: Bahá'í World Center, 1972.

The Institution of the Counsellors. Haifa, Israel: Bahá'í World Center, 2001.

The Promise of World Peace. Haifa, Israel: Bahá'í World Center, 1985.

Turning Point: Selected Messages of the Universal House of Justice and Supplementary Material 1996–2006. West Palm Beach, FL: Palabra Publications, 2006.

Compilations of Bahá'í Writings

Bahá'u'lláh, 'Abdu'l-Bahá, Shoghi Effendi, and the Universal House of Justice. *The Compilation of Compilations: Prepared by the Universal House of Justice, 1963–1990.* 2 vols. Australia: Bahá'í Publications Australia, 1991.

Hornby, Helen, comp. *Lights of Guidance: A Bahá'í Reference File.* 6th ed. New Delhi: Bahá'í Publishing Trust, 2001.

Other Works

Bahá'í International Community, Office of Public Information. *Who is Writing the Future?* Wilmette, IL: Bahá'í Publishing Trust, 1999.

Bahá'í International Community, United Nations' Office. *Iran's Secret Blueprint for the Destruction of a Religious Community: An Examination of the Persecution of the Bahá'ís of Iran.* New York: Bahá'í International Community, 1999.

Balyuzi, H. M. *'Abdu'l-Bahá: The Centre of the Covenant of Bahá'u'lláh.* London: George Ronald, 1971.

———. *The Báb: The Herald of the Day of Days.* Oxford: George Ronald, 1973.

Blomfield, Lady. *The Chosen Highway.* Wilmette, IL: Bahá'í Publishing Trust, n.d.

Cameron, Glen and Wendi Momen. *A Basic Bahá'í Chronology.* Oxford: George Ronald, 1996.

Earle, David M. "A Turning Point in History." *World Order* 2, no. 1 (Fall 1967): 8.

Edwards, Paul, ed. *The Encyclopedia of Philosophy.* New York: Macmillan Publishing, 1967.

Eliade, Mircea, ed. *The Encyclopedia of Religion.* New York: Macmillan Publishing, 1987.

Fox, Dennis R. "Psychology, Ideology, Utopia, and the Commons." *American Psychologist* 40, no. 1: 55.

Garis, Mabel R. *Martha Root: Lioness at the Threshold.* Wilmette, IL: Bahá'í Publishing Trust, 1983.

Hatcher, William S., and J. Douglas Martin. *The Bahá'í Faith: The Emerging Global Religion.* Wilmette, IL: Bahá'í Publishing, 2002.

Hobsbawm, Eric. "Barbarism: A User's Guide." in *On History.* New York: The New Press, 1997.

Hogenson, Kathryn Jewett. *Lighting the Western Sky: The Hearst Pilgrimage and the Establishment of the Bahá'í Faith in the West.* Oxford: George Ronald, 2010.

Hollinger, Richard, ed. *'Abdu'l-Bahá in America: Agnes Parsons' Diary.* Los Angeles: Kalimat, 1996.

Howard, Judith A. "Social Psychology of Identities." *Annual Review of Sociology*. 26 (2000): 367–93.

Jacoby, Russell. *Picture Imperfect: Utopian Thought for an Anti-Utopian Age*. New York: Columbia University Press, 2005.

Khan, Janet A. *Heritage of Light: The Spiritual Destiny of America*. Wilmette, IL: Bahá'í Publishing, 2009.

Khan, Janet A. and Peter J. *Advancement of Women: A Bahá'í Perspective*. Wilmette, IL: Bahá'í Publishing, 2003.

Khan, Peter J. *The Promised Day is Come: Study Guide*. Wilmette, IL: Bahá'í Publishing Trust, 1967.

Kissinger, Henry. *World Order*. New York: Penguin, 2014.

Montgomery, Robert L. *The Lopsided Spread of Christianity: Toward an Understanding of the Diffusion of Religions*. Westport, CT: Praeger, 2002.

Morrison, Gayle. *To move the world, Louis G. Gregory and the advancement of racial unity in America*. Wilmette, IL: Bahá'í Publishing Trust, 1982.

Nabíl-i-A'ẓam. *The Dawn-Breakers: Nabíl's Narrative of the Early Days of the Bahá'í Revelation*. Wilmette, IL: Bahá'í Publishing Trust, 1932.

Nash, Geoffrey. *The Phoenix and the Ashes: The Bahá'í Faith and the Modern Apocalypse*. Oxford: George Ronald, 1984.

Noss, John A. *Man's Religions*. Revised edition. New York: The Macmillan Company, 1960.

Palmer, A. W. *A Dictionary of Modern History, 1789–1945*. Baltimore, MD: Penguin Books, 1964.

Smith, Peter. *A Short History of the Bahá'í Faith*. Oxford: Oneworld, 1996.

Star of the West, various volumes and articles.

Stockman, Robert H. *'Abdu'l-Bahá in America*. Wilmette, IL: Bahá'í Publishing, 2012.

———. *The Bahá'í Faith in America: Origins 1892–1900*. Vol. 1. Wilmette, IL: Bahá'í Publishing Trust, 1985.

———. *The Bahá'í Faith in America: Early Expansion 1900–1912*. Vol. 2. Oxford: George Ronald, 1995.

————. *Thornton Chase: The First American Bahá'í.* Wilmette, IL: Bahá'í Publishing, 2001.

Taherzadeh, Adib. *Child of the Covenant.* Oxford: George Ronald, 2000.

————. *The Revelation of Bahá'u'lláh: Adrianople, 1863–68.* Vol. 2. Oxford: George Ronald, 1977.

————. *The Revelation of Bahá'u'lláh: 'Akká, the Early Years 1868–77.* Vol. 3. Oxford: George Ronald, 1983.

————. *The Revelation of Bahá'u'lláh: Mazra'ih & Bahjí, 1877–92.* Vol. 4. Oxford: George Ronald, 1987.

Taylor, A. J. P. *A History of the First World War.* New York: Berkley Publishing Corporation, 1963.

The Bahá'í World, various volumes and articles.

Unveiling of the Divine Plan: Tablets, Instructions, and Words of Explanation. New York City: Hotel McAlpin, 1919.

Wells, H. G. *A Short History of the World.* Mitcham, Victoria: Penguin Books, 1960.

Wright, Esmond, ed. *The History of the World: The Last Five Hundred Years.* Newnes Books: Twickenham, England, 1986.

Index

A

For more information about the Bahá'í Faith,
or to contact Bahá'ís near you,
visit http://www.bahai.us/
or call
1-800-22-UNITE

BAHÁ'Í PUBLISHING AND THE BAHÁ'Í FAITH

Bahá'í Publishing produces books based on the teachings of the Bahá'í Faith. Founded over 160 years ago, the Bahá'í Faith has spread to some 235 nations and territories and is now accepted by more than five million people. The word "Bahá'í" means "follower of Bahá'u'lláh." Bahá'u'lláh, the founder of the Bahá'í Faith, asserted that He is the Messenger of God for all of humanity in this day. The cornerstone of His teachings is the establishment of the spiritual unity of humankind, which will be achieved by personal transformation and the application of clearly identified spiritual principles. Bahá'ís also believe that there is but one religion and that all the Messengers of God—among them Abraham, Zoroaster, Moses, Krishna, Buddha, Jesus, and Muḥammad—have progressively revealed its nature. Together, the world's great religions are expressions of a single, unfolding divine plan. Human beings, not God's Messengers, are the source of religious divisions, prejudices, and hatreds.

The Bahá'í Faith is not a sect or denomination of another religion, nor is it a cult or a social movement. Rather, it is a globally recognized independent world religion founded on new books of scripture revealed by Bahá'u'lláh.

Bahá'í Publishing is an imprint of the National Spiritual Assembly of the Bahá'ís of the United States.